LANDMARK CASES
IN THE LAW OF TORT

Landmark Cases in the Law of Tort contains 13 original essays on leading tort cases, ranging from the early nineteenth century to the present day. It is the third volume in a series of collected essays on landmark cases (the previous two volumes having dealt with restitution and contract). The cases examined raise a broad range of important issues across the law of tort, including such diverse areas as acts of state and public nuisance, as well as central questions relating to the tort of negligence. Several of the essays place their cases in their historical context in ways that change our understanding of the case's significance. Sometimes the focus is on drawing out previously neglected aspects of cases which have been—undeservedly—assigned minor importance. Other essays explore the judicial methodologies and techniques that shaped leading principles of tort law. So much of tort law turns on cases, and there are so many cases, that all but the most recent decisions have a tendency to become reduced to terse propositions of law, so as to keep the subject manageable. This collection shows how important it is, despite the constant temptation to compression, not to lose sight of the contexts and nuances which qualify and illuminate so many leading authorities.

Landmark Cases
in the Law of Tort

Edited by
Charles Mitchell and Paul Mitchell

·HART·
PUBLISHING

OXFORD AND PORTLAND, OREGON
2010

Published in North America (US and Canada) by
Hart Publishing
c/o International Specialized Book Services
920 NE 58th Avenue, Suite 300
Portland, OR 97213-3786
USA
Tel: +1 503 287 3093 or toll-free: (1) 800 944 6190
Fax: +1 503 280 8832
E-mail: orders@isbs.com
Website: www.isbs.com

Hart Publishing, 16C Worcester Place, Oxford, OX1 2JW
Telephone: +44 (0)1865 517530 Fax: +44 (0) 1865 510710
E-mail: mail@hartpub.co.uk
Website: http://www.hartpub.co.uk

British Library Cataloguing in Publication Data

Data Available

ISBN: 978-1-84946-003-3

Typeset by Forewords, Oxford
Printed and bound in Great Britain by
TJ International Ltd, Padstow, Cornwall

Preface

Landmark Cases in the Law of Tort is the third volume in our series of collected essays on leading cases in the common law. The present volume uses the same techniques as the two earlier volumes (on restitution and contract). Each author was given a free choice of case and method of approach. The essays were presented and discussed at a symposium at King's College London in April 2009, and subsequently revised in the light of that discussion. We are grateful to all the symposium participants for their contributions, and to the King's Law School for supporting the event.

As with our previous volumes, there were no competing demands from authors to write on the same case—which reflects both the sheer number of important decisions in the law of obligations and the differences of scholarly emphasis.

Readers will doubtless have their own views about which authorities should be dealt with in a collection of this kind, and perhaps will be disappointed to find a personal favourite overlooked. However, we should make it clear that none of these volumes ever set out to define the most important cases in a particular area. That would be an extremely difficult, and ultimately rather pointless, task—rather like compiling a list of the ten greatest novels of all time. Rather, the aim has always been to cast new light on some of the many important cases that make up the law of obligations.

Among the thirteen cases dealt with here, readers of the earlier collections will recognise certain familiar themes. If it is true, as Lord Goff once said, that judicial work is 'an educated reflex to facts',[1] then both the facts and the nature of the judge's reflex to them can be profoundly influential. Investigation may reveal that the facts are more nuanced, or more extreme, than the bare, laconic accounts in the law reports suggest. Furthermore, the contemporary context—which very rarely appears in the reports—can give those facts a resonance which is appreciated by the judge, but missed by later readers of his judgment. Conversely, legal principles may compel judges to deal with situations in a deliberately stylised way, where important contextual material is excluded. In such situations the legal process provides an inadequate method for resolving social conflicts. The essays on *Burón v Denman*, *Goldman v Hargrave* and *Hunter v Canary Wharf Ltd* offer powerful illustrations of the importance of a full appreciation of the facts to which the judge is responding.

The facts are, of course, only the starting point. The nature of the 'educated reflex' turns on many other factors. One of the most powerful is

[1] R Goff, 'Judge, Jurist and Legislature' [1987] *Denning Law Journal* 79, 82.

the judge's conception of his own role. In some cases judges have felt obliged, or inclined, to go beyond the immediate facts, so as to lay down broad principles for the future. The essay on *Alcock* (among others) explores some of the motivations behind such expansiveness, and the limits which judges feel themselves bound by. The nature of the response may also be coloured by what legal materials are perceived as relevant. As the essay on *Fairchild* demonstrates, the judges' request in that case to hear argument about the position in European jurisdictions produced an original and distinctive analysis, with a hint that future harmonisation would be welcome. The essay on *Smith v Littlewoods*, by contrast, highlights the delicate issues involved in actually bringing about a convergence of the Scots and English law on liability for the acts of a third party. A further factor influencing the 'educated reflex' may even be the judge's own education (see the essay on *Hedley Byrne*).

The part of a judge's educated reflex that will be furthest removed from the facts involves the use of legal theory. The decision in *Tate & Lyle*, it is argued, made a far-sighted use of the concept of rights, which was ahead of its time. *George v Skivington*, both as decided and as subsequently interpreted by courts and textbook writers, was capable of being understood in a variety of ways, which all raised fundamental questions about the limits of negligence liability. Perhaps most strikingly, several of the cases reveal concerns about legal categories: what should the role of the law of negligence be in relation to the law of nuisance or the law of contract, and what should the role of tort be in relation to a wider regulatory scheme? More broadly, there is an engagement with the question, what is the law of tort for? We believe that the essays collected here illuminate the process of judicial law making generally, and also cast some light on these broader questions.

Charles Mitchell and Paul Mitchell
August 2009

Contents

Contributors

Richard Baker is a barrister at 7 Bedford Row Chambers, London.

Steve Banks is a Lecturer in Law at the University of Reading.

Jonathan Garton is a Senior Lecturer in Law at King's College London.

David Ibbetson is Regius Professor of Civil Law at the University of Cambridge.

Maria Lee is a Professor of Law at University College London.

Michael Lobban is Professor of Legal History at Queen Mary University of London.

Mark Lunney is an Associate Professor of Law at the University of New England.

Charles Mitchell is a Fellow and Tutor in Law at Jesus College, Oxford, and a Professor of Law at the University of Oxford.

Paul Mitchell is a Reader in Law at King's College London.

Jason W Neyers is an Associate Professor of Law and Cassels Brock LLP Faculty Fellow in Contract Law at the University of Western Ontario.

Donal Nolan is a Fellow and Tutor in Law at Worcester College, Oxford, and a CUF Lecturer in Law at the University of Oxford.

Ken Oliphant is Director of the Institute for European Tort Law in the Austrian Academy of Sciences, Vienna and Professor of Tort Law at the University of Bristol.

Elspeth Reid is a Senior Lecturer in Law at the University of Edinburgh.

Charlotte Smith is a Lecturer in Law at the University of Reading.

Leslie Turano is a Lecturer in Law at King's College London.

Mark Wilde is a Lecturer in Law at the University of Reading.

Table of Cases

Australia

Canada

European Court of Human Rights

United States of America

Table of Legislation

Statutory Instruments

Table of Conventions, Treaties, etc

1

R v Pease (1832)

MARK WILDE AND CHARLOTTE SMITH

A. INTRODUCTION

As any schoolboy of previous generations well knows, the Stockton and Darlington Railway is widely regarded as the world's first modern railway.[1] Engineered by the famous George Stephenson,[2] and financed and promoted by the efforts of Edward Pease,[3] it marked a major advance on the many short horse-drawn waggonways which had sprung up in the North Eastern coalfields in the eighteenth century, linking collieries with waterways. It had bridges, cuttings and embankments, carried passengers and, most importantly for our purposes, used steam locomotives.

In 1830 the directors and enginemen of the Stockton and Darlington Railway Company were indicted for public nuisance on the highway. The nuisance in question concerned the startling of horses by steam locomotives on a stretch of highway which ran alongside the railway. The case turned upon whether the statute, which authorised the construction and operation of the line, also authorised potential nuisances caused by the running of steam locomotives. The capacity of a railway to cause ongoing nuisances after the construction phase appears to have been a novel issue.

---

[1] Every 50 years since its opening in 1825 the anniversary has been marked with major celebrations. The sesquicentenary in 1975 was marked by the opening of the National Railway Museum in York.

[2] Widely acknowledged as one of the fathers of railway engineering; leading historical biographies include LTC Rolt, *George and Robert Stephenson, The Railway Revolution* (London, Longmans, 1960).

[3] Edward Pease was a wealthy Quaker woollen manufacturer from Darlington and lead promoter of the Stockton and Darlington. The fusion of his business expertise and vision with Stephenson's engineering genius changed the direction of the initial project and delivered the railway which earned its place in railway history. Many biographical details can be gleaned from his edited diaries: AE Pease (ed), *The Diaries of Edward Pease—The Father of English Railways* (London, Headley Brothers, 1907). See also AF Pollard and C Fell-Smith, rev MW Kirby, 'Pease, Edward (1767–1858)' in *Oxford Dictionary of National Biography* (Oxford, Oxford University Press, 2004), available at http://www.oxforddnb.com/view/article/21728.

In the landmark decision of *R v Pease*[4] the Court of King's Bench held that the authority of the original Act did indeed extend to the authorisation of certain disturbances created by steam locomotives. Yet it is noteworthy that the Act, which had authorised the building of the railway, had explicitly authorised the use of steam locomotives. Had this not been the case the court might have drawn a different conclusion.

Beyond the question of statutory authority, *R v Pease* has wider relevance as being the precursor of the 'railway sparks cases'. Pigou[5] and Coase[6] famously used railway sparks as an illustration of the economic analysis of tort. From an economic perspective, liability in tort should depend upon which solution imposes the least overall costs on society. For example, should the railway company run fewer trains or fit expensive spark-catching equipment? Or should neighbouring farmers avoid cultivating land in reach of the sparks, or even sell it to the railway company? Eventually the courts settled upon a rule of strict liability, although there is little evidence that this was motivated by some economic rationale by reference to which they had decided that the costs should be borne by the railways. In any case, the authority of *R v Pease* prevented the rule of strict liability operating in the vast majority of cases. In this respect, the line of authority flowing from *R v Pease* constitutes an overlooked stage in the development of strict liability.

B. THE DOCTRINAL BACKDROP TO THE CASE

1. Public Nuisance

Given that *R v Pease* concerned criminal proceedings brought in public nuisance, it is necessary to give a brief explanation of the reciprocal relationship between public and private nuisance.

Public or common nuisance (as it was originally termed) is a crime and serves as a receptacle for miscellaneous wrongs which affect a class of Her Majesty's subjects. Actions for public nuisance have been brought in respect of everything from obstructed highways to unlicensed stage plays. It is not clear at what point the term 'nuisance' was first applied to such wrongs. However, the use of the term led to certain links being made with the entirely separate tort of private nuisance. Private nuisance evolved from certain forms of action designed to protect particular interests in

---

[4] (1832) 4 B & Ad 30, 110 ER 366.
[5] AC Pigou, *The Economics of Welfare*, 4th edn (London, Macmillan, 1932) [II.II.5].
[6] RH Coase, 'The Problem of Social Cost' (1960) 3 *Journal of Law & Economics* 1, 28–34.

land.[7] Newark argues that superficial analogies may have been drawn between the types of harm covered by the respective criminal and civil remedies.[8] For example, the obstruction of the King's highway could be likened to the blocking of an easement or other servitude. In a case of 1535,[9] it was established that an individual who suffered particular damage over and above that inflicted upon the general population could maintain a separate action for damages.

Thus, links were forged between the crime of public nuisance and the tort of private nuisance at an early stage in the development of the common law. This led to the cross-fertilisation of ideas between public and private nuisance. One concept, which arose in the context of public nuisance before leaping across into tort, was the defence of statutory authority.

2. Statutory Authority

The extent to which statutory powers should be construed as restricting existing common law rights has been an issue for as long as enabling statutes have been used as a means of facilitating major works.

At this point it is necessary to distinguish between those statutes which imposed certain public duties on private bodies and those which conferred powers on private bodies in order to facilitate grand projects, ostensibly for personal gain. Private bodies, causing damage in the course of carrying out a public duty, enjoyed a limited immunity which derived from Crown immunity.[10] This could be justified on the basis that the duty was intended to serve the public interest and that this would outweigh certain individual harms. It was less easy to apply this logic to private enterprises which enjoyed statutory powers to undertake projects with a view to profit. The relationship between statutory powers and liability for damage caused by the use of such powers was rather more complex.

The canals and the railways fell into the latter category since they were instigated by private enterprise with a view to profit; they were not built at the behest of government in order to implement some grand policy.[11]

7 For an account of the development and respective applications of the forms of action relating to nuisance see CHS Fifoot, *History and Sources of the Common Law: Tort and Contract* (London, Stevens & Sons, 1949) ch 1.

8 FH Newark, 'The Boundaries of Nuisance' (1949) 65 *LQR* 480, 482.

9 *Anon* (1535) YB 27 Hen 8, f 27, pl 10.

10 See AM Linden, 'Strict Liability, Nuisance and Legislative Authorization' (1966) 4 *Osgoode Hall Law Journal* 196, 197–99.

11 The chaotic and unplanned manner in which the British railway system evolved is in marked contrast to the development of many of its continental European counterparts where strategic national plans were drawn up. One of the earliest European systems to develop in the wake of the pioneering work in the UK was in Belgium. After the opening of the first line in 1835 a national plan was devised, the main framework of which consisted of four principal routes

Nevertheless, there was a clear public interest dimension to these projects which could not be ignored. Indeed, in the absence of such public benefits it is doubtful whether the promoters would have gained the necessary statutory backing for the schemes. Projects of this magnitude could only be undertaken with the authorisation of a private Act of Parliament. This provided the promoters with the wherewithal to build the infrastructure and much of the legislation was concerned with land acquisition and compensation. Such powers clearly expropriated the property interests vesting in the land which lay in the path of the development. However, once construction was complete, it was less clear whether the authority to restrict existing rights extended to the day-to-day operation of the enterprise. The issue turned upon whether the harm caused was outweighed by the wider public benefits arising from the scheme.

In *R v Russell*,[12] a case which was to play a decisive role in *Pease*, the defendants were indicted in public nuisance for obstructing the navigable passage in the Tyne through the construction of new coal loading facilities. The Court of King's Bench upheld the trial judge's jury direction[13] that it was appropriate to consider the public benefits of the scheme. These included the national benefits associated with more efficient coal distribution and the resultant lower prices on the London market. By this stage it had long been established, as a matter of common law, that public benefit could be taken into account when considering the reasonableness of a particular land use.[14] If a land use was reasonable it could not amount to an actionable nuisance. In this respect there was certainly nothing groundbreaking about the decision. Some reference was made to various public local Acts which authorised the works. However, they were merely cited as evidence of the fact that the scheme was for public benefit and thus 'not necessarily a nuisance'.[15] In no sense were the Acts regarded as cutting across existing common law rights. Nevertheless, these brief references to statutory powers seem to have sown the seeds of the idea of statutory authority.

Many developments in the common law stem from particular events, changes in society or the proliferation of certain activities which breed

converging on a central hub. Furthermore, the construction was funded by the state. This central planning on the part of certain continental governments was largely due to the fact it was quickly recognized that the railways could have an important strategic military role to play. See F Ferneyhough, *History of the Railways* (Reading, Osprey Publishing, 1975).

[12] (1827) 6 B & C 566, 108 ER 560.
[13] The trial was held at the York Summer Assizes 1824.
[14] An often used early example of the role played by public benefit is *Jones v Powell* (1627) Palm 536, 81 ER 1208. There the burning of sea coal by a brewhouse interfered with the comfort and convenience of a bishop's registrar whose office was situated nearby. The social utility of the business (or its contribution to 'the common wealth', to use the terminology of the judgment) was taken into account.
[15] (1827) 6 B & C 566, 588; 108 ER 560, 568 (Holroyd J).

certain types of dispute.[16] The establishment of statutory authority as a defence to nuisance is largely attributable to the development of railways in the nineteenth century. *R v Pease* was the first public nuisance case to be brought against a steam-operated railway.

C. A BRIEF HISTORY OF THE STOCKTON AND DARLINGTON RAILWAY

The history of the railways is inextricably linked with the eighteenth-century development of the coal industry.[17] The need to transport coal over large distances to feed the ever-expanding London market posed significant logistical problems. In the North East an extensive network of waggonways evolved to transport coal from the pits to the Tyne and Wear Rivers.[18] A horse on a waggonway could draw several times the load of a packhorse or coal wain on the rutted cart tracks.[19] Once on a navigable waterway, the coal could be transported in bulk to far-afield markets. The West Auckland coalfields near Darlington lay beyond the reach of this network, a factor which inhibited the development of the industry.[20] In 1768 a canal had been proposed to link the coalfields with the upstream port of Stockton-on-Tees, but the capital was never raised.[21] In 1810 the opening of a new shipping channel from Stockton to the mouth of the Tees (the Mandale Cut) gave new impetus to the scheme. A committee comprising local businessmen and civic dignitaries was formed to look afresh into creating a transport link with the West Auckland coalfields.[22] The terms of reference

16 An obvious example concerns the extent to which negligence was shaped by an increase in the number of running down cases, as cities became busier; and collisions at sea as maritime trade increased. See MJ Prichard, 'Trespass, Case and the Rule in *Williams v Holland*' [1964] *CLJ* 234.

17 For the widely acknowledged definitive historical account of the Stockton and Darlington see WW Tomlinson, *The North Eastern Railway: Its Rise and Development* (London, Longmans, Green & Co, 1915). A more recent work which examines the project from the perspective of economic history is MW Kirby, *The Origins of Railway Enterprise: The Stockton and Darlington Railway 1821–1863* (Cambridge, Cambridge University Press, 1993).

18 RA, Mott 'English Waggonways in the Eighteenth Century' (1964–65) 37 *Transactions of the Newcomen Society* 1; CE Lee, 'The Waggonways of Tyneside' (1951) 29 *Archeologia Aeliana* 25.

19 It is estimated that even on a crude wooden waggonway one horse could do the work of 24 pack horses or four horse-drawn coal wains: MJT Lewis, *Early Wooden Railways* (London, Routledge, 1970) 299.

20 Local distribution was improved when the 'coal road' between West Auckland, Darlington and Piercebridge was turnpiked in 1751: Kirby, above n 17, 21.

21 For an account of the Brindley–Whitworth survey and subsequent proposals see Kirby, ibid, 21–25.

22 'A committee to inquire into the practicability and advantage of a Railway or Canal from Stockton and Darlington to Winston, for the more easy and expeditious carriage of coals, lead, etc' (hereinafter 'the committee'). The committee arose from a dinner held at Stockton Town Hall to celebrate the opening of the Mandale Cut. It was instigated by the recorder of Stockton, Leonard Raisbeck. See Kirby, above n 17, 27.

of the committee comprised the alternate possibilities of building a canal or a railway. The term 'railway' had largely ousted waggonway by this stage, although there was much loose use of terminology at the time.[23]

Quaker business interests were heavily represented on the committee from the outset. The Pease family had made their fortune in the Darlington woollen and worsted trade. The Backhouses had a similar background although they had diversified more heavily into banking.[24] In fact, the lines of credit available to the Society of Friends, established by their familial and commercial ties, were to prove instrumental in bringing the project to fruition.[25] Edward Pease the elder was influential in ensuring that Darlington would be linked to the new transport link.[26] In this respect, it is clear that the railway was envisaged as far more than a 'canal feeder'. By linking the commercial centres of Darlington and Stockton, it would facilitate trade in other goods and even the carriage of passengers.

Over the next few years, many of the leading engineers of the day were consulted to investigate a canal, a railway, or a combination of the two. At a meeting held on 13 November 1818 the committee took the historic decision to build a railway, surveyed by George Overton,[27] rather than a canal.[28] The cheaper construction costs of a railway may have featured prominently in this decision.[29] Edward Pease's second son, Joseph, was assigned the task of drawing up a prospectus and, before long, the necessary capital had been raised, largely as a result of the network of credit to which the Quakers had access.[30]

Having raised the capital, the next task was to draft a private Bill and navigate it through Parliament. This fell to Leonard Raisbeck, the Recorder of Stockton, and Francis Mewburn, the Peases' family solicitor.[31] The Bill was narrowly defeated in 1819 due to the opposition of the Earl of Eldon (the Vice Chancellor no less) and the Earl of Darlington (later first Duke of Cleveland), whose estates lay in the path of the railway. Lord Eldon was concerned that the compulsory acquisition of his land would

[23] See Tomlinson, above n 17, 12–16.
[24] See Kirby, above n 17, 26.
[25] Ibid.
[26] Ibid, 29–32.
[27] Overton of Lanthelly, near Brecon, was an established builder of tramways serving the South Wales coal industry: Kirby, above n 17, 30.
[28] Tomlinson, above n 17, 54–55.
[29] Kirby, above n 17, 30.
[30] Ibid, 33. The Society of Friends included prominent banking families such as the Gurneys and Barclays of Norwich, both of whom invested in the scheme. Joseph Pease stated to a meeting of 'Friends' in Leeds that 'The Darlington Railway is so popular amongst Friends that about £80,000 stands in the name of members of our Society'. The effect of non-conformist kinship on the flow of capital at this time is explored in A Raistrick, *Quakers in Science and Industry* (Newton Abbot, David & Charles, 1968) esp 34, 45, 335.
[31] The Berwick and Kelso Act, enacted for a line which was never built, provided the template for the Bill. For a detailed account of the passage of the first and second Bills see Tomlinson, above n 17, 60–69.

deprive him of wayleave[32] income, while Lord Darlington was greatly vexed by the loss of his fox covers. Nevertheless, all in Westminster had been taken by surprise by the highly effective lobbying campaign mounted by the Quakers.[33] Mewburn later recalled that an unidentified nobleman had remarked:[34] 'If the Quakers in these times when nobody knows anything about railways can raise up such a phalanx as they have done on this occasion, I should recommend the country gentlemen to be very wary how they oppose them.'

The promoters immediately set to work on a revised Bill, which was submitted in 1821. The route was altered to avoid Lord Darlington's beloved fox covers and Lord Eldon was bought off.[35] The 1821 Bill nearly came to grief due to a shortfall in the capital subscribed to the scheme. Parliamentary standing orders stipulated that a Bill could not proceed unless four-fifths of the capital had been raised. Edward Pease had to step in and provide the £7,000 shortfall out of his own funds, an act which was to consolidate his position as lead promoter. Aside from this, the Bill proceeded smoothly and received the Royal Assent on 19 April 1821. The Stockton and Darlington Railway Company came into being.

There was one important issue, though, which the Act did not address. All along, it had been assumed that horses would provide the motive power for the line, and this was the basis upon which the Bill had been drafted. Until recently there had been no viable alternative, but by 1821 the star of steam was in the ascendant. Steam engine technology, largely pioneered by James Watt,[36] was well established by the early nineteenth century. Stationary winding engines and pumping engines were in common use at collieries and mines, many of which employed enginewrights with fully equipped workshops. The North Eastern collieries and the Cornish copper and tin mines had become hotbeds of innovation in the use of steam power.

33 A type of surface rent charged by landowners to allow passage over their lands.

34 It is reported that they had gone about in pairs door-stopping the honourable members: Kirby, above n 17, 35.

34 Cited in *Memoir of Francis Mewburn, Chief Bailiff of Darlington and First Railway Solicitor, by his Son* (Darlington, 1867) 53. This is a privately published collation of tributes, memoirs, anecdotes and newspaper cuttings assembled by Mewburn's son in celebration of his life upon his death in 1867: PRO ZLIB 29/9.

35 F Mewburn, *The Larchfield Diary: Extracts from the Diary of the Late Mr Mewburn, First Railway Solicitor* (London, Simpkin Marshall, 1876) 177. The terms of the settlement must have been extremely favourable to Lord Eldon in that, through Lord Eldon's solicitor, Mr Wilson, Mewburn got introductions to the Ministerial Whipper-in. Mewburn recalled that with such heavyweight support 'we had little trouble in obtaining our Bill'.

36 Early pioneer of the steam engine and especially the rotary engine, by which the linear motion of the piston is converted to rotary motion. In partnership with Matthew Boulton he developed steam engines as practical machines rather than laboratory experiments and built up the first volume production steam engine manufacturing business: J Tann, 'Watt, James (1736–1819)' in *Oxford Dictionary of National Biography* (Oxford, Oxford University Press, 2004), available at http://www.oxforddnb.com/view/article/28880.

George Stephenson, then employed as an enginewright at the Killingworth Colliery, had been working on the problem of how to turn steam engines into self-propelled locomotives capable of hauling coal wagons along the waggonways. He was not alone in this field and was certainly not the first to build a steam locomotive.[37] His endeavours at Killingworth met with considerable success, however, and his locomotive, *The Blucher*, proved that steam locomotion was a viable technology.[38] He also had a more integrated vision of the railways than many of his peers. Stephenson recognised that railways should be conceived of as complete packages and that in order to get the best out of locomotives it was necessary to design purpose built rails and other infrastructure. Remarkably, Stephenson had a mastery of both the mechanical and civil aspects of railway engineering, an accomplishment matched only by his son Robert and by Isambard Kingdom Brunel. In this respect, George Stephenson is rightly regarded as one of the fathers of railway engineering, a feat made all the more remarkable by the fact that he was illiterate and entirely self taught. Although highly satisfied with his trials at Killingworth, Stephenson was eager to show off his locomotives to a wider audience by running them on more ambitious lines than the short waggonways and canal feeders to which they were currently confined.

On the very day that the second Bill received its Royal Assent, a remarkable meeting took place which arguably changed the course of railway history. George Stephenson, accompanied by Nicholas Wood (the 'viewer' of the Killingworth colliery), arrived at the house of Edward Pease in Northgate, Darlington.[39] Pease had some misgivings about the Overton route and used his enhanced influence in the project to obtain further opinions about the merits of the proposal. Stephenson and Wood arrived in the late afternoon having ridden from Killingworth to Newcastle on

[37] The accolade of inventor of the first workable steam locomotive is normally bestowed upon the Cornish engineer Richard Trevithick. Engravings featuring *His Catch-me-who-can* locomotive, demonstrated on a circular track at Gower Street in London in the summer of 1808, form one of the iconic images depicting railway history. Leading biographies include LTC Rolt, *The Cornish Giant: The Story of Richard Trevithick, Father of the Steam Locomotive* (London, Lutterworth, 1960). As regards the North Eastern waggonways, pioneers included John Blenkinsop, who developed a rack-and-pinion system in order to overcome the problem of traction. Three such engines were put to work at the Middleton Colliery. Other notable engines include Timothy Hackworth's *Puffing Billy*; Hackworth was later to go into partnership with Robert Stephenson & Co.

[38] Stephenson's first locomotive was built at the Killingworth colliery in 1813–14. Over the next five years he built another 16 locomotives at Killingworth: Tomlinson, above n 17, 27–30.

[39] There is some mystery as to how this meeting came about and whether it was by appointment. The edited diaries of Edward Pease suggest that Pease was not expecting the visitors and almost turned them away when a servant told him that there were two mystery gentlemen callers at the door: *Pease Diaries*, above n 3, 85–86. Tomlinson, above n 17, 72 disputes this account, citing evidence that the meeting was arranged by the surveying engineer John Dixon, with whom Stephenson would work on the Stockton and Darlington and future projects. Certainly, it seems unlikely that Stephenson and Wood would have undertaken such an arduous journey on the off chance that Pease might be willing to see them.

horseback before boarding the stagecoach to Stockton. They then walked the entire 12 miles of Overton's route from Stockton to Darlington.

According to Edward Pease's diaries, upon arriving at Pease's house Stephenson and Wood were ushered into the kitchen where an informal and animated discussion ensued with Pease perched on the edge of the kitchen table.[40] This no-nonsense informality would no doubt have appealed to Stephenson. In fact, both men abhorred pretention and it seems that an instant rapport was struck up which endured for life. As Pease later commented in his diaries, 'There was such an honest and sensible look about George Stephenson, and he seemed so modest and unpretending, and he spoke in the strong Northumberland dialect'.[41] As regards the substance of the discussion, Stephenson confirmed Pease's doubts regarding the Overton Route. Stephenson maintained that he could iron out many of the bends and reduce the length of the route to a considerable extent. As regards track, Stephenson impressed upon Pease the advantages of iron rail as opposed to other methods.[42] Furthermore, Stephenson eulogised about the merits of steam locomotive traction and urged Pease to build the line with this form of motive power in mind. He extended an invitation to Pease to 'Come over to Killingworth and see what my *Blucher* can do—seeing is believing, Sir'.[43]

Some time later, Pease took Stephenson up on his invitation.[44] He arrived at Stephenson's cottage accompanied by his cousin, Thomas Richardson. Mrs Stephenson emerged from the cottage and informed the visitors that her husband was at the pit but that she would send for him. Stephenson duly arrived in 'pitman's garb' and took the party to see his locomotives. Pease was highly impressed by the demonstration and was henceforth firmly committed to the use of steam traction on the railway. Furthermore, he recognised that the railways had the potential to create a transport system which went far beyond shuttling coal wagons between pithead and waterway. Reflecting on their experience at Killingworth to Thomas Richardson, Pease observed:[45]

Don't be surprised if I should tell thee there seems to us after careful examination no difficulty laying a railroad from London to Edinburgh on which wagons would travel and take the mail at the rate of 20 miles per hour, when this is accomplished steam vessels may be laid aside! We went along a road upon one

40 *Pease Diaries*, above n 3, 86.

41 Ibid.

42 In partnership with Michael Longridge of the Bedlington Ironworks, Stephenson had developed a design of iron rail along which an iron flanged wheel would pass. The transfer of the guiding flange from the track to the wheel was one of the crucial innovations which made the railways possible: Tomlinson, above n 17, 15–16.

43 *Pease Diaries*, above n 3, 85.

44 Ibid, 86–87.

45 DCRO Hodgkin Papers, D/140/C/63, 'Thomas Richardson', Edward Pease to Thomas Richardson, 10 October 1821.

of these engines conveying about 50 tons at the rate of 7 or 8 miles per hour, and if the same power had been applied to speed which was applied to drag wagons we should have gone 50 miles per hour—previous to seeing this locomotive engine I was at a loss to conceive how the engine could draw such a weight, without having a rack to work into the same or something like legs—but in this engine there is no such thing.

This vision that one day mail trains would thunder between London and Edinburgh proved to be an astonishingly accurate prediction.[46] So enthused was Pease by the technology that he later agreed to invest in the new locomotive building enterprise established by George Stephenson and his son, Robert.[47]

Pease persuaded the committee to allow Stephenson to conduct a new survey of the route, which was duly undertaken in October 1821 with the assistance of Stephenson's son, Robert,[48] and John Dixon.[49] Stephenson had been instructed to keep within the authorisation of the existing Act wherever possible. However, it soon became clear that certain major alterations were required, necessitating a second Act of Parliament. Nevertheless, Stephenson was adamant that the cost savings resulting from a straightened and shorter route would outweigh the time and expense of returning to Parliament. At a shareholders' meeting held on 22 January 1822 Stephenson's revised route was approved and he was appointed as Engineer to the Stockton and Darlington Railway. It was also agreed that a third Bill should be prepared in order to obtain the powers necessary to effect the major route alterations. In the meantime, it was resolved that work should commence on those parts which adhered to the original plans and for which no new authorisation was necessary. By this time it had also been resolved to follow Stephenson's recommendation of constructing an iron railway as opposed to a tramway.

Aside from the route alterations, a new Bill was necessary in order to authorise the use of steam locomotives,[50] and the need to make a decision

---

[46] Although Pease was not the first to recognise that the railways could be used for more than short canal feeders etc. In the 1760s Richard Levell Edgeworth envisaged the concept of 'railways for baggage wagons on the great roads of England': Kirby, above n 17, 16.

[47] See 12 below.

[48] Not to be confused with the Scottish Engineer Robert Stevenson of lighthouse building fame.

[49] As regards Stephenson's survey, see Tomlinson, above n 17, 74–78. According to the *Pease Diaries*, above n 3, 87, Stephenson and Dixon would usually call in on Pease at the end of a long day's surveying and it was on these occasions that many issues of fine detail were discussed, including the design and composition of the rails. The fact that many such issues were thrashed out in private discussions between Pease and Stephenson and then presented as proposals to the management committee demonstrates that the two men were unquestioningly the driving force of the project.

[50] It is not clear who instigated the insertion of the clause. However, it is at least possible that Mewburn may have recognised the need for a special clause. His obituary in the *Newcastle Daily Chronicle* made much of his mastery of detail and ability to foresee many of the pitfalls associated with bringing such a novel and large-scale project to fruition. The piece asserts that it

on this issue was now pressing. Pease had long been converted to the merits of steam locomotion and he set about persuading his fellow directors to seek authorisation for steam traction. The case in favour was further strengthened by the opening of the Hetton Colliery Railway on 18 November 1822, another project overseen by George Stephenson, which successfully demonstrated the potential of the technology.[51] At some point in late 1822 or early 1823 Mewburn inserted a new clause, the first of its type, into the Bill authorising the use of locomotives on the line:[52]

> That it shall and may be lawful to and for the said company of proprietors or any person or persons authorised or permitted by them, from and after the passing of this Act, to make and erect such and so many loco-motive or moveable engines, as the said company of proprietors shall from time to time think proper and expedient, and to use and employ the same in or upon the said railways or tramroads or any of them, by the said recited Act and this Act, directed or authorised to be made, for the purpose of facilitating the transport, conveyance and carriage of goods, merchandise and other articles and things upon and along the same roads, and for the conveyance of passengers upon and along the same roads.

The third Bill began its passage through Parliament in February 1823 and once again a substantial delegation of promoters, accompanied by George Stephenson, travelled to London to oversee the process.[53] According to Mewburn, Lord Shaftsbury, who chaired the Lords standing committee on private bills, could not grasp to what manner of beast or machine the above clause referred: 'he could not comprehend what it meant; he thought it was some strange, unheard of animal, and he struck the clause out of this Act'. Mewburn 'sent Mr Brandling, the MP for Northumberland, and George Stephenson to explain the matter to him. Mr Brandling very soon enlightened his understanding'.[54] The Bill proceeded without encountering major opposition and received the Royal Assent on 23 May 1823.[55]

---

was Mewburn who proposed that a new clause should be inserted to facilitate steam locomotion: *Newcastle Daily Chronicle*, 14 June 1867.

[51] Tomlinson, above n 17, 83–84.

[52] This is the wording of s 8 of the final Act, which remained unchanged from the Bill.

[53] On the passage of the third Bill through Parliament see Tomlinson, above n 17, 84–87.

[54] Ibid. Tomlinson cites the original *Larchfield Diaries* (vol 1, 13) as the source for this anecdote; it does not appear in the published edited extracts, above n 35). The sixth Earl of Shaftsbury chaired the committee from 1814 to 1851. He would no doubt have been impatient with any unusual clause as he was intent upon standardising private Bill procedures and also the clauses used. He devised a series of standard 'Shaftsbury Clauses' which were later brought together in legislation such as the Railway Clauses Consolidation Acts. The length and complexity of private Bills was then reduced by referring to standard clauses in these Acts. See DL Rydz, *The Parliamentary Agents: A History* (London, Royal Historical Society, 1979) 52–55.

[55] An Act to enable the Stockton and Darlington Railway Company to vary and alter the Line of their Railway, and also the Line or Lines of some of the Branches therefrom, and to make an additional branch therefrom, and for altering and enlarging the Powers of the Act passed for making and maintaining said Railway 1823 (4 Geo 4 c 33).

Construction of the line continued apace and the official opening ceremony took place on 27 September 1825.[56] George Stephenson drove *Locomotion No 1* on the inaugural service, hauling an immense train of assorted freight and passengers. The train commenced its journey at Shilden Lane on one of the branches which served the mines. It proceeded to Darlington at an average speed of 8 mph, accompanied on either side by horsemen on well-trained hunters jumping ditches and fences as though taking part in a steeplechase. On reaching Darlington the train was met by 12,000 onlookers, and there was a delay as some passengers disembarked and others boarded. As the train moved off along the mainline bound for Stockton, the Yarm band, who had a wagon to themselves, struck up. The train moved across the impressive Skerne bridge, creating a scene which was later immortalised in the famous painting by John Dobbin. Some three hours and seven minutes after leaving Darlington (which included many stops along the way), the train made its triumphant arrival at the coal wharf in Stockton as the Yarm band played 'God Save the King'.

Although the inaugural service was operated by steam locomotive, horses provided the bulk of the motive power in the very early years of the line. The few steam locomotives had to share the line with horse-drawn trains and on a single track with passing loops; this proved to be a recipe for disaster. There was no signalling, and the fact that the line was operated as a turnpike meant that traffic was chaotic to say the least. In fact, a certain antipathy developed between the enginemen and horse leaders. There are accounts of fisticuffs breaking out when horse and engine met one another between passing loops and neither was prepared to back up.[57] However, steam locomotion was set to displace horse power within a short space of time. In 1823 George and Robert Stephenson established a locomotive manufacturing business in Newcastle into which Pease invested considerable capital. Robert Stephenson assumed the principal engineering role in 1825 and the business took his name, Robert Stephenson and Co. In 1827 the business was joined by the established locomotive engineer Timothy Hackworth, and the two men collaborated on improved designs.[58] Henceforth locomotives provided by Robert Stephenson and Co improved in reliability and power, and by 1828 there were seven engines in operation on the line.[59] As engine performance improved there were many accounts of locomotive hauled trains being delayed by having to follow recalcitrant horse leaders who refused to let

[56] For an account of the grand opening see Tomlinson, above n 17, 105–15.

[57] Kirby, above n 17, 60–61. A number of incidents are recorded in 'Notes of Incidents Connected with the Stockton and Darlington Railway, dictated to Mr H Oxtoby by Mr G Graham Who Drove Engine No 1 "Locomotion" and Whose Father was the Traffic Manager of the Stockton and Darlington Railway': PRO RAIL 667/427.

[58] Kirby, above n 17, 61–68.

[59] The engines in operation at this time were *Locomotion*, *Hope*, *Black Diamond*, *Diligence*, *Globe*, *Chittaprat* and *Royal George*: Tomlinson, above n 17, 142–43.

them by at the passing loops. In 1833 the Company terminated the use of horses on the line and assumed direct control of all services.[60] It is at this point that the Stockton and Darlington became a fully fledged railway in the modern sense of the term.

At the opening of the Stockton and Darlington a numbers of banners fluttered at the departure point bearing certain mottos. One proclaimed the Company's motto as set out in the Company seal, *Periculum privatum utilitas publica* ('at private risk for public service').[61] The motto had been suggested by the Rev Daniel Mitford Peacock and had been adopted by the committee on 25 May 1821.[62] The motto encapsulates a theme which became increasingly prevalent in the nineteenth century, namely, the fact that high-risk schemes undertaken for profit may also be for public benefit. Although the scheme may have been motivated in large part by the wish to benefit the public and despite the display of public enthusiasm at the opening ceremony, the line was not universally welcomed. The operation of the line was to cause disturbances, which led some to question whether it was reasonable that the public benefits of the scheme should justify these harms. Almost six years after the opening of the line, the promoters found themselves indicted in public nuisance as a result of operating their famed steam locomotives.

D. THE LITIGATION

1. Background

At the grand opening of the Stockton and Darlington Railway on 27 September 1825, the *Newcastle Courant* reported on the excitement generated by the inaugural steam service as it ran alongside the Stockton to Yarm Turnpike on the approach to Stockton:[63]

> Numerous horses, carriages, gigs, carts and other vehicles travelled along with the engine, and her immense train of carriages, in some places within a few yards, without the horses seeming the least frightened; and at one time the passengers by the engine had the pleasure of accompanying and cheering their brother passengers by the stage coach, which passed alongside, and of observing the striking contrast exhibited by the power of the engine and of horses; the engine with her six hundred passengers and load, and the coach with four horses, and only sixteen passengers.

[60] Kirby, above n 17, 94–95.
[61] Tomlinson, above n 17, 110.
[62] Ibid, 73.
[63] *Newcastle Courant*, 1 October 1825.

The horses, which were not 'the least frightened' by this fire-breathing iron monster, were clearly made of sterner stuff than those which were to pass along the turnpike over the next few years. Others were terrified by these alien machines, and a first-hand account of the difficulties of controlling a horse in these circumstances is provided by 'Nimrod' in his *Hunting Tours*.[64] Nimrod encountered a steam locomotive whilst riding alongside the Stockton and Darlington on the Yarm turnpike on 14 December 1827:[65]

> The distance from Darlington (which I passed through) to Yarm is five miles, for which I allowed myself somewhat about half an hour, the road being none of the best, but I did not reach it under an hour. The delay arose from my meeting something, which I could only compare to a moving hell. Excuse my profaneness—if such it can be called—for I cannot find any other simile. This turned out to be a locomotive steam-engine, which, running parallel with and close to the road, so alarmed my hack, that it was in vain that I tried to make him face it. This, however, is not to be wondered at: for a horse is naturally a timid animal, and this machine was enough to alarm the Devil himself, if he had met with it, as my horse did, out of his own country. The night was dark, which increased the terrors of it: and it really was a frightful object. The noise of the wheels—perhaps twenty pairs —the working of the engine, the blazing fires of blue and yellow hues, the hissing of the steam, and the black- faced wretches, with their red lips and white teeth, running to and fro, all conspired to heighten the resemblance, and my astonishment increased the more when I reflected on such a nuisance as this being suffered so close to a turnpike road. The only way in which I got past it at last was to get my horse into a hole, with his tail towards the machine, but I never saw an animal so alarmed.

Nimrod's use of the term 'nuisance' to describe the operation of steam locomotives in such close proximity to the turnpike was to prove prophetic. It was only a matter of time before proceedings in public nuisance were instigated in respect of the disruption on the Yarm Turnpike. Indeed, as might be expected, a degree of opposition had emerged to the use of steam locomotives. Unlike canals, it had become apparent that the disruption caused by building a steam railway extended beyond the construction phase. Thomas Creevey, a Member of Parliament who led objections to the Liverpool and Manchester Railway Bill, referred to 'this infernal nuisance—the loco-motive Monster carrying Eighty Tons of goods, and navigated by a tail of smoke and sulphur'.[66] As regards the Stockton and Darlington, certain landowners who had lost land to the

---

[64] Nimrod (ie CJ Apperley), *Nimrod's Hunting Tours—Interspersed with Characteristic Sayings and Doings of Sporting Men* (London, Pittman, 1835). The book is a series of recollections, anecdotes, advice and useful information based upon the author's many years of touring the country and taking part in hunts.

[65] Ibid, 435–36.

[66] Sir H Maxwell (ed), *The Creevey Papers* (London, John Murray, 1903) vol 2, 88, cited by Tomlinson, above n 17, 102.

railway anticipated the disruption. John Russell Rowntree successfully appealed against the level of compensation offered and had it increased to £500 so as to reflect likely nuisance.[67]

2. The Trial

In 1830 Edward Pease, several of his fellow directors and the enginemen were indicted in public nuisance.[68] Those who brought the action were described as 'gentlemen residing in the neighbourhood, Magistrates of the County, and some other persons, who, either in their own persons or by their property, had sustained injury from this undertaking'.[69] There must have been a fair degree of local opposition to the line because the proceedings had to be moved to the York Assizes to ensure a fair trial.[70]

It is not clear to what extent such incidents were regarded as a problem prior to the indictment. However, once proceedings were underway, the management were clearly in no doubt that action had to be taken to mitigate the harm. In a caution to enginemen signed by the company secretary, Richard Otley, on 7 November 1831, it stated at point V:[71] 'Engine-Men to avoid, as much as possible, letting off Steam near public Roads, and should any Horse or Horses take fright at the Engine or Waggons when passing, immediate assistance to be rendered by the Engine-Men and their assistants'.

The trial was held at the York Assizes on 30 March 1831 before Mr Justice Littledale. In his opening address for the prosecution, Mr Williams elected to set the case up as a battle between new technology and the traditional English way of life.[72] Williams acknowledged the technological achievement represented by these machines. He confessed that had any man attempted to explain the concept of a steam locomotive to him 30 years earlier he would have concluded that he must have 'jumped down

---

67 *Durham County Advertiser*, 9 April 1825.

68 The original indictment is in the National Archives: PRO KB11/87, Pt 1, Doc 32. The Directors cited on the indictment include Edward Pease the Elder, Edward Pease the Younger, Joseph Pease, Benjamin Flounders, John Kiching and William Backhouse. The named enginemen include James Stephenson, Joseph Montrey, John Montrey, Robert Murray, Michael Law, Thomas Lanchester and Henry Lanchester.

69 Ibid. The original indictment is dated 7 August 1830. It is then recorded that a plea was entered on 22 October and that the company secretary, Richard Otley, deposited recognizance of £200. The matter went before a Grand Jury at Westminster Hall in November, which found that there was case to answer.

70 *The Morning Chronicle*, 2 April 1831. The proceedings at the York Assizes are also reported in *The Newcastle Courant*, 9 April 1831 and *The Leeds Mercury*, 2 April 1831.

71 'Notice of Traffic Regulations, Stockton and Darlington Railway Company, 1831'. A photograph of one of the original posters displaying the cautions is reproduced by Kirby, above n 17, 92.

72 From notes of evidence taken during the trial, Durham County Records Office (DCRO) Records of the Fleming family of Tudhoe, D/FLE/122, D/FLE/123.

from the moon!' Notwithstanding the reasons for these experiments, 'whether the gratification of philosophy or vanity, or for the purposes of gain' the King's subjects should not be required to pay too high a price. In a curious strategy, which can hardly have endeared him to the jury, Williams then went on to paint a picture of a backward looking merry old England. The 'obsolete and perhaps impracticable people' using horses on the highway should 'not be sacrificed to these scientific projects and locomotive engines'. He went on,

> The old people of England are not easily moved—they do not easily adopt alternatives even if they are improvements; the dull, lagged and quiet people of this realm must beg for a little protection of the law, as long as it may be necessary.[73]

Williams then dealt with the specific nature of the complaints and described the nature of the nuisance on the highway in the following terms. Had any of the jury been in the habit of riding or driving a horse along the turnpike, they would have discovered:[74]

> what antipathy horses have to these new rivals that are set up against them, with what difficulty most of them (some of them have stronger nerves than others) are induced to come into contact with the great roaring, snorting appalling monster vomiting smoke and fire in all directions, and which the horse can by no means recognise as a cater-cousin or relation of his. When they heard of the effect of those machines upon the mails and coaches, for all horses were similarly affected, it would be of no doubt that they were a most tremendous nuisance to persons passing along the Stockton turnpike-road.

Williams then proceeded to outline the nature of the enabling legislation and made the point that it established a corridor of up to 100 yards in width within which the promoters were authorised to build. Had the line been built further back from the turnpike, whilst remaining within this corridor, less disruption may have been caused. This prompted an interjection by the defence counsel, Frederick Pollock,[75] which led to the following exchange:[76]

> [Pollock] It may save my Learned Friend some time, if I state that if we were owners of the land for 100 miles, we have no right to use these engines or even to cross the road except for the Act of Parliament.

---

[73] Ibid.

[74] Ibid.

[75] Later to serve as Attorney General in Sir Robert Peel's first administration before pursuing a highly distinguished and celebrated judicial career as Lord Chief Baron of the Exchequer: JM Rigg, rev P Polden, 'Pollock, Sir (Jonathan) Frederick, First Baronet (1783–1870)' in *Oxford Dictionary of National Biography* (Oxford, Oxford University Press, 2004), available at http://www.oxforddnb.com/view/article/22479.

[76] DCRO, above n 72).

[Littledale J] Then in fact it is a question as to the construction of an Act of Parliament.

[Pollock] Exactly so my Lord.

[Williams] Then gentlemen, I shall trouble you no further but call my witnesses; for a fortiori, if the Defendant's cannot legally cross the road without the act of Parliament, neither can they run parallel to it which they do for nearly 2 miles.

It is not often that one can put one's finger on the exact moment that a common law concept comes into being; this exchange may provide one such rare example. In it we can see the fundamental elements of statutory authority being formulated in the minds of the lawyers. The most critical element is the argument that the existence of statutory powers takes the matter out of the common law and renders it a matter of statutory interpretation.

As his response indicates, Williams had no answer to the argument and pressed ahead with his witness evidence. Charles Harrison, a toll keeper on the turnpike, recounted several incidents in which all manner of wagons and carriages drawn by up to six horses had been overturned. Those on horseback fared little better as 'The same cause frequently made saddle horses, plunge, rear, start aside, or turn around and gallop a considerable distance'.[77] On many occasions he had offered 'alarmed and agitated' horses refuge in his barns until the locomotive had passed. They invariably emerged 'sweating as they do after hearing a distant cannonade'.[78] Thomas Ayres, a wine merchant from Stockton, reported that he was driving a gig past a locomotive when the fireman stirred up the fire, causing the chimney to emit sparks and smoke, with the result that his horse 'took fright'. Emboldened by the success of his statutory authority argument, Pollock again interjected and read out in full section 8 of the 1823 Act authorising steam locomotion. The defendants had a statutory right to conduct the activity and could not be guilty of a nuisance in respect of the consequences thereof. Thus the evidence of a wine merchant incommoded in passing and re-passing along the turnpike was neither here nor there. Pollock then made the crucial assertion that 'It must be supposed that the legislature balanced the evils and inconveniences before the power was given'. Accordingly, the public benefits arising from the scheme must have been deemed to have outweighed the inconveniences suffered by the public.[79]

Pollock pursued the public benefit theme in the case for the defence. Richard Otley, the Secretary of the Stockton and Darlington Railway, gave evidence regarding the vast quantities of coal now carried by the railway. In the year ending 30 January 1830, 171,000 tons of coal had been trans-

---

[77] Ibid.
[78] Ibid.
[79] Ibid.

ported and carriage costs had been considerably reduced. Furthermore, in order to keep pace with demand, there was a pressing need to expand the fleet of locomotives beyond the seven already in use.[80] Pollock emphasised the economic benefits of the line and claimed that these extended beyond local business concerns and encompassed the national interest. Conveying coals cheaply to the Tees would benefit 'not only London but the other great interests connected with the commerce and wealth of the country'.[81] He then questioned the motives of those who had sought to bring about the present prosecution. Whilst he did not wish to characterise the action as 'an outcry against Reform', he regarded it as 'an attempt to put down persons from doing that which they had a right to do under the Act of Parliament'.[82] Furthermore, in operating the railway, the defendants had done everything demanded by discretion, prudence and care to minimise the disruption caused by the locomotives. In this respect, Otley gave evidence to the effect that 'the engines of the Company were constructed on the best principle, and had been from time to time improved'.[83] This latter point appears not to have been contested, and Littledale J shut the door to any argument based upon want of care by concluding that 'upon the evidence of Otley it appeared that due care and caution had been used to make the thing as little nuisance as possible'.[84]

Littledale J was of the view that the case raised a major point of law which needed to be resolved before a verdict could be sought. The judge suggested that if the facts were agreed the jury should be invited to deliver a Special Verdict in order to distil the issues to a particular point of law. After some consultation between the parties it was agreed that the jury should be asked to find that the steam locomotives constituted a public nuisance 'unless authorised by the Acts of Parliament and the facts proved upon his Lordship's notes'.[85] The jury found accordingly and the question was duly referred to the Court of King's Bench. An answer to this question in the defendants' favour would open the way for the defence which would later be termed 'statutory authority'. In other words, activities which prima facie constitute a public nuisance were not actionable if authorised by statute. However, it was also necessary to determine whether the authority of a statute to conduct an activity was limited to harm not arising from any fault on the part of the defendant.

---

80 Ibid.
81 Ibid.
82 Ibid. This comment appears in the newspaper accounts, above n 70). Furthermore, on the back of one set of the notes of the evidence the comment is written in an unknown hand: 'this is nothing but a clamour against Reform'.
83 Ibid.
84 Ibid.
85 Ibid.

3. The Court of Kings Bench

In the Court of King's Bench[86] the case was tried before Lord Tenterden CJ, Littledale, Parke and Taunton JJ. On this occasion the prosecution was led by Cresswell Easterby (later the judge Sir Cresswell Cresswell), who appeared to accept the notion of statutory authority. His main arguments were based upon the idea that such powers should be interpreted very narrowly. A statutory power of this nature should not be construed as conferring blanket immunity and it should not afford the defendant any protection in respect of avoidable harms. For example, as Williams had argued at trial, the corridor of land in which the defendants were entitled to build would have enabled the line to be set further back from the turnpike.[87] Furthermore, where Parliament had intended to expropriate existing rights one would have expected it to make provision for compensation.[88]

Once again the defence was led by Pollock, who took the opportunity to refine his nascent concept of statutory authority. He reiterated the public utility arguments and the fact that Parliament must be taken to have balanced the benefits against individual detriments.[89] Pollock conceded the argument that the immunity conferred by a statute should be confined to inevitable harms. However, he was of the view that the statutory provision should not be so narrowly construed that it rendered the defence meaningless. Some disruption was unavoidable; otherwise there would have been no need to gain statutory powers in the first place.[90] The test should be whether all reasonable steps had been taken to reduce the harm to tolerable levels. In this respect, he cited the evidence of Otley to the effect that the locomotives were of the best construction. Furthermore, the flexibility which the Act allowed, regarding the precise positioning of the line, was not for the purpose of reducing nuisances on the highway. Pollock also ventured that the disruption to traffic on the highway would lessen as horses became accustomed to their new rivals. Finally, he rejected the notion that the absence of provisions for compensation was determinative of whether Parliament had intended to abrogate existing common law rights.[91]

The leading judgment was delivered by Parke J, who agreed that the case raised an issue of statutory interpretation. The wording of section 8 of the 1823 Act, which empowered the company to use steam locomotives, would be given its literal and ordinary meaning unless this would lead to

---

[86] *R v Pease* (1832) 4 B & Ad 30, 110 ER 366.
[87] Ibid, 4 B & Ad 34.
[88] Ibid, 4 B & Ad 36.
[89] Ibid, 4 B & Ad 38.
[90] Ibid, 4 B & Ad 38–39.
[91] Ibid.

unreasonable results. On this basis, he held that that section conferred an 'unqualified authority to use the engines'. It was inevitable that nuisances would arise from the construction of the line as the proximity to the Yarm turnpike was clearly shown in the plans:[92]

> The Legislature, therefore, must be presumed to have known that the railroad would be adjacent for a mile to the public highway, and consequently that travellers upon the highway would be in all probability incommoded by the passage of locomotive engines along the railroad.

Parke J accepted that, had these consequences been deemed an 'unreasonable result' of the use of statutory powers, it would have been necessary to imply some qualification or condition requiring mitigation of the nuisances. Examples of such measures, given by the prosecution, included the erection of screens or building the railway further back from the highway. However, Parke J was not prepared to find that the nuisances suffered by the highway users could be regarded as unreasonable given the wider public benefits arising from the construction of the new railway. The majority of the public would benefit from 'more speedy travelling and conveyance of merchandise along the new railroad'.[93] These benefits were deemed to outweigh the inconvenience suffered by highway users:[94]

> Can any one say that the public interests are unjustly dealt with, when the injury to one line of communication is compensated by the increased benefit of another? So far is such a proceeding from being unreasonable, that it was held by the majority of the Judges in *Rex v Russell* (6 B & C 566), that a nuisance was excusable on that principle at common law; and whether that be the law or not, at least it is clear that an express provision of the Legislature, having that effect, cannot be unreasonable.

Thus public benefit was clearly established as the principal justification for construing a statute in a manner which limited existing rights. Presumably, had Parke J found that the scheme benefited no one other than the promoters, he would have found the nuisances to be an 'unreasonable result' in the absence of any provision in the Act for compensation.

The most significant aspect of the judgment, though, was that statutory authority was formulated as a specific defence to an otherwise actionable nuisance. In this respect, the decision was fundamentally different to *R v Russell*,[95] which was the principal authority cited in argument, and in Parke J's judgment. It will be recalled that that case had turned on well-established principle: that public benefit was relevant to the issue of whether an activity was legitimate and hence reasonable. The public local Acts in question were regarded as strong evidence of the legitimacy of the

---

[92] Ibid, 4 B & Ad 41.
[93] Ibid, 4 B & Ad 42.
[94] Ibid.
[95] (1827) 6 B & C 566, 108 ER 560.

works, but were not in themselves determinative of whether a public nuisance had been committed. The approach adopted in *R v Pease* effectively removed the matter from the common law altogether and rendered it a matter of statutory interpretation.

The notion that a statutory authorisation could operate as a specific defence to a prima facie public nuisance was entirely novel and, in this respect, *R v Pease* can properly be regarded as the starting point for the defence of statutory authority. The decision is especially significant for the reason that Parke J was prepared to regard such an authority as implicit within the statute in the absence of express words. This had a significant effect on the drafting of future statutes; where the legislature intended to preserve common law rights, they felt compelled to insert 'nuisance clauses' for the avoidance of doubt.[96] Furthermore, the decision can be regarded as an early example of judicial deference to the legislature. Parke J was prepared to assume that the sophisticated parliamentary machine would have weighed the competing interests and reached an unimpeachable conclusion that the railway was for the public benefit.

This begs the question of whether the court was right to place such faith in the thoroughness of the parliamentary procedures. In fact, the various standing and select committees which scrutinised private Bills in both Houses of Parliament were exceedingly thorough. Some commentators went so far as to say that the procedure was quasi-judicial in nature. As Erskine May noted:[97]

> In passing private bills, Parliament still exercises its legislative functions: but its proceedings partake also of a judicial character. The persons whose private interests are to be promoted, appear as suitors for the bill; while those who apprehend injury are admitted as adverse parties in the suit. Many of the formalities of a court of justice are maintained; various conditions are required to be observed, and their observance to be strictly proved; and if the parties do not sustain the bill in its progress, by following every regulation and form prescribed, it is not forwarded in the house in which it is pending.

The ability of either side to call seemingly endless witnesses, the complexity of the subject matter and the repetitive nature of Parliamentary procedure became unsustainable during the railway boom of the 1840s. As Pulling commented with discernible bitterness:[98]

---

96 Although whether such clauses were of practical benefit to the plaintiff is doubtful in the light of how they were interpreted. In *AG v Gaslight and Coke Co* (1877) 7 Ch D 217 it was held that a nuisance clause was without prejudice to the general principle established in *R v Pease* to the effect that the defendant could not be liable in respect of any unavoidable harm.

97 T Erskine May, *A Treatise on the Law, Privileges, Proceedings and Usage of Parliament*, 6th edn (London, Butterworths, 1868).

98 A Pulling, *Private Bill Legislation: Can Anything be Now Done to Improve it?* (Longman, Green & Co, London 1859) 7.

The Bill must pass both Houses, and be read three times in each, before it receives the Royal Assent. In order to protect the rights of those who may be affected, the standing orders require a great deal of preliminary procedure on the part of the promoters of Private Bills, as to notices, deposit of plans, books of reference, &c. After a compliance with these requirements has been proved before the Examiner, and the Bill has been introduced into the House in which the proceedings are commenced, and read a second time, the real merits of the measure, for the first time, undergo investigation, the Select Committees, to whom the reference is made, having, we are told, sometimes to hear as many as 400 witnesses adduced by the various parties interested. When the Bill has passed the Lords, or Commons, as the case may be, the same tedious and expensive proceedings have for the most part to be gone through in the other House.

The promoters of the Stockton and Darlington benefited from being pioneers and the general ignorance, on the part of the general public, regarding the nature of steam locomotion. There was little organised opposition aside from that mounted by Lord Eldon and Lord Darlington. Once their Lordships had been appeased by route alterations and financial settlements, the Bills proceeded swiftly through Parliament. There is no evidence that the committee hearings were bogged down by streams of expert witnesses and concerned members of the public.[99] By contrast, the Liverpool and Manchester Railway Bill endured a much stormier passage through Parliament. By this stage, an effective anti-railway campaign had been organised by Thomas Creevey MP.[100] George Stephenson famously crumbled under fierce cross-examination during one of the committee hearings.[101] The promoters got their Act in the end, but not without a very hard struggle.

Thus, in *R v Pease* the court could be reasonably confident that the Bill would have been subject to thorough scrutiny. However, the main problem was that, due to the novelty of the technology, many of the problems would not have been foreseen. One cannot be sure that the full extent of the potential nuisances was fully investigated. Nevertheless, the court was prepared to make a bold assumption that these difficulties must have been anticipated and deemed an acceptable price to pay for the public benefits

[99] As regards the 1821 Bill, Mewburn recalled that once the opposition of Lords Eldon and Darlington had been dealt with there was only a 'feeble show of opposition' from turnpike commissioners (concerned about loss of revenue) and a few landowners: Mewburn, above n 35, 177.

[100] On 31 May 1825 the committee killed off the first Bill by voting to reject the assertion made in the preamble that the scheme would be of benefit to local people. By this stage it was reported that the promoters had spent £30,000 on the surveys and fighting opposition alone: see *Leeds Mercury*, 11 June 1825.

[101] 'I began to wish for a hole to creep into' he ruefully commented afterwards: C Wolmar, *Fire and Steam: How the Railways Transformed Britain* (London, Atlantic Books, 2007) 28; F Ferneyhough, *Liverpool and Manchester Railway 1830–1980* (London, Robert Hale, 1980) 22.

of the scheme. In this sense, the decision appears generous to the promoters. However, set against this, it must be noted that the decision resulted in a duty to minimise the harm.

An important feature of the decision is the fact that it appeared to suggest that the statutory immunity would only extend to harm inevitably arising from the use of statutory powers. To some extent this appeared to introduce an element of fault into the equation, since harm which is not inevitable must a priori have been avoidable. The court in *Pease* did not inquire too closely into whether the locomotives could have been better designed or operated. Given the infancy of the technology, and the extent to which expert knowledge resided in those who built and operated the machines, this was hardly surprising. As railways became more established, and the technology more widely understood, others would question the extent to which the harms caused by steam locomotives should be regarded as inevitable.

E. DEVELOPMENTS AFTER *PEASE* – THE RAILWAY SPARKS CASES

It is easy to forget the astonishing speed with which the railway network began to develop following the opening of the Stockton and Darlington. In the year that the line opened, plans for the Liverpool and Manchester Railway, also engineered by George Stephenson, were already at an advanced stage.[102] By the mid-1830s, projects were afoot throughout the land. Not surprisingly, further disputes were set to arise from the operation of steam locomotives. The issue of spooked horses does not seem to have reappeared as a major issue. To some extent, Pollock's prediction that horses would become accustomed to these machines may have been realised. In any case, due to the rapidity of railway expansion, steam engines very quickly had to be accepted as a fact of life. Both horsemen and enginemen would have had to come to some accommodation regarding their modes of operation when in close proximity. Nevertheless, other forms of harm occasioned by the use of steam engines did lead to further litigation. For example, in 1835 a wine and spirit merchant from South Shields won £104 in damages from the Stanhope and Tyne Railway Company in respect of noise, vibration and 'obnoxious effluvia' caused by passing engines. The vibration damaged the structural fabric of the building and stock in the cellars. The noise of nocturnal engine movements

---

102 As noted above in 1825, the promoters of the Liverpool and Manchester were struggling to get their Bill through Parliament largely due to the effective opposition of Thomas Creevey MP. The grand opening of the line took place on 15 September 1830: Wolmar, above n 101) ch 1.

disturbed the sleep of the plaintiff and his family, and the smoke interfered with their overall enjoyment of the property.[103]

There then followed a series of cases involving fire damage caused by sparks from railway engines.[104] This line of cases led to much agonised consideration of whether liability for fire damage should depend upon negligence or some stricter form of liability. The authority of *R v Pease* was set to have a major influence on the outcome of this debate.

Aldridge v Great Western Railway Co[105] arose from an incident in which sparks from a passing locomotive set fire to a stack of beans in a field near Burnham, Buckinghamshire. A special case was stated to clarify the appropriate cause of action. Channell, for the plaintiff, argued that the damage sounded in trespass. This argument was rebuffed by Tindal CJ, largely on the grounds that a master could not be vicariously liable in trespass for the torts of his servant. Hence the railway company could not be liable for any trespass committed by the driver.[106] It was determined that the jury should be asked to decide whether there had been negligence in the mode of driving the engine.

The courts soon had an opportunity to consider more fully whether sparks from locomotives could be attributable to negligence on the part of the operator. In *Piggot v Eastern Counties Railway Co*[107] sparks from a passing mail train had set fire to farm buildings. By now a number of spark-arresting devices had been developed and the company was found to be at fault for failing to have fitted any such equipment to its locomotives. Tindal CJ, who by now must have become something of an expert on steam locomotives, likened these devices to muzzles. It was clearly established that the owner of an animal likely to bite was under a duty to fit a muzzle,[108] and so a railway company was under a similar duty to muzzle its engines, given their propensity to emit sparks!

The case of *Vaughan v Taff Vale Railway Co*[109] marks the point at which *Pease* was formally adopted by the law of tort. Once again, an action on the case for negligence was brought following the destruction of eight acres of the plaintiff's woodland by sparks from a locomotive.

---

[103] *Bell v Harrison* (unreported, 1835), but see *Durham Advertiser*, 7 August 1835.

[104] By 1836 the issue was of sufficient importance to merit a House of Lords Select Committee on the subject. This took evidence from a number of the great engineers of the day, including Robert Stephenson and Isambard Kingdom Brunel, on the practicability of spark catching devices: *The Times*, 9 December 1836.

[105] (1841) 3 Man & G 514, 133 ER 1246.

[106] The Chief Justice's firm restatement of this principle is hardly surprising, given the fact that he had been responsible for establishing it in the famous case of *Williams v Holland* (1833) 10 Bing 112, 131 ER 848. See Fifoot, above n 7, 186–87; Prichard, above n 16. It was affirmed again in another railway case, this time concerning the running down and killing of the plaintiff's sheep which had escaped onto the line and into the path of the defendant's steam locomotive: *Sharrod v London and North Western Railway Co* (1849) 4 Ex 580, 154 ER 1545.

[107] (1846) 3 CB 228, 136 ER 92.

[108] Citing *Smith v Pelah* (1795) 2 Strange 1264, 93 ER 1171.

[109] (1860) 5 H & N 678, 157 ER 1351.

Clearly, the judgment in *Piggot* must have had some effect in that the defendant's locomotives had been fitted with spark catchers in conjunction with various other precautions. Nevertheless, no system could arrest all sparks and red-hot cinders. A somewhat confusing direction to the jury resulted in a finding in favour of the plaintiff despite the fact it was acknowledged that all reasonable measures had been taken. An application for a retrial was rejected by the Court of Exchequer. Thus the defendant company found itself liable despite the fact that everyone acknowledged that it had done all it reasonably could to mitigate the spark problem. This raised the spectre of strict liability and an appeal was made to Exchequer Chamber.

Strict liability is a highly problematic term. Today we use it to make a clear distinction between fault-based and non-fault-based liability. In the early nineteenth century lawyers did not draw such clear distinctions. Fault was not the essence of the action in trespass and private nuisance, thus one could say that liability was stricter than in negligence. However, it would still be open to argue certain defences, some of which could inject a significant fault element, the major difference being that it placed the onus on the defendant to justify his actions. The present action was not brought in trespass or private nuisance. It was another example of action on the case for negligence. Nevertheless, Grove argued for the plaintiff that 'by the custom of the realm every person is bound to keep his fire so as to prevent it from injuring his neighbour'.[110] This invoked the ancient idea that a man acts at his peril in some cases, an idea which one can possibly trace back to trespass, but which appears somewhat out of place in an action on the case for negligence. For this reason Grove continued that 'if a fire broke out and burnt an adjoining dwelling, *negligence was presumed*'.[111] In other words, conducting certain activities was deemed so hazardous that merely conducting them was regarded as a form of fault.[112] Similar reasoning, he argued, could be applied to spreading fire through operating

---

110 Ibid, 5 H & N 684. In fact it is highly questionable whether strict liability did historically apply to the spread of fire: Fifoot, above n 7, 155–56.

111 Ibid, 5 H & N 684 (emphasis added).

112 F Pollock 'Duties of Insuring Safety: The Rule in *Rylands v Fletcher*' (1886) 2 LQR 52. Pollock regarded strict liability as a blurring of the distinction between the activity itself and the manner in which the activity is carried out. Thus merely conducting the activity and exposing persons to the risk is regarded as a form of fault. This is encapsulated by a passage on the first page of the article: 'The law might have been content with applying the general standard of reasonable care, in the sense that a reasonable man dealing with a dangerous thing—fire, flood-water, poison, deadly weapons, weights projecting or suspended over a thoroughfare, or whatsoever else it be—will exercise a keener foresight and use more anxious precaution that if it were an object unlikely to cause harm, such as a faggot, or a loaf of bread. A prudent man does not handle a loaded gun or a sharp sword in the same fashion as a stick or a shovel. But the course adopted in England has been to preclude questions of detail by making the duty absolute; or, if we prefer to put it in that form, *to consolidate the judgment of fact into an unbending rule of law*.' (emphasis added).

a steam locomotive. By this ingenious device he sought to introduce strict liability in an action on the case for negligence.

The argument appears to have been taken on board by the majority of the court, who accepted that certain activities could give rise to strict liability. Cockburn CJ accepted that certain activities may give rise to liability without fault. However, he cited *Pease* as authority for the proposition that an activity sanctioned by Parliament cannot fall into this category:[113]

> Although it may be true, that if a person keeps an animal of known dangerous propensities, or dangerous instrument, he will be responsible to those who are thereby injured, independently of any negligence in the mode of dealing with the animal or using the instrument; yet when the legislature has sanctioned and authorized the use of a particular thing, and it is used for the purpose for which it was authorized, and every precaution has been observed to prevent injury, the sanction of the legislature carries with it this consequence, that if damage results from the use of such thing independently of negligence, the party using it is not responsible.

In a very short judgment of a few lines, one Sir Colin Blackburn observed that the case reduced the question to one of:[114]

> whether the defendants are responsible for an accident arising from the use of fire when they are guilty of no negligence in using it. *That might have been a difficult question*, but *Rex v Pease* has settled that when the legislature has sanctioned the use of a locomotive engine, there is no liability for injury caused by using it, so long as every precaution is taken consistent with its usage.

Thus Blackburn J was not convinced that, in the absence of statutory powers, the liability of the railway company would turn upon whether they had exercised due care.

Of course, Blackburn J was later to cement his place in legal history by bringing about the rule in *Rylands v Fletcher*[115] which arguably expanded the scope of strict liability. And in fact, after this landmark decision had been affirmed by the House of Lords,[116] Blackburn J would not have long to wait before he was presented with an opportunity to test this 'new' rule in another railway sparks case. In *Jones v Festiniog Railway Co*[117] the plaintiff's haystack had been destroyed by fire caused by a spark emitted by one of the defendant's locomotives. It was accepted that the company had done all that was feasible to prevent the emission of sparks. Blackburn J held that this was a situation in which *Rylands v Fletcher* could apply. 'Carrying a fire along a railway', as he put it, could certainly result in the

---

113 *Vaughan*, above n 109, 5 H & N 685.
114 Ibid, 5 H & N 688 (emphasis added).
115 *Fletcher v Rylands* (1866) LR 1 Ex 265.
116 *Rylands v Fletcher* (1868) LR 3 HL 330.
117 (1867–68) LR 3 QB 733.

escape of mischievous elements, sparks and red-hot cinders in this case. He cited *R v Pease* and *Vaughan v Taff Railway Co* as authority for the proposition that such an activity would give rise to liability irrespective of negligence but for the existence of statutory authority. As regards the latter case, he stated:[118]

> The company were expressly authorized by s 86 of the Railway Clauses Consolidation Act (8 Vict c 20), to employ locomotive engines as a motive power for their carriages and therefore to use and carry the fire along the railway, and the decision of the Exchequer Chamber was, that this express authority of the legislature took the case out of the operation of the common law, and legalized the use of the dangerous engines, subject to the condition that the company took all reasonable precautions, and if, in spite of these precautions sparks escaped, the company were not liable for the consequences.

However, the present case was distinguished on the basis that the Act of 1832, which authorised the construction of the line, did not extend to the operation of steam locomotives. Thus the matter was not taken out of the common law and the rules of strict liability were applied. It is easy to regard this as an attempt by the court to limit the protection afforded by the Act so as to allow the matter to be determined by the common law. In fact, it is important to note that the Act was very old and it had been used to authorise a horse-drawn tramway. There had been no intention to operate steam locomotives at the time. Unfortunately for the company, they had not had the foresight to return to Parliament to seek further authorisation for steam traction.

So there we have it: it would seem that the courts would have subjected the railways to strict liability in respect of damage caused by their locomotives had it not been for the legislature. Indeed, road-going steam carriages and traction engines were commonly subjected to strict liability as they were not operated pursuant to some statutory authority. The driver brought the machine onto the highway at his peril.[119] As regards the railways, the decision in *Jones v Festiniog* did not have a profound effect. Most railway acts had a clause, similar to that drafted by Francis Mewburn, authorising the use of steam locomotion.[120] Had the promoters of the Stockton and Darlington not had the foresight to insert that clause, railway history could have been very different. The last remaining steam engines were finally withdrawn from use on British railways on 11 August

---

118 Ibid, 736–77.

119 See JR Spencer, 'Motor-Cars and the Rule in *Rylands v Fletcher*: A Chapter of Accidents in the History of Law and Motoring' [1983] *CLJ* 65, who offers the surprising insight that the courts came very close to applying similar reasoning to the internal combustion engine.

120 In fact the standard s 86 of the Railway Clauses Consolidation Act cited by Blackburn J in *Jones v Festiniog* derived from Mewburn's s 8 of the second Stockton and Darlington Railway Act. The fact that it was adopted as a standard clause underscores the pioneering nature of Mewburn's work.

1968, some 100 years after the *Festiniog* decision. Fire damage by sparks continued to be an issue throughout that time, although technological means of arresting the sparks continued to improve. Some statutory relief was offered by the statutory compensation scheme introduced by the Railway (Fires) Acts of 1905 and 1923, although they were very restrictive.

Even today there is an occasional echo of the past. On 28 May 2008 a preserved steam locomotive operating a special charter train between Carnforth and Ravenglass had to be taken out of service as it left a trail of fire in its wake due to a defective firebox.[121] No doubt those same preserved steam locomotives still, from time to time, startle horses on the highways and byways of England.

F. CONCLUSION

As noted in the introduction, the railway sparks issue is a classic case study that is often used in the economic analysis of tort. Pigou[122] asserted that the law as it stood tended to throw the costs upon the victim of the fire damage rather than the railway companies. Coase[123] looked a little more closely at the actual substance of the law in England and concluded that the common law would have imposed strict liability, thereby throwing the costs upon the railway companies, but for statutes conferring a partial immunity. Simpson[124] has said that Coase's analysis is wrong and displays a misunderstanding of the legal history of the matter. The courts did not appear to settle upon a rule of strict liability for railway locomotives until the 1868 decision of *Jones v Festiniog Railway*.[125] Thereafter, their inability to impose that rule of strict liability in the majority of cases, due to the existence of statutory authority, was self-inflicted, in that the statutes were generously interpreted in favour of the promoters. The analysis of the railway sparks cases, set out above, certainly supports Simpson's argument. However, it also causes one to reflect upon how the courts were initially

---

121 G Ellison, 'Steam Special Sparks Hotline to Fire Service' available at http://www. whitehaven-news.co.uk/news/1.114574 (last accessed 19 June 2009).

122 Above n 5.

123 Above n 6.

124 AWB Simpson, *Leading Cases in the Common Law* (Oxford, Clarendon Press, 1995) 169.

125 The one scrap of evidence that the courts may have decided to place the costs on railways as a result of some economic analysis is provided by an often cited passage from the judgment of Bramwell B in *Bamford v Turnley* (1862) 7 H & N 160, 158 ER 433. This was not a railways sparks case, but he conveniently used the hypothetical example of a wood burned down by railway sparks in obiter discussion of public utility. He acknowledged that the railways were for public benefit but only if they paid their way by paying for the destruction of woods etc. This does indeed sound very much like an economic 'cost internalisation' argument, although Simpson cautions against projecting an economic rationale onto the passage ex post. In his view, Bramwell B's main concern was ethical and that one should not be 'unjustly enriched' through profiting without paying compensation: Simpson, ibid, 173–75.

persuaded to allow statutes to cut across existing common law rights in so direct a manner. This inevitably brings us back to *R v Pease*, which set the common law upon this course.

The decision in *R v Pease* is something of a watershed in terms of judicial attitudes to legislation. Until the early nineteenth century law was very much regarded as the preserve of judges and the courts. Legislation played a subsidiary role, and much of it proved to be inadequate and ill thought out. The courts were understandably sceptical about legislative reform, and legislation tended to operate without prejudice to existing common law rights. The Industrial Revolution generated a new cadre of professionals in the sciences and business who had a clearer understanding of what needed to be done to facilitate industrial expansion. This brought about a new professionalism in terms of the drafting of both private and public Acts.[126] This is exemplified by the manner in which the Stockton and Darlington Railway was implemented. One is struck by the foresight of Pease and the sophistication of the commercial expertise which he and his fellow Quaker promoters were able to bring to bear upon the project.

Much has been written on the success of the Quakers in business at this time.[127] A detailed analysis is beyond the scope of this paper, although certain themes are clearly demonstrated by the manner in which the Stockton and Darlington came about. There is a certain clarity of vision and purpose in evidence, perhaps attributable to the fact that they were unencumbered by titles and tradition. An obvious point concerns the network of credit created by familial and commercial ties. As regards the detailed planning of the railway, it is perhaps one of those accidents of history which brought together Pease and Stephenson, and it is a matter of pure chance that their personalities were ideally suited. It proved to be a perfect match in terms of combining the engineering brilliance, the commercial expertise and the foresight necessary to bring about such a groundbreaking scheme.

Had it not been for those many private meetings between Pease and Stephenson, the decision might never have been taken to use steam locomotion. However, had Francis Mewburn not been equal to the task of drafting the novel and sophisticated legislation needed to put those plans into effect, the scheme might never have reached fruition. It is likely that Mewburn anticipated the need for a special clause authorising steam locomotion. The fact that the Festiniog Railway sought to rely upon its existing statutory authorisation of 1832, once it started running steam locomotives, demonstrates that it was by no means obvious that such a clause was necessary. Mewburn's obituary rightly regarded his lawyerly

---

126 For an analysis of the changing attitudes towards legislation at this time see PS Attiyah, *Rise and Fall of Freedom of Contract* (Oxford, Oxford University Press, 1979) 252.

127 See Raistrick, above n 30.

skills to be of equal importance to Pease's business acumen and Stephenson's engineering genius in terms of the success of the project. When Mewburn retired from his position with the Stockton and Darlington in 1860, the company chairman, Thomas Meynall, ordered that the following minute be inserted in the company's books:[128]

> That Mr Mewburn be assured that the Board is not forgetful of the energy, ability and success with which the Stockton and Darlington Railway Company's interests, committed to his professional care, were ever watched over and secured, even in those days when, standing as it were alone, before the community as a railway solicitor, new practices and precedents were of necessity to be created.

This level of attention to detail in both the planning and execution of the legislation must have paid dividends when the legislation came to be tested before the courts. It must be remembered that no previous legislation governing infrastructure projects had been subjected to such a degree of judicial scrutiny. In *R v Russell*, the only directly in point authority which either side could produce, the statutes in question only played a subsidiary role in the proceedings. It will be recalled that they were merely adduced as evidence of the fact that the scheme was for public benefit and hence a reasonable use of the waterway. In *R v Pease* the statute took centre stage and the issue was treated as a matter of statutory interpretation rather than one of common law. As Blackburn J later stated in *Jones v Festiniog*, 'the legislature took the case out of the operation of the common law'.[129]

Indeed, the extent to which the public benefits of the scheme were successfully promoted may also have played a crucial part in the judicial treatment of the statute. In *Pease*, Pollock pursued for the defence a theme which had played well in the *Russell* case, namely that the scheme would provide a vital component in the supply chain between the North Eastern coalfields and London. In this respect, the Stockton and Darlington played a vital role in developing the idea of the national infrastructure project, an idea which arguably has its genesis in the canals and Thomas Telford's London to Holyhead road. Overall, it seems that the statute was viewed more in terms of the conferral of statutory powers rather than a statutory authority. In this respect, the statute was linked with the well-established idea that powers conferred by the Crown for executing a public duty could supersede existing common law rights.

On a narrower doctrinal level, a number of other interesting issues also arise from *R v Pease*. In recent times, *R v Pease* and the subsequent railway sparks cases were dusted off and brought into the light by Lord Denning

---

[128] Recorded in *Memoir of Francis Mewburn*, above n 34. However, his son was of the opinion that his contribution was never fully recognised.
[129] Above n 118.

MR in *Allen v Gulf Oil Refining Ltd.*[130] *R v Pease* arose from an indictment in public nuisance and the *Allen* case was brought in private nuisance. By the time of *Allen* it was well established that statutory authority could operate as a defence to private nuisance.[131] Indeed, private nuisance is now the context in which one usually considers statutory authority. However, the defence of statutory authority brought about by the decision had effects on the development of the common law which went beyond nuisance. It is interesting to note that none of the railway sparks cases were actually brought in private nuisance. All the key cases referred to above were actually brought in negligence, including *Jones v Festiniog*, which established the application of strict liability to railway fires. *R v Pease* established that Parliament could authorise certain harms but that it was a reasonable assumption that this would be restricted to harms inevitably arising from the use of the powers. Any harms caused by negligence could be regarded as avoidable and hence beyond the scope of the protection of the statute. The effect of this was that *Pease* established an immunity in respect of any harms where negligence was not an issue. Thus, when strict liability was developed under *Rylands v Fletcher*, the courts were precluded from applying the principle to the railways in any case where the relevant statutory powers had been sought.

In conclusion, it therefore seems that the many Victorian railway promoters who followed Edward Pease had reason to be grateful for his pioneering efforts in securing parliamentary authorisation for grand projects.

---

130 [1980] QB 156 (CA) 164–66.
131 See *Manchester Corporation v Farnworth* [1930] AC 171 (HL).

2

Burón v Denman (1848)

CHARLES MITCHELL AND LESLIE TURANO*

A. INTRODUCTION

Burón v Denman[1] was an unsuccessful action for trespass to goods
brought by a Spanish slave trader against a British naval officer for
the loss sustained when his slaves and trade goods were seized in a
raid on the west coast of Africa in 1840. The case has many interesting
features, including the identity of the defendant's father, Lord Denman.
Throughout his distinguished public career as Whig MP, Attorney-General
and Lord Chief Justice (a post to which he was appointed in 1832), Lord
Denman was a passionate abolitionist who gave many Parliamentary
speeches against the slave trade. In a speech made shortly after the case
was decided, he declared that it was 'the first time' that an English court
had recognised 'the claim of an owner of human beings, made slaves for
the purpose of trade'.[2] In this he was mistaken, for tort actions to protect
property rights in slaves had succeeded in earlier cases.[3] However, the
case was certainly one of the last in which an English court recognised a

* We thank Geoff McLay and Amanda Perreau-Saussine for their comments.

[1] There are two printed reports of the case: 2 Ex 167, 154 ER 450 and 6 St Tr NS 525. The
latter is essentially a reprint of the former, with some interpolated material taken from reports in
The Times and the *Morning Chronicle*. *The Times* reports of the case appeared on 15, 16 and 17
February 1848, on each day at p 7. Additional information about the events which gave rise to
the case, and the preparation of Denman's defence by the government legal officers, can be
found in a file assembled by Admiralty officials that is in the National Archives: ADM 7/605.

[2] Hansard, 96 HL Debs, col 1055 (22 February 1848).

[3] Actions for trover were held to lie for slaves in *Gelly and Cleve* (1694), cited in *Chamberlain
v Harvey* (1792) 1 Ld Raym 146, 147; 91 ER 994, 994 and *Butts v Penny* (1793) 2 Lev 201, 83
ER 518. Findings to the opposite effect were later made in *Smith v Gould* (1795) 2 Salk 666, 91
ER 567 and *Forbes v Cochrane* (1824) 2 B & C 448, 107 ER 450. See also *Madrazo v Willes*
(1830) 3 B & Ald 363, 106 ER 692, a successful action for trespass, discussed in the text to n 41.
Cf *Gregson v Gilbert, The Zong* (1783) 3 Doug 232, 99 ER 629, a claim under a marine policy
for slaves thrown overboard by the master for want of drinking water; in the words of counsel at
3 Doug 233, argument in the case was predicated on the fact that 'It has been decided, whether
wisely or unwisely is not now the question, that a portion of our fellow-creatures may become
the subject of property.' *The Zong* was the subject-matter of a special issue of the *Journal of
Legal History* in honour of Martin Dockray: (2007) 27 *Journal of Legal History* 285ff.

plaintiff's property rights in other human beings;[4] and it has other claims to our attention as well. It is a milestone in the development of the rule, central to our modern law of agency, that ratification of an agent's unauthorised acts can take effect in the same way as prior authorisation. The case also remains a significant authority for the rule that a person who commits a tort in a foreign state against a foreign national has a personal immunity from suit if he acts in an official capacity with the result that his actions constitute an act of state.

B. BACKGROUND

The events which led to *Burón v Denman* took place in 1840, a time when the slave trade and the institution of slavery had been abolished in most of the British Empire,[5] but continued to flourish in the dominions of other countries, including Spain. By 1840 Spain had signed several treaties with Great Britain under which it had agreed to abolish slavery and slave trading in its dominions. In practice, however, enforcement actions against Spanish slave traders fell almost exclusively to Great Britain, to whom Spain had ceded the right to search and arrest Spanish slave ships north of the Equator.[6]

1. Abolition of the Spanish Slave Trade and Anglo-Spanish Relations, 1815–1845

At the Congress of Vienna (1815) and the conference of Aix-la-Chapelle (1818), Viscount Castlereagh attempted but failed to negotiate a multi-

---

[4] See too *Derbishire v Home* (1853) 5 De G M & G 80, 43 ER 32, an action for breach of trust arising out of the misapplication of the sale proceeds of slaves which had taken place thirty years previously. Also *Santos v Illidge* (1860) 8 CB (NS) 861, 144 ER 1404, concerning the sale of slaves on the winding up of a joint stock company that owned a mine in Brazil. According to Blackburn J at 876, the company had legal title to the slaves although their ownership was prohibited by British law, because 'the taking having been of property locally situated in a foreign country, in a manner lawful according to the laws of that country . . . the property actually passed by the sale, and vested in the purchasers, though they committed a felony according to our law by taking it'.

[5] The slave trade was abolished in the British Empire by the Slave Trade Act 1807, and the institution of slavery was abolished in most of the Empire by the Slavery Abolition Act 1833.

[6] In writing this part we have drawn on the following sources in addition to the other works cited in the footnotes: C Lloyd, *The Navy and the Slave Trade* (London, Longmans, Green & Co, 1949) esp ch 4; H Thomas, *The Slave Trade: The History of the Atlantic Slave Trade 1440–1870* (London, Picador, 1997); HL Kern, 'Strategies of Legal Change: Great Britain, International Law, and the Abolition of the Transatlantic Slave Trade' (2004) 6 *Journal of the History of International Law* 233; J Allain, 'The Nineteenth Century Law of the Sea and the British Abolition of the Slave Trade' (2007) 78 *British Yearbook of International Law* 342.

national treaty under which the European powers agreed to abolish the slave trade and slavery, and to grant one another reciprocal powers of search and arrest of slave trading vessels. Thereafter it became a foreign policy objective of successive British administrations to achieve the same effect by negotiating bilateral treaties with other states, including Spain. Great Britain's efforts in this direction, and Spain's ambivalent attitude towards the British campaign against the slave trade, form the backdrop against which our case was played out.[7] The wider context is that this was the most tumultuous century in Spanish history, from the Napoleonic invasion in 1808, through the struggle between absolutism and liberalism that led to the Carlist wars, and ultimately to Spain's struggle in 1898 to retain its last colonies in the face of the US's growing hegemony.

(a) The 1817 Treaty

During the Napoleonic wars, Spain entered a convention with Great Britain which gave British cruisers the right to search and arrest Spanish slave ships. At the end of the wars, this was abrogated, and a treaty was signed on 23 September 1817 under which Spain agreed to end the transport of slaves from Africa to its colonies. This treaty was a compromise which Spain made only reluctantly. Early in 1816, the royal charter granting Spaniards authority to trade in slaves had expired, and Great Britain had then adopted a policy of seizing any Spanish vessel suspected of engaging in the trade, assuming that, once the charter had lapsed, such trade would no longer be sanctioned by Spanish law.[8] Although this was not the case, appeals from the decisions of the Vice-Admiralty courts were difficult for slave-ship owners to obtain. The Spanish government came to realise that, unless Spain formally renounced the slave trade, the British Admiralty courts would come to determine Spanish slave-trading laws.[9]

By this time, Spain had been weakened by 8 years of war. Great Britain had been instrumental in defeating the French and could be useful in keeping them in check. Moreover, Spain was in an exigent financial state, and needed Great Britain to continue its annual subsidy of around £2

[7] The diplomatic difficulties between Spain and Great Britain over the matter are well documented: see esp JA Saco, *Historia de la esclavitud de la raza africana en el Nuevo mundo y en especial en los paises américo-hispanos* (Barcelona, Imprenta de Jaime Jepús, 1875–77); A Corwin, *Spain and the Abolition of Slavery in Cuba 1817–1886* (Austin, TX, University of Texas Press, 1967); D Murray *Odious Commerce: Britain, Spain and the Abolition of the Atlantic Slave Trade* (Cambridge, Cambridge University Press, 1980); R Paquette *Sugar is Made with Blood: The Conspiracy of La Escalera and the Conflict between Empires over Slavery in Cuba* (Middletown, CT, Wesleyan University Press, 1988); D Cantus García, 'Fernando Poo: una aventura colonial española en el África occidental (1778–1900)', unpublished PhD thesis, University of Valencia, 2004.

[8] OF 72/184, Castlereagh to Vaughan, 7 June 1816, cited in Murray, ibid, 48.

[9] Murray, ibid, 49.

million.[10] Hence it was keen to stay in favour with its more powerful and prestigious ally, and felt that it had no alternative but to accede to British demands. But suppression of the slave trade meant undermining the economy of Cuba, one of its most valuable colonies, at a time when revolution was stirring in Spain's other American possessions.[11] Cuban prosperity was essential to Spain's: the Spanish treasury was nearly bankrupt and depended on revenues from sugar and tobacco, and Spain literally could not afford to endanger the interests of the plantation owners, who formed a powerful lobby in the Cortes.[12] Furthermore, King Fernando VII himself was disinclined to see anything wrong with slavery; despite promising to uphold the liberal Constitution of 1812, he proved to be an absolutist monarch who took every opportunity to deny the fundamental rights of his own subjects.[13] His Secretary of State, Pedro Ceballos, even maintained that the Spanish practice of *esclavitud* was different from the British notion of slavery: the confusion resulted from 'the poverty of language that lacks another word to indicate all the modifications of servitude'.[14] Although Fernando VII's government signed the treaty, therefore, its resistance to the spirit of the agreement was patent. The treaty was ratified under domestic law by a royal charter of 19 December 1817 that contained a defence of the institution of slavery as 'beneficial to the African' for bringing them into the fold of Christian society.[15]

The 1817 Treaty enabled the British navy to stop and search any ships suspected of carrying slaves. It also provided for the institution of mixed tribunals in Sierra Leone and Havana to judge seized vessels and cargoes.[16]

10 Ibid, 51. Spain also received an indemnity of £400,000 under the 1817 Treaty to compensate plantation owners for their losses: for (English) Parliamentary discussion, see Hansard, 37 HC Debs, cols 332–38 (11 February 1818). Fernando VII used the money instead to purchase warships from Nicholas I of Russia, which then sank en route to Spain: R Labra y Cardena, *La violación de las leyes en Cuba. Exposición de la Sociedad Abolicionista a Las Cortes* (Madrid, AJ Alaria, 1882) 8.

11 Between 1818 and 1825 Spain had lost all colonies in Central and South America; by 1826 all that remained were Cuba, Puerto Rico and the Philippines. Spain would lose those in 1898.

12 A measure of the strength of feeling against abolition is indicated by the fate of Spain's first abolitionist, New Spain's deputy to the Cortes Miguel Guiridi y Alcocer, who was beaten to death on the streets of Cadiz in 1814 after having defended the suppression of the slave trade in Parliament.

13 Barely two months after his restoration to the throne on 24 March 1814, Fernando revoked the Constitution. Forced to reinstate it in 1820 after a mutiny by liberal army officers, he abolished it again in 1823, his loyal forces having put down the rebellion.

14 Cited in C Navarro Azcue, *La abolición de la esclavitud negra en la legislación española, 1870–1886* (Madrid, Editorial de la Universidad Complutense, 1987) 9.

15 *Real Cédula*, 19 December 1817. See too JM Romero Moreno, 'Derechos fundamentales y abolición de la esclavitud en España' in F de Solano (ed), *Estudios sobre la abolición de la esclavitud* (Madrid, CSIC, 1986) 241, 249.

16 For the history of these and other Mixed Commission Courts, see L Bethell, 'The Mixed Commissions for the Suppression of the Transatlantic Slave Trade in the Nineteenth Century' (1966) 79 *Journal of African History* 79; J S Martinez 'Anti-Slavery Courts and the Dawn of International Human Rights Law' (2008) 117 *Yale Law Journal* 550. These tribunals were a particular source of resentment: in an address to the Cortes, the anti-abolitionist Bernardo

Any condemned ships were taken as fair prize and sold; any captives were freed to the local government. But the trade would not be abolished immediately. The Treaty had provided for a grace period that would expire on 30 May 1820, allowing trade south of the equator until that time. If the slave trade were suppressed immediately, Spain had insisted, Cuba would be left with insufficient labour to satisfy the demands of its sugar industry. Moreover, Cuba's black population was too small and lacking in women to reproduce a Cuban-born labour force.[17] Ironically, however, the prospect of abolition in 3 years' time stimulated a rise in demand from planters for slave labour and a corresponding hike in the price of slaves. The Treaty of 1817 therefore provoked an increase in the slave trade which would prove difficult to suppress when the time came. Shortly after the Treaty was signed, business was booming in the Havana slave markets, and if Spain had found it difficult to end the Cuban slave trade in 1817, it would find it still more so by 1820.

So the Spanish government was caught in a bind which worsened over the years. If anything, Great Britain's abolition of its own slave trade had made it more difficult for Spain to follow suit; Great Britain had been Cuba's principal supplier of slaves under licence from the Spanish Crown until 1789; when the British trade ceased, Spain therefore needed its own subjects to fill the void.[18] It also feared a rival on the horizon: as the sugar and tobacco industries grew after 1817, Cuba began to trade more with the US. Union with the Americans was an attractive prospect for the Cuban slave-owning oligarchy, because the US was better able to resist British abolitionist pressure and Cuba distrusted Spain's liberal government that had taken over after the 1820 officers' rebellion. The

O'Gavan disparaged the 1817 Treaty as 'an agreement wrenched from us at a time of weakness', for having 'imposed on us a foreign tribunal to control, scrutinise and condemn us in our own territory despite our being declared free and independent': *Observaciones sobre la suerte de los negros de África, considerados en su propia patria y transplantados a las Antillas españolas. Reclamación contra el tratado celebrado con los ingleses el año de 1817* (Madrid, Imp del Universal, 1821) 10–11.

[17] A repeated suggestion from Cuban authorities was the requirement that slave ships must reserve a third of their cargo capacity for women captives so as to improve domestic reproduction, but traders refused, as female slaves fetched a lower price since they were deemed incapable of heavy work: Murray, above n 7, 35; Labra y Cardena, above n 10, 8. The point was emphasised repeatedly in Spanish parliamentary debates to suggest that, since Jamaica was by then self-sufficient in slave labour, Britain's real motive in getting other nations to abolish the trade was to give her own possessions in the Caribbean a comparative advantage in the sugar trade. In addition, the Cubans noted that Britain gave better terms to Portugal in their similar 1817 treaty and suspected that it was to protect British business interests in Brazil. This suspicion would sour Cuba's attitude to the British for many years. See R Cepero Bonilla, *Azúcar y abolición: apuntes para una historia crítica del abolicionismo* (Havana, Echevarría, 1948).

[18] *Real Cédula*, 28 February 1789. Until then, Spain had allowed other countries to supply its colonies with slaves since it had never had a colonial foothold on the West African coast; hence its purchase a few years earlier of Fernando Poo and Annobón off the coast of Guinea, on which see the text around n 57.

resurrected Constitution of 1812 made Cubans and conservative Spaniards uneasy about the possible introduction of fundamental rights. But they need not have worried: Article 5 reserved any such rights to free-born Spaniards, while Article 25 expressly excluded those in domestic service from enjoying them. Liberal ideals aside, the need to ensure Cuba's loyalty also persuaded the Cortes to defer any debates on abolition, with the result that, even during the brief interlude of liberal government between 1820 and 1823, Spain made no attempt to comply with its treaty obligations.[19]

Cuba, too, was locked into its colonial relationship with Spain for the time being. Independence might have provided an alternative, but, despite threats by Cuban representatives to the Spanish Cortes that Spain stood to lose its 'ever-faithful isle' if it abolished the slave trade, the Cuban oligarchy knew that independence would compromise their own interests. Their fear was that a revolution in the manner of the new Spanish American republics would introduce ideas of constitutional freedom and fundamental rights, and this would raise the question of civil liberties for all Cubans, including slaves.[20] Hence the oligarchy chose instead to maintain its relationship with Spain, but exacted the price that Spain should not fulfil its treaty obligations to Britain to any meaningful extent.[21]

(b) The 1835 Treaty and the 1845 Penal Code

Even if Spain had been minded to heed Britain's demands, by 1830 it had become impossible to suppress the slave trade in view of the refusal by Cuban authorities to cooperate.[22] In 1826, the British Foreign Secretary, George Canning, urged his Spanish counterpart, Cea Bermúdez, to take new steps to enforce the treaty. The Council of Indies recommended further measures, such as granting freedom to any slave who denounced the vessels in which he had been brought and submitting the log-books of all vessels

19 The Americans, for their part, had rejected Cuba's offer in 1822 to be annexed as a state. Rather than risk antagonising the British, who were interested in seizing the island, they would play a waiting game and urge loyalty to Spain for the time being: H Thomas, *Cuba: The Pursuit of Freedom* (New York, Harper & Row, 1971) 100–01.

20 An abolitionist movement had begun to form among educated, middle-class *criollos* (Cuban-born whites). Some sought independence from Spain; most wished an end to the importation of Africans because they feared a slave insurrection like that of Haiti in 1791 if the black population grew any further. The most prominent abolitionist, José Antonio Saco, became a deputy to the Cortes for a brief period during liberal regency following Fernando's death in 1833, but was exiled from Spain at the behest of Cuban and Spanish anti-abolitionists.

21 The *Real Cédula* of 19 December 1817, ratifying the Treaty, required 10 years' imprisonment for anyone caught in violation, but no such punishment was ever imposed: Saco, above n 7, 340.

22 H Ames, *A History of Slavery in Cuba* (New York, GP Putnam's Sons, 1907) 125. The American Consul in Havana, Nicholas Trist, helped Captain-General Tacón to obtain documentation to enable Cuban and Spanish slavers to sail under the American flag: Cantus, above n 7, 148.

arriving in Cuba for examination by the authorities. These measures were contained in a royal order of 2 January 1826, but were to have little effect in the face of Captain-General Vives's refusal to act on evidence of illicit trade.[23] There followed repeated cycles of infractions, complaints and inaction from Madrid. Protests from London to Fernando's Council of Ministers about the ineffectiveness of the regulations failed to persuade the Council to amend the Treaty, the latter thinking it sufficient to send out yet another order to the Captain-General telling him to adhere to its terms.[24] This tactic usually elicited the excuse that there was nothing that the Cuban authorities could do: Cuba's long coastline made it impossible to prevent illegal landings and they were frustrated in their efforts by the sheer determination of the plantation owners to obtain slaves. [25]

Pressure continued to escalate: a cholera epidemic among the black population in 1833 pushed up the plantation owners' demands for replacements and there seemed to be no way for Spain to meet Britain's demands. Nevertheless, the Foreign Secretary, Lord Palmerston, charged his Minister in Madrid, George Villiers, with the task of securing Spain's agreement to the introduction of a new article to the Treaty, empowering the mixed tribunals to break up condemned slave ships to prevent them from being refitted as such.[26] Spain's attitude towards abolition then began to soften after Fernando's death in 1833, with the introduction of a liberal government under the Queen Regent, María Cristina. But even after the restoration of the 1812 Constitution in 1836, and the introduction of a new one in 1837, the government continued to adhere to the principle that there was one law for Spain and quite another for its dominions. Villiers pressed the government of Martínez de la Rosa to agree to the amendment, but had no illusions about the latter's intention to comply: Spain would sign 'simply as an *obsequio*, as it is called here . . . There can be no greater mistake than supposing that Spain is sincere in wishing to put down the slave trade'.[27] His observation recalls the old Spanish maxim 'Se obedece pero no se cumple' ('one obeys but does not comply'), a motto popular among colonials announcing their indifference to laws handed down by Madrid.

Villiers finally exacted an agreement from a recalcitrant Martínez de la Rosa, which became the Treaty of 1835. The new agreement provided for the seizure of ships and equipment even when there were no slaves found on board. The presence of shackles, handcuffs, hatches with open gratings, quantities of water and food in excess of that needed for the crew was

---

23 Labra y Cardena, above n 10, 7–8.

24 The British were surprised to find that one such order sent on 30 March 1830 had never been published, and that the Spanish government was aware of this; Captain-General Vives had even acknowledged both its receipt and that it had not been made public: Murray, above n 7, 96.

25 Murray, above n 7, 86–88.

26 Ibid, 99.

27 Villiers to Palmerston, 18 July 1834, cited in Murray, above n 7, 99.

evidence justifying seizure. A new Article 2 also required Spain to pass laws banning the trade. Yet this Treaty would fare no better than its predecessor: the Spanish government, ever wary of upsetting loyal Cuban interests, demurred for another 10 years.

The timing of the Treaty was unfortunate as Spain was now in the midst of a civil war. In 1833 the first Carlist War had broken out in response to the ascension to the throne of the infant Queen Isabel II, Fernando's daughter. Those who favoured an absolute monarchy feared that the Queen Regent and her daughter would institute a liberal era, and they turned to Isabel's uncle, Don Carlos, to challenge her claim to the throne. His supporters, the Carlists, among whom were numbered wealthy landowners with holdings in Cuba, vehemently opposed any prohibition of the slave trade. By 1836, the Cortes had expelled several Cuban deputies, there had been a rebellion in the western end of the island and the Spanish government was reluctant to antagonise the Cubans any further. It was thus no surprise that Villiers relaxed his demands over the next few years. The matter was not raised again until 1843 by Palmerston's successor as Foreign Secretary, the Earl of Aberdeen.

In the interim, a new, liberal Captain-General of Cuba, Gerónimo Valdés, had been appointed. The Carlists had been defeated and Isabel II's champion, the radical General Baldomero Espartero, had become Regent.[28] His appointee, Valdés, began to realise that some change in the law on the slave trade was needed to placate the British. By 1843, the British consul, David Turnbull, had been pressing for more extensive powers to be granted to the mixed tribunal in Havana by an amendment to the 1835 Treaty. He could see no other way to end the constant treaty violations, and expressed his frustration in 1840:[29]

> [F]ear of losing their remaining colonies . . . has prompted every successive administration in Spain to resort to the most disingenuous contrivance for the purpose of forcing the slave trade on the island of Cuba . . . Since the year 1817 . . . we have had more than 20 years' experience of their total inefficiency as an engine for the suppression of the slave trade; and now, since the conclusion of the treaty of 1835, which transferred the trade to the flag of Portugal, the courts of Havana and Rio de Janeiro have been reduced to the condition of so many sinecures.

Turnbull's aim was to enable individual Africans to have suits brought on their behalf, seeking their freedom on the grounds that they had been imported illegally, thereby striking at the heart of the slave-owner's vested property right. If a slave-owner's title to his slaves could be challenged,

---

[28] He had ousted the Queen Regent for her suspected conspiracy with the Moderates: R Carr, *Spain: 1808–1975*, 2nd edn (Oxford, Oxford University Press, 1982) 180–82.

[29] D Turnbull, *Travels in the West. Cuba, with Notices of Porto Rico and the Slave Trade* (London, Longman, Orme, Brown, Green & Longmans, 1840) 340.

surely he would be reluctant to invest in importing more?[30] Alarmed by these proposals, Valdés adopted a policy of complying with the existing rules in an effort to stave off British demands for such an amendment. But the British would not desist. David Murray concludes:[31]

> These questions raised the most profound legal and political complexities for the Spanish government and its colonial officials because they dealt with the boundary between the illegal slave trade and the legal institution of slavery. Spain was unquestionably committed to the latter and all the property rights implied by it. How far would she go . . . in her persecution of the Atlantic slave trade? Would she accept the British interpretation that the slave-owner with his newly purchased African slaves was a receiver of stolen goods and therefore guilty of a crime? Or would she confirm the Cuban plantocracy's rationalisation that the legality of the purchase of African slaves could not be challenged . . . ? The answer was really not in doubt . . .

But again, by 1843, Spain was caught in another political upheaval. Espartero had been overthrown by the more conservative General Narváez, and the progressive Valdés was replaced as Captain-General the following year by Leopoldo O'Donnell. Although O'Donnell was a liberal, like others before him he left his liberalism in Spain and went to Cuba to make his fortune.[32] He was an unequivocal supporter of the slave trade, and he resented any British interference with Spanish laws. Martínez de la Rosa, who by now was no longer Prime Minister but a deputy in the Cortes, warned Parliament that any proposed law penalising slave-traders must nevertheless respect the property of slave-owners, as it was fundamental to Cuba's continuing status as a colony. During debates on the Bill that was to become the 1845 Penal Code, he stated:[33]

> I wish to respect slavery as an institution since it already exists, and as it is an institution of private property guaranteed by law; we must not lose sight of the fact that the Antilles request Spain's protection and that entails an absolute preservation of the existing social order and in the guarantee of all types of property.

The law that was eventually passed, therefore, contained an express defence of slave-owners' property rights. Anyone caught transporting slaves could face imprisonment, but the market for their illicit cargo was protected. Under Article 9, once Cuban owners had taken possession of the newly transported slaves, their rights could not be disturbed.[34]

---

30 Murray, above n 7, 134–35.
31 Ibid, 188.
32 Ibid, 201.
33 J Alvarado Planas, 'El régimen de legislación especial para ultramar y la cuestión abolicionista en España durante el siglo XIX' in *La supervivencia del derecho español en Hispanoamérica durante la época independiente* (Mexico, UNAM, 1998) 1, 5.
34 Ley de 2 de marzo de 1845: Labra y Cardena, above n 10, 14. In order to appease a growing abolition movement, Spain had enacted laws governing the treatment of slaves in 1842, but

The Penal Code of 1845, then, did nothing to stem the traffic from Africa. Instead it reinforced the view that the possession of slaves by Spanish subjects anywhere but on the high seas was protected by Spanish law. In fact, Spain would not abolish the institution of slavery within its dominions until 1866, and even then it would remain legal in Cuba for another 20 years. It seemed not to matter that slaves might be found in holding pens on the African coast, clearly ready for transport; until they had actually left the possession of their owners, their status as private property was unassailable. This was the argument that prompted Burón's action against Denman.

2. Slave Trading, Piracy and International Law

One further point should be made by way of preliminary. British aboli-tionists such as Lord Denman were apt to assert that slave trading amounted to piracy under international law. This meant, in their view, that the British navy would be justified in simply seizing the ships and goods belonging to slave traders and freeing their slaves, because their status as pirates placed them outside the law's protection. However, these assertions flew in the face of *Le Louis*,[35] a case decided in 1817 in which a French slaver was captured en route from Martinique to Africa by a British cruiser and condemned by the Vice-Admiralty Court at Sierra Leone. On appeal to the Admiralty Court in London this decision was reversed by Sir William Scott, who could 'find no authority that gives the right of interruption to the navigation of states in amity upon the high seas';[36] held that trading in slaves had not been shown to be illegal under French law;[37] denied that the capture was justifiable on the ground that the ship had been engaged in piracy;[38] and denied that trading in slaves was a crime under international law.[39]

In *Le Louis* the question was left open whether the owner of a slave ship that had been improperly seized would be entitled to damages,[40] but a positive answer to this question was given in *Madrazo v Willes*,[41] where a Spanish slave-ship owner successfully sued a British naval captain who had

these only served to assuage the consciences of the urban middle classes, who had begun to find the institution of slavery distasteful; see J Romero Moreno, above n 15, 250.

[35] (1817) 2 Dods 210, 165 ER 1464. For the legal and historical background to this case, see T Helfman, 'The Court of Vice-Admiralty at Sierra Leone and the Abolition of the West African Slave Trade' (2006) 115 *Yale Law Journal* 1122.

[36] Ibid, 2 Dods 244.

[37] Ibid, 2 Dods 258–64.

[38] Ibid, 2 Dods 246–48.

[39] Ibid, 2 Dods 248–53.

[40] Ibid, 2 Dods 264.

[41] (1830) 3 B & Ald 363, 106 ER 692.

arrested his vessel in 1818 and seized the trade goods and 300 slaves that were on board. At nisi prius Abbott CJ doubted whether the plaintiff could recover the value of the slaves in an English court, and directed the jury to find a verdict separately for each part of the damage, giving the defendant liberty to move to reduce the verdict to the smaller sum, in case the Court of King's Bench should agree with him. The jury therefore found a verdict for the plaintiff, and awarded 3,000l damages for the deterioration of the ship's stores and goods and a further 18,180l for the lost profit on the slaves. A move for a rule nisi to reduce the damages to 3,000l was then dismissed, the Chief Justice deciding on further reflection, and with the agreement of Bayley, Holroyd, and Best JJ, that since slave trading was legal under Spanish law the plaintiff was entitled to the whole sum awarded.

C. THE PARTIES

1. The Plaintiff

Burón v Denman was one of three associated sets of proceedings brought by a group of Spaniards who had been engaged in slave trading at the mouth of the Gallinas River, which is situated near the present-day border between Sierra Leone and Liberia. The other two actions were discontinued following the failure of the proceedings in *Burón*, and the plaintiffs in these other proceedings were Ángel Ximénez, Simón Pérez de Terán, and Domingo Fernández Martínez. All of them may have engaged in some slave trading on their own account, but Ximénez worked as a factor for Martínez,[42] whose main trading interests lay further down the coast,[43] and

---

[42] ADM 7/605, Denman to Herbert, 6 August 1842. At least by 1842 Ximénez was also trading at Gallinas on his own account: Thomas, above n 6, 691.

[43] Assuming that he is the man whose activities are discussed in DA Ross, 'The Career of Domingo Martínez in the Bight of Benin 1833–1864' (1965) 6 *Journal of African History* 79. He may have been related to Pedro Martínez, a shipbuilder at Cádiz with a home in Havana who owned 30 ships himself and who co-owned many others with his associate Pedro Blanco: D Eltis, *Economic Growth and the Ending of the Transatlantic Slave Trade* (Oxford, Oxford University Press, 1987) 148–89; JC Dorsey, *Slave Traffic in the Age of Abolition* (Gainesville, FL, University Press of Florida, 2003) 122–130. See too M Sherwood, 'Britain, the Slave Trade and Slavery, 1808–1843' (2004) 46 *Race & Class* 54, who traces the links between Diego Martínez, Pedro Blanco and Pedro de Zulueta. de Zulueta was exiled to Britain from Spain by Fernando VII in 1823, and founded a firm of merchant bankers who acted as London agents for Blanco and other slavers, including his cousin Julián Zulueta (on whom see Thomas, above n 19, 99). His son, also Pedro, was unsuccessfully prosecuted in 1843 for sending a ship to Gallinas on Martínez's behalf for the purpose of slave trading (*The Times* 30 October 1843, 6b); his great-grandson Francis was Regius Professor of Civil Law at Oxford from 1919 to 1958, and author of *The Roman Law of Sale* (Oxford, Clarendon Press, 1945), which inevitably includes much discussion of contracts for the sale of slaves. For the history of the family, see *Burke's Landed Gentry*, 18th edn (London, Burke's Peerage Ltd, 1965) sv 'De Zulueta'.

it may also be that Pérez de Terán was factor for another slave trader,[44] possibly Martínez, given that he and Ximénez joined together in issuing one of the writs in the case.

The plaintiff in our case was Tomás Rodríguez Burón. The law reports refer to him solely by his metronymic, but that is also how other Spanish sources refer to him, as the name is uncommon.[45] He seems to have been a small-scale trader on the River Gallinas during the period 1820–1840,[46] but he was not the owner of the slaves and goods for the loss of which he sought damages in our case, for in fact these belonged to the man whom he served as agent—Pedro Blanco, a Spaniard from Màlaga, who was probably the most notorious and successful slave-trader of the day.[47] It was Blanco who directed Burón to instigate the proceedings, and presumably also he who paid the costs, although his name does not appear on the record as a party.[48] In our discussion of the case we shall follow the contemporary reports in ascribing ownership of the slaves and goods for which damages were claimed to Burón, but this is for ease of exposition only, and in reality Blanco lay behind it all.

Although Burón receives scant mention in the historical records, he does appear as a character in a fictionalised biography of Pedro Blanco by the

---

[44] This is the implication of Denman's letter to Herbert cited in n 42, where he states that Martínez was a trader in his own right but that the other three plaintiffs worked as agents for other people. On Pérez de Terán see too FO 84/308A, Doherty and Hook (Sierra Leone Commissioners) to Palmerston, 12 March 1840; he seems to have funded a later career as planter out of the profits of his slave-trading business.

[45] Tomás also seems to have had a brother named Vicente, since he jointly deposed testimony with a man by that name for the purposes of the action against Denman: *Testimonio de las diligencias formadas por Dn Pablo Antonio Foñasely para acreditar el atentado cometido en 19 de Noviembre último por los Capitanes y tripulación de algunos buques de S M B en el pueblo de Gallinas contra los intereses de Dn Tomás y Dn Vicente Rodríguez Burón*, Havana, 20 August 1841, fols 51–54, AGA, África-Guinea, Caja 782, cited in Cantus, above n 7, 633.

[46] A Jones, *From Slaves to Palm Kernels: A History of the Galinhas Country (West Africa) 1730–1890* (Wiesbaden, Franz Steiner Verlag, 1983) 43.

[47] Burón's storekeeper, Mariano Diay, stated in evidence that Burón was not Blanco's agent but traded solely on his own account: *The Times*, 15 February 1848, 7c. However, Denman identifies him as Blanco's agent in the letter cited in n 42. Since it seems that Burón had already been dealing in slaves at Gallinas when Blanco arrived, it is likely that he continued to trade for his own profit. However, that does not mean that he did not form an association with Blanco thereafter. Diay seems at pains to deny any link between the two men, but his assertion is undermined by his claims to have no knowledge that Blanco dealt in the slave trade at all, which seems highly disingenuous, given Blanco's notoriety: he was famously described as 'the Rothschild of the slave trade' by his contemporary Théodore Canot: M Cowley (ed), Théodore Canot (aka Theophilus Conneau), *Adventures of an African Slaver: Being a True Account of the Life of Captain Theodore Canot, Trader in Gold, Ivory & Slaves on the Coast of Guinea: His Own Story as Told in the Year 1854 to Brantz Mayer* (London, Routledge & Sons Ltd, [1854] 1928) 299. Moreover, despite Blanco's notoriety, he always tried to remain at arm's length from the trade by employing agents, and Diay's statement is characteristic of the air of denial that surrounded Blanco: G González de la Vega, *Mar Brava: historia de corsarios, piratas y negreros españoles* (Barcelona, Ediciones B, 1999) 384.

[48] Cantus, above n 7, 201 and 238.

author Novas Calvo, published in 1940.[49] By this account, Burón was already established on the Gallinas as the most prominent member of a group of small-time traders when Blanco arrived in 1822.[50] His dominion consisted of a couple of small islands, each with a house on stilts, one for himself and another for his harem of local women, and some small bamboo pens to hold captives for sale. He was initially suspicious of this newly arrived competitor, but soon ceded to Blanco's superior intelligence and ambition.

2. The Defendant

The Hon Joseph Denman was Lord Denman's second son.[51] He was born in 1810, and he joined the navy as a midshipman aged 13. He became a lieutenant at 21 and a commander at 25. In 1840, he was appointed senior naval officer on the Sierra Leone division of the West African Squadron, and in this capacity he led the raid at the mouth of the Gallinas River that gave rise to our case. When news of this action reached London in 1841, Denman was posted captain. He returned home and in 1842 was given the job of drawing up a code of instructions for naval ships employed in the suppression of the slave trade; these were printed and distributed in 1844.[52] Following the trial in 1848, Denman served as a groom in waiting to Queen Victoria, and commanded the royal yacht, the *Victoria and Albert*, between 1853 and 1860. In 1862 he was made a Rear-Admiral, and he ended his career with a flourish as commander of the Pacific station, between 1864 and 1866. He died in 1874.

Denman was determined, strong-minded and energetic. He shared his father's abolitionist views, and corresponded with him on the subject throughout the 1830s and 1840s, supplying him with information about the slave traders' practices and the naval strategies adopted against them. During the 1840s he gave evidence on several occasions to Parliamentary

---

49 L Novas Calvo, *Pedro Blanco, el negrero* (Madrid, Espasa-Calpe, 1940). The novel is thought to be an accurate and unromanticised account of Blanco's life, and what little can be gleaned from the text concerning Burón is corroborated elsewhere. See R Cabrera, 'Aproximaciones al tema de la esclavitud en *Pedro Blanco, el negrero*, de Novas Calvo' in A Kossoff et al (eds), *Actas del VIII Congreso de a Asociación Internacional de Hispanistas: 22–27 agosto 1983* (Madrid, AIH, 1983) vol 1, 293; González de la Vega, above n 47, 373–76. The conclusion that Burón was a minor figure in the employ of a much more important one is consistent with the scarcity and superficiality of references to him by those who had dealings with him.

50 See also González de la Vega, above n 47, 384.

51 WR O'Byrne, *A Naval Biographical Dictionary* (London, John Murray, 1849) vol 1, 278; *Burke's Peerage*, 99th edn (London, Burke's Peerage Ltd, 1949) sv 'Denman'.

52 Denman worked under the auspices of a committee appointed by Lord Aberdeen and chaired by Lushington J. The code was published as *Instructions for the Guidance of Her Majesty's Naval Officers Employed in the Suppression of the Slave Trade* (London, TR Harrison, 1844), and also appears at PP 1844, vol 50.

commissions on the slave trade, and published tracts refuting the findings of William Hutt's House of Commons Committee, a group of free traders, which reported in 1848 that the posting of naval squadrons on the west coast of Africa was expensive, ineffectual and counter-productive.[53]

Denman attributed his strong abolitionist views to his experiences while serving as a lieutenant in command of a ship off the coast of Brazil in 1834.[54] He captured a Portuguese slave ship, which he took into Rio. There the Court of Mixed Commission refused to condemn the vessel as a prize (because she was not Brazilian) and instructed Denman to take her back across the Atlantic to Sierra Leone. There were 500 slaves on board who had already made the Middle Passage from Africa, and it took 46 days to make the return crossing, during which many of the slaves died. Denman 'witnessed the most dreadful sufferings that human beings could endure'. On arrival, the Sierra Leone Mixed Court also refused to condemn the ship (because she had been captured south of the Equator), and so the surviving slaves had to make a third passage back to slavery in Brazil.[55]

[53] The Hon Captain Joseph Denman RN, *West African Interests, African Emigration and the Slave Trade* (London, J Bigg & Son, 1848) esp ch 5, and *The African Squadron and Mr Hutt's Committee*, 2nd edn (London, J Mortimer et al, 1850). Besides giving some influential speeches against Hutt's Committee in the House of Lords on 22 and 28 August 1848, Lord Denman also went into print on this subject, in *A Letter from Lord Denman to Lord Brougham on the Final Extinction of the Slave Trade* (London, J Hatchard & Son, 1848) and *A Second Letter from Lord Denman to Lord Brougham on the Final Extinction of the Slave Trade* (London, J Hatchard & Son, 1849). On the anxiety which both Denmans felt that Hutt's committee was turning public opinion against the maintenance of the West African squadrons, see Sir J Arnould, *Memoir of Thomas, First Lord Denman* (London, Longman, Green & Sons, 1873) 253–61. Opposition to maintenance of the squadron came not only from commercial interests, but also from some abolitionists, who were concerned by the Navy's use of force and the harsh conditions under which freed slaves were taken to Sierra Leone: W Mathieson, *Great Britain and the Slave Trade 1839–1865* (London, Longmans, Green & Co, 1929) 29–57; H Temperley, *British Antislavery 1833–1870* (London, Longmans, 1972) 153–83.

[54] *Report from the Select Committee of the House of Lords, on the African Slave Trade* PP 1850, vol 9, minutes of Captain the Hon Joseph Denman's evidence on 6 July 1849, p 321 (Q 4415). There is a reference to this episode in a letter from Lord Denman to Lord Brougham on 19 February 1834, which now forms part of the Brougham papers at UCL: BROUGHAM HB/43016.

[55] This episode also made a deep impression on the (British) judges on the Sierra Leone court, who wrote to the Foreign Secretary, Lord Palmerston, to express their 'deep regret on witnessing the sailing of that vessel with her cargo of unhappy beings, destined to another miserable voyage across the Atlantic': Sierra Leone Commissioners to Palmerston, 9 April 1834, reprinted in *Irish University Press Series of British Parliamentary Papers: Slave Trade* (Shannon, Irish University Press, 1969) vol 14, 45–46. By this time the British judges were the only judges sitting on the court for, as noted in Bethell, above n 16, 87: 'each of the three [Dutch, Portuguese, and Spanish] commissions at Sierra Leone started out in 1819 with a full complement of officials, but during the next few years all foreign commissioners left, not to return'.

D. THE FACTS

1. The Gallinas Slave Trade

There was only one reason for Europeans to come to the Gallinas River in 1840: slaves. The French slave trader Théodore Canot described the place as follows:[56]

> [a] short and sluggish river, [it] oozes lazily into the Atlantic; and, carrying down in the rainy season a rich alluvion from the interior, sinks the deposit where the tide meets the Atlantic, and forms an interminable mesh of spongy islands. To one who approaches from sea, they loom up from its surface, covered with reeds and mangroves, like an immense field of fungi betokening the damp and dismal field which death and slavery have selected for their grand metropolis. A spot like this, possessed, of course, no peculiar advantages for agriculture or commerce; but its dangerous bar, and its extreme desolation, fitted it for the haunt of the outlaw and slaver.

The Spaniards who made up the majority of slave traders in the Gallinas settled in the area after business in the islands of Annobón and Fernando Poo (present-day Bioko), farther east in the Bight of Benin, had proved too difficult. Spain had acquired these islands from Portugal following the Treaty of Pardo in 1778 for the sole purpose of buying captives for the Cuban and Puerto Rican slave markets. Until that time, Spain had supplied its colonies with slaves not directly but by issuing exclusive import licences, called *asientos*, to other nations, notably France, Denmark and Britain. Spain wished to abolish the *asiento* system (which it did in 1789) and to let Spanish traders export directly to the colonies, and so it needed to establish its own point of supply on the West African coast.[57] But the acquisition was a poisoned chalice. What Spain had not known was that the islands, sparsely populated to begin with, were no longer the best source of captives; Portugal had already abandoned them in favour of Mozambique and Angola, as these were more heavily populated and more convenient for the route to Brazil.[58] Furthermore, Annobón had a particularly unruly population, which refused to recognise Spain's sovereignty and continued to do business with the English and Danish. The climate was intolerable and malaria was rife. Finally, the Treaty of Pardo was unclear about what rights had been granted to Spain; it was not even clear that Portugal had ever established its own sovereignty over the islands in the first place.[59]

---

[56] Canot, above n 47, 295.

[57] Cantus, above n 7, 41.

[58] This was fortunate for Portugal: after the 1815 Congress of Vienna, Britain agreed to allow the slave trade to continue south of the equator, leaving Portuguese traders undisturbed: Cantus, above n 7, 44.

[59] Cantus, above n 7, 52.

Spain therefore never made any attempt to colonise the islands properly. Indeed, their possession had become something of an embarrassment in the wake of Spain's own condemnation of the slave trade expressed in the 1817 treaty.[60] Moreover, unlike the impenetrable mangrove swamps of the Gallinas, the islands were out in the open and easily patrolled by the British navy.[61] Depleted of the only commodity Spain was interested in exploiting, the islands remained in a 'colonial void' for the next 60 years, while Spanish traders moved north to the Gallinas in search of fresh supplies.[62]

By all accounts, the Gallinas was such another colonial void.[63] Although the majority of traders living there were Spanish, the place was home to a variety of nationalities, including British. But, despite its potential, when Pedro Blanco arrived there in 1822 with his associate Pedro Martínez[64] the area had been under-exploited. Most traders just managed to get by, selling a few slaves to any ship that happened to call in only when it had been prevented from doing so farther down the Gold Coast. In addition, the British navy had begun harassing ships on the coast from Sierra Leone, making it difficult for them to load their illicit cargo. However, the famously astute Blanco revolutionised the process whereby Africans were captured and sold to traders by establishing a system of large pens, or barracoons.[65] Previously, ships would arrive and traders would then negotiate the sale of captives with local chiefs. Traders such as Burón kept small pens and filled them only when demand arose. Negotiations with local chiefs could take weeks or even months, and all the while the slavers' ships remained vulnerable to capture and inspection by the British. Under Blanco's system, the pens, in the care of middlemen such as Burón, were enlarged to hold several thousand and were continually filled

---

[60] Nor had Spain any interest in colonising the Gallinas region: see King Manna's letter of 15 September 1846 to Isabel II, begging for protection against the British, who 'burn our houses on the coast': Archivo del Ministerio de Asuntos Exteriores, leg 2066.

[61] The islands' position amidst the shipping lanes of West Africa was so attractive to the British that Spain offered to sell it to them in 1828 and 1841: A Carrasco González, 'El proyecto de venta de Fernando Poo y Annobón a Gran Bretaña en 1841' (1995) 9 *Estudios africanos* 47.

[62] Cantus, above n 7, 131.

[63] See Mariano Diay's remark that 'no one knew about the law' there: *The Times*, 15 February 1848, 7c; also Canot, above n 47, passim.

[64] On Pedro Martínez, see above n 43.

[65] FE Forbes, *Six Months Service in the African Blockade* (London, R Bentley, 1849) 82–83: 'the slave is imprisoned in a barracoon, a shed made of heavy piles, driven deep into the earth, and lashed together with bamboos, thatched with palm leaves'. Within these structures the slaves were shackled together, and heavily ironed if they were strong men, and 'often beaten half to death beforehand to ensure [their] being quiet'. At 79 Forbes also describes the slaving factories out of which trading took place, making the point that destroying these by fire caused the slave-traders a significant capital loss: 'A factory consists of several large dwelling-houses for the members, clerks, &c; of huge stores for the reception of goods, to the amount of sometimes one or two hundred thousand pounds; of counting houses besides, containing bills and valuable documents, once lost, not to be recovered.'

with captives from whatever intertribal war had taken place.[66] All ships had to do was to arrive and take on cargo, thereby reducing the amount of time spent in waters policed by the British.[67] In addition, Blanco replaced his own brigantines with the new, faster clippers. He established contacts in Philadelphia, Baltimore, Boston and New York, enabling him to sail his ships under American flags, to the consternation of the British.[68] And even when the British succeeded in capturing Blanco's ships as fair prize, he was able to buy them back through various agents.[69]

Blanco's career was so successful that, by the time he left Gallinas for Havana in 1839, his fortune was estimated at around one million dollars.[70] He had presided over a boom in the slave trade that had taken place precisely during the time when Britain was increasing pressure on Spain to comply with its obligations to abolish the slave trade under the treaties of 1817 and 1835. The slave business had become so lucrative that, by the time Denman attacked in 1840, most traders had abandoned their intentions to convert their operations to trade in legitimate goods such as palm oil, cocoa and hardwood.[71]

Blanco left Burón in charge of his barracoons. After Denman's attack, Burón and other traders left the Gallinas, and, by August 1841, he was in Havana deposing testimony for proceedings against Denman at Blanco's instigation.[72] He denounced the 'scandalous violation of the most sacred principles of international law . . . in order to appropriate private property', and asserted that, since slave-owning was not illegal, 'as long as

---

66 Defending the slave trade in his deposition against Denman, Burón even claimed that slavery provided a service by improving the lives of prisoners of war: 'En los enunciados Países [África] . . . es un verdadero progreso la esclavitud por cuanto liberta las villas de los prisioneros de guerra': *Testimonio de las diligencias formadas por Dn Pablo Antonio Foñasely*, cited in Cantus, above n 7, 136.

67 Annual imports of slaves into Cuba fell sharply between 1820 and 1821 from almost 23,000 down to 4,000, after the grace period contained in the Treaty of 1817 had expired. After Blanco's arrival, there is a steady climb from 1827 to a peak of 35,000 in 1835, then another drop in 1841–42 back down to 4,000, presumably in the wake of Denman's destruction of the barracoons: Eltis, above n 43, 245. These numbers are of course lower than the total number of slaves exported from Gallinas, since the traders there, including Blanco, also sent slaves to Brazil and Puerto Rico, but they do give an indication of general trends in the volume of traffic over a certain period.

68 This practice went on for some time: see the complaint about it made in a letter dated 31 December 1844 from Aberdeen to the Spanish Consul in Sierra Leone: Archivo Histórico Nacional (AHN), leg 8022/47.

69 Some of these agents were British: A Arnalte, 'Cónsules, comerciantes y negreros (españoles en Sierra Leone en el siglo XIX)' (1996) 10 *Estudios africanos* 66, 71.

70 Blanco went to Havana to set up the legitimate shipping firm Blanco & Carballo. He continued to trade in slaves, however, as the Cuban market was entering its most buoyant period at the time. Complaints against him are made by the British consul in Sierra Leone, RA Melville, to Aberdeen in a letter dated 31 December 1844, AHN, leg 1022/47.

71 Rather than providing an alternative source of income for locals, the trade in palm oil may have helped to bolster the slave trade in that such goods provided a legitimate cover for illicit cargo: Ross, above n 43, 81.

72 Cantus, above n 7, 236.

the slaves did not leave Gallinas, as long as the treaties were not violated, the property in those slaves must be respected'.[73]

2. Denman's Raid

On 4 March 1840, Denman took up duty as the senior naval officer on the Sierra Leone division of the West African station.[74] His instructions were to suppress the slave trade in the region, and he sought to accomplish this by blockading the mouth of the Gallinas River. As we have explained, Denman had no legal power to land his men onshore and release the slaves from their captors by force. Instead, for month after month, he sailed his sloop, the *Wanderer*, and two smaller ships under his command, close in to the coast, to deter the slave traders from embarking their slaves and putting out to sea where he could arrest them. Since Denman and his officers and crews were entitled to head money when they captured a ship with slaves on board, this strategy worked to their financial disadvantage, but he was determined to stamp out the slave traders' activities and he was convinced that a blockade was the most effective way of achieving this. As Lord Denman proudly wrote to his younger sons, George and Lewis, then both at Cambridge University, in March 1841:[75]

> There is something very noble in Joe's conduct. The profits of the Anti-Slave trade enterprises depend on the number of slaves *taken on board* the pirate cruisers, the Government allowing 5l. a head for every negro so taken. The Brit-ish captain's interest, therefore, *is to allow the negroes to be shipped and then capture them*. But this proceeding is attended with infinite suffering to the slaves . . .

A tense waiting game followed. More slave ships arrived from across the Atlantic and more slaves arrived from the African interior, to be penned up in the barracoons. Various provocations took place: some English sailors in a small boat got into trouble in bad weather at the mouth of the Gallinas River and were nearly drowned when the Spaniards prevented anyone from going to their aid; an attempt was made to capture Denman himself when he ventured up the river in a Kroo canoe to scout out the land. However, he was not a man to be trifled with, and he did not

---

[73] Ibid.

[74] ADM 7/605, orders to Commander Denman from Captain Tucker, 4 March 1840. Lloyd, above n 6, gives a full history of the West Africa squadron, and the evolution of naval tactics employed in the region. For a less systematic and less well referenced account, which nevertheless contains some interesting details, see S Rees, *Sweet Water and Bitter: The Ships that Stopped the Slave Trade* (London, Chatto & Windus, 2009).

[75] Quoted in Arnould, above n 53, vol 2, 120 (emphases in the original). On the prize money awarded to those engaged in the suppression of the slave trade, see Lloyd, above n 6, ch 6. George Denman later became a Queen's Bench judge.

hesitate when he was presented with an opportunity to take more active measures. This came at the end of October 1840, when the Governor of Sierra Leone, Sir Richard Doherty, wrote with the news that Prince Manna, son of the local chief, King Siacca, had captured a black woman named Fry Norman and her child[76] and had held them as slaves at Gallinas, even though they were British citizens, having acquired this status in Sierra Leone. Doherty instructed Denman to forward a despatch to King Siacca, requesting the release of the two, and if that proved ineffective, to use force to release them himself.[77] Denman replied that:[78]

> as I have strong reasons to believe that these White Slave Dealers are determined to oppose all intercourse, I consider it impossible to forward your Excellency's despatch except by stealth and in a manner little calculated to impress the natives with respect for British Authority—or by entering the River with a force sufficient to resist any aggression that may be attempted.

On 19 November 1840, Denman therefore led an armed force of 120 seamen and marines in small boats up the Gallinas River, heading towards the barracoon at Dombocorro. At first the Spaniards did not see them coming,[79] and when they realised that an armed force was approaching, they put up no resistance, but sought to escape with their slaves across the river in canoes. Denman's men gave chase and captured around 90 slaves, including two who also turned out to be British subjects from Sierra Leone. Denman then took possession of the Spanish barracoons and warehouses, and entered into negotiations with King Siacca through Prince Manna and three other chiefs. After some prevarication, Fry Norman and her child were handed over, and the chiefs also agreed to a treaty for the abolition of slave trade in their kingdom. Denman seems to have won their agreement by a mixture of brow-beating and bribery.[80] The sweetener was his willingness to look the other way when they seized the Spaniards' trade goods on the ground that slave trading was now illegal in their country—although he ordered that the casks of spirits should be broached and poured away, on the ground that these had been poisoned.[81] The slaves held in the barracoons were handed over, along with handcuffs,

---

[76] She appears as 'Fry Norman' in some sources, as 'Try Norman' in others.

[77] ADM 7/605, Doherty to Denman, 30 October 1840.

[78] ADM 7/605, Denman to Doherty, 17 November 1840.

[79] According to the eye-witness account of the master of an American brig, 'Don Pedro Blanco's establishment is situated on a handsome little island, a short distance up the river, and so surrounded by trees, as to prevent their seeing very distinctly the approach of any boats, unless from a kind of observatory which on this occasion was not occupied': *New York Journal of Commerce*, 2 March 1841.

[80] But note *The Times*, 16 February 1848, 7d, evidence of Captain AW Hill: 'there was not any coercion used, more than their being called on to give satisfaction for what had been done in the detention of the British subjects'.

[81] *The Times*, 15 February 1848, 7f, evidence of Richard Palmer (seaman on the *Wanderer*): the spirits were 'started into the sands, which were so saturated with them that it was almost intoxicating to remain near the place'.

chains, shackles, bar iron used for forging these, and the canoes and boats which were used for transporting slaves out to the slaving ships. These were all destroyed and the factories were burned to the ground. Denman personally fired a rocket into one of these buildings to demonstrate the strength of his firepower.[82] He then took 841 slaves away with him to be freed in Sierra Leone, along with 20 or 30 Spaniards, to whom he also gave passage for protection from the local people.[83] He later had cause to regret this, since the Spaniards included Tomas Burón, the plaintiff in our case.

3. Official Adoption of Denman's Actions

As Baron Parke later observed, the immediate cause of Denman's decision to take his men up the river was Doherty's order to secure the release of Fry Norman and her child, but 'the restoration to liberty of the other slaves might have been in his head as a further object at the same time',[84] and the measures which he took to seize the slaves and burn the factories clearly went beyond his instructions. Denman was certainly aware of this. He had an exact understanding of the limits to his authority, and he negotiated the treaty with King Siacca precisely in order to justify the seizure of the slaves on the ground that slavery was not permitted by local law.[85] Nevertheless, when news of the raid reached London the following March, in a despatch from the governors of Sierra Leone to the Colonial Office, Lord John Russell, the Colonial Secretary, and Lord Palmerston, the Foreign Secretary, were quick to express their approval. This was characteristic of Palmerston, who took a consistently bullish view throughout his career of the legality of British naval actions against Spanish (and Portuguese) slavers, and of the extent to which Spain (and Portugal) could be pressurised into abolishing

---

[82] *The Times*, 15 February 1848, 7e, evidence of Mariano Diay (Burón's store keeper); *The Times*, 16 February, 7a, evidence of Mitchell (seaman on the *Rolla*).

[83] Report from the Select Committee on the West Coast of Africa, PP 1842, vol 12, 512 (Appendix No 39): letter from Denman to the Select Committee, 19 July 1842.

[84] *The Times*, 17 February 1848, 7d.

[85] When Lord Denman reported the story to his younger sons he conceded that 'there may possibly be some irregularity' before going on to say that 'Lord John [Russell] has written me his congratulations on "Joe's" spirited and successful conduct; and Lord Minto tells me that Lord Palmerston thinks the whole affair highly justifiable': Lord Denman to the Hon George and the Hon Lewis Denman, March 1841, quoted in Arnould, above n 53, vol 2, 120. See too Report from the Select Committee on the West Coast of Africa, PP 1842, vol 11, 416–24, where Joseph Denman described the Gallinas raid in evidence to the committee and justified his conduct on the basis (i) that it was necessary to recover Fry Norman and her child and (ii) that his objectives were accomplished 'through the medium of the consent of the native chiefs'. He also stated that 'Nothing of the sort had been done before, and therefore I did it under very heavy responsibility. I could not have struck out a new line without some special grounds to go upon.'

the slave trade within their dominions.[86] In a letter dated 6 April 1841, the Lords of the Admiralty were told that:[87]

> Lord Palmerston is of Opinion, that the Conduct of Commander Denman in his proceedings against the Slave Factories at the Gallinas ought to be approved: And I am to add, that Lord Palmerston would recommend that similar Operations should be executed against all the Piratical Slave Trade Establishments, which may be met with on parts of the Coast not belonging to any Civilized Power.

The following day, a letter to the same effect was sent to the Admiralty from the Colonial Office,[88] and on 15 April Lord John Russell also wrote to Sir John Jeremie, the new governor of Sierra Leone, stating that:[89]

> I entirely approve of the proceeding of your predecessor in urging the interposition of Commander Denman on behalf of the individuals in question, and I have requested that the Lords Commissioners of the Admiralty to express to the Commander the high sense which Her Majesty's government entertain of his very spirited and able conduct and of its important results to the interests of humanity.

When Denman's own account of the raid reached London in July,[90] a letter from the Foreign Office to the Admiralty went even further, restating Palmerston's view that Denman's actions 'were highly meritorious; and that it is extremely desirable, that a similar Course should be pursued in other Places along the Coast of Africa, not being Possessions of any European Power, at which Slave Trade Factories have been established'. The letter went on:[91]

> Lord Palmerston conceives, there can be little doubt that in all such cases an agreement might be made with the Native Chiefs similar to that which was made by Commander Denman with the Gallina Chiefs; but if such an Agreement should in any case be found impossible, the Commanders of Her Majesty's Cruizers would be perfectly justified in considering European Slave Traders established in the Territory of a Native Chief, as persons engaged in a piratical

---

86 Under Denman's direction, several other raids on slave trading depots on the west coast of Africa took place at the same time as the Gallinas raid, or shortly afterwards, at Corisco, Sea Bar and New Cestos. These also received Palmerston's approval: on Corisco, see FO 84/383, fols 245ff, Admiralty to Backhouse, 18 February 1841, enclosing a report by Commodore Tucker dated 11 November 1840; on Sea Bar, see FO 84/384, fols 519ff, Admiralty to Palmerston, 15 July 1841, enclosing a report by Lieutenant Hill, dated 24 February 1841, and also FO 84/384, fol 106, Leveson to Admiralty, 28 July 1841, approving Hill's actions; on New Cestos, see FO 84/384, fols 487ff, Admiralty to Palmerston, 14 July 1841, enclosing a report by Denman dated 30 April 1841.

87 ADM 7/605, Backhouse to Barrow, 6 April 1841. Another copy is at FO 84/383, fol 75.

88 ADM 7/605, More O'Ferrall to Barrow, 7 April 1841.

89 ADM 7/605, Russell to Jeremie, 15 April 1841.

90 FO 84/384, fols 481ff: Admiralty to Palmerston, 14 July 1841, enclosing a report by Denman dated 30 April 1841.

91 ADM 7/605, Leveson to Barrow, 28 July 1841. Another copy of this letter is at FO 84/384, fol 99, and also a draft by Palmerston dated 19 July at fol 477.

undertaking, and the British Commanders would be warranted in landing and in destroying the Barracoons and the Goods contained in them, and in liberating and carrying off to Sierra Leone the Slaves whom they might find therein.

In July 1841 it was resolved that Denman, his officers and his men should be granted a reward of £4000 for their actions,[92] although the change of government that took place the following month led to a good deal of foot-dragging over this, and the money was not finally paid until the Whigs returned to office in 1847.[93] As a further sign of official favour, Denman was posted captain in August 1841.

4. Lord Aberdeen's Letter

In the same month, Lord Melbourne's government came to an end and a Tory government under Sir Robert Peel came to power. The new Prime Minister and his Foreign Secretary, Lord Aberdeen, took a far less free-wheeling attitude than the Whigs towards the legality of actions by the British navy against Spanish (and Portuguese) slavers.[94] In the eyes of their abolitionist critics, including Lord Denman, the Tories were more interested in promoting free trade than they were in stamping out the slave trade, and not all of them took this line for high-minded reasons of economic principle.[95] Viewed from the Tory perspective, however, the Whigs'

[92] *The Times*, 16 February 1848, 7d, evidence of John Parker (secretary to the Treasury).

[93] Estimates, &c Miscellaneous Services for the Year Ending 31 March 1848, VII: Special and Temporary Objects, 8: Rewards for Services in Suppression of the Slave Trade, PP 1847, vol 35, 431–37.

[94] The most obvious example of Palmerston's high-handedness is his action in securing the enactment of an act in 1839, under which British naval ships were empowered to arrest Portuguese slavers, although Portugal had not conceded this right by treaty and although *Le Louis*, above n 35, and *Madrazo*, above n 41, had held that Britain had no such right under international law. On this statute, see L Bethell, 'Britain, Portugal and the Suppression of the Slave Trade: The Origins of Lord Palmerston's Act of 1839' (1965) 80 *English Historical Review* 761; Kern, above n 6, 251–53; Allain, above n 6, 365–67. It is worth noting, however, that Aberdeen himself took almost exactly the same step against Brazil in 1845: on this, see WD Jones, 'The Origins and Passage of Lord Aberdeen's Act' (1962) 42 *Hispanic American Historical Review* 502; L Bethell, *The Abolition of the Brazilian Slave Trade* (Cambridge, Cambridge University Press, 1970) ch 9.

[95] Lord Denman was particularly incensed by the ministerial Sugar Duties Bill of 1846, which was designed to equalise the duties on British colonial and slave-produced sugar; this was passed despite his opposition in Parliament: Hansard, 88 HL Debs, 3rd series, 467–87. On 25 July 1846 he wrote to Sir John Coleridge 'I do hope the Ministry will fail and fall: mischievous as these changes are, they are nothing in comparison to the avowal of a deliberate intention to encourage the Slave Trade of England. If the whole Administration were pounced upon at a whitebait dinner at Greenwich, and carried off, by a just retaliation, to work in African mines by the pirates of Algiers or Barbary, what would be their sufferings compared to those of one cargo of human beings close packed on the Middle Passage?' (quoted in Arnould, above n 53, 210). A further source of dismay, for which the administration could hardly be blamed, was the failure of the murder prosecution in *R v Serva* (1846) 2 Car & K 53, 175 ER 22, following the killing of the prize crew placed on board a captured Brazilian slaver, the *Felicidade*, in 1845: Lord

disregard for the rule of law was deplorable, and their repeated assertions that slave traders were guilty of piracy were not borne out by the rules of international law.[96] Whatever the rights and wrongs of this, however, the most significant result of the shift in official attitude for present purposes was Lord Aberdeen's decision in April 1842 to seek an opinion from Sir John Dodson, the Advocate General, as to the legality of the Gallinas raid and other similar actions.[97] Dodson replied that Denman had overstepped the mark, stating that:[98]

> the very spirited and able conduct of that officer in rescuing [the woman and child] from Slavery is certainly much to be commended; but I scarcely think that the Blockading Rivers, landing and destroying Buildings, and carrying off Persons held in Slavery, in Countries with which Great Britain is not at War, cannot be considered as sanctioned by the Law of Nations, or by the Provisions of any existing Treaties, with which I am acquainted, and, however desirable it may be to put an end to the Slave Trade, an eminent Good should not be attained, otherwise than by lawful means.[99]

On receipt of this advice, Lord Aberdeen wrote to the Admiralty in May 1842:[100]

> I beg to call your Lordships' attention to the subject of the Instructions, given to Her Majesty's Naval Officers employed in suppressing the Slave Trade on the Coast of Africa, and to the proceedings which have taken place with reference thereto . . . Her Majesty's Advocate General . . . has reported, that he cannot take upon himself to advise, that all the proceedings described as having taken place at Gallinas, New Cestos, and Sea Bar are strictly justifiable,[101] or that the Instructions to Her Majesty's Naval Officers as referred to in these Papers are such as can with perfect legality be carried into Execution . . . Accordingly . . . I would submit to the Consideration of your Lordships, that it is desirable, that Her Majesty's Naval Officers employed in suppressing the Slave Trade should be instructed to abstain from destroying Slave Factories, and carrying off Per-

Denman upheld the defendants' conviction at the Exeter Assizes by Platt B, as did Platt B himself, but the other eleven judges on the bench refused to do so, and the men were sent home at the Government's expense after the Advocate General advised that they could no longer be detained in Great Britain, nor sent home to be tried under Brazilian law: FO 83/2354, fols 145ff, Dodson to Palmerston, 23 September 1847.

96 Consider the exchange of views between Palmerston and Peel in Hansard, 76 HC Debs, cols 934, 940–41 and 957–58 (16 July 1844).

97 FO 84/443, fols 113ff, memorandum by Lord Canning; FO 83/2350, fol 93, Canning to Dodson, 7 April 1842.

98 FO 83/2350, fol 95, Dodson to Canning.

99 There is an echo here of Sir William Scott's dictum in *Le Louis*, above n 35, 257, that 'to procure an eminent good by means that are unlawful is as little consonant to private morality as to public justice'. Dodson must have had the case in mind when he wrote his advice and it would have been very familiar to him, since he had acted with Lushington as counsel for the appellants, and indeed was the author of the report of the case cited at n 35.

100 ADM 7/605, Aberdeen to the Admiralty, 20 May 1842. A more strongly worded draft, laying greater stress on the illegality of the actions taken, is at FO 83/2350, fols 122ff.

101 The reference to New Cestos and Sea Bar is explained at n 86.

sons held in Slavery, unless the Power upon whose Territory or within whose Jurisdiction the Factories or the Slaves are found, should, by Treaty with Great Britain or by formal written Agreement with British Officers, have empowered Her Majesty's Naval Forces to take these steps for the Suppression of the Slave Trade . . .

With justification, Denman *père et fils* both thought that adoption of this new policy was a retrograde step that would encourage the slavers to return to their trafficking.[102] Spanish slave traders, including Angel Ximénez, soon returned to Gallinas, and the work of routing them out later had to be done all over again, in 1848 and 1849.[103] On a more personal level, Lord Denman was also angered that Aberdeen should have implied that his son had behaved improperly, and said as much the next year in a House of Lords debate,[104] prompting a reply in which Aberdeen disavowed:[105]

all intention of casting any imputation on the gallant officer . . . in the letter he had written; . . . and even restricted as his own views were as what was authorized to be done by our cruisers on the coast of Africa, that gallant officer in anything he had done had not come within the exception he had laid down; and he must add that there was no one who had more distinguished himself in this important service, nor for whom he entertained a higher respect than that gallant officer.

Lord Denman replied that this statement was 'most gratifying to his feelings'.[106] Nevertheless he continued to deplore what he took to be the Tories' excessively cautious attitude towards suppression of the slave trade, and he must have thought that Aberdeen's letter had produced an additional bad effect when it was published in the *Report from the Select Committee on the West Coast of Africa* in 1842,[107] and three writs were promptly issued against Joseph Denman by a group of Gallinas slave traders.

---

[102] On the bad effects of the new policy, see Lord Denman's comments at Hansard, 68 HL Debs, cols 674–76 (7 April 1843), and also *A Letter from Lord Denman to Lord Brougham on the Final Extinction of the Slave Trade* (London, J Hatchard & Son, 1848) 18–19, noting Captain Matson's evidence to Hutt's Committee. See too HJ Matson, *Remarks on the Slave Trade and the African Squadron* (London, James Ridgway, 1848) 39, 89 and 95.

[103] Thomas, above n 6, 738.

[104] Hansard, 68 HL Debs, col 674 (7 April 1843).

[105] Hansard, 68 HL Debs, col 826 (11 April 1843). Arnould, above n 53, 154 comments that 'this is all mighty well but utterly irreconcilable with the spirit, if not with the terms of the letter of May 20, 1842'.

[106] Ibid.

[107] PP 1842, vol 12, 516.

E. PROCEEDINGS

1. Issue of Writs

These writs were for actions of trespass to goods, and they were served at the suits of Ángel Ximénez and Simón Pérez de Terán, Domingo Fernández Martínez, and Tomas Burón. Ximénez and Pérez de Terán alleged that goods and chattels to the value of £150,000 were carried off or destroyed; Martínez claimed £40,000; and Burón claimed for 4,000 slaves worth £100,000 and goods worth £80,000.[108] These were huge sums. Joseph Denman wrote to the Admiralty immediately, stating that:[109]

> the palpable absurdity of this proceeding seems to me almost incredible as it is utterly impossible that a British Court can entertain the claims of persons who have suffered loss in the persecution of transactions which the Laws of Great Britain regard and punish as Piracy if committed by her own Subjects and it seems to me that proof of the iniquitous nature of their pursuits would effectively prevent them from proceeding any further . . . My proceedings on the occasion in question having been honoured with the full and unqualified approval of Her Majesty's late Government, I have to request that you will move their Lordships to be pleased to give instructions that the case shall be defended by the Law Officers of the Crown at the public Expense.

The Admiralty consulted the Foreign Office, and within ten days Aberdeen answered that the government law officers should undertake Denman's defence at the public cost. Although 'Captain Denman cannot be said to have acted under orders consequent upon the Foreign Office Letter of 6th April 1841, since the Transaction in question took place in November 1840', nevertheless he was entitled to the Government's backing, given 'the decided approval given by Her Majesty's Government of the Conduct of Captain Denman upon that occasion'.[110]

---

[108] As Parke B later observed, no claim was made for the destruction of the barracoons because the action was for trespass to goods, and the buildings were not of the necessary 'transitory character': *The Times*, 17 February 1848, 7d.

[109] ADM 7/605, Denman to Herbert, 6 August 1842.

[110] ADM 7/605, Canning to Barrow, 16 August 1842. This letter contradicts the assertions of some historians that the Tory government behaved badly towards Denman by initially refusing to pay for his defence: Lloyd, above n 6, 99: 'it was only after considerable discussion that the Admiralty agreed that Denman should be defended by the Attorney-General appearing on behalf of the Crown'; Thomas, above n 6, 736: 'not without difficulty Denman arranged to be defended by the government'.

2. Legal Arguments

Although the plaintiffs' writs were issued in August 1842, the case did not finally come on for trial until February 1848. The delay was attributable in part to the difficulty of assembling witnesses and depositions from Spain, Cuba, Sierra Leone and other far-flung places,[111] and in part to procedural skirmishing between the parties.[112] When the case was finally heard,[113] counsel for the plaintiff relied on *Madrazo v Willes*[114] for the proposition that a foreigner who was permitted to engage in slave trading by the laws of his own country could bring proceedings in an English court to recover damages if his slaves and goods were wrongfully seized by a British subject. Two main arguments were made in Denman's defence. The first was that the plaintiff had had no legal right to own slaves in Africa for the purpose of exporting them to the West Indies, and so he had enjoyed no property right in the slaves on which he could now found his action for trespass, and any claim in respect of his trade goods would be tainted with illegality. *Madrazo* was said to be distinguishable on the ground that it turned on the words of the treaty of 1817, by which Spain declared the slave trade illegal, but at the same time reserved to herself the right of trafficking in slaves within her own dominions[115] — something which was now provided against by the treaty of 1835. The second argument was that, even if Denman had committed trespass to the plaintiff's goods, he had done so in an official capacity, with the result that the trespass had been an act of state for which he was not personally liable. This argument depended both on the proposition that the act of state doctrine afforded a defence to tort claims and on the proposition that the government's ratification of Denman's actions had the same effect as a prior authorisation.

---

111 ADM 7/605 contains assorted correspondence relating to these difficulties. See too *Burón v Denman* (1847) 9 LT (OS) 104, which concerned the collection of evidence from witnesses out of the country under a commission, and the opposite party's right to cross-examine them viva voce.

112 In June and November 1844 counsel for the defendant unsuccessfully argued on a demurrer that the plaintiff's replications had admitted an intended violation of the 1817 Treaty: see 2 Ex 171 n (a); and also *The Times*, 14 November 1844, 7 b. Sir Fitzroy Kelly, who represented the plaintiff on this occasion, was appointed Solicitor-General in July 1845, after which he switched sides. This gave rise to some adverse newspaper comment but his conduct (and that of the other government legal officers) was defended in Parliament by the Attorney-General: Hansard, 96 HC Debs, cols 287–89 (8 February 1848).

113 An attempt to hold the trial in December 1847 failed when the requisite number of special jurors failed to appear: *The Times*, 7 December 1847, 7b.

114 See n 41 and text.

115 (1848) 2 Ex 183.

(a) No Property Right

The first argument was unsuccessful. On Denman's behalf, the Attorney-General argued that the chiefs had possessed sufficient law-making authority in their kingdom to render the plaintiff's ownership of slaves illegal by local law when they signed the treaty. However, there were factual difficulties with this because it was unclear what law-making powers the chiefs possessed, and, after the jury failed to reach a verdict on this part of the case, the Attorney-General withdrew the 'Siacca pleas'.[116] Following *Le Louis*,[117] the court also held that slave trading was not an act of piracy under international law. Nor were counsel for the defence able to establish that slave ownership was illegal as a matter of Spanish law, notwithstanding the 1835 treaty between Great Britain and Spain.[118] Since Spain had not complied with its treaty obligations by enacting laws against slavery by 1840, for reasons which we have explained above, the government legal officers could never have obtained evidence to this effect, though in fact they had gone to considerable trouble to obtain testimony on the point, and all to no avail. No-one with a sufficiently expert knowledge of Spanish law could be found in Great Britain, and attempts to ship in an expert witness for the trial had come to nothing,[119] as had the efforts of British Embassy officials to take depositions from Spanish lawyers in Madrid—according to the diplomats, because the Spaniards had taken offence at a slight to their honour;[120] according to Joseph Denman, because they had been bribed.[121]

(b) Act of State

The second argument for the defence succeeded. The court held that Denman would not be liable if he had acted in an official capacity because his actions would then have comprised an act of state. Hence this part of the case turned on the question whether his actions had been ratified by the Crown since they had not been previously authorised. The court held that the Appropriation Act under which Denman and his men had been rewarded £4,000 for their actions was 'no ratification by the Crown'.[122] However, the court also directed that, where an officer of the Crown performed acts on the Crown's behalf that were subsequently ratified, this

116 *The Times*, 17 February 1848, 7d and e.
117 *Le Louis*, above n 35.
118 (1848) 2 Ex 167, 187 (Parke B).
119 ADM 7/605, Stanley to Ward, 24 November 1847.
120 There is an amusingly dry account of the Embassy officials' failure to gain the Spanish lawyers' co-operation at ADM 7/605, Bulwer to Palmerston, 22 October 1847.
121 Report from the Select Committee of the House of Lords, on the African Slave Trade, PP 1850, vol 9, 339, minutes of Joseph Denman's evidence on 6 July 1849 (QQ 4520–21).
122 *The Times*, 17 February 1848, 7d (Parke B).

ratification would be 'equivalent to a prior command to do them', that there was no need for the Crown to give its assent by the Great Seal and that a simple written authority would suffice, and that it did not matter if the Crown had failed to communicate its ratification to the Spanish Queen Regent since it was enough that this had been communicated to Denman. Hence the only question of fact for the jury to determine was whether the letters written by Palmerston, Russell and the Lords of the Admiralty had been written with full knowledge of Denman's actions—and the jury quickly concluded that they had, with the result that a verdict was entered for the defendant on these pleas.[123]

3. Result

In the result, therefore, Denman escaped liability, although he (and his father) would have been happier about this if the court had also held that slave-trading was illegal under Gallinas, Spanish and/or international law. The plaintiff's victory on this point later enabled the plaintiffs in all three actions to negotiate a deal with the Admiralty under which each side bore its own costs and the other two actions were discontinued.[124]

F. RATIFICATION

Owing to the Crown's interest in the case, *Burón v Denman* was tried at bar in the Exchequer Court before Parke, Alderson, Rolfe, and Platt BB.[125] The court's views were given by Parke B, who summed up and directed the jury. Observing that 'the justification of the defendant depends on the subsequent ratification of his acts', he stated that:[126]

> A well-known maxim of the law between private individuals is '*Omnis ratihabitio retrotrahitur et mandato æquiparatur*'.[127] If, for instance, a bailiff distrains goods, he may justify the act either by a previous or subsequent authority from the landlord; for, if an act be done by a person as agent, it is in general immaterial whether the authority be given prior or subsequent to the

---

123 (1848) 2 Ex 167, 187–190; *The Times*, 17 February 1848, 7d–f (Parke B).

124 ADM 7/605, Hay (plaintiffs' solicitor) to Robson (Admiralty solicitor), 26 August 1848; note from Jervis (Attorney-General) to Robson, 28 August 1840; note from Robson to Barrow (Secretary to Admiralty), 7 October 1848. See too Hay's letter to *The Times*, 19 February 1848, 8d, pointing out that a verdict was given for the plaintiff on various pleas.

125 The Crown had an automatic right to trial at bar in actions to which it was a party. Where it was not a party, this right was limited to cases in which it had an actual and immediate interest, and in *Burón* its interest in defending Denman seems to have sufficed for this purpose, as discussed in *Dixon v Farrer* (1886) 18 QBD 43, CA; *cf Lord Bellamont's Case* (1795) 2 Salk 625, 91 ER 529.

126 (1848) 2 Ex 167, 188.

127 'Every ratification relates back and is equivalent to a prior authority.'

act. If the bailiff so authorized be a trespasser, the person whose goods are seized has his remedy against the principal. Therefore, generally speaking, between subject and subject, a subsequent ratification of an act done as agent is equal to a prior authority.

It was a controversial question, though, whether this principle applied to the present case. The other three judges were all 'decidedly of opinion that the ratification of the Crown . . . is equivalent to a prior command',[128] a conclusion that was in line with a previous case on the point, cited by the Attorney-General,[129] but ignored by Parke B in his judgment. This was *The Rolla*,[130] an action for breach of blockade against an American ship in which defending counsel had objected that the commander of the blockading force had acted without authority. Lord Stowell had responded that:[131]

> However irregularly he may have acted towards his own government, the subsequent conduct of Government, in adopting that enterprise, by directing a further extension of that conquest, will have the effect of legitimating the acts done by him, so far at least as the subjects of other countries are concerned.

Nevertheless, Parke B had some doubts about this, observing that:[132]

> there appears to me a considerable distinction between the present case and the ordinary case of ratification by subsequent authority between private individuals. If an individual ratifies an act done on his behalf, the nature of the act remains unchanged, it is still a mere trespass, and the party injured has his option to sue either; if the Crown ratifies an act, the character of the act becomes altered, for the ratification does not give the party injured the double option of bringing his action against the agent who committed the trespass or the principal who ratified it, but a remedy against the Crown only (such as it is), and actually exempts from all liability the person who commits the trespass.

The maxim invoked by Parke B came from Coke's *Institutes*,[133] published more than 200 years earlier, and so the idea of 'relation back' which it encapsulates was scarcely new by the time that *Burón* was decided. Significant aspects of the rule still had to be worked out, though—most notably, whether a principal could ratify a contract entered by his agent after the third party's notified withdrawal, and whether an undisclosed principal could ratify his agent's unauthorised act in entering a contract on his behalf. To the first of these questions the Court of Appeal later gave a

---

128 (1848) 2 Ex 167, 188.
129 Ibid, 184–45.
130 (1807) 6 Rob 364, 165 ER 963.
131 Ibid, 6 Rob 366.
132 (1848) 2 Ex 167, 188–89.
133 Sir E Coke, *Institutes of the Law of England* Book IV (London, M Flesher, for W Lee and D Pakeman, 1634) 317. The influence of earlier writers on Roman and canon law on Coke's understanding of this rule is discussed in G Procaccia, 'On the Theory and History of Ratification in the Law of Agency' (1979) 4 *Tel Aviv University Studies in Law* 9, 13–24.

positive answer in *Bolton Partners v Lambert*,[134] and to the second the House of Lords gave a negative answer in *Keighley Maxsted & Co v Durant*.[135] In both cases reference was made to Parke B's statements of principle in *Burón* and in other cases, including *Bird v Brown*, where it was held that an unauthorised exercise of the power to stop goods in transit could not be ratified after the goods had reached the hands of third parties.[136]

Leaving contract law to one side, and focusing our attention on tort law, *Burón* was an unusual case for several reasons. One is that the government's ratification of Denman's actions was clear on the facts, given the strong terms in which Palmerston and Russell had expressed themselves. Hence Denman did not need to overcome evidential difficulties of the kind that often arose for plaintiffs in cases of this period, where a defendant denied that he had authorised or ratified his agent's tortious acts, and where the courts insisted that clear words were needed to support a finding of ratification, without which there would be no liability. An example is *Eastern Counties Railway Co v Broom*,[137] where there was held to be no evidence to support a finding that the defendant railway company had ratified the actions of its employee in wrongfully arresting a passenger and taking him before the magistrates, although the defendant's solicitor had also attended the magistrates' hearing. The significance of these evidential problems diminished with the development of the vicarious liability doctrine, under which different reasoning came to be used to determine whether a master should be liable for his servant's torts[138] — although problems of a different kind were then created when the courts adopted the 'Salmond test', which required them to consider

---

134 (1889) 41 Ch D 295. Earlier support: *Wilson v Tumman* (1843) 6 Man & G 236, 242–43; 134 ER 879, 882; *Ancona v Marks* (1862) 7 H & N 686, 695–96 and 697; 158 ER 645 and 648.
135 [1901] AC 240, reversing [1900] 1 QB 629.
136 Each of the three printed reports of *Bird v Brown* (decided in 1850) attribute authorship of the court's opinion to a different judge. Although the Law Journal gives it to Parke B (19 LJ (NS) Ex 154), the Exchequer Reports give it to Rolfe B (4 Ex 786, 154 ER 1433) and the Jurist to Pollock CB (14 Jur 132). In *Keighley, Maxsted*, above n 135, 248 Lord Macnaghten observed that 'No one gives it to the fourth judge; but then there were only three sets of reports current at the time. The Weekly Reporter did not begin till later.' Further cases in which Parke considered the ratification doctrine in a contractual context, respectively as Parke J, Parke B and Lord Wensleydale, are: *Vere v Ashby* (1829) 10 B & C 288, 109 ER 457; *Foster v Bates* (1843) 12 M & W 226, 152 ER 1180; *Ridgway v Wharton* (1857) 6 HLC 238, 10 ER 1287.
137 (1851) 6 Ex 314, 155 ER 562. See too *Lewis v Read* (1845) 13 M & W 834, 153 ER 350; *Freeman v Rosher* (1849) 13 QB 780, 116 ER 1462; *Roe v Birkenhead, Lancashire, and Cheshire Junction Railway Co* (1851) 7 Ex 36, 155 ER 845; *Moon v Towers* (1860) 8 CB (NS) 611, 141 ER 1306; *Walker v South Eastern Railway Co* (1870) LR 5 CP 640; *Rowe v London Pianoforte Co Ltd* (1876) 34 LT 450. But cf *Haseler v Lemoyne* (1858) 5 CB (NS) 530, 141 ER 214; *Hilbery v Hatton* (1864) 2 H & C 822, 159 ER 341; *Harrisons & Crossfield Ltd v London & North Western Railway Co* [1917] 2 KB 755.
138 SJ Stoljar, *The Law of Agency: Its History and Present Principles* (London, Sweet & Maxwell, 1961) 179–82; PS Atiyah, *Vicarious Liability in the Law of Torts* (London, Butterworths, 1967) 310.

whether a servant's unauthorised acts amounted to an 'unauthorised mode of doing some act authorised by the master.'[139]

Burón was also unusual because principals and agents were (and still are) usually jointly and severally liable for wrongs committed by the agent with the principal's authority, and it was (and still is) usually no answer to a claim against the agent that his act was authorised by the principal. So, for example, in *Bennett v Bayes*[140] the defendants were agents for the landlord of premises occupied by the plaintiff tenant, who defaulted on the rent. The defendants signed a distress warrant and then wrongfully refused a tender of the rent after the warrant was issued but before it was executed. They were personally liable for the illegal distress. Cases did arise where the ratification of an agent's unauthorised actions absolved him from liability to a third party, by turning his unlawful acts into lawful acts: for example, some cases of unauthorised distress by a bailiff acting for a landlord who had the legal right to distrain on the tenant's goods.[141] However, Parke B does not seem to have thought of *Burón* as a case of this kind, since he thought that the Crown might still be liable to pay compensation even though Denman was not liable to do so. This is discussed further in the next part.

Two points remain to be made here. First, the cases of unauthorised distress used by Parke B to illustrate the private law doctrine of ratification do not all clearly support his reasons for doubting that the doctrine should be applied in *Burón*. His doubts flowed from the fact that ratification of an agent's unauthorised acts in a private law context would not affect the agent's personal liability, but ratification of an act of state would absolve the agent from liability. However, as we have said already, the ratification of the bailiff's unauthorised actions in some of the distress cases *did* absolve him from liability.[142] Secondly, Parke B noted some private law cases where an agent's actions could not be ratified, observing that 'in the case of a tenant from year to year, who has, by law, a right to a half year's notice to quit, if such notice be given by an agent, without the authority of

139 Derived from JW Salmond, *Law of Torts* (London, Stevens & Haynes, 1907) 83, and adopted in *Poland v John Parr & Sons* [1927] 1 KB 236, CA. Cases where the employer had impliedly or expressly prohibited the servant's actions were hard to fit within this test, eg *Ilkiw v Samuels* [1963] 1 WLR 991, CA; *Rose v Plenty* [1976] 1 WLR 141, CA, for which reason the HL switched to a 'close connection' test in *Lister v Hesley Hall Ltd* [2002] 1 AC 215.

140 (1860) 5 H & N 391, 157 ER 1233. See too *Arnot v Biscoe* (1743) 1 Ves Sen 95, 27 ER 914; *Perkins v Smith* (1752) 1 Wils KB 328, 95 ER 644; *Barker v Braham* (1773) 3 Wils KB 368, 95 ER 1104; *Stephens v Elwall* (1815) 4 M & S 259, 105 ER 830; *Green v Elgie* (1843) 5 QB 99, 114 ER 1186; *Hollins v Fowler* (1872) LR 7 HL 757; *Mill v Hawker* (1875) LR 10 Ex 92; *Eaglesfield v Marquis of Londonderry* (1876) 4 Ch D 693, 708; *Consolidated Co v Curtis & Son* [1892] 1 QB 495.

141 *Anon* (1586) Godb 109, 78 ER 67; *Hull v Pickersgill* (1819) 1 Brod & B 282, 129 ER 731; *Whitehead v Taylor* (1839) 10 Ad & E 210, 113 ER 81.

142 See n 140 and text. This point is made in D Lanham, 'Ratification in Public Law' (1981) 5 *Otago Law Review* 35, 43–45.

the landlord, the tenant is not bound by it'.[143] This rule was laid down in *Right v Cuthell*,[144] which, along with *Bird v Brown* and *Keighley Maxsted*, serves as a salutary reminder that even in private law cases the courts will not allow principals to adopt their agents' unauthorised actions if this would produce injustice to third parties.

G. ACTS OF STATE

The rule laid down in *Burón*, that Crown servants owe no liability in tort for acts done in an official capacity against foreign nationals in foreign states, is now subject to certain limits. The rule does not absolve Crown servants from liability for acts committed against friendly foreign nationals within the jurisdiction,[145] nor does it absolve them from liability for acts committed against British subjects outside the jurisdiction.[146] The rule in *Burón* is also inconsistent with the well-established principle that Crown servants are personally liable in tort for acts against British subjects within the jurisdiction.[147]

To explain this inconsistency, some writers have argued that the act of state doctrine renders official actions against foreign nationals in foreign states non-justiciable, owing to the special nature of executive acts performed overseas. One version of this argument holds that acts of state are inherently political and so are not, and should never be, subject to legal assessment.[148] Another holds that acts of state are subject to legal assessment, but that the applicable law is international law rather than English law, and so the English courts are only exceptionally the appropriate forum for applying the relevant rules of international law.[149] On

---

143 (1848) 2 Ex 167, 188.

144 (1804) 5 East 491, 102 ER 1158. See too *Doe d Mann v Walters* (1830) 10 B & C 626, 109 ER 583; *Doe d Lyster v Goldwin* (1841) 2 QB 143, 146; 114 ER 57, 58; *Doe d Rhodes v Robinson* (1837) 3 Bing NC 677, 132 ER 571; *Jones v Phipps* (1868) LR 3 QB 567; *Divall v Harrison* [1992] 2 EGLR 64, CA.

145 *Johnstone v Pedlar* [1921] 2 AC 262. Enemy aliens within the jurisdiction are caught by the rule: *Netz v Ede* [1946] Ch 224; *cf R v Bottrill, ex parte Kuechenmeister* [1947] 1 KB 41, CA.

146 *A-G v Nissan* [1970] AC 179.

147 *Entick v Carrington* (1765) 19 St Tr 1030; *Wilkes v Wood* (1769) 19 St Tr 1406; *Rogers v Rajendro Dutt* (1860) 13 Moo PC 209, 236–37; 15 ER 78, 88–89; *Feather v R* (1865) 6 B & S 257, 296–97; 122 ER 1191, 1205; *Musgrave v Pulido* (1879) 5 App Cas 102, PC; *Raleigh v Goschen* [1898] 1 Ch 73, 77; *Walker v Baird* [1892] AC 491, PC; *Tamaki v Baker* [1901] AC 561, PC; *Hutton v Secretary of State for War* (1926) 43 TLR 106. The leading case since the enactment of the Crown Proceedings Act 1947 is *M v Home Office* [1994] AC 377.

148 Eg JG Collier, 'Act of State as a Defence against a British Subject' (1968) 26 *Cambridge Law Journal* 102, 118ff; P Cane, 'Prerogative Acts, Acts of State, and Justiciability' (1980) 29 *ICLQ* 680; Sir W Wade and C Forsyth, *Administrative Law*, 9th edn (Oxford, Oxford University Press, 2004) 838–40.

149 Eg ECS Wade, 'Acts of State in English Law: Its Relations with International Law' (1934) 15 *British Yearbook of International Law* 98; D Akande, 'Non-justiciability and the Foreign Act

either approach, it follows not only that Crown servants are immunised from liability for acts of state in the English courts, but also that the courts lack jurisdiction to order the Crown to compensate affected parties.

In her fine new study of the act of state doctrine,[150] in which she charts the historical development of the doctrine and contextualises the leading cases to excellent effect, Amanda Perreau-Saussine observes that both of these interpretations have been espoused by the English courts at different periods. The first, distinctly autocratic, approach was taken in various cases relating to the governance of the British Empire in the late eighteenth and nineteenth centuries,[151] and still shows some signs of continued life,[152] but the second approach has dominated in more recent cases.[153] In Perreau-Saussine's view, however, a third approach, which emerges much more patchily from the case law, is preferable to the other two because it holds acts of state to be reviewable by the English courts, and is therefore 'constitutionally healthier'. In this third version, acts of state are legally defensible only insofar as they are just, with the result that, although Crown servants can shift responsibility for their actions onto the Crown, it remains a justiciable issue whether the Crown must pay compensation to individuals who have been injured by the acts done in its name.

Burón is a central case in Perreau-Saussine's rendering of this third approach because, although Denman was not personally liable to pay damages, Parke B left open the possibility that the Crown might still be liable if Burón pursued a remedy by petition of right or else applied to the Spanish government to seek compensation on his behalf.[154] In fact, nothing more was heard from the plaintiff in *Burón* after each side agreed to bear its own costs and the other two actions were discontinued. However, Perreau-Saussine argues that in principle Burón should have been entitled to a remedy against the Crown by petition of right, as Parke B surmised. This might appear to have been ruled out by *Viscount Canterbury v A-G*,[155] where the Speaker of the House of Commons failed to recover damages from the Crown when his house (along with both Houses of Parliament) was negligently burned down by Crown

of State Doctrine in English Law', paper given at the BIICL Conference on 'International Law and the English Legal System', April 2008.

150 A Perreau-Saussine, 'British Acts of State in English Courts' (2007) 78 *British Yearbook of International Law* 176.

151 Eg *Nabob of the Carnatic v East India Company* (1793) 2 Ves Jun 56, esp 60; 30 ER 521, esp 523; *Secretary of State in Council of India v Kamachee Boye Sahaba* (1859) 13 Moo PC 22, 15 ER 9; *Cook v Sprigg* [1899] AC 572, PC; *ex parte Sekgome* [1910] 2 KB 576, CA.

152 Eg *R v Jones (Margaret)* [2006] UKHL 16, [2007] 1 AC 136, esp [62].

153 Eg *A-G v Nissan* [1970] AC 179; *Butte Gas & Oil Co v Hammer (No 3)* [1982] AC 888; *JH Rayner (Mincing Lane) Ltd v DTI* [1990] 2 AC 418, esp 499; *R (Al Jedda) v Secretary of State for Defence* [2007] UKHL 58, [2008] 1 AC 153.

154 (1848) 2 Ex 167, 189–90.

155 (1843) 1 Ph 306, 41 ER 648.

employees.[156] Still more pertinently, the *Canterbury* case was followed in *Tobin v R*,[157] where the court refused to make an unliquidated damages award for trespass to the owners of a ship which had been destroyed by a naval captain off the west coast of Africa in the belief that it was engaged in the slave trade. However, the court in *Tobin* accepted that a petition of right would lie for restitution of property in the event that it was wrongfully seized by a Crown servant or for 'the value thereof if it had been converted to the King's use',[158] and similar conclusions were also drawn the following year, in *Feather v R*,[159] and again, 60 years later, in *Commercial and Estates Company of Egypt v Board of Trade*.[160] In other words, although Burón could not have recovered tort damages to compensate him for his loss, he could have recovered the value of his property in an action that might have been characterised at the time as quasi-contractual, and that might now be identified as a claim in unjust enrichment.

It might be objected that these cases do not support the proposition that Burón could have recovered the value of his trade goods, since these were not taken by Denman but were seized by Prince Manna and the other chiefs. Conceivably, a remedy might have been awarded for the slaves, but that might also have been a difficult claim, since it would presumably have rested on the assertion that the slaves were property that had 'found its way into the possession of the Crown', yet Denman had never purported to 'possess' the slaves, but had treated them as free people from the moment that they were taken from their captors. Obviously, though, the question whether a plaintiff who was caused a loss by an act of state might have recovered from the Crown by petition of right is now of historical interest only, following the abolition of this form of proceeding by the Crown Proceedings Act 1947. Reviewing the case law since then, Perreau-Saussine highlights the House of Lords' refusal to hold in *Burmah Oil Co (Burmah Trading) Ltd v Lord Advocate*[161] that the Crown can take

---

156 The reasoning in the *Canterbury* case reflects an understanding of vicarious liability for torts that has since been superseded. It was assumed that an employer could be liable to his employee's tort victim only if he had committed a wrong in his own right by negligently selecting the employee or had authorised his employee to commit the tort, something which he could only do if he had the legal capacity to incur tortious liability himself; on this theory, the Crown could not be vicariously liable for its employees' torts because it was thought to lack the capacity to commit torts itself: PW Hogg and PJ Monahan, *Liability of the Crown*, 3rd edn (Scarborough, Ontario, Carswell, 2000) 6–7.

157 (1864) 16 CB (NS) 310, 359–60; 143 ER 1148, 1167.

158 Ibid, 16 CB (NS) 358.

159 (1865) 6 B & S 257, 294; 122 ER 1191, 1204–05 (Cockburn CJ). 'The only cases in which the petition of right is open to the subject are, where the land, or goods, or money of a subject have found their way into the possession of the Crown, and the purpose of the petition is to obtain restitution, or if restitution cannot be given, compensation in money, or when a claim arises out of a contract, as for goods supplied to the Crown or to the public service.'

160 [1925] 1 KB 271.

161 [1965] AC 75.

property belonging to foreign nationals by virtue of the prerogative without paying compensation, and the House of Lords' refusal to hold in *A-G v Nissan*[162] that the uncompensated damage done to the plaintiff's hotel by British troops could be defended as an act of state. She concludes that future courts would do well to build on these cases to interpret the act of state doctrine in such a way that the payment of compensation to affected parties is understood to be a prerequisite for the lawful exercise of prerogative powers overseas.

We find this an attractive conclusion, but we would observe that Perreau-Saussine does not explain why Crown officials should not also be personally liable to pay damages for their tortious acts of state against foreign nationals in foreign states, given her belief that such acts should be subject to the rule of law, and given too that public officials are personally liable for torts committed against British citizens within the jurisdiction. The practical significance of this point may be limited, given that claimants will usually prefer to sue a deep-pocketed governmental body rather than individual public officials. It is an interesting question, though, whether it would be desirable to eliminate this inconsistency by abolishing or expanding the rule in *Burón*. In other words, should the personal immunity conferred on public servants who commit acts of state by *Burón* be abolished, or should public servants be given personal immunity for their torts within the jurisdiction as well? The latter development would certainly run against the grain of current judicial attitudes,[163] but it could be justified in the interests of efficient and robust administration, on the basis that it would reduce the risk of over-defensive behaviour by public servants who would otherwise be fearful of unpredictable and disproportionately severe penalties for the negligent performance of their duties.[164] It might also be said that the rules under which Crown servants were rendered personally liable for torts committed in an official capacity emerged from a period when the Crown itself could not be sued directly, and that these rules mitigated the injustice that would otherwise have been wrought by that principle when taken in conjunction with the practice of the government standing behind its officials and paying the judgments that were awarded against them.[165] Fifty years after the enactment of the Crown Proceedings Act 1947, however, that rationale for holding government officials personally liable has surely lost its force.

---

[162] [1970] AC 179.

[163] *Cf D v Home Office* [2005] EWCA Civ 38, [2006] 1 WLR 1003 [57] (Brooke LJ): there is 'nothing in the slightest bit peculiar about an individual bringing a private law claim for damages against an executive official who has unlawfully infringed his private rights'.

[164] A concern voiced in eg *Rowling v Takaro Properties Ltd* [1987] 1 AC 473 (PC) 502; *Hill v Chief Constable of West Yorkshire* [1989] AC 53, 63; *X v Bedfordshire CC* [1995] 2 AC 633, 675.

[165] *Mulcahy v Ministry of Defence* [1996] QB 732 (CA) 740; *Matthews v Ministry of Defence* [2003] UKHL 4, [2003] 1 AC 1163 [4].

Finally we note that some additional support for Perreau-Saussine's conclusions can be drawn from a series of recent developments in the law governing the judicial control of executive action, identified by Philip Sales in a short but insightful article in *Judicial Review*.[166] These include the extension of judicial review proceedings to cover actions taken outside the UK but based on decisions taken within the UK,[167] and the possible availability of claims under the Human Rights Act 1998 in respect of conduct by British officials abroad.[168] Sales also notes *Bici v Ministry of Defence*,[169] a successful claim by Kosovar Albanians who were negligently shot by British peacekeeping troops in Pristina. In that case, the Ministry of Defence conceded that it was vicariously liable for the soldiers' wrongdoing and expressly disavowed any reliance on the act of state doctrine.[170] That it chose to make this concession, however, is suggestive in itself.

H. CONCLUSION

Burón v Denman was decided at a time of great strain in the diplomatic relations between Great Britain and Spain. The facts of the case are emblematic of the opposing attitudes taken by the two nations: Denman's destruction of the barracoons was born of British impatience and growing anger at Spain's dilatoriness in fulfilling its treaty obligations; Burón's (or, more accurately, Blanco's) insistence on his property rights, despite widespread moral objections to slavery, reflected Spanish resentment at Great Britain's interference in Spain's relations with its overseas dominions. From a legal perspective, too, the case is emblematic of its period. It is no coincidence that the principles of ratification as we know them today were worked out at a time before instant (or even quick) communication, when by necessity agents had to act on their own initiative and without consultation, and when the questions therefore arose whether principals could adopt their agent's unauthorised actions or should be permitted to disavow them. Some of the possibilities are illustrated by the differing attitudes taken by Palmerston and Aberdeen towards Joseph Denman, and also, less obviously, by Blanco's relationship with Burón.

---

[166] P Sales, 'Act of State and the Separation of Powers' [2006] *Judicial Review* 94, 94–95.
[167] See now R *(Bancoult) v Secretary of State for Foreign and Commonwealth Affairs* [2008] UKHL 61, [2009] 1 AC 453.
[168] See now R *(Al Skeini) v Secretary of State for Defence* [2007] UKHL 2, [2008] 1 AC 153.
[169] [2004] EWHC 786 (QB).
[170] Ibid, [88].

3

George v Skivington (1869)

DAVID IBBETSON

George v Skivington[1] is not one of those landmark cases which marks a significant deviation in the path of the law. Treated as authority for the proposition that a vendor of goods might owe a duty of care to a person other than the immediate purchaser of them, it was criticised for over half a century, until being finally vindicated in *Donoghue v Stevenson* in 1932, when the liability of the negligent manufacturer of goods was established. 'Few cases can have lived so dangerously and lived so long', said Lord Buckmaster in that case.[2] It is, nonetheless, a case which is worth revisiting. It not only brings out the difficulties associated with liability for defective products as the tort of negligence stuttered into existence, but more importantly links this to problems with the law of contract at this time, particularly when married women were concerned. In the same way that the expansive tort of negligence in the 1980s (and indeed before) was associated with a restrictive law of contract,[3] so too in the middle of the nineteenth century the rigidity of the rules of contract led plaintiffs' lawyers to explore the potential of the law of torts as a route to obtain compensation.

A. THE FACTUAL BACKGROUND

We cannot consider the legal issues of the case independently of the facts. None of the reports give these in great detail, and the case has not been traced in the records of the Court of Exchequer, so some educated guesswork is needed. The basic outline, as winnowed by lawyers and fitted neatly into the seductive categories of the law, appears from the pleadings

---

1 (1869) LR 5 Exch 1, [1869] WN 231, 21 LT 495, 39 LJ Ex 8, 18 WR 118; *The Times*, 16 November 1869.

2 *Donoghue v Stevenson* [1932] AC 562 (HL) 570.

3 B Markesinis, 'An Expanding Tort Law—Price of a Rigid Contract Law' (1987) 103 *LQR* 354.

as reproduced in the various reports.[4] Mr George bought from Mr Skivington a chemical which he had compounded himself and which he represented as being fit to be used for washing the hair;[5] the hairwash was to be used, as the defendant knew, by Mrs George. It had, however, been improperly compounded by the defendant, and when Mrs George used it her hair was destroyed. Such are the bare facts as they can be reconstructed from the pleadings, but it is useful to put a modicum more flesh on the bones.

The Law Journal report of the case tells us that Skivington's attorneys were Williams & Graves of Brighton (the other reports refer simply to Hore & Sons, their London agents), and on the reasonable assumption that he came from the Brighton area we may identify him as Samuel Skivington, or Skevington, a dispensing chemist who lived and worked just off the seafront in Hove.[6] He was in his late forties, and, at least at the time of the 1861 census, was sufficiently prosperous to have had two live-in servants—a cook and a housemaid. The Georges, Joseph[7] and Emma, if we identify them correctly, were from Wapping, near the docks in the east of London; Joseph was a cooper. Both in their early twenties, they had married in 1868.

Presumably the Georges were on holiday in the newly fashionable resort of Hove—perhaps even on their honeymoon—when the purchase of the hairwash took place. We do not know for certain which of them went into the shop, but, since the pleadings (as originally drafted) refer to the sale as having been made to them both,[8] it seems likely that they were together at the time; though clearly the hairwash was bought for the use of the wife. When she used it, in the words of one version of the pleadings, 'her hair was destroyed and injured, and she was and is otherwise injured'.[9] The details are obscure, but the description of the injury points towards some corrosive substance having attacked her hair and scalp. The fact that the claim was brought in the Court of Exchequer rather than the County Court might perhaps point to the injury having been fairly serious, since the upper limit for the jurisdiction of the County Court at the time was £50, whereas there was no lower limit on the jurisdiction of the superior courts (though the successful plaintiff could not recover costs if damages below £10 were awarded in a tort claim[10]). In truth, though, we might

---

[4] See below, n 31.

[5] Whether this was a straightforward shampoo or something more elaborate for perfuming or colouring the hair is not mentioned. The newspapers of the time are replete with advertisements for the latter form of preparation.

[6] The parties' personal details are derived from census data and the registers of births, marriages and deaths.

[7] The husband's Christian name is given as John in the Law Journal, Joseph in the other reports. I cannot trace any John George with a wife named Emma.

[8] 39 LJ Ex 8; see below, n 28, n 31.

[9] 21 LT 495, 496. The other reports are consistent with this.

[10] Stat 30 & 31 Vic, c 142, s 5.

guess that a stronger reason for the Georges' avoidance of the County Court would have been the acute inconvenience they would suffer if they were forced to sue in Brighton.[11]

B. THE CLAIM: MOULDING THE FACTS INTO THE LAW

If Mrs George had been a single woman—or, of course, a man—the matter would have been utterly straightforward. She could have brought an action for damages against Skivington and recovered compensation for her injuries. There might once have been a question whether the action was properly to be seen as lying in contract or in tort—in the former it would have been necessary to have alleged that there had been some payment made as consideration for the hairwash, in the latter not[12]—but by the time that *George v Skivington* was reached it had been settled by the House of Lords that the purchaser could sue in the alternative in either contract or tort.[13] It would have been only slightly more difficult if the sale had occurred while she was single and the action brought after she had married. As a married woman she would not have been able to sue on her own, but the action would have to be brought by her husband. However, since the contract had been made with her, and she had provided the consideration for it, she would be the 'meritorious cause' of the action and could be joined as co-plaintiff. The situation would then in practice be the same as if the action had been brought by her alone, and substantial damages could be recovered to compensate her for the injury which she had suffered.

But contracts with married women were different. Two potential problems arose: first, she might not have provided the consideration for the contract; and secondly, she might not herself have been a party to the contract, and hence her claim might fail for lack of privity. Although these rules were in practice tightly interlinked, it is as well to consider them separately.

The rule that the proper plaintiff in an action on a contract not under seal[14] was the person from whom the consideration had moved was well established; its roots were as old as the doctrine of consideration

11 Stat 9 & 10 Vic, c 95, s 128 had recognised this pressure by providing that the costs penalties for suing in the central courts would not apply if the parties lived more than 20 miles apart, but this had been repealed in 1867: Stat 30 & 31 Vic, c 142, sch C.

12 *Coggs v Barnard* (1703) 2 Ld Raym 909, 92 ER 107 (sub nom *Coggs v Bernard*). See DJ Ibbetson, 'Coggs v Barnard (1703)' in C Mitchell and P Mitchell (eds), *Landmark Cases in the Law of Contract* (Oxford, Hart Publishing, 2008) 1.

13 *Brown v Boorman* (1844) 11 Cl & Fin 1, 8 ER 1003, affirming (1842) 3 QB 525, 114 ER 603.

14 Or, more accurately, in a contract requiring consideration: an action could be brought on a promissory note, for example, without proof of consideration. See *Philliskirk v Pluckwell* (1814) 2 M & S 393, 105 ER 427.

itself,[15] and from the eighteenth century it had been the primary test used to determine who it was who should bring the action.[16] It had the merit of being easy to apply, but its effects were capricious where married women were concerned. Where the consideration was the performance of a service by such a woman, there would have been no difficulty in showing that she had satisfied the requirement: a wife who had exercised her arts to cure the defendant of a wound could be joined with her husband in an action to recover the agreed fee,[17] as could a married woman who had taught the defendant's daughter needlework.[18] It was less straightforward, however, where the consideration was the payment of money, since on marriage the wife's wealth would have vested in her husband,[19] and in the eyes of the law therefore the consideration would have been provided by him rather than her. It was only if some settlement had been made allowing the wife to keep her own separate property that she would, as a matter of law, have been able to provide the consideration and hence bring an action on the contract.

The second hurdle was that, independently of whether or not she had provided the consideration, she might not have been a party to the contract. A married woman was for most purposes treated as the agent, or servant, of her husband; it followed that, even if she was the person physically entering into the transaction, in the eyes of the law it would have been her husband rather than she who was the true party to the transaction. A few years before *George v Skivington* this might not have been a significant difficulty, since a third party for whose benefit a contract had been made might in principle bring an action on the contract;[20] but in 1861 this had been severely questioned in *Tweddle v Atkinson*.[21] There is considerable ambiguity in the reports of this case, some suggesting that the real basis of the decision was the rule that the plaintiff must have provided the consideration, others that there was a separate rule that the action had to be brought by the person with whom the contract had been made.[22] If

---

[15] *Anon* (1575) 110 Seld Soc 457. Sir J Baker, 'Privity of Contract in the Common Law before 1580' in EJH Schrage (ed), *Ius Quaesitum Tertio* (Berlin, Duncker & Humblot, 2008) 35, 43.

[16] *Crow v Rogers* (1724) 1 Stra 592, 93 ER 719; DJ Ibbetson and W Swain, 'Third Party Beneficiaries in English Law: From *Dutton v Poole* to *Tweddle v Atkinson*' in Schrage, ibid, 191, 198–99.

[17] *Brashford v Buckingham* (1608) Cro Jac 77, 205, 79 ER 65, 179; approved in *Fleet v Perrins* (1869) LR 4 QB 500, 507 (Cleasby B). Contrast *Buckley v Collier* (1692) 1 Salk 114, 91 ER 105, holding that the wife could not be joined if the claim was a quantum meruit for the wife's labour, since this was the husband's to dispose of.

[18] *Fountain v Smith* (1659) 2 Sid 128, 82 ER 1293.

[19] Co Litt 351b: 'Marriage is an absolute gift of all chattels personal in possession in her own right . . .'

[20] Ibbetson and Swain, above n 16, 206–10.

[21] (1861) 1 B & S 393, 121 ER 762, 30 LJQB 265, 4 LT 468, 9 WR 781.

[22] Ibbetson and Swain, above n 16, 210–13.

this was the true rule, as some treatise writers at the time assumed,[23] it would follow that, since the wife would as a matter of law not have been a party to the contract, she could not sue on it herself nor could she be joined as co-plaintiff in an action on it.

The legal difficulties associated with married women's contracts were perfectly well known. At the same time as Mrs George was using her hairwash, there was before Parliament a Married Women's Property Bill, the product of deliberations of the Social Science Association, whose preamble referred explicitly to the 'peculiar severity' with which the disabilities imposed by the Common law pressed on the poorer classes of the community.[24] The wealthier classes, it was said, could avoid the legal strictures by the use of marriage settlements, but such an escape route was not in practice open to the poor.[25] Equally impractical for the poor were the various devices which had been developed by the Court of Chancery to ameliorate the legal position of married women: Chancery proceedings were simply too expensive for them to use.[26]

On the facts of *George v Skivington*, and on the law as it stood at the time, a contractual claim by Mrs George would have had little chance of success. We may suspect, too, that Skivington was aware of the problem, for a year earlier he had run into difficulties in the Brighton County Court in a parallel situation where he was suing the (male) head of a household for the price of cosmetics which he had provided; though, in the event, his claim was successful on the grounds that the defendant had paid these bills in the past.[27] It might perhaps have been arguable that *Tweddle v Atkinson* did not apply to cases such as this, or that it was not in fact authority for the proposition attributed to it, but it is highly unlikely that the plaintiffs would have been able to show that the wife had provided the consideration out of her own money: the 23-year-old wife of an East End cooper would not have had any separate property with which to have paid for the goods. It may be that the plaintiffs' attorney flirted with the idea that the wife had been a joint party to the contract, since the pleadings as originally

23 SM Leake, *Elements of the Law of Contracts* (London, Stevens, 1867) 221; F Pollock, *Principles of Contract at Law and in Equity* (London, Stevens, 1876) 190–91; W Anson, *Principles of the English Law of Contract* (Oxford, Clarendon Press, 1879) 200.

24 L Holbrooke, *Wives and Property* (Oxford, Martin Robertson, 1983) 117–26, 141–47, 148–83; ML Shanley, *Feminism, Marriage and Law in Victorian England* (London, Tauris, 1989) 49–78. For the rhetorical significance of this, marginalising the difficulties experienced by middle- and upper-class wives, see in particular pp 58–60, with B Griffin, 'Class, Gender and Liberalism in Parliament, 1868–1882: The Case of the Married Women's Property Acts' (2003) 46 *Historical Journal* 59, 75–76. For a contemporary view, see B Bodichon, *A Brief Summary in Plain English of the Most Important Laws of England concerning Women* (London, Trübner, 1869), 21–22. As Bodichon remarked, at 25–26, Parliament had already amended Indian law to give full property rights to married women: Indian Succession Act 1865, s 4.

25 Hansard, 191 HC Debs, col 1015 (1868). Whether settlements were in fact a benefit even to women of the wealthier class is not uncontroverted.

26 Hansard, 191 HC Debs, col 1359 (1868). The same view was advanced by Lord Penzance and Sir George Jessel: Griffin, above n 24, 75 n 86.

drafted had referred to the sale of the hairwash to the husband *and wife*; but the court insisted on amendment to this, and the final version of the pleadings spoke only of a sale to the husband.[28]

The husband could, of course, have brought a contractual claim in his own name on the basis that the goods were not fit for the purpose for which they had been sold, but, as a note in the *Solicitors' Journal* pointed out, he would not have received substantial damages since he had not personally suffered any loss.[29] There were, for sure, situations in which damages could be recovered for third-party losses, but this was not one of them.[30]

With the claim in contract doomed to failure, the plaintiffs' lawyers had recourse to a claim in tort. The first issue to be decided here was who the proper plaintiff was. Had the wife been very badly injured or killed, the husband might have been able to maintain an action for the loss of her consortium, in which action he would be the sole claimant; but here there was no such loss of consortium. The substance of the claim, therefore, had to be the injury to the wife, and if substantial damages were to be recovered the action had to be brought by her, with the husband joined as co-plaintiff 'for conformity'. The pleadings reflected this analysis: [31]

> Declaration, by Joseph George, and Emma his wife, that the defendant carried on the business of a chemist, and in the course of such business professed to sell a chemical compound made of ingredients known only to the defendant, and which he represented and professed to be fit and proper to be used for washing the hair, which could and might be so used without personal injury to the person using the same, and to have been carefully and skilfully and properly compounded by him, the defendant; and thereupon the plaintiff, Joseph George, bought of the defendant, and the defendant sold to him at a certain price, a bottle of the said compound, to be used by the plaintiff Emma for washing her hair, as the defendant then knew, and on the terms that the same then was fit and proper to be used, and could be safely used, by her for the purpose aforesaid, without personal injury to her, and had been skilfully, carefully, and properly compounded by the defendant; yet the defendant had so unskilfully, negligently, and improperly conducted himself in and about making and selling the said compound, that by the mere unskilfulness, negligence, and improper conduct of the defendant, the said compound was not fit or proper to be used for washing the hair, nor could it be so used without personal injury to the person using the same; by which premises the plaintiff Emma, who used the said compound for

27 *Skevington v Wilson, Brighton Gazette*, 1 October 1868, 6.

28 See 39 LJ Ex 8. The amendment is referred to in *The Times*, 16 November 1869, but there it is erroneously said that the wife should be struck out as joint plaintiff. The final version of the pleadings is abstracted in all of the reports.

29 (1870) 14 SJ 314, 315.

30 *Dunlop v Lambert* (1839) 6 Cl & F 600, 7 ER 824 (consignee of goods); *Lamb v Vice* (1840) 6 M & W 467, 151 ER 495 (court official as trustee); *Robertson v Wait* (1853) 8 Ex 299, 155 ER 1360 (charterparty).

31 Taken from LR 5 Exch 1.

washing her hair, pursuant to the terms upon which the same was sold by the defendant, was by using the same injured in health, &c.

To this the defendant demurred.

HW Lord, counsel for the defendant, argued in support of the demurrer; and then, without calling on the plaintiffs' counsel to address them, the court proceeded to give judgment for the plaintiffs. Clearly, to the Court of Exchequer their claim was so obviously well founded that there was no need to hear anything further. Perhaps a flavour of the course of the proceedings is given in what seems clearly to have been a syndicated news report of the case: [32]

> The Lord Chief Baron having stated that the court would amend the declaration by striking out the words 'and wife' so that the husband should appear to be the purchaser of the compound, said he thought that judgment should be given for the plaintiffs.

Although it is not so stated explicitly, the impression is given that the court wasted no time at all in thinking about the case.

Leaving aside the specifically legal arguments, it is easy to see on the facts why this might have been. It would have been monstrous if substantial damages were not recoverable in situations of this type. No sensible legal system would allow damages to be awarded for injuries to men and single women and refuse them if exactly the same injury occurred to a married woman.[33] Moreover, the judges could not have been ignorant of the moves which had been made in Parliament and elsewhere to improve the position of married women, albeit that these would not have gone so far as to help a woman in the position of Mrs George.[34]

C. THE ARGUMENTS IN THE CASE

What of the legal arguments? With hindsight, we can see that there were three possible lines of argument why the plaintiffs' claim in tort should win, each of which had its own pitfalls. First was that the defendant, as vendor of the hairwash, owed a duty independently of contract to a wider class of persons than the immediate purchaser. Second was that the defendant, again as vendor, might be liable to the wife if he had made a false warranty that the hairwash was fit for purpose. And third was that the defendant, as

---

32 *Liverpool Mercury*, 16 November 1869; *Leeds Mercury*, 16 November 1869.

33 See the judgment of Pigott B, below n 62.

34 In the event, the Married Women's Property Act of 1870 was considerably less far-reaching than the original bill had been. It allowed married women to keep their earnings for themselves but did not provide full rights to separate property (this did not occur until 1882: below n 109). For an assessment of its effect see the works listed in n 24, together with MB Combs, 'Cui Bono? The 1870 British Married Women's Property Act, Bargaining Power, and the Distribution of Resources within Marriage' (2006) 12 *Feminist Economics* 51.

manufacturer of the hairwash, owed a duty to a class of persons defined without reference to any contract. We should consider each of these in turn.

1. Liability of a Vendor to Third Parties

The first possibility to examine is that the defendant, as vendor of the hairwash to Mr George, thereby owed a duty in tort[35] to Mrs George. It had been firmly established by the House of Lords in *Brown v Boorman*[36] that contractual and tortious duties might overlap, so that the fact that a person might have brought an action for breach of contract against another did not in itself preclude the possibility that he or she (or a different person) might bring an action in tort against the same person; but it clearly did not follow from this that a contractual duty owed by A to B would necessarily generate a duty in tort owed by A to C. This situation had been dealt with in *Winterbottom v Wright*, where the Court of Exchequer had held that the supplier of a mail coach to the Postmaster General could not be sued by a mail coachman who was injured as a result of the defective condition of the coach.[37] It is important to note that the defendant in this case was not alleged to have been the maker of the coach, merely the supplier (though it is likely that he was in fact the maker too[38]); and in this context it is easy to understand why no liability should have arisen in tort if a contractual claim would have been excluded for lack of privity between the parties.

It can clearly be seen (at least with hindsight) that the decision in *Winterbottom v Wright* would have been a grave barrier to the success of the plaintiffs' claim in *George v Skivington* if it had been based on the defendant's position as vendor of the hairwash. But the argument was not so based. The report in the Law Times summarises the points which fell to be argued by the defendant, and there is nothing there to point to *Winterbottom v Wright* as a hurdle to be jumped by the plaintiffs; all there is is a lapidary allegation that the pleadings did not show any duty to be owed to the wife, which effectively encapsulates the whole of the defendant's position. While it is true that the reports of the argument and judgments in the case do sometimes refer to the defendant's having sold the goods, this is invariably linked to a characterisation of him as the maker too. This is made abundantly clear by the Law Times's summary of

---

[35] For the non-existence of any duty in contract, see above, 71–73.

[36] (1844) 11 Cl & Fin 1, 8 ER 1003.

[37] (1842) 10 M & W 109, 152 ER 402, 11 LJ Ex 415; following *Tollit v Sherstone* (1839) 5 M & W 283, 151 ER 120. See V Palmer, 'How Privity Entered Tort: *Winterbottom v Wright* Re-examined' (1983) 27 *American Journal of Legal History* 85.

[38] See http://metcam.co.uk.nstempintl.com/history.htm (accessed on 27 October 2009). A contract of 1842 between Wright and the Postmaster General to build and supply mail coaches for seven years survives in the National Archives: POST 10/190.

the argument which would have fallen to be made on behalf of the plaintiffs if their counsel had been called upon to argue:[39]

> The purchase of the hairwash as properly prepared for application related to the original preparation and raised the same duty of the defendant towards the plaintiffs as if they had employed him to prepare it for such purpose.

This linkage between the sale of the article and its manufacture comes through in the judgments, too. The Law Journal report of the judgment of Kelly CB provides an excellent example: 'If a chemist or perfumer, or other compounder of an article of this description, sells it for the purpose of being used by a particular person, named and known to the seller at the time . . .' It was the manufacture of the hairwash that mattered, not its sale: at least on the pleadings, therefore, *George v Skivington* was different from *Winterbottom v Wright*. All the reports of the case reproduce or summarise the argument of HW Lord for the defendant; and none of them reveals him to have been citing it or any similar case,[40] or to have been building on the decision in that case without actually citing it; equally, none of the judges saw any need to sidestep the case in reaching their judgment for the plaintiffs. The conclusion is unavoidable, that *George v Skivington* was not a case in which the defendant was being made liable *qua* vendor of the goods to someone other than the actual legal purchaser of them. If anything, the plaintiffs were at pains to argue that his status as vendor was irrelevant.

2. Liability to Third Parties for Breach of Warranty

The fact that Skivington had sold the hairwash might not have been totally beyond the point if it could be shown that he had given a warranty that it was safe to use and that this warranty inured for the benefit of the wife. The action for breach of warranty would normally be brought by the buyer of the goods, but there were two important and well-known nineteenth-century cases in which it had been held that the action might be brought by someone other than the buyer. The first of these was *Langridge v Levy*.[41] The defendant had sold a gun to the plaintiff's father, knowing that it would be used by the plaintiff and his brothers, and warranting that it was made by the gunsmith Nock and, more importantly, that it was safe to use, these warranties being false to the knowledge of the defendant. The plaintiff used the gun, which was of unsound construction, and his hand

---

[39] 39 LJ Ex 8, 9.

[40] In the Law Times report Channell B does refer to the judgment of Lord Abinger CB in *Winterbottom*, though it is not clear for what point. In the Weekly Reporter it is said that counsel for the defendant referred to the case, but to judge from the position of the reference in the report of the argument it is likely that it was Channell B who did so.

[41] (1837) 2 M & W 519, 150 ER 863; (1838) 4 M & W 337, 150 ER 1458.

was injured so badly that it had to be amputated. Although a wide principle of liability was urged in argument, the Court of Exchequer rejected this: the fact that there was a contract made between the seller and the father did not generate any right in the son, for 'there was no privity in that respect between the plaintiff and defendant'.[42] The court instead chose to characterise the claim as tortious, in what we would call the tort of deceit.[43] What was important was that he had made a representation which he knew was false, and which he knew would be relied upon by the plaintiff, and that the plaintiff had suffered injury by relying upon it. The only real question was whether it was sufficient that the representation had been made to the plaintiff indirectly rather than directly, and it required little to persuade the court that this was an irrelevant distinction. The second case, *Longmeid v Holliday*,[44] was decided on the same principle, though on the facts it fell the other side of the line. The defendant sold to a man a patent lamp to be used by him and his wife in his shop, impliedly warranting that it was sound. It turned out not to be, and the wife was badly burned when it exploded. The husband, the contracting party, recovered damages for breach of contract, but the action brought on behalf of the wife failed. Unlike in *Langridge v Levy*, it was expressly found by the jury here that the defendant did not know of the defect in the lamp and was therefore not fraudulent.

The principle of *Langridge v Levy* and *Longmeid v Holliday* was clear. The representor could be held liable in deceit if he had knowingly made the false statement which was relied on by the plaintiff to his or her detriment; but if he did not know that the statement was false and was therefore not acting fraudulently no liability would arise.

The defendant's argument in *George v Skivington* was substantially addressed to this point. Counsel stressed that it was essential to prove that there was knowledge on the part of the defendant. In the absence of this, he could not be said to have been fraudulent, so that *Langridge v Levy* would be clearly distinguishable and the case would fall squarely within *Longmeid v Holliday*. On the pleadings, though, no knowledge or fraud was alleged, only negligence; since the defendant had demurred, it had to be assumed that they were absent; and hence, it was argued, the plaintiffs should lose. Counsel presumably thought that he was on sufficiently solid ground on this point, but he had an additional makeweight argument that there was not in any event any warranty of fitness for purpose, since the law would not imply one.[45] The plaintiffs had, however, alleged in their pleadings that the defendant had in fact made a representation, and on a

---

[42] (1837) 2 M & W 519, 529, 150 ER 863, 868.
[43] *Pasley v Freeman* (1789) 3 TR 51, 100 ER 450.
[44] (1851) 6 Ex 762, 155 ER 752.
[45] Based on *Emmerton v Mathews* (1862) 7 H & N 586, 158 ER 604, 31 LJ Ex 139; *McFarlane v Taylor* (1865) LR 1 HL (Sc) 245.

demurrer it would not have been possible to argue that this was not express; it would therefore have been difficult to put any weight on this second point.

The only one of the judges to ground his decision on warranty-based reasoning was Cleasby B. He had intervened in counsel's argument with a reference to *Langridge v Levy*, and returned to this in his judgment. He made no effort to distinguish the case, but instead treated *George v Skivington* as falling squarely within it: 'The analogy between that case and the present seems to be complete, except with this difference, that you have only to substitute in this case negligence for fraud.'[46] On the face of it, this elision of the distinction between *Langridge v Levy* and *Longmeid v Holliday*, between fraud and negligence, appears a feat of near-breath-taking legerdemain, but in its day it might not have seemed quite so outrageous. By this time, alongside the notion of fraud as deliberate deceit, there was a distinct notion of 'legal fraud'; this extended to conduct which was far less morally reprehensible than deliberate wrongdoing, though its precise contours were not well defined.[47] Of particular relevance to *George v Skivington*, though, it had been held to apply to situations where a person had made a false representation which he did not believe to be false, but where he should have discovered information which would have revealed its falsity; in effect, that is, a negligent misrepresentation.[48] Moves towards such a broad approach had been made in the Courts of Exchequer and Exchequer Chamber in the 1840s,[49] but after the middle of that decade they were largely confined to the Chancery, building on the decision of Sir William Grant MR in *Burrowes v Lock*.[50] Cleasby B, therefore, was perhaps out of line not so much because of his equation of negligence with fraud, but because of his doing so in the context of a common law claim for damages. Even so, we should not be too quick to blame him: the fusion of common law and equity was in the air, and it was

46 39 LJ Ex at 11; the same point, slightly differently expressed, appears in LR 5 Exch at 5 and 21 LT at 497.

47 See, eg *Rawlins v Wickham* (1858) 3 De G & J 304, 313, 316, 44 ER 1285, 1290, 1291; *Pulsford v Richards* (1853) 17 Beav 87, 94–95, 51 ER 965, 969; *Reese River Silver Mining Co Ltd v Smith* (1869) LR 4 HL 64; L Sheridan, *Fraud in Equity* (Pitman, London 1957) 17–33. Dealing in particular with the common case of fraudulent company prospectuses, Professor Lobban sees 1867 as a turning point in the widening idea of fraud: M Lobban, 'Nineteenth Century Frauds in Company Formation: *Derry v Peek* in Context' (1996) 112 *LQR* 287, 321.

48 *Higgins v Samels* (1862) 2 J & H 460, 70 ER 1139.

49 CM Reed, 'Derry *v* Peek and Negligence' (1987) 8 JLH 64, 69–70, citing *Cornfoot v Fowke* (1840) 6 M & W 358, 151 ER 450; *Shrewsbury v Blount* (1841) 2 Man & G 475, 133 ER 836; *Smout v Ilbery* (1842) 10 M & W 1, 152 ER 357; *Fuller v Wilson* (1842) 3 QB 58, 114 ER 429; *Moens v Heyworth* (1842) 10 M & W 147, 152 ER 418; *Taylor v Ashton* (1843) 11 M & W 401, 152 ER 860; *Ormrod v Huth* (1845) 14 M & W 651, 153 ER 636.

50 (1805) 10 Ves 470, 32 ER 927. Reed, above n 49, 71–74. The closeness of the relationship between fraud and negligence in Chancery is well illustrated by the index to George Spence's *Equitable Jurisdiction of the Court of Chancery* (London, Stevens, 1846–49), where the main entry under 'fraud' is a cross-reference to 'negligence', and the main entry under 'negligence' a cross-reference to 'fraud'.

not completely unreasonable to follow the Chancery precedents in preference to those at Common law.

The other judge who touched on the question whether there was a warranty—and, if so, whether it could ground a claim for a non-party to the contract—was Kelly CB, but he did so only to dismiss it brusquely. 'It is not necessary to enter into that question.'[51] The third judge, Pigott B,[52] did not even go this far: he made no reference either to warranties or to the decisions in *Langridge* and *Longmeid*.

3. Liability for Negligent Manufacture

The third possible line of argument for the plaintiffs, that the defendant should be liable for negligence in the manufacture of the hairwash, was probably the strongest. In this, *George v Skivington* was different from the earlier cases. In *Winterbottom v Wright* the action was brought against the supplier of the mail coach, not its maker (or, at any rate, not against someone who was described as being its maker); in *Langridge v Levy* the defendant was a shopkeeper rather than a gunsmith, and he went out of his way to say that he was not the maker of the gun; and in *Longmeid v Holliday* it was noted expressly by Martin B that the defendant was not, and did not purport to be, the manufacturer of the defective lamp. There were, obiter, suggestions in both *Winterbottom v Wright* and *Longmeid v Holliday* to the effect that no action would have lain against the manufacturer,[53] though it was recognised in the latter case that there were some situations where a person entering into a contract with one person might thereby come under a duty, actionable in tort, to another: a coachman would owe a duty to take reasonable care not to injure his passenger whether the passenger had bought his own ticket or not. The point was finely balanced, and without the benefit of hindsight the argument might not have appeared quite as strong as it seems today. It is noteworthy that the defendant's counsel did not focus on it in his argument in support of the demurrer, concentrating instead on the existence or non-existence of a claim on the supposed warranty, so we might suppose that it did not appear to him to be a major underpinning of the plaintiffs' claim.

The point was not completely ignored, though. The Law Times's note of arguments falling to be made on behalf of the plaintiffs begins, 'that a husband and wife may sue on a contract touching the person of the wife, as on a contract to carry the wife's person, or for medical treatment, and

---

[51] LR 5 Exch, 3. But see below n 60 for his use of *Langridge v Levy* and *Longmeid v Holliday* at a different point in his reasoning.

[52] Channell B, the remaining judge of the court, was absent after the end of the argument and did not give a judgment, merely authorising Kelly CB to say that he concurred.

[53] (1842) 10 M & W 109, 111, 152 ER 402, 404; (1852) 6 Ex 761, 768, 155 ER 752, 756.

the contract declared on is of this class'.[54] The same report (though not the others) shows that it was addressed and picked apart. It was objected that no action could lie to the wife on the contract (presumably for the reasons of privity discussed above), and that she should not have been joined as co-plaintiff. The real question was whether any duty was owed to her *independently of the contract*; and it was said that none was. This situation was different from that of the medical man or carrier, who owed a duty to his patient or passenger no matter who his contract was with. This was really the nub of the matter, though it was soon glossed over.

There was no doubt that there were a number of situations in which professional men owed duties to people other than those with whom they were contracting. This had been clearly established in the case of doctors earlier in the nineteenth century. In *Pippin v Sheppard*[55] the Court of Common Pleas had held that a surgeon could be liable to a wife when he had negligently treated her wounds and made her injuries worse, and in *Gladwell v Steggall*[56] the same conclusion was reached when the defendant (a clergyman who also practised medicine) disastrously treated a ten-year-old child and exacerbated her pre-existing injuries. The latter case hints at the difficulties which might arise when the real world fails to fit neatly into the law's categories: the daughter complained of pains while working in the fields with her father, he took her home to his wife and she called the doctor; in the ordinary course the bill would have been sent to the father, and it was the daughter who was injured. Who was the contract with? Could the daughter bring an action for her injuries? The pleadings had alleged that the doctor had been employed by her, though it was clear that she had not herself entered into any contract with him. Nonetheless, the Court of Common Pleas rejected the defendant's objections to this: it was acceptable to say that he had been 'employed' by her, though it would not have been legitimate to say that he had been 'retained' by her or that he had 'undertaken' to her, since these would have connoted a contract between them. It is important to remember, though, that these had not been easy cases: the law was still in a state of uncertainty as to the boundaries between contract and tort, a confusion which was already evident a century or more earlier in *Coggs v Barnard* and which had been exacerbated by the judgment of Holt CJ in that case. It had similarly been established that a carrier was liable for injuries to the person or property of its passengers, whether or not they had paid for their own journey;[57] though even this case might not have been absolutely clear-cut: we cannot

---

54 21 LT at 496. These situations were among those which had been addressed, and distinguished, in *Longmeid v Holliday*.

55 (1822) 11 Price 400, 147 ER 512; to the same effect, *Lanphier v Phipos* (1838) 8 C & P 475, 173 ER 581.

56 (1839) 5 Bing NC 733, 132 ER 1283, 8 Sc 60.

57 *Collett v London and North Western Railway* (1851) 16 QB 984, 117 ER 158; *Marshall v York Newcastle and Berwick Railway* (1851) 11 CB 655, 138 ER 632.

fail to note that those defendants who argued that there was no liability independent of contract presumably thought that they had a defensible legal position.

The important question was how far this could be generalised. Charles Addison, in his treatise on the law of torts, had formulated a wide abstract principle:[58]

> Every person who exercises an employment is bound . . . to take especial care to do his work so as not to injure another by the negligent performance of that work, whether what he does is merely to please himself or by virtue of a contract made with another.

A similar statement, though perhaps not quite so broad, had been made by Tindal CJ in *Lanphier v Phipos*:[59]

> Every person who enters into a learned profession undertakes to bring to the exercise of it a reasonable degree of care and skill. He does not undertake, if he is an attorney, that at all events you shall gain your case, nor does a surgeon undertake that he will perform a cure; nor does he undertake to use the highest possible degree of skill.

Not everybody would have been so bold: in *Longmeid v Holliday* Parke B had been inclined to limit the scope of these cases, eschewing the general principle favoured earlier by Tindal CJ and later by Addison. The tort of negligence was as yet embryonic, delimited by a multiplicity of fragmented duty situations and resistant to the imposition of broad generalisations about the scope of liability. Faced with the facts of *George v Skivington*, counsel for the defendant distanced himself from the very broad principle and effectively distinguished between the provider of a hairwash and a member of a learned profession. 'A common ordinary tradesman,' he is reported to have argued, 'does not hold himself out to be skilful.'

The court rejected this attempt to limit the scope of the duty situation. Kelly CB described the duty explicitly:[60]

> I take it that everyone who compounds an article for sale has a duty imposed on him to use ordinary care and skill in compounding the article, so as to prevent personal injury to the person who has to use it.

It was because this was so that the warranty point was irrelevant: it was the negligent manufacture of the hairwash which lay at the base of the defendant's liability, not his negligent representation that it had been properly

---

[58] CG Addison, *Wrongs and their Remedies*, 2nd edn (London, Stevens, 1864) 813.

[59] (1838) 8 C & P 475, 479, 173 ER 581, 584.

[60] 39 LJ Ex at 9. Note that it was at this point in his reasoning that Kelly CB dealt with *Langridge v Levy* and *Longmeid v Holliday*. *Langridge* was of great importance, he suggested, because it showed the fact that there was a contract between A and B did not preclude a claim in tort (there in the tort of deceit) by C against A. *Longmeid* was distinguished on the grounds that in that case there was not only no breach of warranty, but more importantly there was no negligence and no breach of duty.

manufactured. Some limit, no doubt, had to be put on the range of the defendant's potential liability, but here he had known at the time of sale that the hairwash was destined to be used by the wife—if we cut through the legal formalities, it is after all probable that she was the person who 'bought' it[61]—so there was no risk of liability to an indeterminate class of individuals into whose hands the product might have fallen. Pigott B followed a near-identical line of reasoning, putting the matter as uncompromisingly plainly as could be:[62]

> The action was founded upon the charge of negligence in the defendant's business as a chemist; and if the action had been brought by the husband alone for any injury that he had sustained by reason of such negligence it cannot be doubted for a moment that the action would be maintainable. And then comes the question, whether, when the goods had been purchased by a husband for his wife, to the knowledge of the defendant, the duty to the wife is imposed on the defendant—whether that duty, in fact, extends to a person who could not contract for herself, who could not purchase these articles, and make a contract for them on her own account, and must do it through her husband? I cannot see how it can be reasonably suggested, that the duty stops with the husband, and does not extend to the wife in the circumstances.

Seen in this light, *George v Skivington* was indeed a more or less easy case. The real issue was whether the manufacturer of a chemical product should be treated on a par with doctors and carriers, owing a duty to people other than those who were in a technical contractual relationship with him. The commonsensical approach articulated by Pigott B led almost inexorably to the answer that he did. Insofar as there was a legal difficulty, it lay in the fluidity of the boundary between contract and tort, but the decision was wholly consistent with the other cases of the middle years of the nineteenth century which had made explicit that there might be overlapping tortious and contractual duties and that the fact that there was a contract between A and B did not preclude a duty arising between A and C. Its importance lay in the application of the rule in these cases to the negligent chemist; and the question for the future, perhaps, was whether it should apply to all manufacturers (as Kelly CB had clearly suggested) or only to some narrower subset of them.

It was as a case on the negligence of the manufacturer-chemist that the decision was most easily admitted into the body of the law. The first edition of Addison's *Law of Torts* to go to press after the decision in *George v Skivington* was published, the fourth (1873), merely added a sentence to its section on the liability of professional men: 'So a chymist will be liable for negligence in compounding hairwash, by which the

---

61 Above n 8.
62 39 LJ Ex at 10.
63 CG Addison, *Wrongs and their Remedies*, 4th edn (London, Stevens, 1873) 403. See also 27, 862, where the case is simply added to footnotes dealing with *Langridge v Levy*.

plaintiff's wife was injured.'[63] Telling, too, is the running head at the top of the page containing this section: 'Of builders, surgeons, chymists etc.' No more was necessary than to add in another trade or profession whose members owed a duty to non-contracting parties, and the 'etc' at the end of the list neatly removed the problem of determining exactly what sort of manufacturers would fall within the principle.

George v Skivington, therefore, was an important landmark case in establishing the liability of at least some negligent manufacturers, and potentially a major landmark in establishing a general rule of manufacturers' liability some 70 years before *Donoghue v Stevenson*.

D. THE RECEPTION OF *GEORGE V SKIVINGTON*: IDENTIFYING THE BASIS OF THE DECISION

'Cursed is he that removeth his neighbour's landmark.'[64]

If *George v Skivington* was a more or less easy case, reaching what was transparently the right conclusion, wherein lay the difficulty? The problem was not with the decision itself, but with the vagaries of nineteenth-century law reporting.[65] Leaving aside the note in *The Times*, we have five reports of the case: in the official Law Reports, the Law Journal, the Law Times, the Weekly Reporter and the Weekly Notes. The last of these is too brief to be of any independent value, but the other four are substantial; and they are all different. The pleadings do not vary, though only the Law Journal notes that they had been amended in the course of argument. The plaintiffs' points for argument appear only in the Law Times; since counsel was not in fact called upon to argue, the reporter must have had private access to what he would have said if he had had the opportunity. The defendant's argument is reported in all the versions, though the Law Times summarises it at greater length than the others and includes one aspect omitted from the others which is (for the historian) crucial to the understanding of the case: the criticism of the analogy between it and the cases where it had been held that wives might join as co-plaintiffs in actions on contracts made for their benefit.[66] Nor are the judgments reported in the same terms in each report. The substance of the argument of Kelly CB appears most clearly in the Law Journal, and the other versions are more or less difficult to follow; in particular, the distinction between the defendant's liability (or non-liability) as vendor and his liability as maker is substantially elided, though all the reports do make clear that he thought the warranty argument was misplaced. The judgment

---

[64] *Book of Common Prayer* (1662), Service of Commination.

[65] *George v Skivington* was by no means the only case in this area which was made difficult to understand by the way in which it was reported. See, eg the criticisms of *Langridge v Levy* by Brett MR in *Heaven v Pender* (1883) 11 QBD 503, 511.

[66] Above n 54.

of Pigott B is also different in its four versions. The Law Times and Law Journal make clear that the defendant's liability was based on his having been the manufacturer of the hairwash; the Weekly Reporter speaks only of the husband having been the purchaser, and can most easily be read as imposing liability on the defendant as vendor of it; and the official law report version is ambiguous, beginning by referring to the action as being 'against a tradesman for negligence and unskilfuness in his business' without saying whether it was crucial that his business involved making up the compound as well as selling it, and then drifting into a focus on the relationship between vendor and purchaser. Only the judgment of Cleasby B is reported consistently and comprehensibly, though, as has been seen, his reasoning was by far the least compelling of the judges'. The historian could perhaps be expected to engage in a microanalysis of the different reports, but the nineteenth-century legal practitioner attempting to advise a client or formulate an argument would not have been expected to unpick the details with quite so much assiduity. The ambiguity of the judges' reasoning as it appeared in the reports, and in particular as it appeared in the official report, weakened it as a decision on which the manufacturer's liability for defective products could be built.

At first, while the case was still fresh in the memory of the judges, this was not a problem. A few months after *George v Skivington*, in *Francis v Cockrell*, Cleasby B summarised the ratio decidendi of the case, accurately adopting the analysis of Kelly CB: [67]

> He said there was a duty in the vendor to use ordinary care in compounding the article sold, and that this extended to the person for whose use he knew it was purchased, and this duty having been violated, and he, having failed to use reasonable care, was liable in an action at the suit of the third person.

After this, however, the basis of the decision became blurred. The case law reveals two distinct strands: in the first, it was interpreted as a case about warranties, or more generally about statements; in the second, it was a case about the manufacture or sale of defective goods.

The first of these strands is visible in *Beattie v Lord Ebury*, where *George v Skivington* was cited in argument as authority for the liability of a vendor who had innocently (ie non-fraudulently) made a false representation,[68] from which the analogy was drawn with other situations of misrepresentation outside the context of the sale of goods. A few years later, in *Heaven v Pender*, counsel for the plaintiff in both the Divisional Court and the Court of Appeal treated it is a case concerning a breach of warranty,[69] and in *Cann v Willson*[70] it was used as an authority to justify a

---

[67] (1870) LR 5 QB 501, 515 (Exchequer Chamber).
[68] (1874) LR 7 HL 102, 106.
[69] (1882) 9 QBD 302, 304–05; (1883) 11 QBD 503, 505.
[70] (1888) 39 Ch D 39.

wide liability for negligent misstatements. But the decision in *Cann v Willson* was itself called into question a year later in *Derry v Peek*,[71] when it was held that only fraudulent misstatements were actionable, and after this *George v Skivington* ceased to be used as authority for the contrary proposition. It was not, however, wholly forgotten. It was arguable that *Derry v Peek* did not apply to situations where a negligent statement had caused physical rather than purely economic loss and, if that was so, *George v Skivington* could remain unassailed.[72] Sir John Salmond, in his treatise on the law of torts first published in 1907, alluded to it in this way, expressing doubts about the correctness of the decision in the first edition of the work but removing those doubts in the second and subsequent editions.[73]

The second strand of interpretation of *George v Skivington* ignored the issue of the warranty or representation, concentrating instead on the more general question of the liability of the vendor or manufacturer. As has been seen, the decision itself appears to have been based on the defendant's status as compounder of the hairwash rather than as vendor, but at a time when small shopkeepers sold products which they themselves had made it was easy to slide between the two characterisations.

The note of the case in the *Solicitors' Journal*,[74] apparently the only contemporary journal which did more than draw attention to the facts and the judgment, reflects this ambiguity. Its description of the ratio decidendi of the case, not distinguishing one judgment from another, focused on the defendant as vendor:

> The Court decided that there was a duty on the defendant to sell hair-wash that was not improperly compounded, and that, as in the case the sale was to the plaintiff for the use of the female plaintiff to the defendant's knowledge, the duty existed towards her as well as towards the other plaintiff . . .

Although stylistically elegant, the use of the passive voice in the first clause extended the range of liability far wider than the case had actually decided: in this form it did not seem to be relevant that the defendant had himself compounded the hairwash in the first place. Seen in this light, the decision marked a giant step from *Langridge v Levy*, since it led to the conclusion that the seller of goods might be liable to a third party if the goods were defective and the third party was injured. It gets very close to seeing it as breaking down the privity of contract rule as it was then being formulated on the authority of *Tweddle v Atkinson*:

---

[71] (1889) 14 App Cas 337. It was formally treated as bad law in *Le Lievre v Gould* [1893] 1 QB 491.

[72] J Smith, 'Liability for Negligent Language' (1900–01) 14 *Harvard Law Review* 184, 192–93.

[73] JW Salmond, *The Law of Torts: a Treatise on the English Law of Liability for Civil Injuries* (London, Stevens & Haynes, 1907) 422n; 2nd edn (London, Stevens & Haynes, 1910) 448n.

[74] 1870 SJ 314.

The fact that the hair-wash in *George v Skivington* was bought for the use of the female plaintiff was held to create a sufficient privity between her and the defendant to support the right of action by her, although there was no fraud by the defendant.

Put this way, the decision in the case was very much at odds with *Winterbottom v Wright*, which had decided precisely the opposite, that the vendor of goods should not be liable to a non-contracting party.

There was no necessary conflict between the decisions, but it was easy to read *George v Skivington* in such a way as to suggest that there was. The friction between them came up to the surface a decade or so later, in *Heaven v Pender*,[75] where the defendant had supplied staging to a shipowner to be used by workers in his dock. At first instance the Divisional Court, consisting of Field and Cave JJ, saw a clear inconsistency between *George v Skivington* and *Winterbottom v Wright*, preferring to follow the latter and holding that no duty was owed by him to the plaintiff, a worker employed by the purchaser of the staging. A note in the *Justice of the Peace* later that year picked up on this, and argued that the decision in *George v Skivington* 'had apparently been repudiated' by the decision in *Heaven v Pender*.[76] On appeal to the Court of Appeal, *Winterbottom v Wright* took rather a backstage position, though counsel for the plaintiff argued that there was no inconsistency between it and *George v Skivington*. The judges in the Court of Appeal were more concerned with the potential conflict with *Langridge v Levy*, but referred only to the unsatisfactory judgment of Cleasby B in *George*, and ignored the other judgments. Perhaps this is unsurprising, since the report to which they referred was that in the official reports, and in this the judgments of Kelly CB and Pigott B were a good deal harder to disentangle than the overtly straightforward analysis of Cleasby B. For Cotton LJ, with whom Bowen LJ agreed, *George* was a simple extension of the warranty reasoning of *Langridge* from fraud to negligence. Brett MR, by contrast, drew from *George* a very wide principle of liability for negligently causing harm, treating *Langridge* as a simple instantiation of this general principle. Since his principle was formulated so widely, it was not necessary to be too precise in detailing the basis of the liability in *George v Skivington*, but it is nonetheless significant that he did not distinguish between the defendant as vendor and the defendant as manufacturer. He had expressed himself more clearly in *Cunnington v Great Northern Railway*,[77] decided between argument and judgment in *Heaven v Pender*. There the defendant's negligence was described as having consisted in the delivery—ie the sale—of the hairwash which had been made up of deleterious compounds: as in the

---

[75] (1882) 9 QBD 302, (1883) 11 QBD 503.
[76] 'Supplying Dangerous Goods' (1883) 47 JP 33, 34.
[77] (1883) 49 LT 392.

note in the *Solicitors' Journal* a decade or more earlier, the shift from the active to the passive voice brought about a subtle but hugely significant shift in the analysis of the case. Brett's broad formulation of a general principle of negligence liability was not to find supporters for another 50 years, but his shifting of the focus of analysis of *George v Skivington* is reflected in the way in which the case came to be treated.

So far as writers in the last two decades of the nineteenth century and the first decade of the twentieth were concerned, the status of *George v Skivington* was problematic. Already by the time of *Heaven v Pender*, the moves towards the identification of a principle of liability of at least some (professional) manufacturers, which had been visible in Addison's treatise on the law of torts, had been reversed. The list of professional men who owed duties independently of contract, with the inclusion of chemists in the third edition of the text and 'chemists etc' in the fourth,[78] disappeared completely from the fifth edition of the work (1879), now in the hands of LW Cave, together with the whole chapter dealing with negligent injuries. *George v Skivington* was reduced to an appearance in the discussion of liability for fraud based on *Langridge v Levy* and *Longmeid v Holliday*.

Thomas Beven was less pusillanimous. In the first edition of his *Principles of Negligence*,[79] he excoriated the treatment of *George v Skivington* in *Heaven v Pender*, pointing out that there was no inconsistency between it and the other decisions, in particular *Winterbottom v Wright*, on the (correct) grounds that in *George* the defendant was under a duty to take reasonable care which arose independently of any contract but in the other cases the defendant was not. In the second edition (1895), this duty independent of contract was more precisely delimited; as well as repeating the general point made in the first edition, Beven included a brief section specifically on the liability of druggists, building on the decision of the Ontario Queen's Bench Division in *Stretton v Holmes et al.*[80] Here the defendant druggist (somewhat ghoulishly named Deadman) was held liable for injury sustained when his employee negligently used hydrocyanic acid rather than hydrochloric acid in making up a prescription, explicitly following the decision in *George v Skivington*. Although it was argued, on the basis of the leading American decision, *Thomas v Winchester*,[81] that the physician who had written the prescription should be liable too, this was rejected by the court on the grounds that he had not been shown to have been guilty of any negligence. The same passages occurred essentially unchanged in the third edition (1908), but in the fourth and last edition,

---

[78] Above n 63.

[79] T Beven, *Principles of the Law of Negligence* (London, Stevens & Haynes, 1889) 56.

[80] (1890) 19 Ont R 286. See T Beven, *Negligence in Law* (London, Stevens & Haynes, 1895) 1406.

[81] (1852) 6 NY 397.

which appeared in 1928,[82] the section on druggists was expunged, and the general discussion of *George v Skivington* was much muted, concluding that no general principle could be deduced from it.

Frederick Pollock was still more robust; and it was his approach which seems to have been most influential in shaping the law right up to *Donoghue v Stevenson*, even if that shaping largely took the form of rejecting his interpretation. He was a strong supporter of the decision in *George v Skivington*, despite the criticisms levelled against it in *Heaven v Pender*. He dealt with the case at two points in his treatise on torts, first published in 1887. On the one hand, he treated it as straightforwardly distinguishable from *Winterbottom v Wright*.[83] That case, he said, had quite correctly held that the breach of a contract between A and B could not in itself automatically generate a right in C; but C might have a claim independently of the contract if there had been bad faith, as in *Langridge v Levy*, or 'misfeasance by want of ordinary care', as in *George v Skivington*. Alternatively, the case could be considered as one of putting in circulation a dangerous thing.[84] This was the basis of *Thomas v Winchester*,[85] a case which was almost certainly not familiar to the mass of English judges and lawyers, but which would have been known to those of a scholarly bent through Melvin Bigelow's *Leading Cases on the Law of Torts*.[86] There a man had bought what was labelled as extract of dandelion for the use of his wife; it turned out to be not dandelion but belladonna, a poison, and when the wife took it she suffered various injuries. An action was brought by the wife against the wholesale druggist who was responsible for the mislabelling. The claim succeeded on the grounds that the defendant had negligently put into circulation a thing which, as a result of the inaccurate labelling, posed a serious risk to the health of any person who drank it. If the user had died, the person responsible for the labelling would have been guilty of manslaughter;[87] a fortiori he should be liable in tort for any injury sustained. By contrast with the approach of the majority of the judges in *Heaven v Pender*, rejecting *George v Skivington* as a case which had gone a step too far, for Pollock it had not gone far enough; it was a 'rather hesitating step' towards what he saw as the true doctrine contained in *Thomas v Winchester*.

---

[82] London, Sweet & Maxwell, 1928.

[83] *The Law of Torts* (London, Stevens, 1887) 448–49.

[84] Ibid, 411–14, reproducing his 'Duties of Insuring Safety: the Rule in Rylands *v* Fletcher' (1886) 2 *LQR* 52, 64–65.

[85] (1852) 6 NY 397.

[86] MM Bigelow, *Leading Cases on the Law of Torts Determined by the Courts of America and England* (Boston, Little Brown, 1875) 602.

[87] *Tessymond's Case* (1828) 1 Lewin 169, 168 ER 1000, where a druggist's apprentice handed over laudanum instead of the far more benign paregoric. The factual similarity between this case and *Thomas v Winchester* could hardly not have proved seductive.

This analysis involved in part the relocation of *George v Skivington* into a rather different strand of English legal authority, a strand which had been ignored in *George v Skivington* itself but which lay expressly at the base of *Thomas v Winchester*. In a series of nineteenth-century cases, beginning with *Dixon v Bell*,[88] it had been held that a person who put into circulation a dangerous thing without taking proper precautions would be liable in tort for resultant personal injuries. Parallel to this, and clearly related to it, such a person might also be criminally liable; in particular, if death resulted, he or she might be guilty of manslaughter.[89] This criminal rule had fed into the arguments in *Langridge v Levy* and *Longmeid v Holliday*, on the basis that a duty imposed by the criminal law must of necessity be a public duty owed to the world in general, though it had not been relied upon in the judgments in those cases.[90] It was, therefore, not far beneath the surface of *George v Skivington*, and Pollock's relocation of the decision into this line of authority would perhaps not have seemed outlandish, even to English lawyers unfamiliar with *Thomas v Winchester*. It did, however, involve an important shift of emphasis. In the cases involving dangerous goods, liability attached to the person who had let the goods loose on the world in their hazardous condition, typically the wholesale or retail vendor, or someone in the same position. Rethinking *George v Skivington* in this way necessarily shifted the focus away from the defendant's status as manufacturer and onto his position as vendor.

The different approaches of Beven and Pollock to the case reflect their different approaches to negligence. At least from the second edition, Beven's work was largely concerned with the detailed analysis of the circumstances in which a duty of care had been held to arise, whereas Pollock's concern was with the identification of underlying principles. For the development of the law, it was the latter which was the more valuable. There remained, though, unresolved ambiguities in Pollock's analysis.[91] Was *George v Skivington* based on a principle of liability for any act of positive malfeasance? Or was it a case of liability for putting into circulation a dangerous thing? And, if the latter, was a 'dangerous thing' to be identified by reference to particular classes of object, or did it include any thing which had a propensity to do harm? If so, would this amount to a

---

[88] (1816) 5 M & S 198, 105 ER 1023; *Illidge v Goodwin* (1831) 5 C & P 190, 172 ER 934; *Lynch v Nurdin* (1841) 1 QB 29, 113 ER 1041; *Brass v Maitland* (1856) 6 El & Bl 470, 119 ER 940; *Farrant v Barnes* (1862) 11 CBNS 553, 142 ER 912; *Mangan v Atterton* (1866) LR 1 Ex 239.

[89] *Tessymond's Case*, above n 87, 168 ER 1000; *R v Carr* (1832) 6 C & P 163, 173 ER 443.

[90] JL Barton, 'Liability for Things in the Nineteenth Century' in JA Guy and HG Beale (eds), *Law and Social Change in British History* (London, Royal Historical Society, 1984) 145, 148–49.

[91] For the tension in Pollock's analysis of negligence see N Duxbury, *Frederick Pollock and the English Juristic Tradition* (Oxford, Oxford University Press, 2004) 262–69.

general liability for injuries caused by things, since a thing which actually did harm must necessarily have had a propensity to do so?

Despite the support given to the result in *George v Skivington* by commentators such as Pollock, the treatment meted out to it in *Heaven v Pender*[92] had weakened it seriously. It resurfaced in legal argument in a series of cases in the early years of the twentieth century, but was increasingly marginalised. The first of the cases in this series was *Clarke v Army and Navy Co-Operative Society*, decided in the Court of Appeal in 1902.[93] The plaintiff had bought a tin of chlorinated lime from the defendants. When she opened it, according to the statement of claim, it exploded in her face and caused injury to her eyes. The defendants had excluded warranties of quality, so the claim had to be characterised as one arising in tort rather than contract. In argument, Collins MR suggested that the judgment of Kelly CB in *George v Skivington* had shown that liability could attach to the vendor independently of any warranty. Counsel for the defendants produced two responses to this.[94] First, the case had been 'unfavourably commented upon'. Secondly, in *George v Skivington* the supplier of the hairwash had been guilty of an act of positive misfeasance — the negligent compounding of the hairwash — whereas here the defendants had merely sold the product. The latter point seems clearly to have been taken from Pollock's analysis of the case, distinguishing it from *Winterbottom v Wright*:[95] Skivington had not been liable simply as vendor, but more importantly as manufacturer. Counsel for the defendant seems also to have relied on Pollock, but on his alternative analysis of *George v Skivington*: that the defendants' liability had flowed from the fact that they had put into circulation a dangerous thing, and in such a situation the non-manufacturer vendor could be liable in tort.[96] The defendants attempted to distinguish this on the facts, denying that there had been any explosion and presumably arguing that the tin was therefore not dangerous; however, when they demonstrated in court how to open a tin from the same batch this proved to require considerable force, and the powder in the tin shot up into the air and came down over the witnesses who were standing nearby. Moreover, it was proved that similar accidents had occurred when other tins had been opened, and that the defendants had been aware of this before Mrs Clarke bought the tin that gave rise to her injuries. Unsurprisingly, therefore, the Court of Appeal gave judgment for the plaintiffs, though using the analysis of *George v Skivington*, which had been favoured by the defendant.

92 Above, text at n 75.
93 [1903] 1 KB 155 (CA).
94 Ibid, 158.
95 Above n 83.
96 [1903] 1 KB 155, 158; above n 84.

Clarke v Army and Navy Co-Operative Society did nothing to undermine *George v Skivington*, but shows the way in which it was being interpreted at the start of the twentieth century: as a decision of perhaps dubious authority, but capable of being analysed in either of the ways suggested by Pollock. The second case in the series, *Earl v Lubbock*,[97] fell the other side of the line. The plaintiff was injured when a wheel came off a van he was driving; the defendant had a contract with the plaintiff's employer to keep his fleet of vans in repair, and it was alleged that his employee had either negligently serviced the van or negligently failed to inspect the van to see what repairs were needed. The van, with its latent defect, was not a thing dangerous in itself, so the reasoning of *Clarke v Army and Navy Co-Operative Society* was inapplicable; and, according to the Court of Appeal, *Winterbottom v Wright* determined the outcome of the case. *George v Skivington* was not cited in the judgment, but the combination of *Earl v Lubbock* with *Clarke v Army and Navy Co-Operative Society* makes clear that, in the eyes of the Court of Appeal, it was to be seen as a case involving a dangerous thing rather than illustrating a more general liability for positive misfeasance in the performance of a contract. The weakness of the authority of *George v Skivington* is brought out well by the almost apologetic way in which it was cited by counsel for the plaintiff in *Earl v Lubbock*: 'it had never been overruled'. It was further marginalised in the Court of Appeal in the same year, in *Cavalier v Pope*,[98] where Collins MR distinguished the lease of a ruinous house (the actual situation in *Cavalier v Pope*) from the sale of dangerous chattels, a situation where liability might have arisen on the authority of *George v Skivington*—'assuming that the latter case can be supported'.[99]

The final blow to the authority of *George v Skivington* was struck in *Blacker v Lake and Elliot* in 1912.[100] The plaintiff was injured when a soldered joint in a blowlamp manufactured by the defendants sheared and the paraffin vapour contained in it exploded over him. He successfully brought an action in the Watford County Court, but the judgment was overturned on appeal to the Divisional Court. Hamilton and Lush JJ subjected *George v Skivington* to careful analysis, holding that it was inconsistent with *Winterbottom v Wright*, *Heaven v Pender* and the subsequent cases.[101] Although it had never been formally overruled by any superior court, neither had it been formally approved; and—perhaps with a sideswipe at Pollock—'when it is referred to by text-book writers, or by courts of inferior authority to that which decided it, the case can only be

---

[97] [1905] 1 KB 253 (CA).
[98] [1905] 2 KB 757 (CA).
[99] [1905] 2 KB 757, 761. See too [1906] AC 428 (HL) 432 (Lord Atkinson).
[100] (1912) 106 LT 533 (DC).
[101] Though Lush J was willing to accept the possibility that it had been rightly decided on its facts, on the basis that it was a dangerous thing falling within the analysis of *Thomas v Winchester*: (1912) 106 LT 533, 541.

referred to for the purpose of following it or showing that it is distinguish-able'.[102] No longer was there any question of extra-contractual liability attaching to the negligent manufacturer as such, though the supplier of a product (whether manufacturer or not) might be liable if there had been a fraudulent warranty that it was safe, if it fell into the category of things which were dangerous in themselves or if it constituted a public nuisance.[103] *Blacker v Lake and Elliot* was not thought fit to report in the Law Reports—it is possible that Pollock, by then general editor, vetoed it, though there is no positive evidence of this[104]—but within a very short time it was being cited as authority for not following *George v Skivington*.[105] Pollock, whether or not he deliberately excluded the case from the Law Reports, seems heartily to have disapproved of it. He did not refer to it in his treatise on torts, and the only concession he gave to the rejection of *George v Skivington* was his description of it as 'not a very profitable case' in the tenth and subsequent editions of the work.[106] Nonetheless, its status as a landmark case was thoroughly extirpated. It was, of course, restored again as good law 20 years later, in *Donoghue v Stevenson*;[107] but it is the latter case that has become the landmark in the establishment of manufacturers' liability rather than *George v Skivington* itself.

E. POSTSCRIPT: MARRIED WOMEN'S CONTRACTS

George v Skivington was a case in tort, and the wane in its fortunes can be seen as reflecting the predominant judicial concern to hold in check the boundaries of tortious liability. It must not be forgotten, though, that the stimulus for the decision in the first place was that a married woman was denied a contractual remedy which was open to men and unmarried women.[108] An alternative, or additional, context for the increasing reluctance to rely on it is provided by the solution to the problem of married women's contracts. This was largely achieved by the Married Women's Property Act of 1882, which provided that a married woman could hold

---

102 (1912) 106 LT 533, 538 (Hamilton J).

103 See in particular (1912) 106 LT 533, 540–41 (Lush J). It is worth noting in passing that even at this time there is no trace of the so-called 'contract fallacy', the proposition that the fact of a contract between A and B precludes a duty between A and C. See in particular the remarks of Hamilton J (1912) 106 LT 533, 536: 'The breach of the defendant's contract with A to use care and skill in and about the manufacture or repair of an article does not *of itself* give any cause of action to B when he is injured by reason of the article proving to be defective in breach of that contract' (emphasis added).

104 Barton, above n 90, 154; Duxbury, above n 91, 306.

105 *White v Steadman* [1913] 3 KB 340 (KB); *Bates v Batey & Co Ltd* [1913] 3 KB 351 (KB).

106 F Pollack, *Law of Torts*, 10th edn (London, Sweet & Maxwell, 1916) 571.

107 [1932] AC 562, 584, 594 (Lord Atkin), 613 (Lord Macmillan); cp 575 (Lord Buckmaster).

108 Above, 71–73.

her own separate property as a matter of law, enter into her own contracts, and sue and be sued on them in her own name.[109] The Act had the effect of releasing the pressure point on the law of tort: no longer was there any need to have recourse to it in order to reach the result which was obviously required as a matter of simple justice. The rule stemming from *George v Skivington*, whatever it was, remained as a scrap of law which had once served a useful purpose, but which was now no longer necessary in order to achieve that end.

---

[109] Married Women's Property Act, 1882, s 1. For a concise survey of the problems which remained, see the Fourth Interim Report of the Law Revision Committee (Cmd 4770, 1934).

4

Daniel v Metropolitan Railway Company (1871)

MICHAEL LOBBAN

A. INTRODUCTION

On 19 December 1866, as the 12.40 from Moorgate Street station was passing under works in progress to build the new Smithfield meat market, a girder crashed onto the train, destroying the last four compartments of the second-class carriage, at the back. Just after the train left Aldersgate Street station, the few passengers in the carriage heard a tremendous crash on the top of the compartment, and saw the girder burst through the roof, crushing everything as it hit the floor. By the time the train stopped, nothing remained in the carriage, for all the sides, seats and roof had been scraped to the back. A 68-year-old widow from Kensington, Sarah Johnson, was killed instantly, as the girder smashed her skull and crushed her body.[1] Also in the compartment had been two men, and a guard at the back, each of whom was swept out of the carriage and onto the ground by the force of the girder.

Workmen from the building site immediately ran over to the scene of the accident, and help was sought from the nearby St Bartholomew's hospital. Two surgeons took the injured passengers to the hospital. As soon as he heard of the crash, the general manager of the Metropolitan railway, Myles Fenton, went to the scene, along with the company's chairman and solicitor. They also inspected the wreckage of the train, which had been removed. Fenton returned to his office, where he penned a letter to send to all the newspapers. In it, he expressed his regret for the crash, but added that '[a]s the accident did not arise from any cause connected with the working of the traffic, there was not any interruption to the ordinary train service of the line'. This businesslike comment did not impress every editor. At the foot of the letter, the editor of *The Times*

---

[1] *The Times*, 22 December 1866, 4e. She kept nothing in her pockets but a corkscrew and lump of sugar, but always carried £200 in banknotes for safety concealed in her stays.

noted, tartly, that '[t]his announcement must be very satisfactory to the survivors and friends of the deceased'.[2]

Four people lost their lives in the accident. The two men taken to hospital did not see the end of the day. Henry Clark Luckey, a 46-year-old linen-draper from Bromley in Kent, whose legs were completely smashed, died from his injuries 10 minutes after arriving at the hospital. He left a wife and family. Charles Passmore, an 18-year-old clerk, died 4 hours later from severe internal injuries.[3] The train guard, Charles Dant, was seriously injured and later died of his injuries.[4] There appeared to be no other injured passengers. It was regarded as near miraculous that the accident had occurred at a time of day when there were few passengers on the train. Four men who were in the front compartments of the carriage escaped injury.[5] None of the reports of the crash mentioned the name of David Daniel, a middle-aged scripture reader and missionary, and a man of modest means, who earned about £200 a year.[6] In August 1867, however, Daniel brought an action against the railway for negligence, in which he claimed £2,000 in damages. His case raised the question of whether a railway company was liable for the negligence of contractors working above their line.

B. THE BUILDING OF SMITHFIELD MARKET

A live cattle market in the open space at Smithfield had existed since the late Middle Ages. By the early nineteenth century, this use of an open space in the heart of the overcrowded city was causing much concern. In 1847, many felt it to be intolerable that all sorts of animals could be driven through the crowded streets of the capital of the British empire, and that hundreds were slaughtered daily in the city, in abattoirs close by the market. 'The very idea is revolting,' *The Times* thundered, 'and it is hardly saying too much that if public health were not concerned, public decency should decide the matter.'[7] Petitions were made by the inhabitants as well as by the Society for the Suppression of Cruelty to Animals to remove the market; counter-petitions were brought by traders. At a time when the government was turning its attention to the health of towns, it was felt that

---

[2] *The Times*, 22 December 1866, 10e.

[3] *The Times*, 22 December 1866, 4e; *Daily News*, 20 December 1866.

[4] Old Bailey Sessions Papers Online, available at http://www.oldbaileyonline.org/, ref t18670128-227 (accessed on 5 November 2009).

[5] They were JW Grimes, JS Ellis, Henry Crane and W Blomfield: *The Times*, 22 December 1866, 10d.

[6] He may have been the David Daniel, born in Waturalizea in Prussia in 1821, who is mentioned in the 1861 and 1871 censuses. He was said to have been an instructor in scriptural languages, including Hebrew: *The Times*, 17 August 1867, 10f.

[7] *The Times*, 18 March 1847, 5f.

it was essential to the health of the city that a new cattle market should be situated on its outskirts, and that the animals should be slaughtered away from the centre. Select committees were appointed in 1847 and 1849, and a royal commission followed in 1850. There were disagreements over how to proceed. The Markets Improvement Committee of the Corporation of London proposed developing a new market slightly to the west of Smithfield, where live cattle would still be sold and slaughtered. However, the commission rejected this, and recommended moving the market out of the centre of town.[8] Legislation followed to close Smithfield cattle market, and the market was moved to Copenhagen Fields in Islington in 1855.

This raised the question of what was to be done with the site at Smithfield. Hit by the loss of business and alarmed by the piling up of rubbish in the area, the local community began to call for a new 'dead meat' market to be erected.[9] When the debate began, the Corporation of London supported the use of the site for such a market, transferring the business from the existing cramped market at Newgate. Against the corporation stood those who argued that, when the cattle market was closed, the land had reverted to the crown, and that it should be left as an open public space, to provide vital lungs for an overcrowded and poor community. St Bartholomew's hospital, which managed to gain the ear of the Board of Trade, was particularly keen for it to remain open, so that it would be available for recuperating patients. The matter was referred to a committee in 1856, which fudged the issue. On the one hand, it stressed the importance to public health of an open space, and recommended that as much of the land as had reverted to the Crown should be adapted for public recreation. On the other hand, it admitted that, for the sake of efficient business competition, there had to be one central market for dead meat, and that neither Copenhagen Fields nor Newgate was suitable for this. The committee suggested that space could be made by clearing buildings around Smithfield.[10]

Little was done after the committee reported in July, and complaints continued about loss of trade in the area. Negotiations continued between the corporation's Markets Improvement Committee and the Treasury, and plans were drawn up for a new market.[11] Eventually, in 1860, a bill (framed by the corporation's Markets Improvement Committee) was brought to enable a new dead meat market to be erected, though part of the site of the old market had to be kept in perpetuity as a public place.[12]

[8] Report of the Commissioners appointed to make inquiries relating to Smithfield Market, PP 1850 [1217] XXXI 355.

[9] *The Times*, 23 January 1857, 7e.

[10] Report of the Committee appointed into the appropriation of the site at Smithfield, PP 1856 [2115] XXXVII 151, x, xii.

[11] *The Times*, 13 November 1857, 8e; 30 July 1858, 7f.

[12] For earlier debates and discussions, see *The Times*, 22 July 1858, 5c; 30 July 1858, 7e; 1 May 1860, 5f; 4 July 1860, 7c; 9 July 1860, 7c.

The Metropolitan Meat and Poultry Market Act did not merely authorise the corporation to build the market; it also authorised the corporation to enter into agreements with railway companies to build a terminus on the site.[13] In the new age of metropolitan railway expansion, the new Smithfield market would be serviced by railways which would connect the market to the abattoirs at Copenhagen Fields, as well as with the wider networks of provincial railways. The corporation's plans were intimately connected with the railway. Before the act was passed, the Markets Improvement Committee had already entered into an agreement with the Great Western and Metropolitan Railway Companies, which provided that a goods station would be built under the new market.[14] The companies were to be given a 100-year lease on the ground under the market at a rent of £2,000 pa, renewable for ever. Under the agreement, railway companies were to excavate the land and construct the substructure at their expense, while the roof of the station, which was also to be the floor of the market, was to be paid for jointly, in agreed proportions.[15] This work would also be supervised by a joint committee, made up of representatives of the corporation and the two railway companies. Above the station was to be the new market, designed by the City Architect, Horace Jones, and the entire building project was estimated to cost £236,800.[16]

The Metropolitan Railway was a key partner in the project. As Lowman Taylor, the chairman of the Markets Improvement Committee, reported in 1861, '[t]he plan for the market was so interwoven with the Metropolitan Railway in particular, that the committee . . . could take no steps' until the company was able to build its line.[17] The progress of the work to build the new market would thus depend on the progress of the building of the terminus and the lines which fed it. The relationship between the Metropolitan Railway and the corporation was a close one. The railway had itself been the brainchild of the City Solicitor, Charles Pearson. In 1853 it obtained an act to build a short line, and in the following year another act was passed to extend the route. The line, which ran from Paddington to Farringdon Street, was opened only at the beginning of 1863, running three and three-quarter miles. It connected with the Great Northern Railway at King's Cross and with the Great Western at Paddington. Its novelty lay in the fact that it was underground. Built by John Fowler, it was hailed as 'the great engineering triumph of the

---

13 Another Act was passed in 1862, to obtain powers necessary to carry out the works required in the earlier act. See *The Times*, 15 November 1861, 5e, 20 December 1861, 5d.

14 The agreement was only sealed in 1862: *The Times*, 27 June 1862, 6f.

15 *The Times*, 18 June 1860, 12b.

16 *The Times*, 25 April 1866, 6f. This did not include the preliminary costs, including parliamentary fees and the cost of the site and approaches.

17 *The Times*, 15 November 1861, 5e.

day'.[18] The railway itself proved very popular and profitable, carrying 30,000 passengers a day within its first month and earning £350 daily.[19]

On the day the line opened, Fowler told the cheering crowds that the next steps would include building the extension to Smithfield. The company had obtained statutory powers to do this in 1861. Following its agreement with the corporation to seek these powers, the corporation bought 20,000 shares in Metropolitan Railway, giving it the right to nominate three directors of the company and to send 40 members of the court to attend shareholders' meetings.[20] The City Architect was appointed inspector of works of the company.[21] At the same time, the Great Western also took shares in the Metropolitan, as part of the deal.[22] Although the line was to be the Metropolitan's, it was to use the broad gauge of the Great Western, which would run its trains on the line. This firm saw enormous advantages to itself in securing a portion of the basement at Smithfield, which would give it a depot in the city and save the high costs currently incurred in transporting goods from their terminus at Paddington.[23] The Metropolitan was also excited by the prospect of the works, which would enable it to create a link between the northern railways (the Great Western and Great Northern) and the southern ones (the South Western, Brighton and Dover lines).[24] The new line would be a central piece in the integration of the metropolitan railway system. The early 1860s were a significant time for the railways of London, as Parliament had to decide whether new lines could be built without a comprehensive plan being set out first. There was much anxiety at this time about the potential of railway building to unsettle the metropolis. However, things boded well for the Metropolitan, for a select committee of the Lords examining the issue favoured the creation of an 'inner circle' by extending the company's lines in both directions.[25]

The Metropolitan remained a highly successful railway company in the 1860s. Its traffic receipts grew from £101,707 in 1863 to £233,180 in 1867. The growth of its profits was faster: from £56,537 to £143,109. So successful was the line that, in February 1863, the corporation sold 18,000

18 *The Times*, 3 November 1862, 5b; 10 January 1863, 10e.

19 *The Times*, 9 February 1863, 6d.

20 *The Times*, 10 February 1860, 10f; 24 February 1860, 8c. The directors' fees were to be paid to the Freemen's Orphan's School: *The Times*, 4 May 1860, 10e.

21 This was controversial for some felt it beneath his dignity: *The Times*, 24 July 1860, 12c.

22 The Great Western was also interested in the success of the Metropolitan from its connection at Paddington. By 1863, the Great Western had invested £175,000 in the Metropolitan, and expected to earn up to £10,000 pa on those shares. *The Times*, 9 February 1863, 6d.

23 *The Times*, 16 August 1860, 10f.

24 *The Times*, 23 June 1860, 10f: The London Railway and Storehouses Bill.

25 Third Report from the Committee of the House of Lords on Metropolitan Railway Communication 1863 (500-II) VIII.9, iv. On the concern over planning, see *The Times*, 14 March 1863, 11c.

of its shares, at a profit of £32,000.[26] At the half-yearly meeting of August 1867, the week before Daniel's case was heard at the Croydon assizes, the chairman of the company assured the shareholders—to rousing cheers—that it would never pay a dividend less than 7%.[27] The week before the case went before the Common Pleas judges, in February 1868, *Herapath's Railway Journal* felt able to 'congratulate the Shareholders, upon having a very good property, in excellent condition, and with the brightest prospects'.[28] The only dark cloud on the company's horizon came later that year, when a shareholder successfully sought an injunction to restrain the company from paying a dividend, on the ground that it was charging costs to the capital account which should have been charged to the revenue account.[29] The case took up far more of the company's attention—and received far more press coverage—than Daniel's case.

Work was begun on the site at Smithfield in September 1864. The work was put in the hands of the engineering firm, Messrs John Fowler & TM Johnson, who regularly did work for both the Great Western and the Metropolitan.[30] The work on the line took some time to complete, not least because of delays in excavating the land to build the new goods station.[31] This led to many complaints. It was not until April 1867 that the contractors building the new market were finally allowed on site, having been excluded for four months, '[t]he works under the control of the railway companies not being in a sufficiently forward state'.[32] The contract to build the new market was initially given to Peto, Betts & Co, but was subsequently taken over by Kelk & Co. Kelk was a well-known builder, who undertook work both in his own capacity and in partnership with others. The firm of Kelk & Lucas had been in the press a great deal in 1862, thanks to a prolonged strike by their builders. The firm was used in the mid-1860s by the Metropolitan Railway for work on the western extension. Kelk himself was the contractor for other work for the railway, notably for the widening of the line at Farringdon Street and for the extension to its line at Finsbury. Kelk was paid substantial sums for his work. In 1867, Kelk & Lucas were paid over £270,000 for work on the western extension, while Kelk himself was paid over £106,000 for other work.[33] Kelk had a number of contracts with the Metropolitan for various

---

26 London Metropolitan Archives (LMA) COL/CCS/SO/04/002ff 554–57.
27 *Railway Gazette*, 10 August 1867, 498.
28 *Herapath's Railway Journal*, 1 February 1868, vol 30, 111.
29 *Bloxam v Metropolitan Railway Co* (1868) LR 3 Ch App 337.
30 See the papers in *Smithfield Dead Meat Market* PP 1866 (103) LIX 183. This firm did other work for the Metropolitan, including the line from Paddington to Farringdon: *The Times*, 30 November 1861, 5d; 24 February 1862, 6e; 6 August 1862, 9b. Fowler was the designer of the projects and Johnson was the resident engineer under whose superintendence the work was done.
31 *The Times*, 9 March 1866, 11 g; 25 April 1866, 6f.
32 *The Times*, 6 December 1867, 3b.
33 LMA ACC/1297/MET1/48.

works, some of which involved building stations and warehouses, and some of which involved works on the line, done under the supervision of Fowler.[34]

The new market was finally opened in August 1868. It was described as 'one of the handsomest modern buildings of the kind in the metropolis'. *The Times* enthused:[35]

> New Smithfield Market is really a wonderful structure. It occupies a space of nearly three acres, and the whole of this great area may be said to hang or rest upon girders over an equal space excavated underneath it. The Metropolitan Railway passes below it in every part, and as at this point there are junctions with the Great Western, Great Northern, Midland, and soon with the London, Chatham and Dover Railway, a large space was required, especially for the great extent of sidings which will be requisite for the meat trucks coming from all parts of England . . . The underground junction is a most wonderful piece of engineering skill, and adds another to the long list of engineering works which, whatever may be its deficiencies in other respects, places London ahead of any other city in the world.

C. THE INQUEST AND DAVID DANIEL'S CLAIM

The operation to build the terminus and market at Smithfield was clearly a joint project between the Metropolitan Railway, the Great Western and the Corporation of London. It was reported in November 1866 that 'Messrs Lucas, Brothers, have taken the share of the contract for the Metropolitan District Railway hitherto held by Messrs Peto, Betts, & Co, in conjunction with Mr Kelk and Mr Waring'.[36] If this reflected the view of the commercial community that the work was being done for the Metropolitan Railway, it is also clear from the dealing between the interested parties that the work in installing the girders which would be both the roof of the terminus and the floor of the market was work for which they were jointly responsible. Nonetheless, in the aftermath of the accident, the railway company sought to argue from the outset that the work above the line had nothing to do with them.

The first reports of the accident exonerated the Metropolitan Railway. The *Daily News* reported:[37]

> It is so far satisfactory to be able to state that the accident has arisen from no fault in the working the railway. The Metropolitan line has heretofore enjoyed a remarkable immunity from fatal accidents, and the present disaster is said to be

---

34 Eg *The Times*, 1 February 1865, 6f.
35 *The Times*, 28 August 1868, 4a.
36 *The Times*, 9 November 1866, 6a; *Daily News*, 10 November 1866. The Metropolitan District Railway was a different company; and it is assumed here that the press meant the Metropolitan.
37 *Daily News*, 20 December 1866.

entirely attributable to neglect on the part of the contractors' men of distinct regulations laid down by the engineers of the railway company, Messrs John Fowler and T Marr Johnson, and not in the remotest degree to any fault in the management of the railway.

The fault lay with workers employed by the Thames Ironworks Company, Kelk's subcontractors, who continued to work as trains were passing below.

The causes of the accident were investigated at the coroner's inquest, which was held in the week after the crash and which was attended by representatives from the Great Western, the Metropolitan Railway, the Thames Ironworks Company and the Corporation of London. The inquest revealed a shockingly relaxed approach to safety by the contractors. The accident had occurred as girders were being put over the line, which would form the support for the floor of the new market. Two main girders had already been fitted over the line, which were to be connected by a series of cross girders, which ran in the direction of the line. Seven of these had already been put in place. The method used to put the last one in place was to drag it at an angle over the ones which had already been installed, so that it would project past the last of the cross girders, and then swing it into place, using a system of pulleys known as sheerlegs, and drop it into position. This was evidently a highly hazardous enterprise, but few precautions were taken to make it safe. This was the first of the girders to be installed in this way; and it was done in this way to save time. The girder was moved by using a donkey engine pulling it by a rope, but no check line was put on the girder to help regulate the pace at which it was dragged. The girder was pulled across in a series of jerks. When the girder neared the balancing point, one workman said they should stop using the engine, but the ganger in charge, Richard Chaney, said it could be used for another foot. Predictably enough, the engine jerked the girder that little bit too far, and it crashed onto the train passing below.

Few precautions had been taken to secure against harming trains. While the foreman of the work had ordered the men to stand still when a train approached, the workers seldom saw the train until it was underneath them, by which time it was too late for the donkey engine to be stopped. The men usually worked with complete disregard to the trains coming from Aldersgate Street. The inquest heard that the order to use the donkey engine was given by the sub-foreman, John Wilmot. When Wilmot was examined, the company's solicitor took care to elicit from him the evidence that 'the railway company's servants had no control over the works of the Thames Iron Company, or the manner in which these works were carried out'.[38]

---

[38] *The Times*, 29 December 1866, 9a.

Commenting on the evidence heard at the inquest, *The Times* asked why the work was not done at night, or when the line was not used. '[I]t will strike every one,' the newspaper opined, 'that there is an inexcusable carelessness in the mere fact of a work of such magnitude being performed in such a manner and at such a time'. In the newspaper's view, all parties had to share some portion of the blame, the Thames Ironworks Company 'for allowing their works to be conducted with such utter recklessness' and the railway company for its failure 'to insist that the Iron Company should not expose their passengers to such imminent peril'.[39] The coroner's jury found a verdict of manslaughter against both Chaney and Wilmot, and they were sent for trial at the Old Bailey. But no trial followed. By the time the case came up for trial, at the end of January, Chaney was dead,[40] and the decision was taken not to proceed against the foreman alone. Observing on the case, Keating J commented that the accident was attributable to a culpable omission to give notice when trains were approaching. It was not, he thought, the task of these men to make such provision, and 'he trusted that a further investigation would take place on whom the blame rested'.[41] No further official investigation took place. The Board of Trade had already reported on the incident, and no other parties were regarded as responsible.[42]

After the accident, however, the City solicitor, TJ Nelson, wrote to the Markets Improvement Committee, pointing out 'that with every precaution, there could be no assurance against accident whilst handling such ponderous weight'. He had therefore written to the Great Western Railway, which ran 10 trains per hour over this line, to suggest that, during the progress of the works, their trains should stop at Farringdon Street, and their passengers transfer onto Metropolitan trains which were not affected by the works. Fred Saunders of the GWR was not impressed. He had been assured by Johnson 'that if only the proper precautions are taken there is no reason why the work at Smithfield should not be carried on during the time the trains are running without any unusual risk of accident'. In any event, if trains could not run while the work was being done, then the works would have to take place at night. Under these circumstances, Kelk was given instructions by Johnson to work only at night.[43]

It is not clear whether any compensation was paid to the families of the victims of the crash. The family of the unfortunately named Luckey, partner in the firm of Nash & Luckey, would surely have had a strong

39 *The Times*, 29 December 1866, 7a.
40 According to the *Pall Mall Gazette*, 23 January 1867, '[h]e had been unwell since the inquest, and was very nervous about the result of his forthcoming trial'.
41 *The Times*, 31 January 1867, 11e.
42 The National Archives (TNA) RAIL 1053/58/60 (1866, 78–79).
43 LMA COL/CCS/50/04/002 ff 556–57.

claim under Lord Campbell's Act. It may well be that the Thames Ironworks Company paid something to the family. Perhaps the Metropolitan paid something. On 9 January 1867, £1,000 was paid into Fenton's manager's account for compensations.[44] Four days earlier, a collision had taken place at Farringdon Street station between two trains, when a thick fog had reduced visibility. Two men received severe cuts in the crash but were able to be taken home after being treated at the scene.[45] In the company's half-yearly report, delivered to shareholders on 7 August, it was reported that £1,700 had been paid out in compensation for injuries which occurred in consequence of the accident in the fog.[46] This sum seems very high in light of what seem light injuries sustained in consequence of this accident. In 1867, the average sum recovered in trials for negligence causing death or personal injury was £394.[47] It may well be, therefore, that the railway company paid money to the families of those killed in the Smithfield accident, but without wishing to publicise having done so.[48]

By the time of the half-yearly meeting, David Daniel had already commenced his suit against the company.[49] Daniel claimed to have been injured in the accident as a result of the company's negligence. He claimed to have 'suffered great pain' and to have lost income because he had been 'unable to follow his employment'. His claim might have taken the company by surprise. After all, apart from the four casualties, no one else appeared to have been injured in the crash. It may well be that Daniel was making a claim for what is now called post-traumatic stress disorder. He claimed that he had been violently thrown backwards and forwards by the shock to the carriages, and had injured his knee. He also claimed that, as a result of the accident, he could not read or pursue his other avocations as usual. The railway company did not deny that there was some injury; but it did deny the extent.[50] Both Daniel's claim and the company's response are consistent with the behaviour of parties to suits

---

[44] LMA ACC/1297/MET1/48, fol 13.

[45] *Daily News*, 7 January 1867; TNA RAIL 1053/58/60 (1866, 78–79).

[46] *The Times*, 8 August 1867, 7d.

[47] There were 133 verdicts for plaintiffs in such cases, and £52,413 awarded in damages: Judicial Statistics, 1867, PP 1867–68 [4062] LXVII 519.

[48] At this time, railway companies were agitating strongly for a reform of Lord Campbell's Act. For an example where a railway company was prepared to pay compensation, while denying any legal liability for a claim brought under Lord Campbell's Act, see *Stretton v London and North-Western Railway Co* (1855) 16 CB 40, 139 ER 669.

[49] Damages for personal injury were often higher than for death, since families could only recover for their own pecuniary losses. At the Croydon assizes where Daniel brought his suit, another plaintiff recovered £4000 in damages (subject to a reference) for injuries sustained in a train crash: *Hampshire Telegraph and Sussex Chronicle*, 17 August 1867. This case was covered in many newspapers.

[50] *The Times*, 17 August 1867, 10f.

involving claims for injuries arising from train crashes, which were known as 'railway spine'.[51]

This condition was much in the public mind in early 1867, when Daniel commenced his suit, for in 1866, John Eric Erichsen, Professor of Clinical Surgery at University College, London and author of the influential book *The Science and Art of Surgery*,[52] published a treatise *On Railway and other Injuries of the Nervous System*, based on his lectures. Erichsen was interested in the fact that people who had suffered only very minor physical injuries in railway accidents often displayed severe symptoms, which developed after the accident. According to Erichsen, the victim began to feel unwell only after getting home:[53]

> A revulsion of feeling takes place. He bursts into tears, becomes unusually talk-ative, and is excited. He cannot sleep, or if he does, he wakes up suddenly with a vague sense of alarm. The next day he complains of feeling shaken or bruised all over . . . After a time, . . . he finds that he is unfit for exertion and unable to attend business.

Other symptoms included headaches, irritability, numbness and loss of balance. Erichsen to sought give a physical explanation for these symptoms. He argued that these psychological reactions to the railway accident were the result of a shock to the spine, which was suffered in the accident. According to his diagnosis, the victim suffered a concussion of the spinal cord, or marrow, from which nerves of sensation and motion were sent throughout the body. The concussion shook the nervous force out of the victim, just as a hammer striking a magnet could knock the magnetic force out from it.[54] Paradoxically, the less apparent the injury, the greater it might be. Although an accident victim whose arms or legs were broken might feel shock, he would suffer no further injury, since it was not communicated to the spine. According to Erichsen, just as watch-makers said that a watch which fell on the ground would often be

---

51 For discussions of this condition, see D Mendelson, *The Interfaces of Medicine and Law: The History of the Liability for Negligently Caused Psychiatric Injury (Nervous Shock)* (Aldershot, Ashgate, 1998) ch 2; R Harrington, 'The Railway Accident: Trains, Trauma and Technological Crises in Nineteenth Century Britain' in MS Micale and P Lerner (eds), *Traumatic Pasts: History, Psychiatry and Trauma in the Modern Age, 1870–1930* (Cambridge, Cambridge University Press, 2001) 31; KM Odden, '"Able and Intelligent Medical Men Meeting Together": The Victorian Railway Crash, Medical Jurisprudence, and the Rise of Medical Authority' (2003) 8 *Journal of Victorian Culture* 33; R Harrington, 'Railway Safety and Railway Slaughter: Railway Accidents, Government and Public in Victorian Britain' (2003) 8 *Journal of Victorian Culture* 187. For the similar debates in America, see E Caplan, *Mind Games: American Culture and the Birth of Psychotherapy* (Berkeley, CA, University of California Press, 1998); BY Welke, *Recasting American Liberty: Gender, Race, Law and the Railroad Revolution, 1865–1920* (New York, Cambridge University Press, 2001).
52 JE Erichsen, *The Science and Art of Surgery* (London, Longmans, 1853).
53 JE Erichsen, *On Railway and other Injuries of the Nervous System* (Philadelphia, PA, Henry C Lea, 1867) 74.
54 Ibid, 73.

undamaged if the glass broke whereas it would be broken if it appeared intact—since the mechanism would bear the force of the fall—so in an accident leaving the person apparently undamaged there would be an invisible harm. Although Erichsen argued that such spinal concussion could occur in any ordinary accident, he associated such injuries particularly with railway accidents. 'The rapidity of the movement, the momentum of the person injured, the suddenness of its arrest, the helplessness of the sufferers, and the natural perturbation of mind that must disturb the bravest,' he noted, 'are all circumstances that of a necessity greatly increase the severity of the resulting injury to the nervous system, and that justly cause these cases to be considered as somewhat exceptional from ordinary accidents.'[55]

Erichsen was very aware of the legal implications of his work. Observing that the 'secondary effects of slight primary injuries to the nervous system' had not attracted the attention they deserved from surgeons, he noted that this was extraordinary, since this phenomenon had become 'a most important branch of medico-legal investigation'. Having long acted himself as a medical witness in accident cases, he was well aware that there was no area in which doctors' evidence was more used than in cases arising from railway collisions, and no area in which there was more disagreement among surgeons.[56] Erichsen's book sought to show that there was a somatic explanation for the condition: it was a real, physical, medical condition. Historians have sometimes assumed that his work opened the path for 'nervous shock' claims to be brought in railway cases because he allowed the claimant to jump through the loophole that a physical injury was needed by showing that the injury was physical, and not purely mental. In fact, the notion of nervous shock was not a new one. Medical writers had long contended not only that the nervous shock provoked by a physical event such as a gunshot wound or operation could kill, but even that:[57]

> An extraordinary excitement of mind, such as is produced by dread, or by the screwing up of the system for the endurance of painful operations, when it is already much depressed and enervated by continued suffering, or apprehension of it, sometimes proves suddenly fatal.

Mid-nineteenth-century courts had seen convictions in criminal cases for deaths resulting from the nervous shock which followed an attack,[58] as

---

[55] Erichsen, above n 53, 22.

[56] Ibid, 18.

[57] B Travers, *An Inquiry concerning that Disturbed State of the Vital Functions usually called Constitutional Irritation* (London, Longman, Rees, Orme, Brown & Green, 1826) 22. For the effect of gunshot wounds, see GJ Guthrie, *A Treatise on Gun-Shot Wounds, on Injuries of Nerves, and on Wounds of the Extremities*, 2nd edn (London, Burgess & Hill, 1820).

[58] Eg *R v James Kenyon*, *The Times*, 25 February 1856, 11f, where the prisoner was convicted of manslaughter. Medical witnesses testified that the violence of the prisoner against his wife

well as cases where those injured in accidents recovered damages in civil suits for nervous harms. Provided that a jury could be persuaded that a nervous injury had been sustained in an accident, damages would be awarded.[59] In these cases, no attempts were made to argue that a psychological injury was distinct from a physical one, and therefore not the subject of compensation;[60] indeed, mid-nineteenth-century medical opinion tended to the view that nervous injuries had underlying neurological causes.[61] Disagreements usually centred on whether the particular psychological injury had been caused by the accident or whether it was a fabrication of a claimant seeking money. There were also disputes over how long the injury would last and how much compensation should consequently be awarded. Where the apparent immediate harm was slight, railways and their advisers were generally sceptical of claims. The importance of Erichsen's book hence lay less in the fact that it identified a wholly new condition than in the fact that it seemed to make it easier to prove that the plaintiff's nervous condition in these cases was a genuine one, resulting from an accident, and that the condition would persist.

It did not take long for reviewers to notice the practical relevance of Erichsen's diagnosis. *The Examiner* wrote that medical witnesses in actions for damages against railway companies would have reason to thank the professor for directing their attention to the significance of these obscure symptoms.[62] Railway companies also soon saw the danger in a book which would encourage more claims for potentially permanent nervous conditions. One doctor wrote that now any train crash victim would only have to read Erichsen's book, lie in bed a few days and go to court looking pale and wan, and he would get huge damages.[63] Railway companies were especially anxious since the sums awarded in nervous shock cases were very high. For instance, in 1865, the average amount recovered in trials on

(who suffered from consumption) had hastened her death 'partly by the nervous shock and the reaction consequent upon it causing weakness and depression'. *Cf R v John Crabbe, The Ipswich Journal*, 25 March 1848, who was convicted of manslaughter: he had beaten his wife, whose death 'was rather to be attributed to the shock sustained by the nervous system than to any of those injuries'.

59 Eg *Ramson v Birkenhead, Lancashire and Cheshire Railway Co, The Times*, 7 November 1859, 11c, where the railway company paid out for symptoms of a nervous injury sustained in a train crash, only to challenge it subsequently on discovering that the symptoms were caused by the plaintiff's existing sciatica. See also *Appleby v London and North Western Railway Co, The Times*, 22 August 1861, 9c.

60 This notion derived from *Victorian Railway Commissioners v Coultas* (1888) 13 App Cas 222. In contrast to this case, which involved a near miss, in all the railway cases discussed here, an accident had occurred in which the plaintiff had been involved.

61 Nonetheless, as Edwin Morris put it, 'in the whole range of structural anatomy there is no part so difficult as the brain and nerves to comprehend. Of the active principle in the nervous system, we in reality know little or nothing.': *A Practical Treatise on Shock after surgical operations and Injuries* (London, R Harwicke, 1867) 18.

62 *The Examiner* 10 November 1866

63 Caplan, above n 51, 28.

circuit for personal injury was £218; under Lord Campbell's Act, the average amount was £936. But in July of that year, *The Times* reported the case of *Percy v Great Eastern Railway*, where the jury awarded £6,300 to an artist who was also a drawing master on the school ship *Britannia*. Percy had been in a train crash, when a train had run down an embankment, and had been knocked out. Having regained consciousness, he got a train back to London. He had a painful leg and a numb foot, and had clearly suffered concussion. He was then told by his doctors that he had suffered a severe concussion of the brain and a severe nervous shock. The company admitted liability, but disputed the amount he should be paid. Medical witnesses disputed whether the condition had caused permanent physiological damage. Dr Coulson, for the company, said that there had been '"functional derangement", and there was an hysterical tendency, often seen in persons who had suffered a great nervous shock; but, on the whole, he thought him certain to recover'. Another doctor, Mr Skey of St Bart's, said he had suffered a general shock to the system, but there was no concussion of the brain or injury to the spinal chord. Unfortunately for Mr Skey, he could not tell the jury the difference between the general shock and the other states, though he was sure there was one. The discussion between the medics was over whether there was an organic injury—from which he might not recover—or not. Although the consensus seemed to be for recovery, the jury awarded very high damages.[64]

With high damages potentially available, and with Erichsen's book as an authority that even apparently slight physical shocks could generate serious nervous conditions, there was every reason for Daniel to make a claim. There was equally every reason for the railway to dispute it. The company's best line of defence was not simply to deny the extent of the damage to Daniel (although it did do this) but rather to shift the blame onto the contractors for the works. The plaintiff, it was argued, should seek his remedy against others, notably the Thames Ironworks Company. In fact, it appears that he had initially brought an action against that company for negligence, but was persuaded to drop that case and pursue the railway. It is noteworthy that he was represented at the trial by Serjeant Ballantine, for he was the counsel who had represented the Thames Ironworks Company at the inquest. Why did Daniel change his suit? In this case, where there were a number of parties who were potentially liable, Daniel may have been persuaded that it was best to sue the company from whom he bought his ticket.[65] This made all the more sense, since judges had recently seemed sympathetic to rail passengers injured when travelling on dangerous tracks. Equally, he may have been persuaded that in a case such as this, where the workmen would never know when

64 *The Times*, 8 July 1865, 10g.

65 This would account for his not choosing to sue the Great Western, in whose train he was traveling.

trains were approaching, it was for the railway company to signal the danger. Finally, if his claim was in fact one for 'railway spine', he may have felt that a jury was more likely to award damages against a profitable railway company than against a firm of builders.

D. THE CASE IN THE COURTS

Daniel may have been encouraged to sue the railway because of the growing willingness of judges to impose liability vicariously on railway companies for the negligence of those it had contracted with. Although it had been settled by 1840 that a defendant could only be held vicariously liable for the wrongs of his servants and not for those of independent contractors,[66] this principle was in the process of being qualified when Daniel brought his suit. In a number of areas, the 1860s saw the development of a series of what would later be called 'non-delegable' duties. It had already been recognised that, where a statutory duty was imposed on someone, he could not avoid liability for its proper performance by subcontracting its performance.[67] Equally, the principle was established that a person could be held liable for any damage flowing from his authorising a contractor to commit a wrongful act, such as a public nuisance.[68] In 1861, the Common Pleas confirmed that if a defendant employed a contractor to perform a wrongful act, or if he entrusted a contractor with performing a duty which lay on him, then he was liable for any harms which resulted. In the case before them, *Pickard v Smith*, the court found for a passenger who had fallen into a coal cellar on a station platform after the flap had been left open by the merchant who was delivering coal for the defendant. In the court's view, it was the occupier of the premises whose duty it was to keep them safe for the public. As Williams J put it, 'It was his obvious duty . . . if he used the hole in a way necessarily to create such danger, to take reasonable precautions not to injure persons lawfully using the platform: *Sic utere tuo ut alienum non laedas*'.[69] It was also agreed in the early 1860s that if the act contracted for did not itself generate danger, even though it was a task which might be performed dangerously, there was no duty on the employer to see that care was taken. Where a contractor was employed to perform a lawful act, it was to be presumed that he was employed to do it in a careful and proper manner.[70]

---

[66] *Quarman v Burnett* (1840) 6 M & W 499, 151 ER 509.

[67] *Gray v Pullen* (1864) 5 B & S 970, 122 ER 1091.

[68] *Ellis v Sheffield Gas Consumers Co* (1852) 2 E & B 767, 118 ER 955; *Hole v Sittingbourne and Sheerness Railway Co* (1861) 6 H & N 488, 158 ER 201.

[69] *Pickard v Smith* (1861)10 CB NS 470, 479; 142 ER 535, 539.

[70] *Butler v Hunter* (1862) 7 H & N 826, 158 ER 702.

At the same time, a number of courts looked more closely at the nature of the liability of railway companies for accidents suffered by their passengers. By the time of Daniel's accident, the courts had distinguished between the various kinds of liability owed by occupiers to those who came on their land. It had become settled that occupiers had a duty to inform 'licensees' of concealed traps of which they were aware; and that they had a (higher) duty to take care to prevent harm to 'invitees' as a result of unusual dangers not known to the invitee. The highest duty was owed to those who came onto their property by virtue of a contract, as passengers did. The nature of this liability, in the railway context, was debated in the 1860s, when courts explored the question of the company's liability for defective trains. In April 1867, in *Readhead v Midland Railway Co*, Blackburn J, in a dissenting judgment in the Queen's Bench, suggested that railway companies were under a strict obligation to provide carriages reasonably sufficient for the journey, and could therefore be liable even for undetectable latent defects in the rolling stock. The majority of the court set the bar lower, holding the company to have a duty to take the utmost care, but without considering them liable for defects which could not be discovered. The majority's view was upheld in the Exchequer Chamber,[71] which confirmed that the railway company had a duty to use due care—including skill and foresight—to carry the passenger safely. In the judgment of the court (given by Montague Smith J), the contract of carriage could not be seen to include an implied warranty that the carriage was fit; but there was an implied term in the contract that due care would be taken. This entailed 'a high degree of care, and casts on carriers the duty of exercising all vigilance to see that whatever is required for the safe conveyance of their passengers is in fit and proper order'.[72] *Readhead* did not raise any question of vicarious liability—for the duty was on the railway company to check its rolling stock—but in the following year, in a case brought against the committee which had organised the Cheltenham race meeting, Hannen J intimated that railway tickets did contain an implied term that due care had been taken in constructing the vehicle. This was to suggest a contractual liability to assume the risk of negligence by a contractor.[73] By the time Daniel's case came to court, his counsel could therefore draw on case law which set a high duty of care on railway carriers to ensure that their carriages would be safe.

The nature of railway companies' contractual liability for the negligence of others was also explored in cases where accidents arose from the negligence of other railway companies or their employees. It was decided in 1862 in *Great Western Railway Co v Blake* that a railway company which

---

[71] *Readhead v Midland Railway Co* (1869) LR 4 QB 379.
[72] Ibid, 393.
[73] *Francis v Cockrell* (1870) LR 5 QB 184, 194.

had the power to run its trains over the lines of another railway was liable to its passengers for injuries they received as a consequence of accidents caused by the negligence of the other company in maintaining the line. The decision rested on an analogy with carriers' contractual liabilities for loss and damage to goods. Just as carriers who had contracted to carry goods to a final destination were held liable if the goods were damaged or lost when being carried by another firm, so they should be liable contractually for personal injuries suffered on lines not their own. 'If a railway Company chooses to contract to carry passengers not only over their own line, but also over the line of another Company, either in whole or in part,' Cockburn CJ ruled, 'the Company so contracting incurs all the liability which would attach to them if they had contracted solely to carry over their own line.' By using the line of another company, 'they make the other Company their agent, and on their part they undertake that the other Company shall keep their line in a proper condition'.[74] The doctrine announced in 1862 was developed over a number of cases in the decade, and was confirmed in February 1871 in *Thomas v Rhymney Railway Co.* The cases showed that, in the contract of carriage, the carrier assumed an obligation 'that the passenger shall be carried with due and reasonable care along the whole line from one end of the journey to the other'.[75] Aware of these cases, Daniel's lawyers were careful to include a count stating that he had been invited onto their railway, to be carried for hire.

But Daniel's case was significantly different from these precedents. There were no problems with the train or the line, and no other company's carriages collided with his. Rather, the accident was the result of negligence on the part of those engaged in work that had nothing to do with operating the line or carrying passengers. Given this state of facts, counsel for the railway argued that they could not be liable, since the work done was not under their control. They denied that they could be vicariously liable for the workmen's negligence, since they were not their servants but the servants of another company. Martin B confirmed that the railway could only be liable for the negligence of its own servants and not for the negligence of the Thames Ironworks Company's servants. The judge accepted that the latter company was to be regarded as an independent contractor and refused to hear any evidence as to the various contracts under which the work was done. It was agreed that the defendants could only be held liable if they were found to be negligent in not taking precautions to prevent trains running during the works.

The trial court heard evidence from (among others) the train driver, one of the workmen and the foreman in charge of the works. The driver, John Simkins, who had earlier told the inquest that girders should not be

74 *Great Western Railway Co v Blake* (1862) 7 H & N 987, 991–93; 158 ER 773, 774–75.
75 *Thomas v Rhymney Railway Co* (1871) LR 6 QB 266, 273.

erected while trains were running, testified that there were no orders from the railway company not to run the trains while the works were proceeding. Under cross-examination, he told the court that he had on some days driven trains under the works six times a day, and had had no reason to expect an accident.[76] Henry Smith, a hoister, told the court that moving the girders was a very dangerous process, and testified that, when he had done similar work on other lines, the railway always had someone to warn of approaching trains. At the end of Ballantine's re-examination, the following exchange took place:[77]

> Mr Baron MARTIN.—Has it frequently happened, or has it occasionally happened that a girder has fallen while you were employed in this way?
>
> A. I never had a girder fall where I was before in my life; I have been in the work for years; I have had some slight accident such as a man's arm broken, or something of that kind, but never lost any lives, never any one killed—we are all liable to that in our employment.
>
> Mr Serjeant BALLANTINE—It does not matter so long as it is confined to the workmen.
>
> Mr Baron MARTIN.—This is a very intelligent man.
>
> Mr Serjeant BALLANTINE—He is, my Lord.

John Malding, the foreman in charge, confirmed that, where such work was done, railways usually placed a man to signal the approach of trains. In his view, where a girder was finely balanced, it could easily be dislodged by the vibration of a train or even by the force of smoke from the funnel. He also told the court that '[w]e are so liable to accident from these heavy weights that I should not think it was safe' to run trains below.[78] The Thames Iron Company's engineer, Thomas Edward Hussey, also confirmed that it was unsafe to run trains under such works and that the normal practice was to have a man placed by the railway to signal.

At the end of the plaintiff's case, the company argued that there was no evidence of negligence to go to a jury. Everything hinged on the question whether the company ought to have had a man on lookout. This, Martin B felt, was one of law which needed reference to the full bench.[79] At the judge's suggestion, the trial ended with an unusual procedure. A verdict was entered by consent for the plaintiff (with damages to be assessed by an arbitrator), subject to leave being reserved to the defendants to move to set it aside and have either a nonsuit or a verdict entered for them. The court was to be at liberty to draw inferences of fact and judge on the evidence.

---

[76] *The Times*, 22 December 1866, 4e; Parliamentary Archives HL/PO/JU/4/3/264, case papers for *Daniel v Metropolitan Railway*, 22–25.

[77] Parliamentary Archives HL/PO/JU/4/3/264, p 35.

[78] Parliamentary Archives HL/PO/JU/4/3/264, p 38.

[79] *The Times*, 17 August 1867, 10f.

The usual procedure would have been for the trial judge to decide if there was any evidence to go to the jury of the breach of a duty owed by the defendants, leaving it to the jury to decide on the facts if he felt there was evidence, and allowing the defendants to move for a new trial for a misdirection. If he felt there was no evidence, he should have directed a nonsuit, reserving to the plaintiff the liberty of moving for a verdict to be entered for him. As Lord Chelmsford pointed out when the case reached the Lords, the procedure adopted by the trial judge made for confusion. On the one hand, the terms of the arrangement asked the higher courts to find for the defendant if they felt there was no evidence to go to a jury—a question of law—while on the other, it invited them to make a decision on the facts.

When the case went to the Common Pleas, counsel for Daniel used the language of non-delegable duties in answering Montague Smith J's question whether the company was bound to anticipate carelessness by the Thames Ironworks Company's men: 'They had no right to speculate upon others performing a duty which the law casts upon themselves, viz to use due care and diligence to carry their passengers in safety.'[80] By contrast, counsel for the company stressed that the work in question had been done for the Corporation of London, under its statutory powers, by contractors over whom they had no control. The mere fact that an accident had occurred could not make the company liable, it was argued. There had to be some substantive evidence that the accident was caused by some specific an act or omission on their part. In the company's view, they had a perfect right to rely on the Thames company doing its work competently, noting that it was 'only dangerous if unskilfully or negligently conducted'.

The Common Pleas, however, found for the plaintiff. The leading judgment was given by Willes. He endorsed the principle that the company could not be regarded as even prima facie liable simply because an accident had occurred:[81]

> It is necessary for the plaintiff to establish by evidence circumstances from which it may fairly be inferred that there is reasonable probability that the accident resulted from the want of some precaution which the defendants might and ought to have resorted to: and I go further, and say that the plaintiff should also shew with reasonable certainty what particular precaution should have been taken.

This was an important qualification of the *res ipsa loquitur* principle which threatened to impose serious liabilities on railway companies. Willes J also agreed that a defendant could not be held liable for the negligence of strangers. However, in his view, those who carried others for hire were under a duty to take care to avoid unusual dangers of which they were

---

[80] *Daniel v Metropolitan Railway Co* (1868) LR 3 CP 216, 220.
[81] Ibid, 222.

aware and which they were in a position to avoid. To clarify his point, Willes compared the situation of a railway with that of a coach proprietor, whose coach was hit by bales falling off an overladen van passing by. In the latter case, the proprietor could not be liable for a breach of duty for not avoiding the risk, since the risk was one common to all people using the highway, and since no precaution he could have taken would have averted the danger. By contrast, in the case before him, the railway company was both aware of the risk (in a way the passenger could not be) and was in a position to take precautions against accident. In coming to this conclusion, he drew attention to the evidence which had been given at the trial that, when such work was in progress, the railway usually employed men to signal when trains were coming. As for the degree of care needed, Willes said:[82]

> I do not mean to lay it down as a proposition of law that that which is usually done is a reasonable thing to do, because there are silly and void usages. But that which is usual amongst practical men in the ordinary transactions of life, is cogent evidence of that which it is reasonable to do in similar circumstances; and the omission to do so is evidence of negligence.

Willes concluded that there was a duty to take care, and a breach of that duty. He came to the conclusion, on 'a mixed question of law and fact', that the jury might reasonably have found a verdict for the plaintiff.

The Common Pleas decision effectively ruled that there was duty arising from the relationship of passenger and carrier that the company would not run apparent unusual risks which were not evident to the passenger, and that there was evidence of the breach of this duty to go to a jury. On these grounds, Daniel won his case. When the case went to the Exchequer Chamber in June, Daniel lost his case, largely because the judges in this forum did not think, as a matter of fact, that the duty had been breached. As Blackburn J put it, 'we are bound upon this appeal to find such a verdict as we think a jury ought upon the evidence laid before us to have found'. Giving judgment for the whole court, Blackburn accepted the law as laid down by the Common Pleas to be correct. He further admitted that there was evidence of a breach of duty to go to a jury, and that there would 'possibly' have been no rule given that a verdict for the plaintiff would have been against the evidence. However, on the evidence, the Exchequer Chamber held that the persons who had the duty to take precautions were those doing the work. The key point, in Blackburn' view, was that

> though the defendants as reasonable persons must have known that girders if negligently handled are likely to fall, they could have no reason to suppose that the persons who were doing the work would do it so negligently as to hazard the happening of such an event.[83]

---

[82] Ibid, 224.
[83] *Daniel v Metropolitan Railway Co* (1868) LR 3 CP 591, 593–94.

This was to take the view that there was as a matter of fact no apparent unusual risk.

Three years later, the case went to the Lords. By now, a number of judges and commentators were beginning to express disquiet at the expansion of railway liabilities represented by cases like *Blake*. While feeling bound by the decision in the latter case, the Queen's Bench judges in *Thomas v Rhymney Railway Co* had said that a railway company should not be liable over those it could not control.[84] In the Exchequer Chamber, Kelly CB sought to draw a line, holding that a railway company would be liable if the company over whose line it was running had been negligent in maintaining it, but that it would not be if a stranger threw a log on the line. Even this did not persuade the *Law Times*, which pointed out that a railway with running powers over another's company's lines had no more control over the workmen of the other firm than it had over strangers, and which concluded that there could be no reason for liability to exist in one case and not in the other. While the rule from *Blake* was convenient for passengers who might be unsure over whom to sue, the journal argued that it had no foundation in law or justice, and it led to circuity of action.[85]

In the Lords, counsel for Daniel, who now included the Solicitor General, Sir John Duke Coleridge, made some attempt to build on the cases which had extended the liability of railways, but without success. They cited *Readhead v Midland Railway Co*, as well as a number of earlier nineteenth-century cases, which established that the law imposed an obligation to take a high degree of care in cases where passengers were conveyed. The rule from *Readhead* was said to:[86]

> make it necessary that where two companies exist and are acting independently of each other, should a mischief happen, the company carrying the passenger, though having no control over the other company, will be liable, because a danger existed and was known to exist, and yet every proper precaution was not taken against it.

If this comment bore a hint that the Metropolitan Railway might be vicariously liable for the failure of the Thames Iron Company to take care, as well as liable for its own failure to take care, it was not a hint the judges were keen to take. Lord Hatherley summarised the law in a way Kelly CB would have approved of. In his view, the rule to be inferred from the earlier cases (and from Willes's example of non-liability for harms done by overloaded coaches on the road) was that 'those who undertake the carriage of passengers are bound to take all reasonable precaution and

[84] *Thomas v Rhymney Railway Co* (1870) LR 5 QB 226.
[85] 50 *Law Times* 415 (1 April 1871).
[86] *Daniel v Metropolitan Railway Co* (1871) LR 5 HL 45, 49. Reference was made to *Thomas v Rhymney Railway Co*.

care with reference to any danger which may reasonably be expected upon the line of road over which they travel'. This meant that:[87]

> They would be obliged to see that their own line of road was in perfect order, and they would be responsible for any negligence which occurred on the other line of road, whether under their control or not, if they have contracted to carry passengers over that particular piece of road; but they would not be answerable, as I apprehend, for any mischief occasioned by any matter extraneous altogether to the work in which they were engaged, and as to which they had no reasonable ground for supposing that ordinary and proper care had not been taken by those persons whose duty it was to take such care.

To hold the railway liable for the negligence of others in this way would be to extend the liability for negligence further than common sense would warrant.[88]

The court did not look closely at the relationship between the Metropolitan Railway and the contractors doing the work. The Lords accepted that the work being done by the Thames Ironworks Company had nothing to do with the railway's business, and was being executed under a contract entered into by the Corporation of London under its statutory powers. Although a closer analysis of the facts might have supported it, they did not view the task undertaken by the Thames company as an inherently dangerous one which was done at the request of the Metropolitan Railway, and which might as a consequence have generated a 'non-delegable' duty on the defendants to ensure that the task was carefully performed. As yet, the law of 'non-delegable' duties was little developed; and the Lords had no appetite to develop it further.

The Lords (like Martin B) did, however, take the view that it made no difference whether or not the Thames Company was working under a contract with the Metropolitan Railway or the Corporation. Even if they were subcontractors for the railway, they held, since they were independent of the railway, there was no duty on the railway company to ensure that the subcontracted work was carefully done, which would make it strictly vicariously liable for any negligence. The company would only be liable for its own negligence, in failing to take care to avert an evident danger. In fact, the very ambiguity of the Thames Ironworks Company's position allowed the judges to set limits on the growth of the vicarious liability of railways. For instance, Lord Westbury—who thought that little turned on whether the Thames Ironworks Company had a contract with the Metropolitan Railway or others—nonetheless stressed the fact that they were competent, experienced contractors engaged in work done wherever railway bridges had been built. In his view, the error of the Common Pleas was to ignore the fact that the Thames Company was

[87] Ibid, 54–55.
[88] Ibid, 56.

acting under a contract. This led them (in his view) to ignore the fact that the contractors were under an obligation to take care. It led them to 'a complete *petitio principii*' in assuming that the railway company was under an obligation, when the contractors were already under one. The crucial question for him was whether the railway company had a right to rely on the contractors fulfilling their obligation. Clearly they could, since:[89]

> the ordinary business of life could not go on if we had not a right to rely upon things being properly done when we have committed and entrusted them to persons whose duty it is to do things of that nature, and who are selected for the purpose with prudence and care, as being experienced in the matter, and are held responsible for the execution of the work.

Westbury's point was not merely Kelly's argument that companies were not to be held liable for the torts of complete strangers, but the point that employers should be allowed to trust their contractors. It was an argument which was intended to place a cap on the development of a form of vicarious liability that would make an employer strictly vicariously liable for the negligence of contractors.

Like the Exchequer Chamber judges, the Lords found against Daniel on the facts. They agreed that the railway company would be liable to passengers if it ran apparent risks of danger. Lord Chelmsford felt that both lower courts had taken a view of the law which suggested that there could be an obligation to provide against possible dangers which might arise out of the performance by others of dangerous work—a kind of non-delegable duty to ensure that work was safe.[90] While holding that this was wrong, he admitted that if the work was known to present an imminent danger, an obligation might be thrown on the company. Lord Colonsay agreed that:[91]

> if the operation which the Thames Ironworks Company was performing was one which, according to previous knowledge and experience, however carefully performed, was likely to lead to mischief, I think it would then have been incumbent on the railway company to foresee it and to take precautions against it.

What most influenced the Lords in their decision was their conviction that continuing with the work of installing girders weighing five tons above an operating railway was not itself unsafe. In coming to this decision, the evidential material which came before them was limited. They had transcripts of the evidence given at the trial by four men, but heard

---

[89] Ibid, 61.
[90] This was in his view the Common Pleas's position, affirmed by the Exchequer Chamber in holding they concurred with the lower court's view of the law.
[91] *Daniel v Metropolitan Railway Co* (1871) LR 5 HL 45, 63.

nothing about the nature of the relationship between the parties.[92] The judges were also selective in the evidence they found persuasive. In Hatherley's view, the most important witness was Smith, and the most important of his evidence was the point that in 20 years he had never seen a girder fall: 'Now I think we have the exact measure of the degree of danger to be ascribed to this operation.' It showed that if due care were taken, there was no reason to anticipate any harm. The only reason the accident had occurred was because the contractors had for the first time used a donkey engine that worked by jerks. Malding's evidence that railway companies usually signalled to workmen when trains approached was dismissed, since it related to works where those working on the railway were the same as those carrying out other works 'and who, therefore, would be careful to attend both to the one and the other'. This was a point which might well have applied to the case before him—since the work at Smithfield was clearly a joint operation—but did not apply to the examples alluded to in the evidence.[93] For Hatherley, although the work might be considered dangerous, it was being done by competent men who had never known an accident to happen before, and who had themselves changed their mode of operation from a cautious one to a dangerous one.

The other judges agreed that this was simply not a dangerous task. It was an unusual accident, caused by clear negligence by the workmen. As Lord Westbury put it, '[t]his was a kind of work which every person as a contractor has almost daily been in the habit of doing'.[94] The judges were happy to see the claim fail. Westbury commented that he had 'much satisfaction in thinking that this decision will greatly tend ultimately to bring the liability of railway companies to a position in which it may be found to be more consistent with law, and less with feeling and excitement'.[95] Hatherley agreed that to hold the company liable here would be extending its liability 'in consequence of supposed negligence in not taking precautions against every remote and contingent possibility of accident, to an extent' beyond that which common sense would warrant.[96]

---

[92] Hatherley LC said that the whole of the evidence had been printed and that the court had the whole case in front of them in *Daniel v Metropolitan Railway* (1871) LR 5 HL 45, 51. However, the material in the Parliamentary Archives HL/PO/JU/4/3/264 is much more limited.

[93] Malding said: 'I put a bridge over at Brixton, for the Thames Ironworks Company, over the London and Brighton Line (I believe it was); and we put the bridge over the line at the time when the trains were running. They always had a servant at one side of the bridge to give signals to us and the trains.' Parliamentary Archives HL/PO/JU/4/3/264, p 38.

[94] *Daniel v Metropolitan Railway Co* (1871) LR 5 HL 45, 62.

[95] Ibid, 62.

[96] Ibid, 56.

E. AFTERMATH

Work continued to develop Smithfield. A vegetable market was established there under the London Central Market Act of 1875, on land acquired by the corporation from the Metropolitan Railway.[97] Eleven years later, more legislation was passed to make provision for a fish market on Snow Hill, next to Smithfield. Building work would continue to take place over railway lines. By this time, however, a much tougher safety regime was in place. Lessons had been learned from the 1866 accident. When the new fish market was built, work was carried out at night and the railway line was closed. Under the statute, the Metropolitan Railway was paid £50 per hour for any losses caused by any interruption to the traffic, as when works overran. The Metropolitan was not slow to make claims when the work overran—even if no trains were scheduled to run—and was prepared to go to litigation to recover the statutory penalty.[98] By this time, it was accepted that it was simply unsafe for railways to continue to operate under building works, and it was for parties to sort out by their contracts with builders, who was to bear the loss when works overran.

By the mid-1870s, other judges followed the Lords' lead in seeking to rein in the vicarious liability of railway companies. In 1873, in *Wright v Midland Railway Co*, the Exchequer barons held that a railway company could not be held liable if another company's carriages with the right of running over its lines collided with one of its trains. In Bramwell B's judgment, a train company contracted 'that all persons connected with the carrying and with the means and appliances of the carrying, with the carriages, the road, the signalling, and otherwise, shall use due diligence, so that no accident shall happen'. But they contracted no further, for '[i]f they were to contract that everybody should use care and diligence, their duty would extend to strangers'.[99]

If the judges of the later 1870s wanted to stem the creeping tide of railway liability, judges hearing non-railway cases at the same time began to develop the notion that a defendant could be vicariously liable for the acts of independent contractors, where 'non-delegable duties' were imposed. In 1876, in *Bower v Peate*, the Queen's Bench Division articulated the general principle that, where a man ordered work to be done

---

The Times, 12 February 1875, 11f.
98 See LMA ACC 1297/MET/10/44.
99 *Wright v Midland Railway Co* (1873) LR 8 Exch 137, 140. However, in *Richardson v Great Eastern Railway Co* (1875) LR 10 CP 486, (1876) 1 CPD 342 it was held that railway companies had a duty to make some checks to see that the rolling stock of other companies running on their lines was safe.

which would necessarily generate dangers, he had a duty to take steps to prevent the mischief. As Cockburn CJ put it:[100]

> There is an obvious difference between committing work to a contractor to be executed from which, if properly done, no injurious consequence can arise, and handing over to him work to be done from which mischievous consequences will arise unless preventive measures are adopted. While it may be just to hold the party authorizing the work in the former case exempt from liability for injury, resulting from negligence which he had no reason to anticipate, there is, on the other hand, good ground for holding him liable for injury caused by an act certain to be attended with injurious consequences, if such consequences are not in fact prevented, no matter through whose default the omission to take the necessary measures for such prevention may arise.

In the same year, the court also held that, where a defendant knew that a lamp projecting from his house over a highway was unsafe, it became his duty to make it reasonably safe, which could not be discharged by entrusting the performance of the duty to another.[101] This principle was confirmed in *Dalton v Angus*, where Lord Blackburn held that 'a person causing something to be done, the doing of which casts on him a duty, cannot escape from the responsibility attaching on him of seeing that duty performed by delegating it to a contractor'.[102] At the same time, some judges were worried by the breadth of Cockburn's formulation. It was one thing for the court to recognise some duties as 'non-delegable'—such as those derived from contracts, easements or the law of nuisance—but quite another to formulate the principle so widely that a passenger in a cab would be liable for the recklessness of the driver. Concerns like these made Lord Blackburn criticise Cockburn's formulation in 1883,[103] though other judges continued to defend the formulation.[104]

Jurists also began explain this developing doctrine. Thomas Beven argued that such a principle of vicarious liability attached to occupiers of property, and did so in four situations. It attached where the work contracted for was illegal and where there was a statutory duty imposed on the defendant. It also arose in two further situations. The first was where 'injury has arisen from the doing of a delegated act (whether in itself dangerous or not, is immaterial) if the act is one whereby in fact danger is caused'.[105] This was to suggest that if harm ensued from doing the precise

---

[100] *Bower v Peate* [1876] 1 QBD 321, 326–27. In this case, the defendant who had hired a contractor to pull down his house and build another was liable to his neighbour when his contractor failed to ensure that the house was properly supported.

[101] *Tarry v Ashton* [1876] 1 QBD 314.

[102] *Dalton v Angus & Co* (1881) 6 App Cas 740, 828.

[103] *Hughes v Percival* (1883) 8 App Cas 443, 446.

[104] In *Hardaker v Idle District Council* [1896] 1 QB 335 (CA) 347, AL Smith LJ pointed out that hiring a cab was not itself a dangerous activity.

[105] T Beven, *Negligence in Law*, 4th edn (ed WJ Byrne and AD Gibb) (London, Sweet & Maxwell, 1928) vol I, 529. Beven had in mind *Pickard v Smith* (1861) 10 CB NS 470, 142 ER

act delegated, then there would be liability. The second was where the work undertaken was necessarily dangerous, or could become so if precautions were not taken. Beven's discussion seemed to suggest that, in such cases, liability was imposed without fault. It was this view which was taken of 'non-delegable' duties, when the phrase was first coined in 1916.[106] The notion that such duties existed developed in an age before the articulation of a general principle that a duty of care existed in negligence, when the law of tort was still regarded as made up of distinct sets of duties.[107] The doctrine evolved in the particular contexts of disputes arising from public nuisances, failures to fulfil statutory duties, or cases of private nuisance or wrongs to property, such as the removal of support.

Where the defendant had authorised a nuisance or the violation of a right of support, or had failed to perform a statutory duty, such strict liability made sense, since the primary obligation on the defendant was generally a strict one. Things were more complicated in cases where the nuisance was authorised (as when statutory bodies dug up streets) or where the issue was one of occupiers' liability. In these instances, it was harder to justify liability without fault. In the former case, courts developed a version of the doctrine by stressing the fact that the defendant knew or should have known of the danger of the work. For instance, in *Penny v Wimbledon UDC*, the Court of Appeal endorsed the principle that, where a person hired a contractor to do work in a place frequented by the public, which might pose a danger to the public, 'an obligation is thrown upon the person who orders the work to be done to see that the necessary precautions are taken'. If the precautions were not taken, he could not escape liability by seeking to blame the contractor.[108] Similarly, in *Holliday v National Telephone Co*, the Court of Appeal held the defendants liable when a contractor they had used was negligent while soldering pipes together in work on a public street, as a result of which the plaintiff was injured. The company was held liable, since they were engaged in dangerous work near a highway. As Lord Halsbury LC put it, 'works were being executed in proximity to a highway, in which in the ordinary course

535 as an example of this, with Beven broadening the principle. He also cited *Daniel* as an example which fell in neither of these classes, though on the facts we have seen, it might be argued to have fallen within both.

106 The phrase 'non-delegable duties' was coined by ER Thayer in 'Liability without Fault' (1916) 29 *Harvard Law Review* 801, 809–10.

107 *Bower v Peate* and *Dalton v Angus* were both decided before *Heaven v Pender* (1883) 11 QBD 503, generally taken as the precursor of *Donoghue v Stevenson* [1932] AC 562. As Glanville Williams pointed out, Blackburn's formulation in the latter case 'if literally applied, would create vicarious liability for any and every act of negligence performed by an independent contractor in the course of doing the work': G Williams, 'Liability for Independent Contractors' [1956] *CLJ* 180, 181. Williams added that 'Blackburn presumably did not intend to go so far as this'—something we can infer from his comments in *Hughes v Percival*.

108 *Penny v Wimbledon UDC* [1898] 2 QB 212, 217, [1899] 2 QB 72. Cf *The Snark* [1900] P 105.

of things an explosion might take place'.[109] Similarly, in 1934, Stephen Chapman wrote that:

> it is the dangerous nature of the works, presumed in the case of works on a highway, coupled with the fact that as a reasonable man he ought to foresee the presence of others on the highway, which gives rise to the duty.[110]

The question of occupiers' vicarious liability remained unsettled for much of the early twentieth century. Although Frederick Pollock wanted to see vicarious liability generally reined in, he argued that the duty owed by occupiers to invitees should be non-delegable.[111] But his view took a long time to get accepted. It was finally acted on by the House of Lords in 1941. In *Thomson v Cremin*, Lord Wright ruled that the duty owed by an invitor to an invitee was a personal one, under which he warranted that due care and skill had been used to ensure that the premises were reasonably safe.[112] This was, in effect, to take a view of the liabilities of occupiers which was different from that decided, for the railway context, by the House of Lords in *Daniel*. But in 1957, this new view was reined in by the legislature. The Occupiers Liability Act 1957 was framed in such a way as to exonerate the occupier who used a subcontractor, if he acted reasonably in subcontracting, and if he had taken reasonable steps to satisfy himself that the contractor was competent and the work properly done. The Act was aimed at removing the historical distinctions between the different classes of visitor and imposing a simpler single duty on the occupier to take reasonable care that his premises were reasonably safe. On the issue of the non-delegable duty recognised in 1941, the Law Reform Committee recommended that:[113]

> Where the occupier of premises has entrusted the performance of any work of construction, maintenance or repair or other like operation on the premises to an independent contractor, and the negligent performance of such work by the contractor gives rise to some danger by which a visitor to the premises is injured, the contractor's negligence should not necessarily be held to constitute a breach by the occupier of the common duty of care towards the visitor, but it should in each case be material to consider whether the occupier acted reasonably in entrusting the work in question to an independent contractor, and took such steps as, having regard to the nature of the work, were reasonably practicable to satisfy himself that the work was properly done so as to leave the premises in a safe condition.

109 *Holliday v National Telephone Co* [1899] 2 QB 392, 399.
110 S Chapman, 'Liability for the Negligence of Independent Contractors' (1934) 50 *MLR* 71, 78.
111 F Pollock, *The Law of Torts*, 13th edn (London, Stevens & Sons, 1929) 530: 'I can see no reason for thinking that the duty declared in *Indermaur v Dames* can be escaped by delegating its performance to an independent contractor.'
112 *Thomas v Cremin* (1941) [1953] 2 All ER 1185, 1191; cf *Wilkinson v Rea, Ltd* [1941] 2 All ER 50; but contrast *Haseldine v Daw* [1941] 2 KB 343.
113 Quoted in PM North, *Occupiers' Liability* (London, Butterworths, 1971) 11–12.

This was to look for an element of fault in the occupier before holding him liable, as the Lords had wanted in *Daniel*.

However, by then, the Court of Appeal had taken a further step to expand the doctrine of non-delegable duties in cases involving dangerous activities. In *Honeywill v Larkin*, the plaintiffs, who had obtained permission to photograph a cinema owned by Denman Picture Houses Ltd, hired the defendants to take the pictures. The flash used by the latter had set fire to the curtains, as a result of which the plaintiffs paid compensation to the cinema owners. When they tried to recover this from their sub-contractors, the latter claimed that the plaintiffs were under no liability to the owners to pay for their contractors' carelessness. This rather unmeritorious argument was rejected by the Court of Appeal. Giving judgment, Slesser LJ observed that liability for the acts of independent contractors was limited to a number of defined situations, but included cases where the activity engaged in was 'extra-hazardous' and presented particular dangers. The court felt that taking photographs with magnesium flash was one such activity:[114]

> The appellants, in procuring this work to be performed by their contractors, the respondents, assumed an obligation to the cinema company which was, as we think, absolute, but which was at least an obligation to use reasonable precautions, to see that no damage resulted to the cinema company from these dangerous operations: that obligation they could not delegate by employing the respondents as independent contractors, but they were liable in this regard for the respondents' acts.

This was to hold that, where the defendant authorised action which was dangerous in nature, he was held strictly liable to ensure that care was taken by those carrying out the action. It was a significant expansion of the doctrine, for it suggested that the notion of non-delegable duties could be applied not only where a nuisance had been committed or a statutory duty breached, or where a specific duty was owed to the plaintiff (whether from contract, occupancy or as a neighbour giving support), but to any activity which resulted in harm to a stranger. Not only did it allow courts to continue to hold occupiers strictly liable, after 1957, for authorising dangerous activities to be conducted on their premises, even when they would not have been liable without fault for the dangerous condition of the premises themselves, but it allowed courts to hold liable parties who authorised any dangerous activity which harmed anyone.[115] It was a broad vicarious liability in negligence, which was only to apply when courts regarded the activity as hazardous. Since the liability was a strict one, the

---

114 *Honeywill and Stein, Ltd v Larkin Brothers (London's Commercial Photographers), Ltd* [1934] 1 KB 191, 200.
115 On the distinction between occupancy duties (covered by the principles of occupier liability and the 1957 Act) and activity duties (covered by the law of negligence), see North, above n 113, 72ff.

fact that the defendant may not have been aware of the danger (and hence not in any way at fault) was irrelevant.

Judges and jurists have remained troubled by the notion vicarious liability for 'extra-hazardous' conduct, not least because what is considered dangerous may change and is hard to define.[116] The doctrine was strongly criticised by PS Atiyah in 1967, in a work which has proved influential on the judiciary.[117] It was also criticised by Mason J in the High Court of Australia, which held in 1986 that the doctrine had no place in Australian law. As he saw it, 'the traditional common law response to the creation of a special danger is not to impose strict liability but to insist on a higher standard of care in the performance of an existing duty'.[118] British judges have continued to question the doctrine articulated in *Honeywill v Larkin*, while recognising that it is a matter for the House of Lords to settle.[119] The recently expressed view of the English Court of Appeal is that 'the doctrine enunciated in *Honeywill* is so unsatisfactory that its application should be kept as narrow as possible. It should be applied only to activities that are exceptionally dangerous whatever precautions are taken.'[120]

Atiyah felt he had already found a House of Lords case which could be used to slay the dragon of *Honeywill*: *Daniel v Metropolitan Railway Co*. Seeking to correct those who saw the case as concerned with the potential liability for the acts of strangers, Atiyah stressed the point made by the judges that the case would have been no different had the Thames Ironworks Company been contractors for the railway. For Atiyah, the judgments in that case seemed to show precisely that the employer was not liable for the negligence of contractors who engaged in dangerous work. The employer was entitled to assume that the contractor would take care. As he put it, '[a]lthough it is difficult to conceive of a more dangerous operation the House of Lords held that the defendants were entitled to leave everything to the contractors, and were not liable simply because they had not been negligent'.[121]

As the last sentence shows, Atiyah recognised that in *Daniel* the Lords had no desire to make the defendants *strictly* liable for someone else's faults. Rather, they had a duty to their customers to take precautions against any dangers of which they were or should have been aware. In *Daniel*, the defendants would have been regarded as liable had the court felt that the activity engaged in was dangerous to their knowledge. Had

---

[116] *Salsbury v Woodland* [1970] 1 QB 324, 347.

[117] PS Atiyah, *Vicarious Liability in the Law of Torts* (London, Butterworths, 1967) 371–73.

[118] *Stevens v Brodriff Sawmilling Co Pty Ltd* (1986) 160 CLR 16, 30.

[119] *Bottomley v Todmorden Cricket Club* [2003] EWCA 1575, [2004] PIQR 18; *Biffa Waste Services Ltd v Maschinenfabrik Ernst Hese GmbH* [2008] EWCA Civ 1257, [2009] Bus LR 696; *Stewart v Malik* (2009) SLT 205.

[120] *Biffa*, above n 119, [78].

[121] Atiyah, above n 117, 372.

the higher courts been persuaded (as the Common Pleas judges were) that here there was an obvious danger which the company should have guarded against, then the company would have been held to have owed a duty of care, which would have been discharged by the company's placing a railwayman on the line to signal the approach of trains to the workmen, so that they would stop work. If those workmen had carried on, recklessly or negligently ignoring the signal, and had dropped a girder on the line, the company would not have been regarded as liable. This would therefore not have been regarded as a strict, non-delegable liability, under which the defendants would have been liable without fault, as the defendants were in *Honeywill*.

The idea that an occupier should be held liable for permitting obviously dangerous activities to be conducted on his premises was accepted by the Lords in 1943. In *Corporation of Glasgow v Muir*, Lord Wright said there was a real distinction to be made between things which were obviously and necessarily dangerous and those which were not. An occupier who allowed a flying trapeze artist onto his premises owed a duty to the public to protect them from the obvious risk of harm by netting. An occupier who allowed someone to carry a tea urn through his premises was not bound to take any care against an accident on their part.[122] But this was to see the matter from the point of view of what a reasonable party should have foreseen; it was not a case of holding a party strictly liable for an activity which a court considered, after the event, to be dangerous.

---

[122] *Corporation of Glasgow v Muir* [1943] AC 448, 463–64.

5

Woodley v Metropolitan District Railway Company (1877)

STEVE BANKS

A. INTRODUCTION

Of the many bars to recovery laid in the nineteenth century before an employee wishing to sue for an injury in the course of his employment, I intend here to consider but one, that expressed by the maxim *volenti non fit injuria*. This maxim was much employed by the judges, not least because, unlike the question of contributory negligence, the issue of *volenti* did not need to be put before juries unduly sympathetic to injured plaintiffs. The scope of the defence was, however, always subject to debate, involving as it did difficult questions about knowledge, assent and free bargaining. By the final quarter of the century clear differences had emerged within the judiciary as to the scope of the defence and its relationship to the implied contract presumed between master and servant. From 1877 and *Woodley v Metropolitan District Railway Co*[1] until 1891, when *Smith v Charles Baker & Sons*[2] appeared to resolve the matter, the judges frequently found themselves in disagreement about the appropriate application of the *volenti* defence. Sometimes those disagreements were profound, since they were predicated upon very different views of the employment relation. Here, then, I shall be exploring those differing views and the legal disagreements that they engendered, and I shall be doing so most particularly through the medium of the *Woodley* case. I hope to assess the significance of the outcome of the contest between the judges for the future development of the law and also to locate the place of the judiciary within the broader social and political debate that ultimately led to the reshaping of employer liabilities at the end of the century.

Some judges, it will be observed, seemed intent on retaining a view of master and servant relations that refused to acknowledge the gross

---

1 (1877) 2 Ex D 384, [1874–80] All ER Rep 125.
2 [1891] AC 325.

disparity of bargaining power inherent in so-called free contracts for labour. Others adopted a rather more realistic view of the ability of the workman to bargain and to contract to assume risk, and they were informed both by principle and by pragmatism. Judges were not unaware that politicians were beginning to recognise the power, and therefore the legitimacy, of organised labour and that they were contemplating measures to placate it. By the 1870s, thoughtful judges might well have been disposed to consider that it was no longer truly judicious to erect so many barriers to recovery for the injured workman. Others, however, for the moment in the majority, were adamant that to extend liability for workplace injuries would be but to harm the industrial base and prosperity of the nation and must therefore be resisted at all costs. It is useful to begin, then, by asking why there was such a conviction that to ease recovery for injured workmen would prove so deleterious to the interests of manufacture.

B. INJURED INDUSTRIALISTS: ASSUMPTIONS OF RISKS AND FREE CONTRACTUAL BARGAINING

In 1881 a paper was read to the London Statistical Society by the distinguished statistician Cornelius Walford.[3] In his introduction he promised to report his conclusions in respect of the effects of the recently passed Employers' Liability Act 1880. To Walford, this was an act, 'I cannot say I think to be based upon the wisdom of Parliament'.[4] He would demonstrate statistically that industrial injuries were so common that no employer could be expected either to compensate for them out of his own pocket or to pay the premiums required to insure against them. The act, to which I shall later return, was then for Walford but a recipe for employer penury:[5]

> What a prodigious crop of litigation may be foreseen out of all this! It is surely incumbent upon all who believe in the welfare of their race to ponder seriously upon this fact, in view of concerting means for harmonizing the interests of employers and employees in this matter.

To support his doleful view of the consequences of the act, Walford deployed an array of statistics that alarmed his audience. Whether their fears were well founded is a rather different matter, however—from the first, there was such a partiality about his sources of information and his uncritical employment of them as should have called his conclusions into

---

[3] C Walford, 'On the Numbers of Deaths from Accident, Negligence, Violence and Misadventure in the United Kingdom and some other Countries, Read before the London Statistical Society, 15th February 1881' (1881) 44 *Journal of the Statistical Society of London* 444.
[4] Ibid, 514.
[5] Ibid, 512.

question. For example, he accepted from the insurance companies the unproven assertion that '1 in 10 of all persons insured meets with an accidental injury, slight or serious, up to fatal, every year'. He offered no evidence to support this, nor any information as to the number of persons those companies actually compensated during the course of a year. He was content to leave his audience with the clear and simple understanding that the liabilities of the unfortunate companies were unduly onerous.[6] In fact, both Walford's paper and the debate that followed were characterised by a mix of superficially impressive statistics blended with untested assumptions. All of those assumptions led to the conclusion that employer liabilities were already almost insupportable and any increase must at all costs be resisted.

In the audience he found a ready ally in a fellow statistician, FG Nelson. Nelson readily declared his interests: his own research was financed by employers opposed to the Employer's Liability Act. That research was even more alarming in its implications than that of Walford. He told the audience that the most dangerous industry in the land was not, as often supposed, mining, but rather the railways. Upon passenger lines 25 out of 10,000 employees were killed each year, whereas upon goods lines the figure was 35 out of 10,000. In a career of 20 years upon the railway, then, if those figures were right, it seemed that a man had a 5–7% chance of being killed. Furthermore, Nelson told his audience that he accepted a statement of Walford himself that there were some 99 injuries of a less or more serious nature for every single fatality. The conclusions to be drawn from this were never made explicit, but the audience were statisticians, so presumably they could do the maths. Based upon what was in fact a mere unproven assertion of Walford's, it was implied that perhaps 25–35% of all railway employees were injured each year.

The term 'injury' covers a wide degree of harms, of course, but it seems that a goodly proportion of those injuries were of a serious nature. Walford had already tried to discover in what proportion serious injuries occurred as opposed to fatal ones by deploying evidence from a report in the *Medical Annual* for 1839. This had suggested that for every accident victim who died in hospital there were 18 others who survived. All those admitted to hospital had to be regarded as seriously injured since '[i]njuries of the more ordinary kind, such as broken arms and legs, sprains and contusions, burns and scalds, unless in very severe shape, do not go into hospital'.[7] If a man had a 5–7% chance of being killed in 20 years as a servant of the railway, and if, as was being suggested, there were 18 times more serious injuries than fatalities, then it seemed that serious incapacity was the fate of very many railway workers. Furthermore, the

---

[6] Ibid, 514.
[7] Ibid, 512.

evidence purported to show the average injury rates amongst all railway employees, including the safer occupations of station manager, porter and so forth as well as the more dangerous occupations such as shunter. Can any of the men in the more risky occupations have survived? All this was of course based upon assertion, loose reasoning and dubious extrapolations from uncertain facts. The common sense observation that there seemed to be many who had worked on the railway for some time who had survived the experience intact escaped these statisticians.

The railways were, of course, not nearly as dangerous as was being suggested. PW Kingsford notes that in 1876 some 1,946 injuries or deaths were reported out of a workforce of some 280,000, or, as Kingsford calculates, some 1 in 167.[8] Under-reporting of minor accidents was common, but Kingsford also studied the reports of the Casualty Fund of the Railway Benevolent Institution. In 1871 the fund gave relief to some 793 of its 29,220 members, or about 1 in 37. Most of those injuries were probably minor, since the payments were made for only short periods. In 1875 the General Secretary of the Amalgamated Society of Railway Servants estimated at the TUC Congress that a railway employee had a 1 in 40 chance of being injured or killed each year. Of course, these figures are quite shocking to modern sensibilities; no one can say that, by modern standards, the Victorian railways were not extremely dangerous places to work. My point, though, is that Kingsford's sober review of the evidence suggests that injury rates were perhaps only a tenth of the rates implied by some of the evidence given to the Statistical Society. The importance of the evidence given to the Statistical Society was not that it was true—it was not—but that it seemed to be true and laid a seemingly respectable foundation for widespread assumptions about the impracticality of compensating injured labour.

Significantly, the high casualty rates in industry did not suggest to any of the assembled statisticians that employers needed to be affixed with greater liability in order to induce them to take greater care of their workmen. Instead, a reformation in the behaviour of employees was what the facts dictated. Walford attributed many accidents to negligence upon the part of employees and stated that 'no rate of premium will cover the risk of intemperance'.[9] Nelson was sceptical about the legitimacy of many claims raised against employers:[10]

> when the coal trade was bad, the rate of non-fatal accidents increased wonderfully, and men whose backs were strained in times of depression were never heard of in times of prosperity; but always when the price of labour went down, the men got their backs sprained with greater intensity.

[8] PW Kingsford, *Victorian Railwaymen: The Emergence and Growth of Railway Labour, 1830–1870* (London, Frank Cass, 1970) 47.
[9] Walford, above n 3, 515.
[10] Ibid, 523–24.

Perhaps the most significant observation, however, was made by another statistician, LL Cohen, who asserted that what he had heard had but proved that intervention in industry by the legislature was 'superfluous' and that:[11]

> it was only necessary that the teachings of economical science should be brought sufficiently home to masters and men, to lead them to understand that legislative interference was not in any way necessary, and they would understand how they could themselves cover all the risks which might be cast upon them. If a man chose to take employment which was dangerous, that was a question in which it was not for anyone to control him; but if he took that employment he ought to know as nearly as science could teach him the extent of his risks, and he should be taught that it was part of his business that he should protect himself from those risks, and exact from his master a sufficient wage to provide against them.

Quite who was to find and teach the new labouring economic scientist was not clear. However, the judges had already assumed such a calculating creature to be in existence, as evidenced by their frequent assertions that workmen injured in hazardous employ had voluntarily assumed the risks. Such assertions were, of course, based upon the free bargaining contract theory as envisaged above, upon the influence of Adam Smith (and others), and upon what Michael Stein has called 'the dominant influence of political economy as an intellectual schema'.[12] George Wilshere, Baron Bramwell, put it thus:[13] 'Everyone knows that the total aggregate happiness of mankind is increased by every man being left to the unbiased, unfettered determination of his own [free] will and judgment as to how he will employ his industry.'

Left to their own devices, men would assess risk and freely contract, pricing in risk in such a way as to produce an economically efficient market for the manufacture, sale and distribution of goods. A wholesome society would emerge in which the members of Mandeville's grumbling hive would, by pursuing their own interests, nevertheless produce the greatest good for the greatest number.

The modern eye notes that such a theory of free contracting and risk was predicated upon the assumption that knowledge as to risk was evenly distributed and also that it ignored the asymmetrical distribution of power between employers and unorganised labour. Nineteenth-century judges, however, preferred to focus upon the danger to the free contract model posed by those who failed to honour their contracts as to risk. The employee who had bargained and accepted risk, pricing his service accordingly, and who then sought to place liability upon his employer when the

11 Ibid, 522.
12 MA Stein, 'Victorian Tort Liability for Workplace Injuries' [2008] *Illinois Law Review* 933, 936.
13 *R v Bailey* (1867) 16 LT 859.

risk materialised was in effect seeking to retrospectively and unilaterally repudiate the bargain. He was seeking the aid of the law in forcing the employer to accept a liability for risk that the employer thought he had bargained away. Hence the complaint of Willes B in *Saxton v Hawksworth*,[14] that a great number of cases had come before the courts 'where a servant chooses to enter into employment of which the system is well known . . . [but after the accident] suddenly finds out that the master was exceedingly wrong'. Courts were, in broad terms, unwilling to disturb a bargain based upon free contracting. However, these were not written contemporaneous agreements but contracts construed by the court ex post facto. The courts necessarily had to consider the knowledge of the parties at the time of their agreement and thereby what risks a plaintiff might be construed as having consented to.

In *Priestley v Fowler*,[15] Abinger CB had argued that the plaintiff servant did not fall to be treated as a mere passenger conveyed in a wagon, since he had been able to inspect the obviously overloaded vehicle. Knowledge of risk, and the imputed consent that flowed from such knowledge, were not only assessed at the moment of entering service: the continued performance of service when new hazards arose were interpreted as a further consent to run that further risk. The servant was 'not bound to risk his safety in the service of his master . . . [but could] decline any service in which he reasonably apprehend[ed] injury to himself'.[16] In *Hutchinson v York, Newcastle and Berwick Railway Co*,[17] however, this principle had been extended after counsel for the plaintiff had sought to use Abinger's own reasoning in *Priestley*. In *Hutchinson* the deceased had been travelling in a railway carriage and had been killed by a collision with another of the defendant's carriages. In *Priestley* it had been said that the deceased could have avoided the risk 'by common prudence and caution', but in *Hutchinson* the deceased had had no knowledge of the negligence of other parties and therefore of the particular risk that he was running. The prosecution had therefore asserted that he could not be said to have assumed that risk. However, Alderson B had concurred with the argument for the defence that workers assumed all the normal risks of their occupation as part of their implied terms of employment, and that normal risks were to be construed broadly. Hence Pollock's claim in *Dynen v Leach* that in the workplace 'a master is not bound to use the safest method'[18] to protect his employees, and Chief Baron Kelly's assertion in *Saxton* that a steelworker had consented to the risk of being injured by a machine, not under his care, that had disintegrated in another part of the works: 'Can we believe a

---

[14] (1872) 26 LT 851, 853.
[15] (1837) 3 M & W 1, 150 ER 1030.
[16] Ibid, 3 M & W 6.
[17] (1850) 5 Exch 343, 155 ER 150.
[18] (1857) 26 LJ Ex 221, 222.

Sheffield man to be ignorant of the risks that he ran in steel manufacture?'
he asked.[19]

Faced with such unsympathetic declarations, it becomes easy to accept
that, as Witt puts it, '[n]ineteenth century work accident law cynically
deployed notions of the value of worker responsibility and self-reliance in
such a way as to obscure employer power and enforce employee discipline
in the workplace'.[20] This may be true in part, but many judges
undoubtedly believed that they were acting according to principle, and
there were many proofs available to them of the efficacy of contemporary
labour arrangements. Was not the Great Exhibition delivered by the
labours of a myriad of contractors, on time and on budget? Smith reminds
us that '[t]he astonishing thing about looking back even over so short a
time-span as a hundred years is the realisation of how little collectivist
theory had then permeated thinking in the Western world'.[21] Solutions to
what would now be considered social or economic problems were instinc-
tively sought in the correct ordering of individual relationships. Witt
reminds us that many aspects of large-scale production were governed by
customary practice, and workers in many industries were self-directing.[22]
Workers policed themselves and each other.

> Want of vigilance on the part of a man on duty may lead to accidents, but other
> men are watchful and check the other. For instance if a man at a station neglects
> his signal, the guard and the driver watch it and they report the case . . . and the
> guilty party is punished'[23]

The notion of independent workers collaborating and consenting to risk
was convenient for employers, but it was not a wholly fanciful one. The
courts similarly were 'engaged in something other than wilful hypocrisy'
for 'Nineteenth Century work accident cases articulated a remarkably
narrow conception of the possibilities for pervasive and far reaching
managerial control of the workplace'.[24]

Perhaps one should not make too much of this. Great industrial
magnates had long demonstrated, in places such as Etruria, the possibility
of closely supervised systems of labour. But this was not the general
experience and not what the judges saw when observing labour around
them. Haskell has argued, to my mind convincingly, that sympathy, sensibility and humanitarian impulses in respect of many social ills did not

---

19 *Saxton*, above n 14, 853.

20 J Witt, 'The Transformation of Work and the Law of Workplace Accidents, 1842–1910'
(1998) 107 *Yale Law Journal* 1467, 1468.

21 H Smith, 'Judges and the Lagging Law of Compensation for Personal Injuries in the
Nineteenth Century' (1981) *Journal of Legal History* 258, 258.

22 Witt, above n 20, 1470–75.

23 *Report of the Select Committee on Accidents on Railways* HC (1857–58) 362 XIV.
Evidence of J Beattie.

24 Witt, above n 20, 1477.

emerge until after the development of social and managerial techniques had demonstrated the possibility, and thence the duty, of acting.[25] I think, then, that we must accept that the doctrines of *volenti*, common employment and contributory negligence were rather more than simple contrivances cynically devised to prevent recovery. They reflected ways of ordering the working relationship and conceptualising a society in which the full possibilities of managerial practice and risk elimination had not yet been revealed.

Having envisaged a world of free contractual bargaining, though, the creators were sometimes liable to find themselves being constrained by the logic of their own creation. LL Cohen in 1882 was seemingly unsympathetic to the position of labour but nevertheless asserted that the worker should have full knowledge of risks and be able to bargain upon that basis. Judges, for their part, had to consider how to act where the knowledge of a contracting plaintiff as to risk had been seriously flawed or, worse, where he had been actively deceived. This raised the difficult question of how accurately a man should have been able to have foreseen the causal sequence of events that led to him being harmed before it could be said that he had agreed to run the risk. Did a man who worked on a high-rise building consent to the risk of falling into the unmarked pit that his employer had dug nearby? In *Priestley*, of course, the causal sequence was rather short and simple, and the plaintiff knew precisely the hazard to which his continuing service exposed him. By contrast, Alderson B in *Hutchinson* seemed to suggest that an employee consented to exposing himself to any hazard, however unlikely and difficult to foresee. Some judges, however, were prepared to allow recovery where risks had been actively concealed. Thus, in *Paterson v Wallace & Co*, Lord Cranworth held that an employer was 'bound to take all reasonable precautions for the safety of his workers' and owed a duty not to induce an employee into thinking that working conditions were safe if he knew or ought to have known otherwise.[26]

In general, in the 1850s it remained the case that the more open and obvious the danger (and so to modern thinking the higher was the duty to ameliorate the risk), the more likely the defence of *volenti* was to succeed. Yet by the end of the decade some of the judges were preparing to contemplate an exception in the case of dangerous machinery. Bramwell was not amongst them. If the hazards posed by the machinery were known or obvious, then continued performance of service signalled a voluntary assumption of risk. Thus, in *Dynen v Leach* the plaintiff could not recover because 'the workman has known all the facts and is as well acquainted as

---

[25] See generally TL Haskell, 'Capitalism and the Origins of the Humanitarian Sensibility' (1985) 90 *American Historical Review* 389, 547.
[26] (1854) 1 Macq 748, 751.

the master with the nature of the machinery and voluntarily use[d] it'.[27] Similarly, in *Williams v Clough* it was held that a master 'cannot be held liable for an accident to his servant whilst using machinery in his employment, simply because the master knows that such machinery is unsafe, if the servant has the same knowledge as the master'.[28] However, three years later, in *Mellors v Shaw*, Crompton J asserted that a master would be liable if he knew that machinery to be used by an employee was improper or unsafe, 'notwithstanding that knowledge sanctions its use'.[29] In *Clarke v Holmes* it was said that

> The knowledge of the plaintiff that the machinery was unfenced . . . is only a fact in the case to be taken into consideration by the jury, with all the other circumstances, in determining the question whether the plaintiff has himself helped to bring about the accident in respect of which he seeks to charge the defendant.[30]

Clarke v Holmes, though, fitted neatly into bargaining theory, for the defendant had promised to shield the harmful machinery and had then not done so: he had reneged on his part of the bargain.

The creation of the dangerous machinery exception seems to have signified some thawing of judicial attitudes in respect of recovery, for which a number of explanations can be posited. In part, the courts may have been reacting to a more sympathetic or socially realistic view of the power of individualised labour to contract. They may also have been recognising that there were now new interests in society that demanded to be accommodated. Trade unions were increasingly tolerated in the period between the Friendly Societies Act 1855 and the Trade Union Act 1871, and they soon began to exert real pressure upon the body politic. Social reformers and policy makers were probably also exerting some influence. As Chadwick had pointed out, the injured but unrecompensed employee merely became a charge upon the Poor Law. The ratepayer, in effect, was subsidising the employer. Finally, it may simply have been that the old homilies about the master and servant relationship were becoming increasing untenable in a society that was becoming ever more familiar with the large industrial enterprise. As enterprises increased in their complexity, and as the worker became but an anonymous cog in a larger machine, the notion that the worker, 'knows, or ought to know to what risks he is exposing himself'[31] became more difficult to sustain. As Witt puts it, such a notion had 'diverged sharply from the sociological conditions of the workplace'.[32]

27 *Dynen*, above n 18, 223.
28 (1858) 3 H & N 258, 260; 157 ER 468, 469.
29 (1861) 1 B & S 437, 444; 121 ER 778, 781.
30 (1862) 7 H & N 937, 945; 158 ER 751, 754.
31 *Bartonshill Coal Co. v Reid* (1858) 3 Macq 266, 282–83.
32 Witt, above n 20, 1482.

However, the sociological conditions of the workplace did not unduly disturb Bramwell's view of free contractual relations. 'How can a contract be forced on a man?' he asked in 1884. Interfering with contracts 'treats people as helpless, and, instead of teaching them to struggle for themselves, adds to their feebleness by a mischievous taking care of them'.[33] Frederick Pollock was still claiming in 1887 that a servant 'contracted with the risk before his eyes, and that the dangers of service, taken all around, were considered in the fixing of payment'.[34] In truth, all or almost all of the judges were committed to the free contract model through the second half of the nineteenth century. In none had theories of paternalism yet advanced so far as to say that there were some risks that men were not competent to contract to assume. Contractual reasoning did not, however, necessarily lead the judges to the same conclusions as each other when considering the application of the doctrine of *volenti*. There were those, supported by a raft of cases from *Hutchinson* onwards, who adopted the broad-brush approach. They were prepared to impute to the servant knowledge of types of risk that, in truth, he could have barely contemplated. In addition, such judges were inclined to extend the remit of the doctrine of *volenti non fit injuria* to cover situations of labour in which the parties had neither a formal contractual agreement nor a traditionally implied contract as between master and servant. Other judges, however, took a rather narrower view, one in which the doctrine of *volenti* was to be confined to true assumption of risk, determined by factual analysis. They were more inclined to ask whether the employee could reasonably be supposed to have contemplated the species of risk within which the harm that had arisen lay. Such judges were more likely to seek to confine the doctrine either to traditionally implied master and servant contracts or to situations outside contract where there had been express agreement to run a particular risk. Some, as in *Clarke*, were even prepared to ask a more socially sophisticated question. They were prepared to ask whether, in the circumstances of the labouring poor, knowledge of risk could be equated with willingness to run it. These two contrasting judicial views as to the appropriate ambit of the *volenti* defence were on display in the case of *Woodley v Metropolitan District Railway Co.*

C. WOODLEY AND THE WILLING WORKMAN

In brief, the facts of the *Woodley* case were as follows. The plaintiff had been the employee of a contractor and he had been engaged to repair the brickwork in an unlit tunnel on a railway line. Trains had been scheduled

[33] C Fairfield, *Some Account of George William Wilshere, Baron Bramwell of Hever and his Opinions* (London, Macmillan, 1898) 146.
[34] F Pollock, *The Law of Torts* (London, Steven and Sons, 1887) 85.

to travel through the tunnel every 6–10 minutes but, because of the noise of the work, the plaintiff had been unable to hear them. In addition, because the tunnel was situated upon a curve in the line, the plaintiff had also been unable to see the trains until they were within some 20–30 yards. No one had instructed the drivers to slow down whilst passing through the tunnel. The onus, then, had been wholly upon Woodley to notice the arrival of the service and then to shrink against the tunnel wall, there being just enough space to allow a train to pass without harming him. The plaintiff had been severely injured when he had reached over the line to pick up a tool and, as Cockburn CJ put it, '[i]t is unnecessary to say that the service upon which the plaintiff was employed was one of extreme danger'.[35] It was of some significance that when similar work had been carried out upon the tunnel previously a watchman had been employed to warn of the approaching locomotives but upon this occasion that precaution had not been taken.

At first instance a jury found for the plaintiff, who was awarded 300l. Metropolitan appealed to the Court of Exchequer, which unanimously affirmed the verdict, although not without some reservations expressed by Cleasby B. The lead judgment was given by Kelly CB, who was at pains to point out that his judgment was limited to the very specific facts of the case before him:[36]

> I do not propose to lay down any rule upon the subject; certainly not to hold that in all cases where work is done in a dark tunnel and by a stranger, not a servant of the company, or by some one who has no connection with the company, it is the duty of the company to employ a lookout man to see when trains are approaching.

However, Kelly CB noted that the company had previously employed such a man and this was a case in which the workman

> had no means of either seeing or hearing in time to enable him to get out of the way . . . Under these circumstances and dealing with the facts of this particular case, I am of the opinion that the jury were fully justified.

Cleasby B did not dissent but made apparent his unease. It was clear that the plaintiff had had to rely very much upon himself for his own safety and that he had placed himself in that position voluntarily. 'One might apply the maxim *volenti non fit injuria*: he takes the risk upon himself, and there is no wrong if the consequence arises which is likely to arise upon his taking it.' But, he relented, his fellow judges, 'see sufficient evidence to shew that by the conduct of the defendants, and I may say the improper conduct, the plaintiff was exposed to greater dangers than those which he took upon himself in the way I have mentioned'.[37] Amphlett B

---

35 *Woodley*, above n 1, 387.
36 Ibid, 386.
37 Ibid, 386.

did no more than concur with Kelly CB, 'limiting it, as he has done in his judgment, to the particular facts of the case and laying down no general rule'. This, then, was a cautious judgment, limited in its applicability, and one, furthermore, that did not investigate the nature of the relationship between a company and the employees of a contractor upon the company's premises. Naturally, the company appealed.

In the Court of Appeal, Cockburn CJ commenced his judgment by declaring that:[38]

> morally speaking, great culpability attached to the defendants in omitting to take measures for the protection of the plaintiff. Where there was any evidence of negligence, a finding of negligence was, following on from the decision of the House of Lords in *Bridges v North London Railway Co*, a matter for the jury. For his own part he thought that their verdict had been perfectly right. However, if the plaintiff, in doing the work on the railway, is to be looked upon as the servant of the company, the decision of the Court of Exchequer in his favour cannot, as it seems to me, be upheld.

No deception, he pointed out, had been practised upon the plaintiff as to the nature and danger of the work, and he had been engaged upon that work for a fortnight before the injury occurred.

> If he had been misled in supposing that precautionary measures such as the dangerous nature of the service rendered reasonably necessary would be taken, he had a right to throw up his engagement and decline to go on with the work.[39]

If, he hypothesized, a man was deceived as to the nature of a risk, or was promised that precautions would be taken to minimise the risk but was injured before the extent of the risk or the absence of precautions were known, then he might hold his employer liable. However, once he became aware of risks which he had not contemplated upon taking up employment, 'His proper course is to quit the employment. If he continues in it, he is in the same position as though he had accepted it with full knowledge of its danger in the first place.' Finally, he anticipated that it might be said that that defendant was not in the service of the railway at all, but a lawful visitor injured by negligence of the company. However:[40]

> that which would be negligence in a company . . . so as to give a right to compensation for an injury resulting therefrom to a stranger lawfully resorting to their premises in ignorance of the danger, will give no such right to one, who being aware of the danger, voluntarily encounters it. The same observation arises as before: with full knowledge of the manner in which the traffic was carried on, and of the danger attendant on it, the plaintiff thought it proper to remain in the employment.

---

[38] Ibid, 388.
[39] Ibid, 388.
[40] Ibid, 390.

The plaintiff, then, was to be regarded as a servant, *volenti* in respect of the risks undertaken in service, or else he was to be considered a lawful visitor who was unable to recover because he was aware of the hazards of the premises.

Was Cockburn correct in asserting that Woodley was a servant of the railway company? It could not be said that he had freely contracted for his labour with the knowledge of the risks before him. The price of his labour had been set in negotiations between his employer and the railway. Treating him as a servant, though, obviated the necessity of considering whether indeed the doctrine of *volenti* was founded in and confined to the context of contractual relations or whether it was of broader application. One wonders, of course, what would have happened if Woodley had committed some tortious act whilst upon the railway and a plaintiff had attempted to sue the railway upon the basis of *respondeat superior*. According to Pollock:[41]

> The relationship of master and servant exists only between persons of whom one has the order and control of the work done by the other . . . A master is one who not only prescribes to the workman the end of his work, but directs or at any moment may direct the means also . . . An independent contractor is one who undertakes to produce a given result, but so that in the actual execution of the work he is not under the order or control of the person for whom he does it.

Cleasby B had pointed out in the lower court that the fact that Woodley was left entirely on his own to carry out the work, without supervision or assistance from the railway, suggested that he had willing assumed the risk. Others might have argued that those same facts proved that Woodley was not a servant of the railway and that, in their view, in the absence of a master servant relationship, the maxim *volenti non fit injuria* could not be applicable.

Two of his fellow Court of Appeal judges, Mellor J and Grove J, concurred with Cockburn's finding that the decision of the Court of Exchequer could not be upheld. Grove J did not offer a separate judgment and Mellor J, whilst arriving at the same conclusion as Cockburn, did so by means of a rather different analysis, one that some might think opportunistic and inconsistent. Cockburn had proceeded upon a straightforward contractual approach, assuming that the company had been negligent but holding that the plaintiff had bargained away his right of recovery. Mellor first asserted, without qualification, that the company and the plaintiff had not been in any form of contractual relationship. The conclusion that he drew from this, however, was that, in the absence of such a relationship, no duty had arisen as between the company and the plaintiff. In drawing this conclusion, he dissented from Cleasby's assertion in the Court of Exchequer that the company had owed an obligation to station a man to

41 F Pollock, 'Liability for Torts of Agents and Servants?' (1885) 1 *LQR* 207, 210.

warn of the approach of trains. He could 'see no implied obligation on the part of the company, at their expense, to employ such a person . . . No such person was in any sense necessary for the proper and ordinary working of the defendant's trains.'[42] He surely had in mind *Skipp v Eastern Counties Railways Co*, where Parke J had refused to hold that the jury owed the 'duty of fixing the number of servants which a railway company ought to have . . . The company themselves are the proper judges of the number that they require for carrying on the business of the line.'[43] The company, Mellor observed, had carried on its ordinary business in its ordinary way and no duty could be imputed to it in respect of a plaintiff towards whom it had assumed no responsibilities.

However, after negating the existence of a duty, Mellor immediately made reference to the master servant relationship and the doctrine of common employment:[44]

> It is now completely settled that a master is not liable to one servant for the consequences resulting from the negligence of a fellow servant in the course of the same employment, on the ground that the servant undertakes, as between himself and his master, the natural risks and perils incident to the performance of his duty.

The fellow servant referred to can have been only the contractor, both the contractor and the plaintiff being treated as fellow servants of the same master, the railway company. But if this were the case, then this surely gave rise to a duty upon the part of the master, the presence of which Mellor had previously denied. This is not to say that the plaintiff would necessarily be entitled to recover, merely to say that it was illogical to have invoked the doctrine of common employment as a defence to an action by a plaintiff who had previously been determined not to have been in an employment relationship.

Mellor then moved on to *volenti*: 'He ought either to have stipulated with his master, or the company, to provide some additional means or precautions . . . He ought to have refused the task unless they were provided.'[45] To hammer home the point, he speculated as to the outcome of an action by the plaintiff against his immediate employer. He began with the disclaimer that 'whether the master has done anything which may make him liable as between himself and the plaintiff we are not concerned to decide'. Of course, he then proceeded to offer his opinion, invoking *Priestley v Fowler* before concluding that the master would not be liable. Since the plaintiff

---

[42] *Woodley*, above n 1, 396.
[43] (1853) 9 Ex 223, 226; 156 ER 95, 96.
[44] *Woodley*, above n 1, 396.
[45] Ibid, 397.

must be presumed to know the ordinary traffic of the company and the limited space within which he had to work, [he] came within the maxim of *volenti non fit injuria*, and has at all events no remedy against the company.[46]

Mellor then found no duty as between the plaintiff and the defendant. He further suggested that, if indeed there had been a duty, both the contractor and the plaintiff might fall to be treated as fellow servants, so that the plaintiff's action was potentially barred by the negligence of the contractor. With respect to *volenti*, he supposed that the plaintiff had certainly assumed the risks incident to working on the railway and was most likely barred by this assumption of risk from recovery against his immediate master.

Mellish LJ in his dissenting judgment exposed the inconsistencies of the position adopted by both Cockburn and Mellor. Cockburn had inferred the existence of a contract between master and servant to allocate risk when in fact none had been in place. Mellor had by turns doubted the existence of such a contract and utilised its absence to argue that there was no duty between the parties, and he had then discovered a species of contractual relationship between the parties in order to assert that the plaintiff had bargained away his right to recover. Mellish for his part denied the existence of the contract and discovered the existence of a general duty:[47]

> No one has the right to carry on his trade in such a manner as is likely to cause personal injury to others. This liability is not founded on contract. It may be modified or taken way by contract, but it is founded on the right which is inherent in everyone not to be subject to personal injury from the wrongful or careless act of another. In the case of a servant who enters into the service of a master who carries on a dangerous trade, the right of the servant to be protected in his person is largely modified by the contract between master and servant . . . but the servant of the contractor enters into no such contract with the railway company because he enters into no contract with the railway company at all . . . I am unable to discover any principle by which railway companies are freed from the liability of taking reasonable care that the servants of contractors are not injured by passing trains.

However, could the plaintiff be said to have given a bare license to the defendants to run their trains in the manner that they had? Mellish concluded that this was not a necessary inference of law. First, he referred to the question of knowledge, holding that 'It is by no means certain that the plaintiff, an ordinary bricklayer's labourer, understood at all what the extent of the risk was which he was running'.[48] Secondly, he acknowledged the realities of social bargaining:

---

46 Ibid, 398.
47 Ibid, 391.
48 Ibid, 393.

It seems to me it would be extremely unjust to hold that he was obliged either at once to quit his master's employment or else to lose his right of action against the railway company for negligently running him over.[49]

However, Mellish quickly returned to contractual analysis. Suppose, he argued, that a man was contracted to sweep the streets and each day a cab sped by, negligently driven. If the cab eventually ran the sweeper over, it would, Mellish declared, be no defence for the cabman to assert, 'You knew my style of driving. You had seen me drive for a fortnight; I was only driving in my usual style.' In Mellish's view, the street sweeper's case 'does not differ from the case we have to determine, there being no contract between the defendants and the plaintiff any more than between the cabman and the scraper of the streets'.[50] Mellish's view, then, was both narrower and broader than that espoused by either Cockburn or Mellor: narrower because he was not prepared to invent contractual relations in order to assert that the right to recovery had been bargained away, but broader insofar as he looked to the reality of knowledge of risk and even went so far as to note that assent to risk did not necessarily equate with a willingness to run that risk:[51]

> I think he is entitled to say, 'I know I was running a great risk, and did not like it at all, but I could not afford to give up my good place from which I get my livelihood, and I supposed that if I was injured by their carelessness I should have an action against the company'.

Baggallay LJ agreed with Mellish that 'the plaintiff cannot be regarded as the servant of the company'.[52] The majority of his judgment was therefore directed towards the issue of the status of the plaintiff whilst on the railway company's premises. Cockburn had declared that as a lawful visitor the plaintiff could not recover because he had voluntarily encountered the danger inherent in performing the contracted work. He and the contractor 'were in a very different position from that in which they would have stood had they been at work in ignorance of the danger'. Baggallay, however, was clear that the case could not be distinguished from the unanimous decision of the Court of Common Pleas in *Indermaur v Dames*.[53] In *Indermaur* the plaintiff had been a gas fitter sent by his employer to carry out a contract upon the defendant's premises, a sugar mill. The mill had been pierced by a number of unfenced holes, into one of which the workman had fallen. The defence in *Indermaur* had argued that the workman had been a mere licensee, and that the only obligation upon the defendant had been to keep his premises in the condition usual in his

[49] Ibid, 393.
[50] Ibid, 394.
[51] Ibid, 393.
[52] *Woodley*, above n 1, 394.
[53] (1866) LR 2 CP 311.

business. Kelly CB, however, had demurred since the plaintiff had been in the mill on lawful business, fulfilling a contract in which both plaintiff and defendant had had an interest. He had then not been in the mill upon a bare permission and in respect of such a person:[54]

> We consider it settled law that he, using reasonable care on his part for his own safety, is entitled to expect that the occupier shall on his part use reasonable care to prevent damage from unusual danger which he knows or ought to know; and that when there is evidence of neglect, the question of whether such reasonable care has been taken by notice, lighting, guarding or otherwise, and whether there was such contributory negligence in the sufferer must be determined by a jury as a matter of fact.

Where Mellish had found a general duty, Baggallay found a more specific one in the obligations owed by an occupier to a lawful visitor as expounded in *Indermaur*. It was significant that neither in *Indermaur* nor in *Woodley* had the plaintiff been injured by harm arising within his area of competence, that is to say, by gas fitting or by damage sustained from falling brickwork in the tunnel; rather, both had been injured by hazards arising within the course of the defendants' normal operations, hazards of which the defendants had had notice.

The plaintiff in *Woodley* did not, of course, recover, but the case is interesting because it serves to demonstrate the dichotomy between those judges who were prepared to countenance the construction of fictitious contractual relations, and draw the broadest conclusions as to supposed assumptions of risk, and those judges who insisted upon the reality of the contractual bargain. It is significant that it was those judges who were prepared to examine the historicity of the supposed contractual exchange who were the first to question the very notion of free bargaining itself. *Clarke v Holmes* and then *Woodley* were important steps on the way towards the conclusion that *sciens* did not in law mean *volens*. In the meantime, however, those taking a broad-brush approach to the assumption of risk continued to avow, with Bramwell, that a contract could not be imposed upon any man, and for a moment they held the upper hand.

D. *WOODLEY* TO *SMITH V BAKER*: POLITICS, PROGRESS AND POSTURING

Whichever side they took, in what was becoming an increasingly partisan debate, the judges could hardly have been unaware that outside the courtroom a body of respectable opinion was slowly coalescing in favour of somewhat easing the path to recovery. The debate focused initially upon

---

[54] Ibid, 313.

common employment. In 1876 a report from a select committee declared itself in favour of retaining the doctrine.[55] However, in February of that year, supported by the TUC, Alexander Macdonald MP introduced the Employer's Liability for Injury Bill under which the defence would be abolished.[56] The bill did not gain its second reading until April 1878,[57] and was therefore still under consideration at the time of the *Woodley* decision. Although it was not subsequently enacted, Macdonald's speech on the occasion of the second reading of the bill illustrated the changing temper of the times. He mocked the suggestion that in an enterprise each employee was able to supervise the activities of the others and so guard more surely against harm than would be the case if the negligence of one servant was indemnified by the right of action against the common employer:[58]

> He would ask how one of a number of men wheeling barrows along a plank could guard against the man behind him, whom he could not see, pushing him from the plank . . . How a labourer working for a slater could guard against the slater letting a slate fall upon him?

More broadly, he also asked how it could be said that the risks of an occupation were compensated by higher wages when it was a fact that some of the lowest wages were paid in mining and the railways:[59] 'All agreed that the most dangerous employment was that of shunter, and yet he had the longest hours and was the worst paid. Yet they were told, forsooth, that the wages covered the risk.'

Responding, opponents fell back on domestic homilies and a professed concern for the labouring man. If the rules of recovery were eased, then masters would be induced to pay lower wages, since they had hitherto compensated workmen for the risks of their trades. The doctrine of common employment, they argued, simply protected the working man from common unemployment. If a man with two maidservants was made potentially liable for the negligence of one in leaving a coalscuttle on the stairs over which the other might trip, why, then, logic would cause him to reduce his potential liability by dismissing one of those servants before such an accident occurred. What then would happen to all the unemployed maidservants?[60] However, given that rather more generous compensation regimes were in place in France, Germany and many of the American states, defending the argument that employers could not afford the imposition of further liability was becoming both logically and politically

---

[55] Report from the Select Committee on Employers Liability for Injuries to their Servants, HC (1876) 372, 688.
[56] Hansard, 227 HC Debs col 118 (9 February 1876).
[57] Hansard, 239 HC Debs cols 1043–71 (10 April 1878).
[58] Ibid, col 1045.
[59] Ibid, col 1046.
[60] Ibid, cols 1057–59.

difficult to sustain. Hence, perhaps, Sir Henry Jackson's defensive comment that it was:[61]

> entirely wrong to say that the law was made against the working classes. This statement was untrue historically, and untrue in fact. The well paid Chairman or Manager of a Railway Company was just as much within the law as a plate-layer.

This remark cannot but put one in mind of Anatole France's famous observation about the rich, the poor and the law in respect of sleeping under bridges.

Jackson's primary concern was the management of employer liability:[62] 'If a proper limit could be put to the general liability of a master for acts for which he was not morally responsible . . . then strangers and workmen might reasonably be put on the same footing.' He promised to support a government bill to such an end, but in the event it was left to the incoming liberal administration and Joseph Chamberlain to introduce government legislation in 1880. In brief, the Employer's Liability Act 1880 curtailed the ambit of the common employment defence by making an employer liable for harm that arose out of the negligence of a workman who had been placed in a position of superintendence over others. However, it also made him liable for accidents arising out of defects in 'the conditions of the ways, works, machinery and plant'. Noticeably excluded from the protection of the act were domestic servants, seamen, all those not engaged in manual labour and, of course, employees of the Crown.

Although it was reasonably clear that the act had limited the application of the defence of common employment, it remained unclear as to where the act had left the maxim of *volenti non fit injuria*. Could a negligent employer still argue that a plaintiff who had had knowledge of defects in his master's premises had assumed the risk of the harms that might in consequence arise? This was the issue in *Thomas v Quartermaine*.[63] The case concerned a brewery worker charged with attending to two hot and unfenced vats either side of a narrow walkway. In pulling out a lid from under one of the vats he had fallen backwards into the other and had been severely scalded. The Surrey County Court had concluded that, although the hazards posed by the vats had been known to both plaintiff and defendant, it could not be said that the plaintiff had been guilty of contributory negligence. The County Court awarded him 75l but the Divisional Court then set aside that award. In the Court of Appeal, Bowen LJ asked whether the 1880 Act:[64]

---

[61] Ibid, col 1058.
[62] Ibid, col 1063.
[63] (1887) 18 QBD 685.
[64] Ibid, 691.

has only placed an injured workman (as regards his remedies) in the same position (with specified exceptions) as he would have occupied if he had not been in
the master's employ? Or has the act gone further, and imposed on masters' new
duties and liabilities towards their servants, which the masters would not be
under towards the general public or servants of anyone else?

His conclusion was that the former was clearly the case since section 1
of the Act had specified that 'The workman shall have the same right of
compensation and remedies against the employer as if the workman had
not been a workman of, nor in the service of, the employer'. The
workman, then, was possessed of the same rights as a lawful visitor, no
more and no less. Bowen then relied upon Cockburn CJ's determination in
Woodley that no right of compensation was available to a lawful visitor
who 'being aware of the danger voluntarily encounters it, and fails to take
the extra care necessary for avoiding it'. In so doing, he anticipated two
objections: first, that the jury had found no contributory negligence upon
the part of the plaintiff, and secondly, that if the effect of the act was to
dissolve the contract of employment between master and servant, then, as
the minority had held in *Woodley*, the doctrine of *volenti* should not apply.
His response was that:[65]

> the doctrine of *volenti non fit injuria* stands outside of the doctrine of contribu-
> tory negligence and is in no way limited by it . . . Neither of these is a defence
> that arises merely by implication out of the workman's contract of service. For
> many months, the plaintiff, a man of full intelligence, had seen this vat—known
> all about it—appreciated its danger—elected to continue working near it. It
> seems to me that the legal language has no meaning unless it were held that
> knowledge such as this amounts to a voluntary encountering of the risk.

Bowen, it is true, noted that 'the maxim be it observed is not *scienti non
fit injuria* but *volenti*'.[66] In his mind, however, the term *volenti* seems to
have had nothing to do with the reality of the master and servant relation,
or with a genuine consent to take risk, but rather seems to have concerned
the capacity to appreciate risk:[67]

> It is plain that mere knowledge may not be conclusive defence. There may be a
> perception of the existence of the danger without comprehension of the risk; as
> where the workman is of imperfect intelligence, or, though he knows the danger,
> remains imperfectly informed as to its nature and extent.

Fry LJ concurred with Bowen and added little. He too depended upon
Woodley, reiterating that the plaintiff was to be treated as the lawful
visitor: 'Can such a person maintain an action in respect of an injury

[65] Ibid, 697–99.
[66] Ibid, 696.
[67] Ibid, 696.

arising from a defect, of which defect and of the resulting damage he was as well informed as the defendant? I think not.'[68] Thomas did not recover.

Esher MR, however, dissented, and he based his dissent upon the minority opinion in *Woodley* which had tied the presumption that the plaintiff had assumed the risks incidental to his calling to the existence of a contractual relationship between the parties. The 1880 Act, he asserted, dissolved the contractual relationship between the servant and the master:[69]

> It has been suggested that this act has only the effect of doing away with the doctrine of the immunity of the master from damage arising from the negligence of another servant in the common employment of the master. To my mind it is clear that the statute has taken away from the master another defence. It was, no doubt held that a servant could not sue a master for injuries arising from the negligence of a fellow-servant, but it was also held that a man who went into any employment undertook to take all the ordinary risks incident thereto, unless they were concealed or were known to the master and not to the servant. It seems to me clear that this Act has taken away that defence from the master. I can see no difference between contracting to take a risk upon oneself and under-taking an employment to which risk attaches. No one ever suggested that there could be such a contract in the case of any person other than a servant, so that when a servant is put on a footing with other persons that defence of the master is gone.

The presumption of assumption of risk had therefore been ousted. Esher was not quite saying that the workman was incapable of assuming risk but was rather implying that this must be specially evidenced. The question to which he devoted the second half of his judgment was whether, in assenting to work under such circumstances, the plaintiff could be said not to have been *volenti* in respect of the risk, but to have acted with contributory negligence? *Clarke v Holmes*, he concluded, had been correctly decided, the issue of contributory negligence was one for the jury, and the fact that the servant had had knowledge was 'not conclusive against him'.[70]

Six months later, Esher returned to the issue of knowledge, this time carrying the majority in *Yarmouth v France*.[71] He did not doubt that the defence of *volenti* might exist, but the example he gave of a situation in which it might apply was as follows:[72]

> if a thing is put before a workman and he is told, 'Now I do not ask you to do this unless you like; but I will give you more wages if you do. You see what it is. There is a rotten ladder; it is ten to one that it will break under you: but if you

---

[68] Ibid, 700–01.
[69] Ibid, 688.
[70] Ibid, 690.
[71] (1887) 19 QBD 647.
[72] Ibid, 653.

choose to run that risk I will give you extra wages.' If the workman, seeing the risk elects to incur it, no one could doubt that he would be precluded from recovering damages from his employer.

It is immediately apparent how different was Esher's conception of the defence from that advanced by the majority in *Woodley*, or indeed in *Thomas*. In his v™iew, mere knowledge of the danger creating a risk of harm, coupled with a decision to run that risk, was not enough to bar recovery. He based this conclusion upon section 2(3) of the 1880 Act. This denied recovery

> in any case where the workman knew of the defect or negligence which caused his injury, and failed within a reasonable time to give or cause to be given infor-mation thereof to the employer, or some person superior to himself in the service of the employer, unless he was aware that the employer already knew of the said defect or negligence.

A workman noticing a danger that was unknown to his employer and failing to inform his employer could not complain if that danger resulted in harm to himself. Esher reasoned that the section therefore envisaged that in the contrary case the workman would be able to recover—that is, where the workman had complained of the danger or where his employer had had knowledge of it.

> Mere knowledge of the danger will not do: there must be an assent on the part of the workman to run the risk, with a full appreciation of its extent, to bring the workman within the maxim *of volenti non fit injuria.*[73]

Hawkins J relied upon *Yarmouth* the following year in *Thrusell v Handyside*[74] to decide the case of a plaintiff woodworker who had been injured by a hot rivet, dropped by a contractor metalworker from a construction above. The negligence of the defendant lay in failing to erect a staging or lay out a canopy to catch the falling rivets. The defence, relying on *Woodley* and *Thomas*, pointed out that the hazard had existed for some time prior to the accident. The plaintiff had had full knowledge of it and so had allegedly consented to run the risk. Hawkins, however, distinguished *Woodley*, arguing that in that case the worker had been able to rely upon his own skill to avoid the passage of trains, whereas in this case no skill on the part of the woodworker would have allowed him to avoid the danger of falling metal. Furthermore, relying on *Yarmouth*, and developing the point made in *Thomas* in respect of *scienti* and *volenti*, Hawkins observed that:[75]

> It is difficult to say, where a man is lawfully working, subject to the orders of his employers and to the risk of dismissal if he disobeys, that if, after asking for

---

[73] Ibid, 657.
[74] (1888) 20 QBD 359.
[75] Ibid, 364.

and failing to obtain protection from the danger caused by other people's work, he suffers injury; the maxim '*Volenti non fit injuria*' applies. It is true he knows of the danger, but he does not wilfully incur it . . . His poverty, not his will, consented to incur the danger.

Ten years on from *Woodley*, the opinions advanced by the minority in that case had begun to prevail. There was no room in Esher's construct of *volenti* for implied assumptions of risk, assumed for a fictitious consideration, to be imputed into non-contractual relationships in situations of imperfect knowledge. Rather, in the context of the workplace at least, Esher envisaged a genuine meeting of minds, an informed knowledge of and willing assumption of risk based upon a quantifiable advancement of consideration. *Yarmouth v France* and *Thrusell v Handyside* reinforced and advanced the further proposition that for the defence of *volenti* to be valid the context in which the risk had been assumed had to have been outside of the ordinary labour relation. That is to say that the will of the workman must have been unconstrained and his readiness to run the risk must not have been a condition of his continuing employment. It is perhaps somewhat ironic that in *Thrussell* Hawkins J relied upon Bowen LJ's deployment of the difference between *volenti* and *scienti*, since it is far from clear that Bowen had in mind the reasoning that was later attributed to him in *Thrussell*—and, indeed, in *Smith v Charles Baker & Sons*.[76]

E. CONTRACTING OUT OF THE COURTROOM: THE AFTERMATH OF *SMITH V BAKER*

Smith v Baker is too well known to consider in any great detail in the short space permitted here. Much was built upon the minority in *Woodley* and upon the cases thereafter. Lord Halsbury for the majority was clear that 'in both *Thomas v Quartermaine* and *Yarmouth v France* it has been taken for granted that mere knowledge of the risk does not necessarily involve consent to the risk'.[77] Lord Watson accepted in part the construction of the 1880 Act as previously offered by Esher, holding that 'the Legislature did not intend that the statutory remedy given to the workman should be taken away simply by reason of his continuing in the same employment after he became aware of the defect from which he ultimately suffered'.[78]

By contrast, Lord Bramwell, in a splendidly bad tempered judgment, had no doubt that where a man undertook a hazardous employ and was aware of the risks of doing so the defence of *volenti* applied. If the case had come before him in the first instance, 'I should hold it to be the plainest possible, and that the plaintiff had no claim in law or

[76] [1891] AC 325.
[77] Ibid, 337.
[78] Ibid, 356.

morality'.[79] One doubts that he endeared himself greatly to his fellow judges, four to one against him, by his declaration that,

> The case is now before your Lordships, and there cannot be a doubt how it ought to be decided, unless, by some miscarriage of jury, or judge or counsel, the defendants are to be made liable where they are absolutely free from legal blame.[80]

Bramwell was assuredly right when he boldly declared that although he knew the court did not concur with him he knew many judges that would. The Court of Appeal had favoured the defendants and, although Lord Morris concurred with the majority in concluding that the maxim of *volenti non fit injuria* did not apply in the case at hand, he did so without any great enthusiasm and continued to support the opinion of the majority in *Quartermaine*:[81]

> The principle as laid down by Bowen LJ is clear and conclusive, viz: 'Where the danger is visible and the risk appreciated, and where the injured person, knowing and appreciating both the risk and danger, voluntarily encounters them, there is, in the absence of further acts of omission or commission, no evidence of negligence.'

On the facts of *Smith v Baker*, the jury had concluded that the defendant's machinery had been negligently constructed or maintained. Hence Morris could not address that issue as he was bound by the jury's verdict. Instead, he founded his judgment on knowledge; the plaintiff could not have known about the condition of the machinery operating above him and therefore could not have assumed the risk of being injured because of its supposed defects.

Significantly, none of the judges accepted Esher's conclusion in *Quartermaine* that the 1880 Act ousted *volenti non fit injuria* from actions under the act. Indeed, it is notable that Esher himself did not reassert this in *Yarmouth*. Yet thereafter it became rather more unusual for courts to conclude that workmen had willingly assumed those risks against which the courts held employers to owe a duty to protect them. Some judges had developed their own, increasingly sophisticated understanding of the free assumption of risk, one that both addressed issues of knowledge and at least began to address the disparity of the parties' bargaining positions. In one sense this was but a working through of the logic of free contractual relations that had caused the application of the *volenti* doctrine in the first place.

One suspects, however, that the judges were prepared to see some easing of the difficulties of recovery because by the mid-1880s it was becoming

---

[79] Ibid, 339.
[80] Ibid, 343.
[81] Ibid, 369.

apparent that, notwithstanding the fears of Walford, the Employer's Liability Act 1880 was not going to impose unsustainable burdens upon employers. Between 1881 and 1886 there were 3,000 actions under the statute in the county courts and in total a mere £120,000 damages were awarded.[82] According to the 1886 select committee, 'the apprehensions as to [the Act's] possible results in provoking litigation and imposing heavy charges upon employers have proved groundless'.[83] However, it was still difficult to recover in the courts. Furthermore, employers had moved swiftly to defeat the intentions of the act by contracting out. An attempt was made to prevent this practice with the introduction of the Liability Act (1880) Amendment Bill 1883. During the second reading, Mr Burt MP pointed out that 'No sooner was the act [the Employers' Liability Act 1880] passed than some employers and corporate bodies—especially some of the Railway Companies—put very extraordinary pressure on their workmen to compel them to contract out of its provisions'.[84] This led to a strike in Lancashire—itself an indication of the growing power of labour to resist. Mr Broadhurst MP, supporting, pointed out that in the building trade unemployed men could be induced to work under almost any conditions. He reported that no sooner had the 1880 Act been passed than a large building company had put up a placard informing its employees that they must consider themselves to have made an express agreement with their employer to the effect that the employer had no liability under the Act—or else they were to quit their employment.[85] Numerous other building companies, he alleged, had done the same. Ultimately, though, the bill was defeated by 149 votes to 38, Sir Joseph Pease addressing the house as perhaps Bramwell might have done in his shoes:[86]

> The Question put broadly before the house was, whether or not the working classes of this country were able to take care of themselves? Were the employed too prejudiced, too ignorant, or to foolish to make their own contracts with their employers . . . There could be only two reasons for this bill. One was, that the men were subject to undue pressure from their employers-were, in fact, slaves to their masters; and the other was, that they were so unwise and so imprudent that they contracted themselves out of the Act without receiving any equivalent. No such case had been or could be made out.

In 1883 both the legislature and the courts were thinking in terms of free contractual bargains, and they were still doing so in 1897 when the legislature enacted the Workmen's Compensation Act. Recovery without

---

82 V Markham Lester, 'The Employer' Liability/Workman's Compensation Debate of the 1890's Revisited' (2001) 44 *Historical Journal* 471, 478.
83 Report from the Select Committee on the Employer's Liability Act (1880) Amendment Bill (192-session 1), PP 1886, VIII, iii (11 June 1886).
84 Hansard, 280 HC Debs cols 504–505 (13 June 1883).
85 Ibid, col 510.
86 Ibid, col 507.

any proof of negligence was offered to the injured employee, but on a sliding scale of compensation so modest that few employers bothered to exercise their continuing right to contract out. An injured employee could either claim compensation under the 1897 Act or he could litigate under the 1880 Act. However, if he chose to do the latter then he still faced both the burden of proving negligence and of overcoming the tripartite defences of common employment, *volenti* and contributory negligence. Under such circumstances, few thereafter assumed the risk of bringing an action under the 1880 Act. Significantly, it was only in the most egregious cases of neglect that trade unions were prepared to fund such actions. Thus, the number of cases against employers in which the courts were obliged to consider a *volenti* defence was henceforth rather small. In effect, in return for a very modest compensation, injured employees had been induced to contract out of the courts. This had indeed been a very uneven bargain, but it was allegedly a free one and one which, no doubt, many of the judiciary greeted with great satisfaction.

6

Cavalier v Pope (1906)

RICHARD BAKER AND JONATHAN GARTON

A. INTRODUCTION

This chapter considers the continuing significance of *Cavalier v Pope*,[1] in which the House of Lords established the principle of *'caveat* lessee' and held that a landlord owes no duty of care to his tenants or their guests in respect of defective premises. Although the case predates *Donoghue v Stevenson*[2] and the foundation of the modern law of negligence by over a quarter of a century, and allows no room for the considerations of reasonable foreseeability, proximity or fairness, justice and reasonableness that characterise our contemporary understanding of the duty of care concept, it continues to define the limits of a landlord's liability at common law. For this reason, its central principle was famously described by Denning LJ as a 'relic' and an 'out-worn fallacy'.[3] However, whilst the approach of effectively granting blanket immunity to all landlords in respect of harm caused by their defective premises is no longer appropriate, it is by no means clear that if a situation governed by *Pope* was now dealt with in the same way as a typical negligence case it would be fair, just and reasonable for the court to impose a duty of care.

B. THE CASE

The facts of *Cavalier v Pope* are straightforward. Mr Cavalier rented an unfurnished home on a monthly basis from Mr Pope and resided there with his wife. On moving in, the tenants repeatedly called their landlord's attention to the dilapidated condition of the kitchen floor and, in response, the agent contracted with Mr Cavalier to effect the appropriate repairs in return for which he withdrew a threat to end the tenancy. However, before

---

1 [1906] AC 428.
2 [1932] AC 562.
3 *Greene v Chelsea Borough Council* [1954] 3 WLR 127 (CA) 138.

the repairs were carried out Mrs Cavalier was injured when the floor gave way as she was standing on a chair. Both husband and wife sought damages for breach of contract.

At first instance, Phillimore J found for Mr Cavalier on the basis that his wife's injury was a loss suffered by him as a result of the breach of contract,[4] and found for Mrs Cavalier on the basis that Mr Pope owed her a common law duty of care by reason of the defective nature of the floor. This was despite the fact that she was not privy to the contract for repair.[5] The judge based his decision on the dicta of Denman and Lopes JJ in the Divisional Court in *Nelson v Liverpool Brewery Co,*[6] who stated that a landlord would be liable to a third party for the defective state of his premises if there was a contract for repair which was enforceable against him by his tenant.[7] *Nelson* itself followed a line of authorities in which landlords who retained responsibility for certain repairs, and hence control over that aspect of their property, were held liable to third parties for the calamitous consequences of their failure to repair. An example is *Todd v Flight,*[8] in which a landlord was liable for his failure to repair defective chimneys, which he knew to be 'ruinous and in danger of falling',[9] when they fell and caused damage to an adjoining property. Another is *Payne v Rogers,*[10] in which a landlord was liable for the injuries sustained by a third party as a result of his failure to repair a cellar trapdoor.

The landlord appealed in relation to the duty owed to Mrs Cavalier, and a majority of the Court of Appeal rejected the trial judge's approach and held that in fact Mr Pope owed her no duty. Collins MR distinguished the authorities relied on by Phillimore J from the facts of the instant case on the ground that the former involved instances of nuisance to neighbouring land or public highways from properties over which the landlord had control, whilst the latter concerned 'merely a defect in the interior of the house'.[11] His Lordship held that no liability should lie here for two connected reasons: first, an occupier of land would at that time have owed no duty of care to those invited onto his land, save where his nonfeasance amounted to the setting of a trap, which was not the case here as Mrs

4 [1905] 2 KB 757 (CA) 761 (Collins MR, noting the judgment of the trial judge).
5 Ibid, 761–62 (Collins MR, noting the judgment of the trial judge).
6 (1877) 2 CPD 311.
7 (1877) 2 CPD 311, 313 (Lopes J, delivering the judgment of Denman and Lopes JJ). No duty of care was owed in *Nelson*, where the plaintiff tenant of the defendant brewery's public house was injured when a chimney pot fell on him, as, although the pot had been in a precarious condition for some weeks prior to the accident and both parties were aware of this, there was no undertaking to repair, and the business custom whereby breweries would typically undertake such repairs was not sufficiently 'uniform, certain and well-established' to give rise to liability: ibid, 313 (Lopes J).
8 (1860) 9 CB (NS) 377, 142 ER 148.
9 Ibid, 9 CB (NS) 388 (Erle CJ).
10 (1794) 2 H Bl 350, 126 ER 589.
11 [1905] 2 KB 757 (CA) 763.

Cavalier was clearly aware of the danger;[12] and secondly, Mr Pope's duty to a third party as landlord should in any case not be as onerous as the duty owed to someone invited by the tortfeasor onto the land.[13] Authority for this proposition was *Lane v Cox*,[14] in which no duty was owed by a landlord to his tenant's workman when he was injured by a defective staircase as there was insufficient 'proximity' between them.[15] Collins MR drew particular attention to the words of Lord Esher MR in that earlier case:[16]

> It has been held that there is no duty imposed on a landlord, by his relation to his tenant, not to let an unfurnished house in a dilapidated condition, because the condition of the house is the subject of contract between them. If there is no duty in such a case to the tenant there cannot be a duty to a stranger.

Collins MR also considered that it would be unfair to impose a duty on a nonfeasant landlord who had undertaken to carry out repairs to the property when a similarly nonfeasant independent tradesman having made such an agreement would owe no such duty.[17]

Romer LJ agreed with Collins MR and put Mrs Cavalier's case in the following succinct terms:[18]

> To enable her to succeed, she must establish that her injury was caused by [the landlord's] neglect of some private duty he owed towards her in reference to the dilapidated condition of the flooring in the interior of the house. Now, I take it to be clear that if a person takes as tenant an unfurnished house, he cannot, in the absence (as here) of a warranty or other special circumstances, hold the landlord liable because of damage arising to him during and by reason of his occupancy as a tenant through the house being out of repair or dilapidated. And if the tenant brings his wife with him to live in the house, she cannot be in a better position than her husband by reason of her occupancy of the house.

His Lordship held that the landlord's agreement to carry out repairs did not 'alter or affect any duty previously owing' to either Mr or Mrs Cavalier,[19] and merely gave the husband the right to sue for breach of contract. He observed that '[t]he contract with the husband to repair could not create a special private duty on the part of the landlord to the wife which would have had no existence in the absence of that contract',[20] and

12 Ibid, 763.
13 Ibid, 763.
14 [1897] 1 QB 415 (CA).
15 Ibid, 417 (Lord Esher MR), noted by Collins MR in *Cavalier* (CA), above n 11, 763.
16 Ibid. See also the words of Erle CJ in *Robbins v Jones* (1863) 15 CB (NS) 221, 240, 143 ER 768: 'A landlord who lets a house in a dangerous state, is not liable to the tenant's customers or guests for accidents happening during the term; for, fraud apart, there is no law against letting a tumble-down house'; noted by Collins MR in *Cavalier* (CA), above n 11, 763–64.
17 *Cavalier* (CA), above n 11, 764.
18 Ibid, 764–65.
19 Ibid, 765.
20 Ibid, 765.

rejected the suggestion that the husband or wife had been invited to remain on the premises 'on the footing that . . . the repairs were to be taken to be effected', with the result that a duty of care had arisen.[21]

In the minority, Mathew LJ upheld Mrs Cavalier's appeal, but for a different reason to Phillimore J. His Lordship agreed with the majority that the analogy between the instant case and the nuisance cases could not stand,[22] but he held that the promise made by the landlord's agent to carry out the repairs amounted to a misrepresentation inducing the couple to remain in the property, as the evidence was that the landlord had never intended to carry out such repairs; hence a claim in deceit arose.[23] Although the Cavaliers were clearly aware of the dilapidated nature of the kitchen floor, Mathew LJ rejected the idea that they released Mr Pope from making good on his representation by remaining in the property for some time afterwards despite the lack of repair, as they had little choice in the matter:[24]

> It was said that their remedy was to the leave the premises; but, as the landlords of such property well know, it is not easy for humble people to change their residence . . . It is true that the plaintiffs knew of the condition of the premises, but they did not willingly incur the risk to which they were exposed by the conduct of the landlord.

His Lordship drew an analogy with *Langridge v Levy* in support of this point.[25] There the seller of a 'bad, unsafe, ill manufactured and dangerous gun'[26] induced its purchase and subsequent use by misrepresenting its quality and safety, and was held to be liable when the gun injured a third party attempting to fire it.

Mrs Cavalier was granted leave to appeal to the House of Lords, where, in a series of notably brief opinions, the majority decision of the Court of Appeal was affirmed and the House held that no duty of care is owed to the occupier of dilapidated premises in respect of personal injury caused by the dilapidation where the occupier is aware of the state of the premises and is not privy to any contract for repair. Giving the leading judgment, Lord MacNaghten, with whom Lords Davey and Robertson concurred,[27] held that Mrs Cavalier could not have a better claim than a customer or guest on the property given that she had the 'advantage or disadvantage' of knowing about the condition of the property,[28] and rejected Mathew LJ's account that the promise made by the agent amounted to fraud, even

---

21 Ibid, 765.
22 Ibid, 766.
23 Ibid, 766.
24 Ibid, 766–67.
25 (1837) 2 M & W 519, 150 ER 863; noted by Mathew LJ in *Cavalier* (CA), above n 11, 767.
26 Ibid, 2 M & W 519.
27 [1906] AC 428, 430 and 431.
28 Ibid, 430.

if it was never intended for the repairs to be carried out.[29] Lord Atkinson took a similar approach[30] but also, along with Lord James, considered the issue of control, with which Collins MR had characterised the *Nelson* line of authorities. Both judges were of the view that, in the instant case, the landlord did not control the premises in any meaningful sense,[31] Lord Atkinson equating control with exclusive possession and the right to admit or exclude people from the premises,[32] and Lord James noting, albeit with some reluctance given the injury sustained by Mrs Cavalier, that any constructive control that might have been taken by Mr Pope by virtue of the agreement to undertake repairs was negated by the actual possession of the tenants.[33]

Cavalier v Pope thus establishes the principle of '*caveat* lessee' and holds that no common law duty of care is owed by a landlord to his tenants or their guests in relation to defective premises. This reach of this principle was subsequently extended by the Court of Appeal in *Bottomley v Bannister*,[34] where the purchasers of a property who had moved in prior to completion under a tenancy at will were killed by carbon monoxide poisoning as a result of a dangerous flueless gas boiler installed by the vendor, a building company also responsible for the construction of the property. In denying the claim, the Court held not only that a vendor owes no duty of care in respect of defective premises to his purchaser, at least where that purchaser moves in prior to completion, but also that no duty is owed even if the landlord or vendor was himself responsible for the defect. In the words of Greer LJ:[35]

> It seems to me that this principle equally applies to the case of a builder or other owner of property, when the question is whether he owes any duty towards people who may with his consent either as purchasers, tenants, or licensees of purchasers or tenants, come onto his property and be damaged by its defective condition.

This was despite the fact that if the boiler had been installed by an independent contractor then its negligent installation would have resulted in the contractor's liability.[36]

The principle has also been extended, somewhat ironically given the reluctance of the Court of Appeal in *Cavalier v Pope* to draw an analogy with the nuisance cases cited by Phillimore J, to provide landlords with

---

[29] Ibid, 430.
[30] Ibid, 432–23.
[31] Ibid, 431 (Lord James) and 433–34 (Lord Atkinson).
[32] Ibid, 433.
[33] Ibid, 431.
[34] [1932] 1 KB 458.
[35] [1932] 1 KB 458 (CA) 476–77. However, note the subsequent decision of *Rimmer v Liverpool City Council* [1985] QB 1 (CA) in the context of landlords qua builders: see text to nn 57–64 below.
[36] Ibid, 478 (Greer LJ).

immunity in cases where their defective premises cause or exacerbate a private nuisance. In *Baxter v London Borough of Camden*[37] a tenant had no claim in private nuisance against her landlord where this was caused by poor sound insulation, and in *Jackson v JH Property Investment Ltd*[38] a tenant had no claim in private nuisance against his landlord when his property suffered water damage as a result of a defective light-well in the landlord's adjoining property.

C. THE IMPACT OF *CAVALIER V POPE* ON THE COMMON LAW

The identification of general guiding principles for establishing a common law duty of care in negligence in *Donoghue v Stevenson*[39] did not take place for more than 25 years after the House of Lords set out their opinion in *Cavalier v Pope*. The conflict between the new and the old, however, was evident from the start. In dissenting from the majority in *Donoghue*, Lord Buckmaster observed:[40]

> If such a duty exists, it seems to me it must cover the construction of every article, and I cannot see any reason why it should not apply to the construction of a house. If one step, why not fifty? Yet if a house be, as it sometimes is, negligently built, and in consequence of that negligence the ceiling falls and injures the occupier or any one else, no action against the builder exists according to the English law, although I believe such a right did exist according to the laws of Babylon.

The development of common law negligence following *Donoghue v Stevenson* saw the gradual erosion of many of the effects of *Cavalier v Pope* so that the immunity for malfeasance,[41] and for negligent acts or omissions that had taken place before or after the demise and which created a danger within the premises,[42] was removed by *AC Billings & Sons v Riden*,[43] in which liability was attached to a landlord's contractors who interfered with the safe access to the demised premises causing the occupiers to take a more perilous side route and as a consequence of which one of their visitors suffered injury.[44]

That a landlord's duties should be considered in light of broader principles of negligence in place of contract was confirmed in *Greene v*

---

[37] [2001] QB 1 (CA).
[38] [2008] EWHC 14 (Ch), [2008] Env LR 30.
[39] [1932] AC 562.
[40] Ibid, 577–78.
[41] *Davis v Foots* [1940] 1 KB 116 (CA).
[42] On which, see: *Malone v Laskey* [1907] 2 KB 141 (CA); *Ball v London County Council* [1949] 2 KB 159 (CA).
[43] [1958] AC 240.
[44] The usefulness of this authority would be broadly eclipsed by subsequent legislation.

Chelsea Borough Council.[45] In this case the plaintiff and her late husband were permitted to occupy part of premises under a licence on the basis that their landlord was permitted to enter the premises to inspect them and carry out such repairs as were necessary. The tenant notified her landlord of deterioration in the ceiling within the premises and asked for repairs to be done; no repairs were carried out and after a time part of the ceiling collapsed, injuring the tenant. *Cavalier v Pope* was raised in an effort to defeat the claim. Denning LJ responded:[46]

> During the nineteenth century there was a doctrine current in the law which I will call the 'privity-of-contract' doctrine. In those days it was thought that if the defendant became connected with the matter because of a contract he had made, then his obligations were to be measured by the contract and nothing else. He owed, it was said, no duty of care to anyone who was not a party to the contract. This doctrine received its quietus by the decision of the House of Lords in *Donoghue v Stevenson*, but it has been asserted again before us today. We must, I think, firmly resist the revival of this out-worn fallacy. *Cavalier v Pope* is a relic of it which must be kept in a close confinement.

This call to restrict *Cavalier v Pope* was repeated and approved by the Court of Appeal in *Rimmer v Liverpool City Council*,[47] which we consider below,[48] yet, despite such calls, there have been no significant attempts by the courts to address the immunity, either immediately in the aftermath of *Donoghue v Stevenson* or following the subsequent cases that defined the manner in which the courts should examine the duty of care.[49] In *Anns v Merton London Borough*,[50] the high watermark of incremental expansion, whilst stating that *Cavalier v Pope* was far from the principles in consideration, Lord Salmon was able to comment that 'the immunity of a landlord who sells or lets his house which is dangerous or unfit for habitation is deeply entrenched in our law'.[51]

Indeed, the Court of Appeal felt compelled to follow *Pope* as recently as 1999, in *Boldack v East Lindsey DCC*.[52] This case concerned a four-year-old boy who was injured when a paving slab, which had been propped up against the outside wall of his mother's council house, fell on his foot. The case fell outside the scope of the landlord's duty under the Defective Premises Act 1972, section 4[53] for several reasons, not least the facts that it was not established that the council knew or ought to have

45 [1954] 2 QB 127 (CA).
46 Ibid, 138.
47 [1985] QB 1 (CA).
48 See text to nn 57–64 below.
49 See, eg *Hedley Byrne & Co Ltd v Heller & Partners Ltd* [1964] AC 465; *Dorset Yacht Co Ltd v Home Office* [1970] AC 1004; *Caparo Industries plc v Dickman* [1990] 2 AC 605.
50 [1978] AC 728.
51 Ibid, 768.
52 (1999) 31 HLR 41 (CA).
53 See text to nn 71–72 below.

known about the paving slab and that the tenancy agreement contained no relevant express covenant to repair.[54] When considering the possibility of liability at common law on the basis that it was reasonably foreseeable that a small child might be injured by the paving slab, May LJ observed:[55]

> [Counsel for the plaintiff] was bold enough to suggest at one stage that this court might simply ignore *Cavalier v Pope*; but certainly text book writers have indicated that opportunities should be taken to reconsider it. Nevertheless it is, in my judgment, quite plain that *Cavalier v Pope*, a decision of the House of Lords, remains binding on this court and that it is not open on this court to take the bold and somewhat 'flamboyant' step that [counsel] has invited us to take . . . *Cavalier v Pope* remains entrenched so far as it has not been confined by statute or other authorities.

Accordingly, the council owed no duty to the child.

The only significant common law exception to *Cavalier v Pope* which has been developed concerns cases of landlords qua architects or builders.[56] In *Rimmer v Liverpool City Council*,[57] the Court of Appeal considered an appeal from the Queen's Bench Division after a council tenant was awarded damages for personal injuries following an accident that occurred in December 1975. The facts of the case were that in 1959, Liverpool City Council designed and built a block of 24 flats through their architects and direct works department. Each of the flats had, as part of the internal wall, a glass panel, three millimetres thick, directly opposite the lounge door. The plaintiff had been granted a weekly tenancy of one of the flats. At the start of the tenancy he complained to the defendant's technical officer that the glass panel was dangerously thin and that it represented a danger to his five-year-old son. He was told that it was of standard design and nothing could be done about it. Inevitably, one day the plaintiff tripped over some of his son's toys and fell. As he did so he put out his left hand, which broke the glass panel and caused him serious injury.

As the flats had been built in 1959, the case fell outside of the statutory provisions relating to builders set out in the Defective Premises Act 1972, section 1(1). The defendant argued that defective design was not part of the plaintiff's pleaded case and that, applying *Cavalier v Pope*, there could be no common law duty. The plaintiff addressed the appellant's arguments

---

[54] *Boldack*, above n 52, 48 (May LJ).

[55] Ibid, 49.

[56] A landlord owes a duty of care under the Occupiers' Liability Act 1957 in respect of common parts within premises, of which he has retained control: *Wheat v Lacon* [1966] AC 552. Whilst this could reasonably be described as an undermining of a landlord's immunity from claims in negligence, it does not strictly go to the same issues that were addressed in *Cavalier v Pope*, namely whether a landlord owes duties in respect of the condition of demised premises. The principle that a person who occupies or controls premises owes a duty to visitors to those premises grows from a different line of authority and pre-dates the 1957 Act.

[57] [1985] QB 1.

by placing *Cavalier v Pope* in the balance with *Donoghue v Stevenson*. Stephenson LJ outlined the issues behind the Court's consideration thus:[58]

> The question raised by this appeal is whether the authority of *Cavalier v Pope* binds this court to hold the council immune from liability to the plaintiff, or whether it does not, either because it is inconsistent with later decisions of the House of Lords, which was (we think) the judge's view, or because it can be distinguished from this case, which is our own view.

The Court of Appeal in *Rimmer* were in no position to overrule the principle set down by the House of Lords in *Cavalier v Pope*; their options were therefore limited and, despite their agreement with Denning LJ's disapproval of the authority in *Greene*,[59] they had to recognise that the authority was 'deeply entrenched' in the common law and left the issue as one that their Lordships had 'left for another day'.[60] Nonetheless, the court relied on a line of authority that followed *Cavalier v Pope* and could be said to stand against it. In the words of Stephenson LJ:[61]

> It is also now the law, authoritatively stated by Lord Macmillan in *Donoghue v Stevenson* [1932] AC 562, 610, that one person may owe another a common law duty of care co-existing with a contractual duty and a contractual relationship does not necessarily exclude a relationship of proximity giving rise to the duty formulated in that case. It is unnecessary to go into the important effects that this co-existence of duties may have on the measure of damages and the period of limitation. Suffice it to note for the purpose of this appeal that this development of the law has been applied by this court to lessees of a house built on land without proper support and consequently unfit for habitation so as to enable them to recover damages for financial loss both from the builders of the house for their negligence and from the developers of the land, who employed the builders and let the house, for their negligence as well as for their breach of contract: *Batty v Metropolitan Property Realisations Ltd* [1978] QB 554, a case relied on by the judge and approved by the House of Lords in *Junior Books Ltd v Veitchi Co Ltd* [1983] 1 AC 520.

Stephenson LJ went on to quote at length from the authority of *Anns v London Borough of Merton*,[62] before setting out the Court's conclusion as follows:[63]

> From these authorities we take the law to be that an opportunity for inspection of a dangerous defect, even if successfully taken by A who is injured by it, will not destroy his proximity to B who created the danger, or exonerate B from liability to A, unless A was free to remove or avoid the danger in the sense that it was reasonable to expect him to do so, and unreasonable for him to run the risk

---

[58] Ibid, 8.
[59] See text to n 46 above.
[60] *Rimmer*, above n 57, 15.
[61] Ibid, 11.
[62] [1978] AC 728.
[63] *Rimmer*, above n 57, 14.

of being injured by the danger. It was not reasonable or practical for the plaintiff to leave the flat or to alter the glass panel. He remained in law the council's
neighbour, although he had complained that the glass was too thin.

He then balanced this conclusion against *Cavalier v Pope* by saying:[64]

In our judgment, the judge formulated the duty too widely so as to include the
bare landlord as well as the builder owner. It may be that to impose a duty on
all landowners who let or sell their land and dwellings, whether or not they are
their own designers or builders, would be so great a change in the law as
to require legislation. But, in our judgment, this court can and should hold,
following *Batty v Metropolitan Property Realisations Ltd* . . . and distinguishing *Cavalier v Pope* . . . that the council, as their own architect and builder,
owed the plaintiff a duty to take reasonable care in designing and constructing
the flat to see that it was reasonably safe when they let it to him.

The common law has not progressed any further in creating exceptions
to the rule in *Cavalier v Pope* and it has been left to Parliament to further
reduce the effect of the immunity.

D. STATUTORY EXCEPTIONS

Part I of the Housing Act 1936 created the first exception to the rule that
denied a tenant any remedy if he was injured as a consequence of a
landlord's failure to maintain and repair premises. The modern successor to
this is the Landlord and Tenant Act 1985, section 8, which provides that in
a tenancy agreement of a house let for human habitation, notwithstanding
any express term to the contrary, there is (i) a condition that the house is fit
for human habitation at the start of the tenancy and (ii) an undertaking
that this fitness will be maintained by the landlord for the life of the
tenancy. However, a landlord cannot be liable for a breach of this implied
condition unless he has notice of the defect that is alleged to render the
premises unfit for human habitation,[65] and thus the condition does not
impose a positive duty upon the landlord as would exist under the common
law, where foreseeability of harm forms the basis for duty in place of notice
of or actual foresight of harm.

The second, and more wide reaching, statutory exception to the '*caveat
lessee*' principle is the Defective Premises Act 1972, which came into force
on 1 January 1974. This followed the publication of a report by the Law
Commission in which the following recommendations were made:[66]

64 Ibid, 16.
65 *O'Brien v Robinson* [1973] AC 912.
66 Law Commission, *The Civil Liability of Vendors and Lessors for Defective Premises* (Law
Com No 40, 1970) para [70].

1. Those who build, or undertake work in connection with the provision of, new dwellinghouses (whether by new construction, enlargement or conversion) should be under a statutory duty, owed to any person who acquires a proprietary interest in the property, as well as to the person (if any) for whom they have contracted to provide the dwelling, to see that the work which they take on is done in a workmanlike or professional manner (as the case may be), with proper materials and so that the dwelling will be fit for habitation. The same duty should be owed by those who in the course of trade or business or under statutory powers arrange for such work to be undertaken[.]

2. The vendor's and lessor's immunity from liability for the consequences of his own negligent acts should be abolished; that is to say '*caveat emptor*' should not longer provide a defence to a claim against a vendor or lessor which is founded upon his negligence[.]

3. A person who sells or lets premises should be under a general duty of care in respect of defects which may result in injury to persons or damage to property and which are actually known to him at the date of the sale or letting[.]

4. A landlord who is under a repairing obligation or has a right to do repairs to premises let should be under the general duty of care to the risk of injury or damage arising from a failure to carry out the obligation or exercise that right with proper diligence; but a landlord should not, by reason of a right to enter and repair on the tenant's default, be liable to the tenant for injury suffered by the tenant's default[.]

The report expressly considered the landlord's immunity for letting defective premises. After addressing its origins and development through the common law, the Law Commission observed that whilst it would be open to the House of Lords in a future case to reject it as being inconsistent with the principles of modern negligence liability, the immunity was unlikely to be abolished by a lower court,[67] and concluded:[68]

It is clear from the cases mentioned above that the immunity can cause great injustice and the law is applied by the courts of first instance with considerable regret. The rights of an injured person may depend upon distinctions which can only be regarded as capricious . . . We think that these distinctions are indefensible and that the law should be amended by statute.

The Commission therefore clearly intended that the immunity encapsulated in *Cavalier v Pope*, and adopted and entrenched in subsequent authorities, should be abolished.[69]

---

67 Ibid, para [44].

68 Ibid, paras [45]–[46].

69 Concern regarding the continuation of the immunity has also been reflected in the reports of reform bodies in other jurisdictions, eg: Law Reform Committee for Scotland, 'The Law relating to (a) the Liability of an Occupier of Land or other Property to Persons suffering Injury while on the Property, and (b) the Obligations of a Lessor towards Third Parties invited, or allowed, by the Lessee to be on the Subjects Let' (Cmnd 88, 1957); Law Reform Commission of Ireland, 'Report on Defective Premises' (LRC 3, 1982).

Section 1(1) of the Act places a duty on persons

> taking on work for or in connection with the provision of a dwelling . . . to see that the work which he takes on is done in a workmanlike or, as the case may be, professional manner, with proper materials and so that as regards that work the dwelling will be fit for habitation when completed.

Section 3 removes the immunity from liability for negligent acts that were performed before the letting of premises. Thus, if a landlord carried out work on premises prior to a letting, he owes a duty to take reasonable care to avoid causing injury to persons whom he might reasonably expect will be affected. In effect, this creates a duty in the terms of *Donoghue v Stevenson* and the subsequent negligence authorities, thus overturning in part the contractual doctrine that formed the basis of *Cavalier v Pope* and, in particular, the immunity of the landlord for any claim arising from the condition of the premises at the time of the letting. The duty is, however, plainly limited to the issue of malfeasance and does not create any liability in respect of the landlord's nonfeasance. Thus, a landlord who negligently performs adaptations to a property can be liable if his tenant suffers injury, whereas a landlord who does not adapt premises and lets them in a hazardous condition would still be able to rely upon the immunity afforded to him by *Cavalier v Pope*.

Parliament may have believed that the absence of any duty in respect of nonfeasance under section 3 of the Act was mitigated by the duty under section 4, which provides that, where a landlord covenants in a tenancy agreement to maintain or repair the premises, he owes a duty to take 'such care as is reasonable in all the circumstances to see that [the tenants] are reasonably safe' from personal injury or property damage caused by a 'relevant defect' in the state of the premises[70] where he knows or ought to have known of that defect.[71] The Act defines a relevant defect as follows:[72]

> [A] defect in the state of the premises existing at or after the material time and arising from, or continuing because of, an act or omission by the landlord which constitutes or would if he had had notice of the defect, have constituted a failure by him to carry out his obligation to the tenant for the maintenance or repair of the premises; and for the purposes of the foregoing provision 'the material time' means: (a) where the tenancy commenced before this Act, the commencement of this Act; and (b) in all other cases, the earliest of the following times, that is to say (i) the time when the tenancy commences; (ii) the time when the tenancy agreement is entered into; (iii) the time when possession is taken of the premises in contemplation of the letting.

The provision creating a duty in respect of defects that exist at the time when the tenancy commences would plainly bind a landlord for

---

[70] Defective Premises Act 1972, s 4(1).
[71] Ibid, s 4(2).
[72] Ibid, s 4(3).

nonfeasance in respect of premises that were let in a state of disrepair. However, the definition of defect is expressly restricted to defects that arise from a failure to maintain or repair premises, rather than defects that are created by the design or construction of premises.73 Thus a landlord who lets premises containing a dangerously steep staircase without handrails or, as in the case of *Rimmer*, a glass panel made from dangerously thin glass would not owe any duty under the Act. This was recently confirmed by the Court of Appeal in *Alker v Collingwood Housing Association*.74 In the words of Laws LJ:75

> There is, as my Lord, Lord Justice Carnwath pointed out in the course of argument, much learning on this dichotomy between maintain and repair. It is not necessary to go into it in this case. No doubt the two concepts overlap. Neither of them, however, can in my judgment possibly be said to encompass or to include a duty or obligation to make safe. Moreover a duty to keep 'in good condition', the words used here, even if it encompasses a duty to put into good condition, again cannot encompass a duty to put in safe condition. A house may offer many hazards: a very steep stairway with no railings; a hidden step; some other hazard inside or outside the house of the kind often found perhaps in particular older properties. I do not think it can be said that the Act requires a landlord on proof only of the conditions I have described for the application of section 4 to make safe any such dangerous feature.

Although a fair and proper interpretation of the language used within the statute, the case of *Alker* indicates the inadequacies of the Defective Premises Act 1972 in abolishing the *Cavalier v Pope* immunity. The language of the Act does not reflect the language used by the Law Commission, which referred simply to 'defects' throughout its report, nor the fact that the term traditionally had a broader meaning within the law of tort than the term 'disrepair': in *Tate v Latham and Son*76 it was defined as meaning 'a lack or absence of something essential to completeness',77 whilst in *McGiffin v Palmer's Shipbuilding and Iron Co Ltd*78 it was defined in the context of machinery as 'the absence of some part of the machinery, or a crack, or anything of that kind'.79 There is no obvious justification for Parliament to have defined a defect as being a hazard within premises arising from disrepair, as opposed to a simple hazard within premises.

---

73 See, eg *Quick v Taff Ely BC* [1986] QB 809 (CA); *Post Office v Aquarius Properties Ltd* [1987] 1 All ER 1055 (CA).
74 [2007] EWCA Civ 343; [2007] 1 WLR 2230.
75 Ibid, [14].
76 [1897] 1 QB 502 (QBD), aff'd [1897] 1 QB 502 (CA).
77 Ibid, 506 (Bruce J).
78 (1883) LR 10 QBD 5.
79 Ibid, 9 (Stephen J).

E. THE FUTURE OF *CAVALIER V POPE*

If Parliament intended to mitigate the harshness of *Cavalier v Pope* and remove the doctrine of '*caveat* lessee' from English law through the Defective Premises Act 1972, then it plainly failed. It might not be said that a landlord is necessarily free to let a tumbledown house to a tenant without risk of liability, but a landlord who is not the builder of the premises is still immune from liability for personal injury in circumstances where he lets hazardous premises. This creates a plain and unjustifiable contradiction in the law. Why, in principle, should the liability of a landlord who constructs premises containing an integral defect for an injury sustained by a tenant many years later be assessed according to the neighbour principle and the requirements of the duty of care concept laid down in *Caparo v Dickman*[80] while the liability of a landlord who purchases and lets an identical property is automatically excluded without any consideration of the issues of reasonable foreseeability, proximity and policy considerations? Why should a landlord be under a duty to ensure that premises were not rendered unsafe by disrepair but never owe a duty to act in respect of other hazards within the premises? These contradictions exist because the duties that arise through the relationship between landlord and tenant were fixed before the common law had adequately developed the concept of a duty of care through the neighbour principle. Whilst it might be said that *Cavalier v Pope* represents a relic, as was said of the case in 1954,[81] it nonetheless continues to define the limits of the duties owed by landlords to their tenants. Reliance on *Cavalier v Pope* without further consideration of the principles that underpin a landlord's duties towards their tenants is no longer defensible, if it ever was following the development of modern law of negligence.

However, it does not follow that its application necessarily leads to unjust results in every case. The concept of '*caveat* lessee' might very well be justifiable within the context of a private arrangement between a landlord and a tenant who has a degree of choice over whether they choose to take premises that contain an inherent hazard. In this sense, the case could be seen as part of the same line of jurisprudence as *Murphy v Brentwood DC*,[82] where the House of Lords held that a local authority charged with a statutory duty to approve building plans will not be liable for personal injury caused by its negligent approval of the plans of a defective building where the defect is patent to the injured person. Speaking more broadly, Lord Keith observed:[83]

---

[80] [1990] 2 AC 605.
[81] See text to n 46.
[82] [1991] 1 AC 398.
[83] Ibid, 464.

[T]here can be no doubt that, whatever the rationale, a person who is injured through consuming or using a product of the defective nature of which he is well aware has no remedy against the manufacturer. In the case of a building, it is right to accept that a careless builder is liable, on the principle of *Donoghue v Stevenson*, where a latent defect results in physical injury to anyone, whether owner, occupier, visitor or passer-by, or to the property of any such person. But that principle is not apt to bring home liability towards an occupier who knows the full extent of the defect yet continues to occupy the building.

Of course, even on these terms the nature of the *Cavalier v Pope* immunity remains anomalous by virtue of its failure to address the neighbour principle and the issues associated with it: in *Murphy*, the House was at pains to determine the existence (or lack thereof) and scope of any duty of care by reference to *Stevenson* and matters of policy,[84] adopting what is clearly recognisable today as an embryonic *Caparo* approach.

Cavalier v Pope has less merit, however, in the context of the relationship between a local authority or housing association and its tenant, who will have little real choice over what premises they take, a fact acknowledged by Mathew LJ's minority judgment in *Pope* itself.[85] Social landlords, who in accordance with the Housing Acts 1985 and 1996 provide services beyond mere accommodation, might also be said to have a broader relationship with their tenants than a private landlord. Given that this type of relationship did not exist at the time when *Cavalier v Pope* was decided, the blanket immunity warrants reassessment in light of modern principles of duty of care. However, whilst a review of the principles underpinning the immunity is warranted, it is by no means certain that a straightforward application of the *Caparo* three-stage test would necessarily warrant the imposition of a duty of care between landlord and tenant to fill the lacuna. Although it is likely that the relationship would be sufficiently proximate and the risk of harm foreseeable, in the context of council housing, problems would likely arise in response to the question of whether it is just and reasonable to impose a duty:[86] the creation of a duty arising from a local authority's statutory obligations to provide accommodation would risk offending the line of authority running through *X v Bedfordshire County Council*[87] and *O'Rourke v Camden London Borough Council*,[88] which effectively prohibits a court from creating a common law duty of care to fulfil statutory obligations in circumstances where Parliament has not opted to provide a civil right of action under the terms of the statute.

---

84 Ibid, 461–62 (Lord Keith) and 473–75 (Lord Bridge).
85 See above n 24 and associated text.
86 As per the third element of the test for establishing a duty of care in *Caparo v Dickman* [1990] 2 AC 605.
87 [1995] 2 AC 633.
88 [1998] AC 188.

This problem was vividly illustrated in the recent case of *X and Y v London Borough of Hounslow*.[89] The question before the court was whether the defendant council owed a common law duty to rehouse the claimant tenants, who had learning disabilities, where the council had learned that they were in imminent physical danger (which was subsequently realised in the course of a weekend of kidnap, assault and abuse involving some of the most disturbing events that it is possible to read about in the law reports) from a group of local youths who were exploiting the couple. At first instance, Maddison J considered that the actions of the council in housing and providing support for the couple went beyond the mere provision of their statutory obligations and applied the *Caparo* test in order to consider whether a duty of care should be said to exist. Having considered that the test was satisfied upon the facts of that case, he found that the law should take a small incremental step and impose a duty of care to move the claimants. This approach was rejected by the Court of Appeal. Sir Anthony Clark MR said:[90]

> In these circumstances, as we see it, the question is whether this case falls within Lord Hoffman's category of care in which public authorities have actually done acts or entered into relationships or undertaken responsibilities which give rise to a common law duty of care . . . Only in such a case would it be fair, just and reasonable to hold that a local authority such as the Council on facts such as these owe a duty of care to the respondents. This is not a case of control like *Dorset Yacht*. Nor is it a case where the defendant has created or increased the danger to the respondents. Moreover it is not a case of assumption of responsibility unless it can properly be held that there was a voluntary assumption of responsibility: see *Rowley v Secretary of State for Work and Pensions* [2007] EWCA Civ 598, [2007] 1 WLR 2861, especially per Dyson LJ at [51] to [54]. This is because, as the cases cited above show, a public authority will not be held to have assumed a common law duty merely by doing what the statute requires or what it has power to do under a statute, at any rate unless the duty arises out of the relationship created as a result, such as in Lord Hoffman's example of a doctor patient relationship.

Similarly, in *Mitchell v Glasgow City Council*,[91] the House of Lords considered whether a local authority owed a duty of care to its tenant to warn him about the violent conduct of another tenant who had expressed an intention at a meeting with the council to cause him harm. The House did not consider it appropriate to impose a duty of care, having determined that to do so would not be fair, just and reasonable. Nonetheless, in reaching this decision, the House considered it appropriate to consider the relationship between social landlord and tenant under the umbrella of the *Caparo* test.

---

[89] [2009] EWCA Civ 286, [2009] Fam Law 487.
[90] Ibid, [2009] Fam Law 487 [60].
[91] [2009] UKHL 11, [2009] 2 WLR 481.

X and Y and *Mitchell* demonstrate that, even assuming that a local authority or housing association, in providing accommodation to tenants, could be said to have assumed responsibility for providing property that would not be injurious to their health, it does not necessarily follow that a duty of care would arise in a situation currently governed by *Cavalier v Pope* if we were to apply the *Caparo v Dickman* test. The very fact that the higher courts are considering these very specific aspects of the duties arising between social landlord and their tenants, though, brings into focus the broad illogicality of their continued immunity for hazardous defects within the premises that they are obliged to provide.

F. CONCLUSION

Referring to *Cavalier v Pope* as a landmark case may at first glance seem to be misleading, as it might better be regarded as an anomaly or relic within the modern law of negligence. It has nonetheless taken on an air of indestructibility, standing as 'a rock which has escaped the floodtide of liability released by *Donoghue v Stevenson*',[92] having survived both the common law and Parliament's efforts to destroy it. There seems little reason to suspect that it will be overturned in respect of a private landlord and tenant, for whom the doctrine of '*caveat* lessee' might well find a place within the *Caparo* consideration so as to mean that it would not be just, fair or reasonable to create a duty of care. The creation of a duty as between local authority landlords and their tenants, on the other hand, would remedy the injustice that '*caveat* lessee' creates within that relationship, though such steps might be rejected for the same reasons as in *X and* Y. Whether the common law should be extended to create a duty in either of these situations is ultimately a matter for the courts to address; irrespective of their conclusion, however, *Cavalier v Pope* does not provide a legitimate basis for a persisting immunity.

---

92 JW Salmond and RFV Heuston, *The Law of Torts*, 16th edn (London, Sweet & Maxwell, 1969) 378.

7

Hedley Byrne & Co Ltd v Heller & Partners Ltd (1963)

PAUL MITCHELL

A. INTRODUCTION

In *Hedley Byrne & Co Ltd v Heller & Partners Ltd*[1] the House of Lords made an extremely important contribution to the law of negligence. A duty of care would arise, it held, where a defendant assumed responsibility to the claimant for the accuracy of a statement and the claimant suffered purely economic loss as a result of relying on that statement. Subsequent cases have expanded the range of the *Hedley Byrne* principle, applying it to situations involving the negligent performance of services,[2] reliance on a negligent statement by a third party[3] and, most controversially, an omission to act resulting in purely economic loss.[4] The principle has also been invoked to support duties of care where the claimant's damage was physical, whether that harm arose from misperformance[5] or non-performance.[6] In the 40 years since it was decided, the principle from *Hedley Byrne* has been enormously influential.

However, it has also been highly controversial. Two main themes have emerged. First, it has been doubted whether the assumption of responsibility test is sufficiently coherent to explain the outcomes of cases in which it has been applied.[7] Secondly, it has been questioned whether the *Hedley Byrne* principle really belongs in the law of negligence at all.[8]

The first criticism was given force by cases in which the courts have said that the question is not whether responsibility *has been* assumed, but

---

1 [1964] AC 465 (HL).
2 *Henderson v Merrett Syndicates Ltd* [1995] 2 AC 145 (HL).
3 *Spring v Guardian Assurance plc* [1995] 2 AC 296 (HL).
4 *White v Jones* [1995] 2 AC 207 (HL).
5 *Phelps v Hillingdon London Borough Council* [2001] 2 AC 619 (HL).
6 *Barrett v Ministry of Defence* [1995] 1 WLR 1217 (CA).
7 K Barker, 'Unreliable Assumptions in the Modern Law of Negligence' (1993) 109 *LQR* 461.
8 Eg J Weir, 'Liability for Syntax' [1963] *CLJ* 216; N McBride and A Hughes, '*Hedley Byrne* in the House of Lords: an Interpretation' (1995) 15 *Legal Studies* 376.

whether it should be *deemed* to be assumed in the circumstances.[9] 'Deeming' that responsibility has been assumed suggests that the decision to recognise a duty of care has been taken for reasons that are being concealed. Ultimately this concern that the assumption of responsibility test was not an accurate reflection of the real reasons for a decision led to the formulation of a new, rival test in *Caparo Industries plc v Dickman*, where it was asked whether damage to the claimant was foreseeable; whether there was sufficient proximity of relationship between the claimant and the defendant; and whether it was fair, just and reasonable to impose a duty of care.[10] The *Hedley Byrne* test and this new test coexisted unhappily until the decision in *Customs and Excise Commissioners v Barclays Bank plc*.[11] There the Court of Appeal obliterated *Hedley Byrne*, making no reference to it in its judgments and asserting that the assumption of responsibility test must always yield the same results as the *Caparo* test.[12] Fortunately the case was appealed to the House of Lords, where the distinctive significance of the *Hedley Byrne* principle was acknowledged. In passing, their Lordships also indicated that the 'deeming' of an assumption of responsibility was not the right approach: the *Hedley Byrne* principle would lose its utility if it was stretched too far by forcing situations into it.[13]

The second criticism of the *Hedley Byrne* principle has wider theoretical and practical ramifications. As a matter of theory, it has been a source of unease in some quarters that *Hedley Byrne* creates liability where no contractual claim would lie. The focus, it is argued, should be on reforming those contract doctrines which have made the use of the *Hedley Byrne* test necessary.[14] On the other hand, some judges have taken the view that the circumvention of contractual requirements such as consideration and privity, which can be achieved by using the *Hedley Byrne* principle, is a bonus.[15] More fundamentally, there have been arguments that *Hedley Byrne* does not truly belong in negligence at all: it is really either part of fiduciary relationships[16] or the law of contract.[17] Of course, there are similarities between contract, fiduciary relationships and the

---

[9] *Smith v Eric S Bush* [1990] 1 AC 831, 862 (Lord Griffiths). The tension between the rival approaches is particularly vivid in *Merrett v Babb* [2001] QB 1174 (CA).

[10] [1990] 2 AC 605, 617–18 (Lord Bridge).

[11] [2004] EWHC 122 (Comm), [2004] 1 WLR 2027; [2004] EWCA Civ 1555, [2005] 1 WLR 2082; [2006] UKHL 28, [2007] 1 AC 181.

[12] See in particular [2004] EWCA Civ, [2005] 1 WLR 2082 [23] (Longmore LJ). For criticism of the Court of Appeal's decision see C Mitchell and P Mitchell, 'Negligence Liability for Pure Economic Loss' (2005) 121 *LQR* 194.

[13] See in particular [2006] UKHL 28, [2007] 1 AC 181 [35] (Lord Hoffmann) and [52] (Lord Rodger).

[14] J Fleming 'Comparative Law of Torts' (1984) 4 *OJLS* 235, 240–41.

[15] *Hedley Byrne*, above n 1, 517 (Lord Devlin) (consideration); *White v Jones*, above n 4, 262–63 (per Lord Goff) (consideration and privity).

[16] McBride and Hughes, above n 8.

[17] A Beever, *Rediscovering the Law of Negligence* (Oxford, Hart Publishing, 2007) ch 8.

Hedley Byrne principle, but there are also differences. Contracts always require consideration, the *Hedley Byrne* principle does not; *Hedley Byrne* liability requires proof of damage, liability for breach of contract does not.[18] Breach of fiduciary duty does not require proof of fault; liability under *Hedley Byrne* is fault-based. The merits of eliminating those differences are beyond the scope of this chapter. The point is that, even after more than 40 years shaping the development of the law of negligence, the *Hedley Byrne* principle has still somehow not been fully accepted. It is a paradox.

This chapter goes about elucidating the importance and role of the *Hedley Byrne* case in three stages. First, it analyses how the House of Lords came to its decision, looking both at the principles created and the authorities used. Secondly, it looks at the immediate factors influencing the form and substance of the decision. Finally, it places the decision in the context of assumpsit duties. As will be seen, assumpsit duties have a long and continuous history in the common law, which is only hinted at in the speeches in *Hedley Byrne*. In essence, such duties arose where one party gratuitously undertook to act for the benefit of another and carelessly misperformed. They do not fit neatly into tort, contract or any other modern legal category because they predate the creation of those categories. *Hedley Byrne*, it will be argued, is best understood as a reassertion of a very old idea about liability in a world of modern legal categories. Its novelty lies, paradoxically, in its articulation of a principle that would have been obvious to a fourteenth century lawyer.

B. THE DECISIONS

1. Facts

Easipower Ltd, a manufacturer of electrical goods, wished to advertise its products in the press and on television. It approached the claimants, an advertising agency, to act for it. By agreeing to act, the claimants inevitably exposed themselves to financial risk, because, at that time, television companies and newspaper proprietors insisted that only 'recognised advertising agents' could place orders for advertising space, on terms by which the advertising agents would be personally liable.[19] It was, therefore, crucial for the claimants to be confident that Easipower would be able to reimburse it for any advertising space it purchased.

---

18 See the compelling criticisms of J Neyers, 'On the Right(s) Path' (2008) 19 *King's Law Journal* 413, 417–21.
19 House of Lords Library, *Appeal Cases* 1963, no 1107, Appendix, 36 (judgment of McNair J).

The claimants placed various orders on Easipower's behalf. They then sought reassurance about the risk by asking their bank, the National Provincial, to make inquiries with Heller and Partners, Easipower's bank, about whether Easipower should be able to meet the £8,000–9,000 liability to which these contracts committed it. The National Provincial did as requested, making a telephone call to the defendants. Heller's note of the conversation was as follows:[20]

> Person called L Heller, re Easipower Ltd. They wanted to know in confidence, and without responsibility on our part, the respectability and standing of Easipower Ltd, and whether it would be good for an advertising contract of £8,000 to £9,000. I replied that the company recently opened an account with us. Believed to be respectably constituted and considered good for its normal business engagements. The company is a subsidiary of Pena Industries Ltd, which is in liquidation, but we understand that the managing director, FR Williams, is endeavouring to buy the shares of Easipower from the liquidator. We believe that the company would not undertake any commitments it is unable to fulfil.

The substance of the reference was passed on to the claimants. Easipower went into liquidation shortly afterwards, its liabilities to the claimants unsatisfied. The claimants stated that, had a more accurate account of Easipower's financial position been given, they would have cancelled the contracts and, therefore, reduced their exposure.

2. Trial

At the trial before McNair J both the existence of a duty and its breach were disputed. The breach point turned on the particular wording of the reference. Essentially it was said that the reference was in fact carefully guarded and neutral; the National Provincial Bank should have realised this and read between the lines. McNair J rejected this argument. In his view, the reference as a whole could not be read in the limited way for which the defendant contended.[21]

The duty issue raised wider questions. Could a duty of care be owed in negligence in this kind of situation? McNair J approached this question by applying the House of Lords' decision in *Nocton v Lord Ashburton*,[22] where it had been held that a duty to take care in respect of negligent statements could arise in a contractual relationship and in a fiduciary one. Here, the judge observed, there was neither a contract (no consideration) nor a fiduciary relationship. Nor did the fact that Easipower was

---

[20] *Hedley Byrne & Co Ltd v Heller & Partners Ltd* [1962] 1 QB 396 (CA) 398.
[21] House of Lords Library, *Appeal Cases* 1963, no 1107, Appendix, 43–44.
[22] [1914] AC 932 (HL).

dependent on its bankers for financial support create any special relationship between the claimants and the defendants. McNair J also hinted that, even if there had been some special relationship between the parties, it was not open to him, given the authorities, to recognise a duty of care.[23]

3. Court of Appeal

When the case reached the Court of Appeal,[24] the state of the authorities played a similarly powerful role. The claimants indicated that they wished to argue that the general principle of duty of care formulated by Lord Atkin in *Donoghue v Stevenson*[25] should apply. They also acknowledged, however, that it was not open to them to make such an argument in the Court of Appeal, since that Court was bound by its own earlier decision in *Candler v Crane, Christmas & Co*[26] that the general *Donoghue* principle did not apply.[27] Pearson LJ, giving a judgment in which both Ormerod and Harman LJJ concurred, agreed.[28] Similarly, he said that the authorities gave no support to the idea that a special relation between the defendant and the subject of a reference could give rise to a duty.[29] At the very end of this judgment, however, he indicated that the state of the authorities was not a cause for regret. It would have been 'wholly unreasonable' to require a banker in the position of the defendants to spend time searching records and weighing up the evidence before producing 'a well-balanced and well-worded report'.[30]

4. House of Lords

(a) Principles

In the House of Lords, three distinct points were addressed. First, could a duty of care arise in respect of a statement causing purely economic loss? Secondly, did the circumstances of this case give rise to a duty? Thirdly, was the defendant's giving the reference 'without responsibility' sufficient to exclude any liability? The House of Lords unanimously held that a duty of care could arise in respect of negligent statements causing purely economic

---

23 House of Lords Library, *Appeal Cases 1963*, no 1107, Appendix, 49.
24 [1962] 1 QB 396 (CA).
25 [1932] AC 562 (HL).
26 [1951] 2 KB 164 (CA).
27 [1962] 1 QB 396, 399–400.
28 Ibid, 412.
29 Ibid, 414.
30 Ibid.

loss; and that the disclaimer was effective to exclude liability. They tentatively found, by a majority, that there was no duty on the facts in any case.

The first issue, the point of general principle, was dealt with in slightly different ways by the five Law Lords. Each of them agreed that it was not a simple matter of applying the neighbour principle from *Donoghue v Stevenson*. For Lord Reid this was because negligent words and negligent acts were different. Words could be, and often were, spoken casually, on informal or social occasions, when it would be unreasonable to impose liability. Defective articles, by contrast, were only rarely put into circulation. Furthermore, defective articles would typically cause a single accident, following which the defendant's liability would come to an end. Words, on the other hand, could easily be repeated, and it would be 'going very far'[31] to impose liability to everyone who relied on those words to his or her detriment. Lord Hodson took a similar view, commenting that, whilst the principle in *Donoghue* was not confined to physical damage and damage to property, it had never been applied to statements.[32]

Lord Devlin's approach was distinctively different. For him, the attempt to apply *Donoghue v Stevenson* to the facts was misconceived, because Lord Atkin's principle was a 'general conception' that should be used 'to open up a category of cases'.[33] Those categories required their own detailed rules, which should draw on existing categories. In short, *Donoghue* showed 'how the law can be developed to solve particular problems',[34] but did not specify how the particular problem in *Hedley Byrne* should be solved. Lord Pearce took elements of both Lord Reid's and Lord Devlin's approaches, saying that *Donoghue* could not be read as if it was dealing with 'negligence in word causing economic damage'.[35] It had nothing to say about the 'problems peculiar to negligence in words'[36] and could, therefore, only be read as 'affording some analogy from the broad outlook which it imposed on the law relating to physical negligence'.[37]

What, then, could be used to develop liability in place of the *Donoghue* principle? Lord Reid thought that the 'most natural requirement would be that expressly or by implication from the circumstances the speaker or writer has undertaken some responsibility'.[38] Lord Morris agreed with this general idea, and valuably elaborated on when such an undertaking of responsibility might be implicit: he had in mind advice given by professional people such as accountants, solicitors or doctors. The essence of it

31 [1964] AC 465, 483.
32 Ibid, 506.
33 Ibid, 524.
34 Ibid, 525.
35 Ibid, 536.
36 Ibid.
37 Ibid.
38 Ibid, 483.

was that the advice 'should be the result of an exercise of the skill and judgment required by [the defendant] in his calling' and the defendant 'knows and intends that its accuracy will be relied upon by another'.[39] Lord Hodson put the same point slightly differently: a duty was to be imposed 'where persons hold themselves out as possessing special skills and are thus under a duty to exercise it with reasonable care'.[40] For Lord Devlin the key was that there was 'a responsibility that is voluntarily accepted or undertaken'.[41] It was impossible to set out exhaustively the circumstances from which a voluntary undertaking could be implied, but Lord Devlin was happy to adopt the formulation of any of the other judges. Lord Pearce's speech reiterated the themes of Lord Morris's and Lord Hodson's speeches: 'if persons holding themselves out in a calling or situation or profession take on a task within that calling or situation or profession, they have a duty of skill and care'.[42]

When it came to applying this general principle to the facts of the case, the analysis was perfunctory. Their Lordships were unanimous that the basis on which the reference had been given was 'without responsibility'. Therefore, no duty could arise. Whether there would have been a duty in the absence of an understanding that there was no responsibility is rather difficult to pin down. Lord Morris tentatively[43] and Lord Hodson more confidently[44] held that there would have been no duty anyway; Lord Devlin disagreed.[45] Lord Reid and Lord Pearce did not commit themselves either way.

(b) Authorities

Both the trial judge and the Court of Appeal had felt constrained by the authorities. In the House of Lords, those same authorities represented a significant, though not insuperable, obstacle to the recognition of a duty of care. Their Lordships distinguished and reinterpreted some authorities that stood in the way, overruled others and reinstated decisions that had previously been disapproved.

The two main obstacles were the Court of Appeal's decision in *Candler*[46] and the House of Lords' decision in *Derry v Peek*.[47] The *Candler* case concerned negligent statements by an accountant about the financial position of a company. The recipient of the statements was a

[39] Ibid, 497.
[40] Ibid, 510.
[41] Ibid, 529.
[42] Ibid, 538.
[43] Ibid, 504.
[44] Ibid, 512–13.
[45] Ibid, 532.
[46] Above n 26.
[47] (1889) 14 App Cas 337 (HL).

potential investor, and the accountant was fully aware that his statements would be relied on in making the decision whether to invest or not. A majority of the Court of Appeal held that no duty arose: there was no general duty of care for statements. Denning LJ dissented. For him, a duty was owed by accountants, surveyors, valuers and analysts both to their employers and to third parties to whom either they or their employers showed their reports, knowing that the purpose was to prompt an investment decision. Whilst the Court of Appeal in *Hedley Byrne* was bound by the majority's decision, the House of Lords was able to approve Lord Denning's dissent.

The House of Lords' decision in *Derry* was more problematic for two reasons. First, the House of Lords was not yet free to depart from its earlier decisions—that would not occur until the Practice Direction in 1966. Secondly, several cases had expounded the significance of *Derry* for the tort of negligence: any reinterpretation of the case would also necessitate a readjustment of those subsequent cases.

Derry concerned liability in deceit. It held that the fraud necessary for liability in that tort must consist of actual knowledge that the statement was false or recklessness as to whether it was true or not. A defendant who genuinely, although unreasonably, believed the truth of what he said was not fraudulent. Thus, a negligently made false statement gave rise to no liability in deceit.

In terms of the tort of deceit, the decision was a controversial one—as Pollock was quick to point out.[48] Over the course of the nineteenth century, a broader idea of what could be regarded as fraud had been emerging, most recently in the Court of Appeal's decision in *Peek v Derry*;[49] that broader idea embraced negligent misrepresentations. Several US jurisdictions would remain unpersuaded by the House of Lords' narrower test.[50] However, the House of Lords' decision was also seen as having a broader message, namely, that tortious liability for statements required fraud in the strict sense. Thus, on the facts of *Derry* itself—which concerned a misrepresentation in a company's prospectus—the House of Lords was taken as having held, implicitly, that no duty of care in negligence existed between the company's directors and a purchaser of shares who had relied on the misrepresentation.[51] This broad reading of the decision in *Derry's* case was used to overturn earlier cases, where a duty had been identified to take care

---

[48] F Pollock, 'Derry v Peek in the House of Lords' (1889) 5 *LQR* 410.

[49] (1887) 37 ChD 541 (CA).

[50] See further, the criticisms in S Williston, 'Liability for Honest Misrepresentation' (1910–11) 24 *Harvard Law Review* 415. Some of the problems faced by jurisdictions rejecting the narrower view of fraud are highlighted in F Bohlen, 'Misrepresentation as Deceit, Negligence or Warranty' (1929) 42 *Harvard Law Review* 733.

[51] *Low v Bouverie* [1891] 3 Ch 82 (CA) 105 (Bowen LJ); *Le Lievre v Gould* [1893] 1 QB 491 (CA) 501–02 (Bowen LJ); J Smith, 'Liability for Negligent Language' (1900–01) 14 *Harvard Law Review* 184, 185.

in making statements that resulted in purely financial loss. In *Cann v Willson*,[52] for instance, Chitty J had held that a valuer making a valuation for a mortgage owed a duty to the mortgagee. The judge had relied on the Court of Appeal's decision in *Peek v Derry*, and a general idea of duty of care derived from *Heaven v Pender*.[53] In *Le Lievre v Gould*,[54] decided after the House of Lords had decided *Derry*, the Court of Appeal held that reliance on the Court of Appeal's decision in *Derry* was now wrong; and any general notion of duty only applied to physical damage. *Cann* was, therefore, wrongly decided.

In one important respect, the cases interpreting the significance of *Derry* for liability in negligence went even further than the House of Lords itself had indicated. Lord Herschell had been careful to say that the requirement of fraud did not apply to situations where

> a person within whose special province it lay to know a particular fact, has given an erroneous answer to an inquiry made with regard to it by a person desirous of ascertaining the fact for the purpose of determining his course.[55]

That seemed to leave open the possibility of imposing negligence liability on those claiming expert knowledge about a subject, and advising others about it. In *Low v Bouverie*,[56] however, it was held that no duty was owed by a trustee who negligently misinformed the claimant about incumbrances on the trust fund, which induced the claimant to deal with the beneficiary under the trust. As with the decision in *Le Lievre*, the Court of Appeal disapproved earlier authorities in order to reach this restrictive conclusion.[57]

Eventually the tide turned against this expansive reading of *Derry v Peek*. In *Nocton v Lord Ashburton*[58] the House of Lords warned against interpreting *Derry* too broadly.[59] It should not, for instance, be seen as imposing a requirement of fraud where there was a fiduciary relationship. Other observations in *Nocton* could be seen as expanding the exceptions to *Derry* further. Of particular significance was Lord Shaw's remark that a duty would arise where the situation was equivalent to contract.[60] A year later, in *Robinson v The National Bank of Scotland Limited*[61] Lord Haldane was emphatic:[62]

---

[52] (1888) 39 ChD 39 (Ch).
[53] (1883) 11 QBD 503 (CA).
[54] [1893] 1 QB 491 (CA).
[55] *Derry*, above n 47, 360.
[56] [1891] 3 Ch 82 (CA).
[57] *Burrowes v Lock* (1805) 10 Ves Jun 470, 32 ER 927; *Slim v Croucher* (1860) 1 De G F & J 518, 45 ER 462.
[58] [1914] AC 932 (HL).
[59] See in particular Lord Haldane at 947–48 and Lord Shaw at 969–71.
[60] Ibid, 972.
[61] 1916 SC (HL) 154.
[62] Ibid, 157.

an exaggerated view was taken by a good many people of the scope of the decision in *Derry v Peek*. The whole of the doctrine as to fiduciary relationships, as to the duty of care arising from implied as well as express contracts, as to the duty of care arising from other special relationships which the Courts may find to exist in particular cases, still remains, and I should be very sorry if any word fell from me which should suggest that the Courts are in any way hampered in recognising that the duty of care may be established when such cases really occur.

When the House of Lords in *Hedley Byrne* came to deal with this mass of authorities on *Derry* it seized on the indications given in *Nocton* and *Robinson*. Lord Devlin gave particular emphasis to the importance of separating what had actually been decided in *Derry* from what it was widely assumed to have decided; only the former was binding[63]. Of course, that was not to say that *Nocton* and *Robinson* supplied the voluntary assumption of responsibility test; they did not. Nor was it obvious what was to be included in addition to fiduciary relationships. The reference to contracts in *Robinson* was not helpful at first sight, since contractual liability was not in issue. Lord Reid, however, saw it as significant that *Robinson* was a Scottish appeal (Scots law did not require consideration for a valid contract), so the House of Lords could be seen as envisaging liability for gratuitous undertakings.[64] Similarly, Lord Devlin made use of Lord Shaw's comments in *Nocton* that liability would arise in situations equivalent to contract.[65] This less restrictive approach to *Derry* allowed their Lordships to reinstate the decision in *Cann v Willson*,[66] and cleared the way for the principle of assumption of responsibility.

By contrast with this mass of interrelated authorities on a duty of care for statements, the English authorities cited in support of the assumption of responsibility principle itself were meagre and elderly. Even Lord Hodson admitted that they were 'old'.[67] None of them had been decided within the previous century, and none involved negligent advice. In themselves, they seemed a slender basis for an important new development. The most convincing case referred to was *Glanzer v Shepard*,[68] but that, as a decision of the Court of Appeals of New York, could only be illustrative of how English law might be developed.

More will be said about the status of the principle of assumption of responsibility in the final section of this chapter. Before that, however, a different question must be addressed: why did the House of Lords go to all this trouble, finding its way through a morass of case law, when it was going to dispose of the case on the simple 'without responsibility' point?

---

63 *Hedley Byrne*, above n 1, 519.
64 Ibid, 492.
65 Ibid, 530.
66 Above n 52.
67 *Hedley Byrne*, above n 1, 510.
68 135 NE 275 (1922).

C. THE JUDICIAL PROCESS

What *Hedley Byrne* decided, and how it reached its conclusion, is inextricably linked to timing and personnel. In 1963 the House of Lords as a judicial body was in transition. Throughout the 1950s, under the leadership of Viscount Simonds, the House had taken a very limited view of its role in developing the common law. Certainty and precedent were the dominant themes.[69] By the early 1960s, however, a more nuanced approach was starting to appear. Bold creativity of the kind practised by Lord Denning was still untypical, but there was an emerging sense that certain legal areas, at least, were suitable for judicial development. Lord Reid, for instance, worked out a careful strategy in which the law of tort was regarded as a suitable candidate for elaboration.[70] Lord Radcliffe—in lectures given to American students—argued that judges should subtly change the law whilst making it appear the same.[71] This was hardly militant judicial activism, and it would not be until 1966 that the House of Lords would claim to be able to overrule its own decisions. But the scope for, and appropriateness of, a little judicial creativity was being recognised.

Certain features of the *Hedley Byrne* decision clearly reflect this transitional phase in the House of Lords. The most obvious is the treatment of authority. The Law Lords were being more assertive in their attitude to authority, as some commentators immediately noticed.[72] At the same time, however, they could not be as independent as they might have liked. It was still not permissible to say that if *Derry* decided that there could be no tortious liability for statements in the absence of fraud, it was wrong. Instead, *Derry* had to be distinguished, and the only way to do that was to say that if the claimant had brought a claim in negligence, the result might have been different. As Goodhart pointed out, this was rather difficult to believe.[73] A second feature of *Hedley Byrne* that reflects prevailing ideas about the House of Lords' own role in judicial development was the reasoning supporting a duty. Lord Pearce spoke of a social policy dimension in recognising a duty of care,[74] but this was very much the

---

69 A Paterson, *The Law Lords* (Basingstoke, Macmillan, 1982) ch 6; R Stevens, '*Hedley Byrne v Heller*: Judicial Creativity and Doctrinal Possibility' (1964) 27 *MLR* 121, 126–30; Simonds, 'Law' in E Barker (ed), *The Character of England* (Oxford, Clarendon Press, 1947) 112, esp 115–17.

70 Lord Reid, 'The Law and the Reasonable Man' (1968) 54 *Proceedings of the British Academy* 189; Lord Reid, 'The Judge as Law Maker' (1972) 22 *Journal of the Society of Public Teachers of Law* ns 22.

71 Lord Radcliffe, *The Law and its Compass* (London, 1961) esp 39.

72 H Street, 'The Twentieth Century Development and Function of the Law of Tort in England' (1965) 14 *ICLQ* 862, 863; V Palmer, 'Offenses and Quasi-offences—Negligence—The Duty of Careful Statement' (1963) 38 *Tulane Law Review* 197; Stevens, above n 69, 133.

73 A Goodhart, 'Liability for Innocent but Negligent Misrepresentations' (1964) 74 *Yale Law Journal* 286, 291.

74 *Hedley Byrne*, above n 1, 536.

exception. The other speeches focused instead on drawing together threads from cases that were 100 years old or more. Here it seems that the judges were being careful to avoid becoming embroiled in anything that looked like social engineering. Certainly, the approach is strikingly different to the current overt discussion of matters of policy in novel duty cases.

So far as the personnel involved were concerned, there is a fascinating background of alternatives and alterations. To begin with counsel, the defendants were represented throughout by John Foster QC, but the claimants changed their counsel for the House of Lords. In the Court of Appeal they had been represented by SBR Cooke QC, a future High Court judge and chairman of the Law Commission; for the appeal to the House of Lords they brought in Gerald Gardiner QC. Why Cooke was replaced is unclear; certainly there is no radical difference of approach between Cooke and Gardiner, so far as the summaries of the arguments show. It may have been a matter of availability, but it could also have been a strategic change. Gardiner was well known for his interest in law reform, having been a member of the Law Reform Committee for over a decade. Among the Committee's proposals was a recommendation, made in 1962 (after the Court of Appeal's judgment, before the appeal to the Lords), to expand liability for misrepresentations that induced the misrepresentee to enter a contract. The key feature of these proposals was that negligence, rather than fraud, should be the basis of the misrepresentor's liability.[75] Gardiner had also taken over the editorship (with Andrew Martin) of a volume of essays on law reform, which was produced under the auspices of the Society for Labour Lawyers.[76] That volume would not appear until 11 July 1963,[77] which was two months after the House of Lords delivered judgment in *Hedley Byrne*. However, it is striking that the chapter on contract and tort, by Aubrey Diamond, called for recognition of liability for pure economic loss along the lines advocated by Lord Denning in *Candler*.[78] That proposal was, of course, obsolete before it appeared in print, but Gardiner, as editor, would have been aware of it before he argued *Hedley Byrne*. The attraction of instructing a reform-minded QC on a point that he already regarded as one of 'those reforms in our law, which [he] would like to see carried out by the next Labour Government'[79] was obvious. Rumours of Gardiner's being a future Labour Lord Chancellor might also have been influential.[80]

---

[75] Law Reform Committee, Tenth Report: Innocent Misrepresentation (1962). The Committee's recommendations were eventually enacted in 1967 as the Misrepresentation Act.
[76] G Gardiner and A Martin (eds), *Law Reform NOW* (London, Victor Gollancz, 1963).
[77] The review in *The Times*, on that date, described the book as "published today".
[78] A Diamond, 'The Law of Contract and Tort' in Gardiner and Martin, ibid, 57, 74–75.
[79] Gardiner and Martin, ibid, x.
[80] M Box, *Rebel Advocate; A Biography of Gerald Gardiner* (London, Victor Gollancz, 1983) 141–42 describes Gardiner being approached by Arnold Goodman and Harold Wilson about becoming Lord Chancellor immediately after the appearance of *Law Reform NOW*. Harry

Gardiner, of course, could only present the arguments; it was for the judges to decide whether to accept them. Who those judges were was a surprisingly complex story. One of them might easily have been Lord Denning, who reported that, although he had been asked to sit, he had declined on the ground that his judgment in *Candler*'s case would come under scrutiny.[81] Denning did not say who had issued the invitation, but it was most likely to have come from George Coldstream, the Permanent Secretary at the Lord Chancellor's Office. Coldstream made a point of extensive consultation with the judiciary, calling on senior judges as part of his daily routine.[82] The panel, as originally constituted, consisted of Lord Radcliffe, Lord Cohen, Lord MacDermott, Lord Jenkins and Lord Guest.[83] Cohen clearly did not feel inhibited by the prospect of his judgment in *Candler* being scrutinised. However, after the first day of argument, Lord Radcliffe was appointed to the Vassell Tribunal, necessitating a fresh start. The new panel consisted of Lord Reid, Lord Morris, Lord Hodson, Lord Devlin and Lord Pearce.

What might have happened if Lord Denning had said yes, or the Vassell Tribunal had appointed someone else, is difficult to say, but it seems unlikely that any decision about a duty would have been unanimous, since there was no sign that either Lord Cohen or Lord Denning had changed their minds since their disagreement in *Candler*'s case. Lord Radcliffe might well have found himself unable to subscribe to Denning's overt activism.[84] The most likely outcome would probably have been a short judgment for the defendant on the basis that no responsibility had been assumed.

Among the judges to whom it ultimately fell to decide the case, a range of backgrounds and styles could be seen. Lord Hodson was perhaps the least well placed to deal with this kind of case, having studied classics then specialising in divorce law. Lord Devlin's entry on Hodson in the *Oxford Dictionary of National Biography* rather cuttingly describes him as having 'left little or no mark on the law. He took the law as he found it, whether he liked it or not.'[85] Whatever the merits of this criticism as applied to other cases, it certainly does not reflect Hodson's contribution to *Hedley Byrne*. Here he engaged in a full analysis of the broader issues, particularly the assumption of responsibility. Lord Morris and Lord Pearce, with

Street, reviewing *Law Reform NOW*, regarded Gardiner as an obvious choice for the post—(1964) 27 *MLR* 237.

81 A Denning, *The Discipline of Law* (London, Butterworths, 1979) 245.

82 D Oulton, 'Coldstream, Sir George Phillips' in *Oxford Dictionary of National Biography* (online edn).

83 Stevens, above n 69, 130 note 34.

84 See Radcliffe's cautious exposition of judicial creativity in *The Law and its Compass*, above n 71.

85 Lord Devlin, 'Hodson, Francis Lord Charlton [Charles]' in *Oxford Dictionary of National Biography* (online edn).

backgrounds as common law judges,[86] could be expected to be comfortable with the broader issues. Similarly, Lord Reid regarded it as an important part of his role to move the law in the right direction,[87] so it is not unsurprising that he considered the broad principle of duty of care for statements causing purely economic loss.

However, there still remains the question why their Lordships chose to engage in such elaborate analyses when, on the facts, no duty arose. To conclude, after this elaborate analysis, that there was only liability for fraud was, as Tony Honoré put it, to go 'to the village church via the moon'.[88] The driving force was Lord Devlin.

Devlin's crucial role is highlighted in Lord Reid's notebook on the *Hedley Byrne* case.[89] Reid's detailed notes indicate the depth into which counsel went, and reveal his own ideas forming. Early on, for instance, he asks 'Is it words v acts or financial v physical loss?',[90] a question not completely resolved by his own speech.[91] Most importantly, however, Reid noted the preliminary views of his colleagues once the argument had concluded.[92] Both Lord Pearce and Lord Hodson placed the 'without responsibility' point at the forefront of their analyses. Lord Pearce hinted at some of the ideas that would appear in his speech—such as the link between duty of care and social policy—but Lord Hodson remained quite fact-specific. Lord Morris took a more general approach, but there was no indication of the ideas about the basis for liability which would subsequently appear in his decision. Lord Devlin, judging from Reid's notes, spoke for longest. This is what Reid recorded:[93]

Deal with general point.

Nocton explains Derry + overrules reasoning in Lievre

Was fiduciary the only one—NO. Special

Donoghue shews p[roper?] approach to special duty but not precise criteria

Overrule Candler

1. *voluntary* undertaking—requires care

---

[86] Lord Edmund-Davies, 'Morris, John William' in *Oxford Dictionary of National Biography* (online edn); J Comyn, 'Pearce, Edward Holroyd' in *Oxford Dictionary of National Biography* (online edn).

[87] Paterson, above n 69, 170–75.

[88] A Honoré, '*Hedley Byrne & Co Ltd v Heller & Partners, Ltd*' (1964–1965) 8 *Journal of the Society of Public Teachers of Law* ns 284, 291.

[89] House of Lords Archive. Pages not numbered. Subsequent page references ascertained by the author.

[90] Ibid, 16.

[91] J Stapleton, 'Duty of Care and Economic Loss: A Wider Agenda' (1991) 107 *LQR* 249, 259–60.

[92] Paterson, above n 69, ch 5, particularly 92.

[93] Notebook, 32.

Contract but for consideration

2. Like Restatement—course of business etc.

Both take existing *line* of authority.

Without resp. not as if contract duty already

Beginning of that w[or]k w[oul]d create relationship

Devlin already had a clear and compelling view of the case, which would be reflected in his speech. Two points are particularly striking: first, the emphasis on dealing with the general point; and secondly, the insistence that the solution be built on an existing line of authority. Both were characteristic of Devlin's judicial approach.

A major theme of Lord Devlin's extrajudicial writings, both before and after the *Hedley Byrne* case, was the very limited scope for judicial development of the common law. Thus, in 1962 he had written that 'I doubt if judges will now of their own motion contribute much more to the development of the law'.[94] Things had been better in the past, but now, in Devlin's view, the appellate courts were swamped with cases on statutory construction.[95] Devlin used cases reported in the Appeal Cases volume from 1959 to illustrate his point; by 1963 things were no better, although the 1964 volume (which included *Hedley Byrne*) showed some improvement.[96] Readers of Devlin's work across the Atlantic thought that he was being too pessimistic,[97] but in 1964 he took early retirement. Tony Honoré, writing Devlin's entry in the *Oxford Dictionary of National Biography*, records that he had found the work of an appellate judge 'dreary'.[98]

Devlin viewed the lack of opportunity to develop the law of tort with particular regret. As it stood (in 1962), it was unsatisfactory: liability for physical damage had started to become more systematic following Lord Atkin's exposition of duty of care in *Donoghue v Stevenson*, but the handling of economic damage was still 'rudimentary'.[99] This part of the law, he continued, [100]

---

94 P Devlin, *Samples of Lawmaking* (London, Oxford University Press, 1962) 23.

95 Ibid, 5.

96 The 1964 Appeal Cases volume included *Lewis v Daily Telegraph Ltd* [1964] AC 234 (defamation), *H West & Son v Shephard* [1964] AC 326 (personal injury), *Dingle v Associated Newspapers Ltd* [1964] AC 371 (defamation) and *Rookes v Barnard* [1964] AC 1129 (economic torts, and exemplary damages), in addition to *Hedley Byrne*.

97 J Dawson, 'Review of P Devlin *Samples of Lawmaking*' (1963–64) 15 *University of Toronto Law Journal* 478, 480; H Friendly, 'The Gap in Lawmaking—Judges Who Can't and Legislators Who Won't' (1963) 63 *Columbia Law Review* 787: 'This resigned attitude is hardly what would be expected of a man with the fighting name of Patrick Devlin' (787).

98 T Honoré, 'Devlin, Patrick Arthur' in *Oxford Dictionary of National Biography* (online edn).

99 Devlin, above n 94, 8.

100 Ibid.

still awaits a unifying principle. Is there any reason in logic why the duty laid down in *Donoghue* . . . should not be extended to every sort of injury of which the law takes cognizance? So far negligence has failed to jump the fence between the physical and the non-physical.

The absence of principle was almost a cause of personal embarrassment: 'Most of us are apologetic about the apparent inability of the common law to give relief for the consequence of injurious carelessness of this sort.' He had made the same point in a lecture to students the previous year.[101] The solution, he suggested, was available judicially: the argument for a duty of care in respect of pure economic loss had failed in *Candler*[102] 'not on its merits, being defeated by force of authority, so that it might fare differently in the House of Lords'.[103] Devlin clearly thought that Denning's conclusion was the right one.

However, whilst Devlin agreed with Denning's conclusion, he would not follow Denning's methods. Respect for precedent was fundamental—otherwise cases would turn, arbitrarily, on one individual judge's view.[104] The way forward was not to disregard precedent, but to encourage it to divide and expand: precedent was both the 'life force' of the common law and the factor that prevented it collapsing into a collection of single instances. What guided the expansion of precedent was existing principle: it was the courts' role to recognise new instances of existing principles, and Parliament's role to create any new principles.[105] In this way, Devlin thought, the common law would grow organically.[106]

In *Hedley Byrne* Lord Devlin can be seen to be implementing his own previously declared legal philosophy. He regarded liability for negligently inflicted pure economic loss as a prime subject for judicial development, and when the rare opportunity arose to contribute to that development he seized it. The method of development was to invoke an existing legal principle—the assumption of responsibility—and apply it to a new instance. Judicial legislation was out of the question. Devlin's powerful analysis, which can be seen fully formed at the conclusion of the arguments, convinced and galvanised his colleagues.

---

[101] P Devlin 'Morals and the Quasi-Criminal Law and the Law of Tort' in P Devlin *The Enforcement of Morals* (Oxford, Oxford University Press, 1965) 26, 41–42. The lecture was originally delivered in 1961 (see asterisked footnote on page 26).

[102] Above n 26.

[103] Devlin, above n 94, 9.

[104] Ibid, 19–23 and 115.

[105] Ibid, 22–23.

[106] See in particular the biological metaphors used at 115: the common law is said to be an 'organism', made up of the 'cells' of precedent, which divide and multiply; further down the page precedents are said to be like branches of a tree, from which 'young shoots . . . can be trained this way or that'.

D. ASSUMPSIT DUTIES

Lord Devlin had convinced his colleagues of the merits of the assumption of responsibility principle, but he did not convince the commentators. A flood of articles and notes followed the decision, in many of which there was a note of regret that more emphasis had not been given to simple foreseeability as the basis of the duty. At their most extreme, these articles and notes claimed that *Hedley Byrne* actually was,[107] or in effect was,[108] based on foreseeability. A more accurate reading was given by Goodhart, but he went on to lament that a broader duty test had not been used, coupled with a more rigorous test of breach of duty.[109]

Patrick Atiyah and Tony Weir criticised the assumption of responsibility test directly. Atiyah doubted how its use could be consistent with Devlin's extrajudicial pronouncements that no new principle could be judicially created.[110] Weir attacked the suitability of the test head-on: [111]

> This sounds very curiously in a tort suit. One does not say that a careless motorist is liable to his victim for undertaking to drive; liability is imposed because he drove carelessly. Surely, then, the man who makes careless statements is liable in negligence not because he undertook to speak but because he spoke heedlessly. This seems clear first because there would presumably be no liability for undertaking to speak and then keeping quiet, and secondly because the defendant may be liable for speaking even if he failed, unreasonably, to realise that his words were likely to be acted on. The 'undertaking', then, is nothing but the positive aspect of the absence of waiver; it is an explanatory construction, not a fact which must be separately found.

This attempt to marginalise the assumption of responsibility test, and to see it as merely a by-product of the factual situation with which the House of Lords was faced, was prompted by the sense that the test did not 'fit' the tort of negligence. More than 30 years later, Weir was even less impressed. 'Never,' he asserted, 'has there been such a judicial jamboree as *Hedley Byrne* where one almost has the feeling that their Lordships had been on a trip to Mount Olympus and perhaps smoked a joint on the

---

107 H Street, 'The Twentieth Century Development and Function of the Law of Tort in England' (1965) 14 *ICLQ* 862, 866.

108 R Atkey, 'Negligent Words: A Look at *Hedley Byrne & Co Ltd v Heller & Partners Ltd*' (1964) 3 *Western Law Review* 104, 108; A Rigrod, 'Negligence: Negligent Misrepresentation: The Concept of the Special Relation: *Hedley Byrne & Co v Heller & Partners Ltd*' (1965) 50 *Cornell Law Quarterly* 331, 332.

109 A Goodhart, 'Liability for Innocent but Negligent Misrepresentations' (1964) 74 *Yale Law Journal* 286, particularly 300. See also the similar analysis by G Dworkin, 'The Value of a Banker's Reference' (1962) 25 *MLR* 246, 248 (commenting on the Court of Appeal's decision in *Hedley Byrne*).

110 P Atiyah, 'Judges and Policy' (1980) 15 *Israel Law Review* 346, 355 note 25.

111 J Weir, 'Liability for Syntax' [1963] *CLJ* 216, 217.

112 T Weir, 'Errare Humanum Est' in P Birks (ed), *Frontiers of Liability* (Oxford, Oxford University Press, 1994) vol 2, 103, 105 n 12.

bus.'[112] A similar concern about fit could be seen in Robert Stevens's contemporary comment that the test was a 'hermaphrodite', owing something to both contract and tort.[113] Even in the most recent work on *Hedley Byrne*, nearly 50 years later, the sense remains that the case does not fit into the tort category.[114]

This section shows that this concern about 'fit' is quite right. The *Hedley Byrne* principle cannot be easily accommodated within the tort of negligence; nor does it belong in contract. That is not to say that it should be discarded, however, or obliterated by a general test of foreseeability. On the contrary, *Hedley Byrne* is the second most important case in the well-established category of liability for misperformance of gratuitous undertakings—or 'assumpsit duties', as Hobhouse J once described them.[115]

1. The Origins of Assumpsit Duties

The use of an undertaking as the basis for liability dates from at least the fourteenth century.[116] Claimants bringing actions on the case against ferrymen, surgeons, farriers and the like pleaded that the defendant undertook ('assumpsit') to carry, cure, etc carefully, but failed to do so, to the claimant's damage.[117] To a modern reader these cases are immediately recognisable as archetypal instances of negligence liability, but it must be emphasised that that was not how fourteenth-century lawyers categorised them—the emergence of the tort of negligence was several centuries away.[118] Rather, to fourteenth-century lawyers these cases were merely part of the action on the case. The lawyers recognised, of course, that certain kinds of claims brought using the action on the case had certain common

---

113 Stevens, above n 69, 161.

114 R Buxton, 'How the Common Law Gets Made: *Hedley Byrne* and Other Cautionary Tales' (2009) 125 *LQR* 60, 61, describing the case as 'difficult to fit into the general law of negligence'.

115 *General Accident Fire and Life Assurance Corporation v Tanter (The Zephyr)* [1984] 1 Lloyd's Rep 58, 84; quoted with approval by Mustill LJ on appeal: [1985] 2 Lloyd's Rep 529, 534 and 538.

116 See generally J Ames, 'The History of Assumpsit' (1888) 2 *Harvard Law Review* 1; J Baker, *An Introduction to English Legal History*, 4th edn (London, Butterworths, 2002) 329–31, 395–96 and 406–07; D Ibbetson, *A Historical Introduction to the Law of Obligations* (Oxford, Oxford University Press, 1999) ch 3. Liability based on misperformance of an undertaking was recognised in local courts before it became part of the royal courts' jurisdiction: see Baker, 329.

117 *Bukton v Townsend* (1348) YB 22 Lib Ass p 41 (ferry); *Waldon v Mareschal* (1369) YB Mich 43 Edw III fol 33 pl 38 (veterinary surgeon); *Stratton v Swanlond* (1374) YB Hil 48 Edw III fol 6 pl 11 (surgeon). See J Baker and S Milsom, *Sources of English Legal History; Private Law to 1750* (London, Butterworths, 1986) 358, 359 and 360 respectively.

118 P Winfield, 'The History of Negligence in the Law of Torts' (1926) 42 *LQR* 184, particularly 194ff (highlighting the role of abridgements).

substantive features, and that there was a potentially troubling overlap with contractual actions,[119] but the kinds of claims that could be brought by such an action were not defined by any substantive principles or criteria; they simply reflected recognised types of claim that could not be enforced by the established writs (such as the writ of trespass). The action on the case was a residual, procedural category, not a principle-based cause of action.

This had advantages and disadvantages. The main advantage was that the absence of substantive limitations enabled judges to develop the law to embrace new kinds of claim.[120] Thus, actions for misperformance of undertakings had no natural home in the scheme of writs. The closest writ to our modern tort actions was trespass, but that required an allegation of the use of force and arms, which was obviously not appropriate when the claim was about non-forcible accidents.[121] The action on the case allowed such complaints to be dealt with in the royal courts. On the other hand, the absence of substantive limitations also meant that it was impossible to identify any scientific basis for the content of the action on the case. As Winfield commented: 'The action on the case has been the life-blood of the English law of torts, but is calculated to make any professor of jurisprudence desperate.'[122]

As the action on the case developed, various strands of liability with a resemblance to *Hedley Byrne* emerged. One important strand was that of defendants professing a common calling. Where that was the case, no allegation of an express undertaking was required—an undertaking would be implied from the circumstances. The same implied undertaking was made where the defendant was exercising a public office.[123] A second strand of liability concerned undertakings by sellers as to the nature or qualities of their goods. Here the courts were careful to distinguish between mere affirmations (which incurred no liability) and undertakings or warranties (which did).[124] Eventually this category of liability would become part of the law of contract, with the decisive question in litigation being whether the defendant intended to promise that what he was asserting was true.[125]

---

119 See, eg the argument in *Bukton v Townsend*, above n 117, over whether the claim should have been brought in covenant.

120 See Ibbetson, above n 116, 56, describing trespass on the case as having 'no inbuilt boundaries and . . . an almost unlimited potential to expand'.

121 See further Ibbetson, above n 116, 48–51.

122 Winfield, above n 118, 197.

123 Ibid, 185–89; see also P Winfield, 'Duty in Tortious Negligence' (1934) 34 *Columbia Law Review* 41, 44–47.

124 Ames, above n 116, 8–10. The leading case was *Chandelor v Lopus* (1607) Cro Jac 4, 79 ER 3.

125 *De Lassalle v Guildford* [1901] 2 KB 215; *Heilbut Symons & Co v Buckleton* [1913] AC 30; *Oscar Chess Ltd v Williams* [1957] 1 WLR 370. For compelling criticism of this categorisation see Williston, above n 50, 419–20.

A third, crucial, strand was bailment. Here the leading case was *Coggs v Bernard*,[126] in which an action on the case was brought for negligently transporting a barrel of brandy, causing it to be damaged. In a decision that would be enormously influential, both within and beyond the law of bailment, the Court of King's Bench held that the defendant was liable irrespective of the absence of consideration. For Gould J the basis of the liability was 'the particular trust reposed in the defendant, to which he has concurred by his assumption, and in the executing which he has miscarried by his neglect'.[127] Powell J was equally clear about the basis of liability: 'Now to give the reason of these cases, the gist of these actions is the undertaking.'[128] Holt CJ, in his famous exposition of the standard of care required of the different types of bailees,[129] did not offer a general basis for liability in all cases, but he did offer some important observations on liability where goods were bailed to be carried or delivered gratuitously. The basis of liability in these cases, he said, was that the obligation was imposed 'upon persons in cases of trust'. The precise legal categorisation, however, required further analysis:[130]

> what will you call this? In Bracton . . . it is called mandatum. It is an obligation which arises ex mandato. It is what we call in English an acting by commission. And if a man acts by commission for another gratis, and in the executing his commission behaves himself negligently, he is answerable.

Holt CJ saw this liability as turning on two points: first, it was 'a deceipt to the bailor'[131] for the bailee to undertake to be careful, but then act carelessly; and secondly, it could be said that there was consideration in the handing over of the goods by the bailor.[132] As we have seen, broad ideas about what counted as deceit would be eliminated by the House of Lords' decision in *Derry v Peek*.[133] The argument about consideration was awkward, and rather forced: handing the goods over for free carriage or work to be done was a benefit to the bailor, unless the rather unrealistic view was taken that any loss of possession was always a detriment.[134] If that was the case, no bailment was ever gratuitous. Whatever the merits of the consideration analysis, it highlighted a point that would remain problematic: a sufficiently creative judge could exploit the flexibility

---

126 (1703) 2 Ld Raym 909, 92 ER 107.

127 Ibid, 909, 108.

128 Ibid, 910, 109.

129 On the composition of Holt CJ's judgment see D Ibbetson, 'Coggs v Barnard (1703)' in C Mitchell and P Mitchell (eds), *Landmark Cases in the Law of Contract* (Oxford, Hart Publishing, 2008) 1.

130 *Coggs*, above n 126, 918, 114.

131 Ibid, 919, 114.

132 Ibid.

133 (1889) 14 App Cas 337.

134 H Beale (ed), *Chitty on Contracts* (London, Sweet & Maxwell, 2008) 3–177; J Beale, 'Gratuitous Undertakings' (1891–92) 5 *Harvard Law Review* 222, 224.

inherent in the doctrine of consideration to find consideration where the transaction was, in reality, gratuitous. Imposing liability in such cases could then be done under the guise of orthodox contractual principles, thus removing the case from the category of misperformance of gratuitous undertakings.[135]

These three strands of liability—the common calling cases, sellers' warranties and bailments—all had similarities with the situation which would arise in *Hedley Byrne*, and exemplified the principle on which *Hedley Byrne* would be decided. They also, however, highlighted an ambiguity concerning the idea of liability for undertakings, which *Hedley Byrne* would not entirely resolve. In the sellers' warranties cases the defendant was undertaking that a particular state of affairs actually existed, or would be achieved. In the common calling and bailment cases, by contrast, the defendant only undertook to act; the legal obligation to use care was superimposed on that undertaking. In other words, whilst liability in the sellers' warranty cases was based squarely on what the defendant himself had undertaken, liability in the common calling and bailment cases ultimately rested on a duty imposed by law.[136] The same ambiguity would resurface in *Hedley Byrne* itself, when the judges talked of responsibility being assumed either through direct communication between the parties or by the parties entering a relationship in which the assumption of responsibility was implicit.[137] Two different techniques for imposing liability were being treated under the same heading.[138]

---

135 Eg *Whitehead v Greetham* (1825) 2 Bing 464, 130 ER 385; *Ralli Bros v Walford Lines Ltd* (1922) 10 Ll L Rep 451, (1922) 13 Ll L Rep 223. See also the explanation of *Gomer v Pitt & Scott* (1922) 10 Ll L Rep 668, (1922) 12 Ll L Rep 115 in *General Accident Fire and Life Assurance Corporation v Tanter (The Zephyr)* [1985] 2 Lloyd's Rep 529 in terms of 'the existence in the background of a relationship which at least initially was otherwise than gratuitous' (539, per Mustill LJ). Similar techniques were at work in the United States—see A Monahan, 'Contracts: Gratuitous Undertakings: Liability of Promisor for Nonfeasance' (1923–24) 9 *Cornell Law Quarterly* 54; N Arterburn, 'Liability for Breach of Gratuitous Promises' (1927–28) 22 *Illinois Law Review* 161, 166–67.

136 Baker, above n 116, 406. *Cf* the awkward phraseology used by J Beale to explain the common calling situations: 'By undertaking the special duty, he warrants his special preparation for it' ('The Carrier's Liability: Its History' (1897–98) 11 *Harvard Law Review* 158, 163).

137 See, eg per Lord Devlin at [1964] AC 465, 529: 'It is a responsibility that is voluntarily accepted or undertaken, either generally where a general relationship, such as that of solicitor and client or banker and customer, is created, or specifically in relation to a particular transaction.'

138 *Cf* the approach to similar situations in South Africa: express undertakings were dealt with contractually, whilst implied undertakings based on the general relationship between the parties were a matter for the law of delict. R McKerron, 'Liability for Negligent Statements: *Hedley Byrne v Heller*' (1963) 80 *South African Law Journal* 483, 486.

2. The General Principles of Assumpsit Duties

By the end of the eighteenth century the action on the case for misperformance of an undertaking was firmly established. The leading case was, and would continue to be, *Coggs v Bernard*,[139] with the ideas it articulated being applied across a range of transactions.[140] Two crucial points had also become clear. First, the kind of loss suffered by the claimant was irrelevant—it could be physical or purely economic. Examples of the latter could be seen in successful claims against negligent attornies for failing to keep a judgment debtor in prison,[141] and against a carpenter for having used new materials rather than the old ones he had been instructed to use.[142] Secondly, the action on the case only lay for misperformance, not non-performance. The point was made emphatically in *Elsee v Gatward*,[143] the carpenter case referred to above. There the claimant's declaration contained two counts: the first alleged failure to complete the agreed work; the second alleged wrongful use of new materials, causing the claimant increased expense. The Court of King's Bench, citing *Coggs*, held that the first count was bad, since no consideration was pleaded, but the second count was good. As Ashhurst J explained,[144]

> The distinction is this: if a party undertake to perform work, and proceed on the employment, he makes himself liable for any misfeasance in the course of that work: but if he undertake, and do not proceed on the work, no action will lie against him for nonfeasance.

The basis of liability thus remained halfway between the modern categories of contract (the importance of the undertaking) and tort (damage caused by a careless act). To the eighteenth-century lawyer this did not matter—as a matter of practical reality, claims were brought using the action on the case—but once the procedural classifications (the forms of action) were replaced by substantive categories (causes of action), liability for gratuitous undertakings would have no natural home.

As the nineteenth century progressed, the principle of liability for misperformance of a gratuitous undertaking was applied to situations as diverse as the purchase of an inadequately secured annuity,[145] railway

---

[139] It was described as 'the leading case on the subject of gratuitous undertakings' by Beale, above n 134, 227.

[140] See, in particular, *Shiells v Blackburne* (1789) 1 H Bl 158, 161, 126 ER 94, 97 (Heath J); also, *Elsee v Gatward* (1793) 5 TR 143, 101 ER 82. For a nineteenth-century reassertion of the importance of *Coggs v Bernard* as articulating a general principle see *Skelton v London and North Western Railway Company* (1867) LR 2 CP 631, 636.

[141] *Russell v Palmer* (1767) 2 Wils KB 325, 95 ER 837; *Pitt v Yalden* (1767) 4 Burr 2060, 98 ER 74.

[142] *Elsee v Gatward*, above n 140.

[143] Ibid.

[144] Ibid, 150, 87.

[145] *Dartnall v Howard* (1825) 4 B & C 345, 107 ER 1088.

safety[146] and lapses by stewards at a horse race.[147] One particularly important instance concerned negligence by gratuitous agents in obtaining insurance cover for their principals. The early cases focused on what was necessary for a defendant to be held to have given an undertaking to insure. Clearly a letter accepting the principal's instructions would be enough,[148] but in *Smith v Lascelles*[149] the Court of King's Bench went further, holding that no express assent was needed. As Ashhurst J put it,[150]

> It is true indeed that one person cannot compel another to make an insurance for him against his consent: but if the directions to insure be given to him, to whom the application would naturally be made in the usual course of trade, and he do not give notice of his dissent, he must be answerable for his neglect, because he deprives the other of any opportunity of applying elsewhere to procure the insurance.

Buller J agreed, saying that, where a merchant abroad gave instructions to an agent in Britain,[151]

> if the course of dealing between them be such, that the one has been used to send orders for insurance, and the other to comply with them, the former has a right to expect that his orders for insurance will still be obeyed, unless the latter give him notice to discontinue that course of dealing.

These principles had already been hinted at in *Wallace v Tellfair*,[152] and were confirmed in *Smith v Cologan*.[153] An undertaking was, in effect, being inferred from the agent's silence. Later courts would struggle with that idea,[154] but what is more striking about it for our purposes is that it shows how well established the basic doctrine was.

Later cases on insurance tended to focus on whether the agent had been in breach,[155] or on questions of quantum;[156] the general rule was not challenged. There was, however, one exception: *Wilkinson v Coverdale*.[157] There the vendor of premises was alleged to have undertaken to renew the existing fire insurance policy for the purchaser's benefit. He failed to have the renewed policy properly endorsed, and it was, therefore, ineffective.

---

146 *Skelton*, above n 140.
147 *Balfe v West* (1853) 13 CB 466, 138 ER 1281.
148 *Delany v Stoddart* (1785) 1 TR 22, 99 ER 950.
149 (1788) 2 TR 187, 100 ER 101.
150 Ibid, 188, 103.
151 Ibid, 189–90, 103.
152 (1786) 2 TR 188n, 100 ER 102.
153 (1788) 2 TR 188n, 100 ER 102.
154 *Paal Wilson & Co A/S v Partenreederei Hannah Blumenthal (The Hannah Blumenthal)* [1983] 1 AC 854; *Allied Marine Transport v Vale do Rio Doce Navegacao SA (The Leonidas D)* [1985] 1 WLR 925.
155 *Comber v Anderson* (1808) 1 Camp 523, 170 ER 1044; *Fomin v Oswell* (1813) 3 Camp 357, 170 ER 1410. The focus in both *Wallace v Tellfair*, above n 152, and *Smith v Cologan*, above n 153, was breach of duty.
156 *Webster v de Tastet* (1797) 7 TR 157, 101 ER 908.
157 (1793) 1 Esp 75, 170 ER 284.

The premises burned down. Lord Kenyon CJ is reported as having doubted whether there could be liability in the absence of consideration, but was persuaded otherwise by counsel's citation of a manuscript note of *Wallace v Tellfair*. It is rather surprising that Lord Kenyon CJ felt any doubt at all, having been party to the decision in *Elsee v Gatward* earlier the same year.[158] Nonetheless, despite the doubt, *Wilkinson*'s case was a good illustration of the general principle, in particular of its application to purely economic loss.

In the twentieth century the principle was again reasserted in relation to the negligent misperformance of an undertaking to insure,[159] and, more importantly, the Court of Appeal made it clear that the necessary undertaking must be to act for the benefit of the claimant.[160] Thus, where a landlady's statement that she would remove a gas fire from premises before the start of the tenancy was made for her own benefit, not for the benefit of the tenant, there was no liability when the removal was carried out ineptly and resulted in the tenant being poisoned.

These later cases, whilst reasserting and elaborating on the general principle, also reveal occasional signs of uncertainty about where the principle belonged in the categories of the law of obligations. Thus, in *Balfe v West*,[161] where it was sought to apply the principle to stewards of a horse race who had, allegedly, failed to identify the winner correctly, the court was concerned that the only relevant undertaking was that made by the stewards to whoever had appointed them. It was, in effect, seen as a type of contractual liability. Similarly, in *Davis v Foots* Mackinnon LJ regarded the application of the principle as showing a 'contractual obligation'.[162] Most strikingly, in *Gomer v Pitt & Scott*[163] both the High Court and the Court of Appeal analysed an insurance situation identical to *Wilkinson* (which was not cited) as a case of 'mandate', and imposed liability on the gratuitous agent.[164] Nor were the courts alone in being attracted to a contractual analysis. Smith's *Mercantile Law*, which was cited in *Balfe*, claimed that the gratuitous agent's liability in cases like *Wilkinson* was, in fact, supported by consideration:

> by entering upon the business, he has prevented the employment of some better qualified person, and the detriment thus occasioned to his principal is a suffi-

158 See above, text accompanying n 143ff.
159 *Ralli Bros v Walford Lines Ltd* (1922) 10 Ll L Rep 451.
160 *Davis v Foots* [1940] 1 KB 116.
161 *Balfe v West*, above n 147.
162 [1940] 1 KB 116, 122.
163 (1922) 10 Ll L Rep 668; (1922) 12 Ll L Rep 115.
164 Subsequently the case was reinterpreted as turning on 'the existence in the background of a relationship which at least initially was otherwise than gratuitous' (*General Accident*, above n 135, 539).

cient consideration to uphold an undertaking on his part to act with care and fidelity.[165]

Anson introduced a different contractual analysis. To him, cases like *Wilkinson* could be seen as a deliberate English borrowing from the Roman law of mandate.[166] That was an ingenious suggestion, and could be supported by Holt CJ's comments in *Coggs*.[167] It also appealed to some American commentators.[168] However, if it was true, it meant that English law was like Roman law in having gratuitous contractual liability. This was such a radical position that not even Anson's own editors were prepared to endorse it.[169]

The truth was that assumption of responsibility predated categorisation into contract and tort, and could not sensibly be forced into either category. This was widely recognised in America,[170] and also acknowledged, although less widely, in England. Thus, Scrutton LJ in *Ralli Bros v Walford Lines Ltd*[171] approved Pollock's rejection of a contractual explanation for *Wilkinson*, adding that *Wilkinson* was, in fact, 'an application of the principle stated by Lord Holt in *Coggs v Barnard*'.[172] Winfield understood the point too. In the chapter of *The Province of the Law of Tort* dealing with bailment,[173] he identified that actions against bailees, surgeons and carpenters were all originally based on undertakings, and went on to explain that bailment had never been finally categorised: 'the peculiar origin of assumpsit would have puzzled any one who tried to draw a distinction between tort and contract'.[174] In a lecture predating

---

165 J Smith, *A Compendium of Mercantile Law*, 4th edn by G Dowdeswell (London, Benning, 1848) 112.

166 On mandate in general see J Thomas, *Textbook of Roman Law* (Amsterdam, North-Holland, 1976) 304–09; A Borkowski and P du Plessis, *Textbook on Roman Law* 3rd edn (Oxford, Oxford University Press, 2005) 281–84.

167 See above, text accompanying n 132.

168 Eg Anon, 'Gratuitous Undertakings' (1903–04) 17 *Harvard Law Review* 126; Monahan, above n 135.

169 The passage on mandate appears in the 20th edition by J Brierly (Oxford, Clarendon Press, 1952) at 112–13. In the 21st edition (1959), by A Guest, it is deleted. The 22nd edition, appearing in 1964, heralded *Hedley Byrne* as 'the most significant decision affecting this branch of the law' (v), but that did not prompt the reinstatement of any of the material on gratuitous undertakings and mandate. *Cf* the significance of *Hedley Byrne* in South Africa, where the discussion of express voluntary assumptions of responsibility was seen as being of little interest, being straightforwardly contractual under Roman-Dutch law: R McKerron, 'Liability for Negligent Statements: *Hedley Byrne v Heller*' (1963) 80 *South African Law Journal* 483, 486.

170 Eg Beale, above n 139; Anon, above n 168; Monahan, above n 135; Arterburn, above n 135; W Shattuck, 'Gratuitous Promises—A New Writ?' (1936–37) 35 *Michigan Law Review* 908, 915–18. Arterburn and Shattuck were prompted by the work of the American Law Institute on the Restatement of the Law of Contracts, s 90, which dealt with the enforcement of gratuitous promises on which the promisee had relied.

171 (1922) 10 Ll L Rep 451.

172 Ibid, 456.

173 P Winfield, *The Province of the Law of Tort* (Cambridge, Cambridge University Press, 1931) ch V.

174 Ibid, 96.

The Province, entitled 'Points of Contact between the Law of Torts and Other Parts of the Legal System',[175] he had gone further. Bailment, he explained, had been subjected to both tortious and contractual theories. It had been seen as tortious because bailees were liable in actions on the case for negligence, and contractual because judges had been prepared to invent consideration. This readiness to invent consideration, Winfield argued, had caused problems in *Coggs*, 'and you will find it causing difficulties in the theory of consideration in the text-books on contract which you read. See *Wilkinson v Coverdale* (1793) which is not accurately handled by Anson.'[176] Ultimately, he concluded, bailment could only be coherently seen as part of the law of personal property.

Winfield's insights into the role and significance of assumpsit duties are compelling and important in themselves. They may also have had an influence on the decision in *Hedley Byrne* that is not apparent on the surface. Patrick Devlin had been a law student in Cambridge in 1926 and 1927, where he was tutored by AL Goodhart and, as he put it in his autobiography, attended the lectures by 'the personalities'.[177] Winfield was, at that time, offering all the lectures on tort, supplemented by problem classes,[178] and would have delivered the lecture quoted above when Devlin should have attended it. Winfield had also just finished his definitive article on the history of negligence, in which he placed great emphasis on the importance of undertakings.[179] He may well have included material from that article in his lectures—he was certainly doing so when giving lectures on legal history in the 1930s.[180] Devlin may even have read the article himself: the *Law Quarterly Review*, in which it appeared, was edited by his tutor, and Devlin assisted him in the editorial work.[181] At the very least, Devlin had been exposed to the ideas of the best tort lawyer of his day, at a time when Winfield was intensely interested in the role of assumptions of responsibility.

---

[175] Manuscript in Cambridge University Library. I am grateful to Professor David Ibbetson for drawing this to my attention. The manuscript cannot be dated precisely, but at p 19 there is a 'Later Note' by Winfield, dated 14 May 1928.

[176] Ibid, 21–22.

[177] P Devlin, *Taken at the Flood* (East Harling, Taverner Publications, 1996) 56.

[178] *Cambridge University Reporter 1925–1926*, 69; *Cambridge University Reporter 1926–1927*, 117.

[179] Winfield, above n 118.

[180] Cambridge University Library, pamphlet headed 'Professor Winfield's Class', entitled Legal History (not dated—but the most recent item cited is an article in 1937 *Yale Law Journal*).

[181] T Honoré, 'Devlin, Patrick Arthur' in *Oxford Dictionary of National Biography* (online edn).

E. CONCLUSION

Seen with the benefit of the historical background, the House of Lords' use of assumption of responsibility in *Hedley Byrne* was not a radical departure at all. On the contrary, it was a return to first principle. The decision should be seen as exemplifying an existing principle, not creating a new one.[182]

Although it was a first principle, however, it had become a controversial one, because, despite formidable historical roots, it did not have an obvious role in the scheme of the modern law of obligations. That was partly a result of the nineteenth-century division of obligations into contract and tort, with the shadowy category of quasi-contract in the background. Contractual obligations required consideration, and were based on the agreement of the parties; tortious obligations were imposed.[183] It was also partly a result of Lord Atkin's speech in *Donoghue v Stevenson*,[184] which had claimed to identify a single unifying principle of duty of care, namely foreseeability of damage to the claimant. Assumption of responsibility fitted into none of these categories, and, therefore, appeared to be highly novel. Perhaps if greater attention had been given to its longevity and general application the speeches in *Hedley Byrne* would have appeared less surprising.

What the House of Lords' decision in *Hedley Byrne* really showed was that these assumptions about the structure of the law of obligations and the unifying principle of duty of care were wrong. Torts need not be restricted to obligations imposed by law, as opposed to obligations assumed by the parties themselves. Lord Atkin was wrong when he said that 'there must be . . . and is'[185] a general conception of duty of care: there need not be, and, in fact, there is not one single principle but at least two. Nor is it inappropriate that duties should arise on different bases depending on whether there is a pre-existing relationship between the parties. *Hedley Byrne* was a reassertion of a fourteenth-century principle, which appeared radical because it was seen against an oversimplified, reductive and unhistorical background of the law of obligations.[186] It is such a landmark not because it established something very new, but, paradoxically, because it repeated something very old.

---

182 R Stevens, *Torts and Rights* (Oxford, Oxford University Press, 2007) 9–14 and 33–37, particularly 34.

183 D Ibbetson, 'The Tort of Negligence in the Common Law in the Nineteenth and Twentieth Centuries' in E Schrage (ed), *Negligence: The Comparative Legal History of the Law of Torts*, CSC 22 (Duncker & Humblot, Berlin, 2001) 229, 236–38.

184 [1932] AC 562.

185 Ibid, 580.

186 For a similar instance involving the categories of contract and unjust enrichment, see J Gleeson and N Owens, 'Dissolving Fictions: What to Do with the Implied Indemnity?' (2009) 25 *Journal of Contract Law* 135.

8

Goldman v Hargrave (1967)

MARK LUNNEY*

A. INTRODUCTION

In June 1966 the Privy Council upheld the decision of the High Court of Australia in *Goldman v Hargrave* that an occupier of land was liable for failing to prevent the spread of a fire from his land.[1] The fire had started as a result of a lightning strike and had spread onto the property of his neighbours, causing damage to property. The cause of action recognised by the Privy Council as establishing liability was negligence and whether there was any overlap with the boundaries of nuisance was 'a question of classification which need not here be resolved.'[2] The shift from nuisance to negligence represented by *Goldman* is the justification for treating it as a leading case, and this chapter explores the reasons for a negligence-based analysis. This exploration is justified if for no other reason than the primary authorities on which the extension was based were actions in private nuisance, and the leading authority, *Sedleigh-Denfield v O'Callaghan*,[3] suggested that there were significant differences between liability in negligence and in private nuisance.

The chapter also considers the wider historical question of why this particular scenario was litigated and why it proved a good vehicle for extending the liability of an occupier, whether in private nuisance or in negligence. It argues that the extensive bushfires in Western Australia in the summer of 1960/61, and the particularly unusual circumstances surrounding the defendant, Alan Goldman, made the fire that spread from his property an ideal test case for liability arising from natural hazards on one's land. In doing so, the chapter challenges the notion that develop-

---

* The author would like to thank the library staff of the State Library of Western Australia, the National Archives of Australia and Mr Clive Duffield of the Judicial Committee of the Privy Council, who arranged for access to the court file. The Registrar of the Supreme Court of Western Australia kindly gave permission to view the court file and his assistance is gratefully acknowledged.

[1] [1967] AC 645 (PC), affirming (1963) 110 CLR 40 (HCA).

[2] *Goldman* (PC), above n 1, 657.

[3] [1940] AC 880.

ments in the law can be understood in isolation from their wider historical context. This is not to suggest that legal principles play no, or even a predominate, role in legal reasoning, but merely to argue that attempts to explain legal reasoning solely within a theoretically satisfying conceptual structure risk being ahistorical.[4]

B. GIDGEGANNUP IN LATE FEBRUARY 1961

Gidgegannup was, and remains, a small village in the Perth Hills, about 40 kilometres from the Perth Central Business District.[5] In February 1961 the area consisted of small- to medium-sized (by Australian standards) rural and semi-rural properties. Alan Goldman owned a property slightly west of Gidgegannup village of just over 600 acres, separated from the village by a main road. In the early evening of 25 February an electrical storm hit the Gidgegannup area which resulted in a number of lightning strikes but no rain. One of these lightning strikes hit a ring-barked, dead tree in a stockrace[6] on Goldman's property and caused a fire in the 'branchy' top of the tree in a fork, about 80 feet from the ground. Goldman, who lived alone, discovered the fire the next day and recognised that it represented a danger, illustrated by its spread to another tree in the stockrace later that morning. Early in the morning he telephoned the local fire control officer and eventually it was agreed that a tree-feller would come to cut the tree down. It took some time, and complaints from Goldman, before the tree-feller and his assistant arrived, but the tree was felled about midday. In the meantime Goldman had created a firebreak around the tree and watered the area from a moveable six hundred gallon water tank with a pipe and sprinklers. When the tree was felled the fire in the fork flared and was enhanced further when Goldman bulldozed the pieces of the burning tree that had fallen into his firebreak area when the tree fell. This practice was consistent with Goldman's expressed view that the only way to deal with this kind of fire was to 'burn it out'.[7] During the remainder of the afternoon Goldman continued to monitor the fire and some visitors also assisted by again watering the area around the trees (the second tree that had been set alight also fell over and needed to be contained), before the stopcock on the watertank was inexplicably broken off, rendering the tank useless. The next morning Goldman claimed that he inspected the burning

---

[4] See, eg A Beever, *Rediscovering the Law of Negligence* (Oxford, Hart Publishing, 2007); R Stevens, *Torts and Rights* (Oxford, Oxford University Press, 2007).

[5] For a history of Gidgegannup see http://www.gidgegannup.info/home/history.htm (accessed on 27 March 2009).

[6] The term has a variety of meanings but in this context seems to refer to a central paddock which gave access to a number of surrounding paddocks. The stockrace on Goldman's property was 180 yards long and 40 feet wide.

[7] *The West Australian*, 11 May 1961, 2.

trees and doused them with water, but this was contradicted by visitors to his property that morning, who claimed that he had left immediately after they had.[8] He was also away for most of the following day. On Wednesday, 1 March, Goldman was working with another man, Jones, on a different part of his property when he was alerted by his companion to smoke rising from near his homestead (hence near the fallen trees as the stockrace was near the house). Goldman left immediately to go to the house and when Jones and his wife arrived there later in the day they found Goldman sitting on a tractor near where a tree was burning. They observed 'a big burnt strip of land indicating where a fairly big fire had already gone down towards the west'.[9] Jones thought that the fire had spread from the burning log. This fire then spread rapidly for the remainder of the day. Firefighters struggled to contain the outbreak for the next day and a half, but by 2.00 am on 4 March the fire was under control, although by then it had destroyed property and stock.[10]

This description of the facts is largely drawn from the report of the first instance decision of Jackson J in the Supreme Court of Western Australia.[11] However, this sanitised version fails to convey the seriousness with which bushfires generally, and this bushfire in particular, were viewed. Bushfires have long been of concern in rural and regional Australia, and the summer of 1960–61 in south and southwestern Western Australia was a notoriously bad season for bushfires.[12] Several major bushfires began in December 1960 and January 1961, but the most extreme conditions set in at the end of February 1961. In early March *The West Australian* was reporting major bushfires in a number of areas.[13] The Gidgegannup fire was only one of a number that broke out in the Perth Hills, forcing some residents to run for their lives.[14] Some of these fires were closer to Perth than the Gidgegannup fire, but it was considered a significant threat as it moved towards the vineyards of the Swan Valley.[15] A breakaway fire started to the east of the township, creating a new fire front. Apart from this breakaway fire, the main fire threatened stock and property in the area and on 2 March destroyed a number of properties and associated farm equipment, as well as a small sawmill.[16] At its worst,

---

8 This is omitted in the report of the trial but is contained in the joint judgment of Taylor and Owen JJ in the High Court: *Goldman* (HCA), above n 1, 47–48.

9 *Daily News*, 2 May 1961, 2.

10 A detailed description of the fire is contained in *Report of Royal Commission upon the Bush Fires of December 1960 and January, February, and March 1961 in Western Australia*, 14.

11 *Hargrave v Goldman* [1963] WAR 102. Some references are from newspaper reports of the Coroner's inquest that followed the fire and which is discussed in more detail below.

12 The summer temperatures were considered a 'near record': *The West Australian*, 1 March 1961, 1.

13 *The West Australian*, 2 March 1961, 1; 3 March 1961, 1 and 7; 4 March 1961, 1 and 8.

14 *The West Australian*, 2 March 1961, 1.

15 Ibid.

16 *The West Australian*, 3 March 1961, 1.

authorities feared it would jump a firebreak and threaten a further 20 properties. Firefighters worked for more than 24 hours straight to save property and relief crews had to be drafted in from surrounding areas. The newly formed State Emergency Service arranged for a mobile Red Cross unit to be deployed to the area to treat, amongst others, smoke injuries, and several ambulances and a doctor remained on call in Gidgegannup itself. The Australian Army also assisted by providing 30 Special Air Services troops to help with firefighting and communications in the area.[17] The fire gained some notoriety, with authorities reporting that sightseers were hampering firefighters; special police patrols and roadblocks were established to prevent non-essential traffic from reaching the area.[18] It was later suggested that 18,250 acres had been burnt out in the Gidgegannup fire and the damage to buildings, fencing, pasture, stock and timber was estimated at £13,600 with a conservative estimate of £6,000 spent on suppressing the fire.[19]

Although these figures may appear high, they pale into insignificance when compared to other bushfires of the 1960–61 season, as the map in Figure 1 indicates. However, no other actions, certainly that went to trial, were brought in respect of these bushfires. Why, then, was the Gidgegannup fire singled out for being the subject of litigation?

C. THE AFTERMATH OF THE FIRE

The litigation in *Hargrave v Goldman* was commenced at the end of 1961, but much had happened between the fire and that time. Just before the Gidgegannup fire began, the Western Australian Government announced that a Royal Commission would be established to enquire into the causes of the 1960–61 bushfires,[20] and by the time it began it included the fires of March 1961 (including Gidgegannup). It commenced in May 1961 and reported in August. At the same time as it began, the Perth City Coroner started an inquest into the cause of the fire. The tenor of the inquest was set at the first session. Although Goldman had been told he needed to attend, he did not do so, forcing his counsel to seek leave to represent him, without notice, on the day of the inquest. The Coroner told counsel he could blame his own client for this, commenting: 'Apparently he thinks we've got nothing to do.'[21] The evidence given to the inquest made it clear that Goldman was to blame for the spread of the fire. A variety of witnesses

---

17 Ibid.
18 *The West Australian*, 4 March 1961, 8.
19 *Royal Commission Report*, above n 10, 15. It was also reported that the fire had destroyed 7,400 acres of pasture and 125 miles of fencing: *The West Australian*, 8 March 1961, 12.
20 *The West Australian*, 1 March 1961, 3.
21 *Daily News*, 1 May 1961, 2.

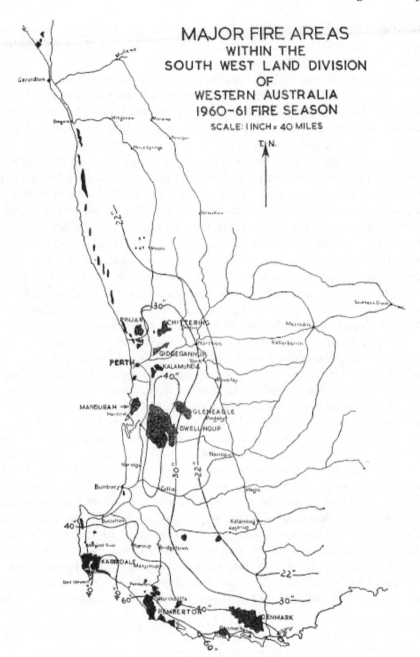

MAJOR FIRE AREAS
WITHIN THE
SOUTH WEST LAND DIVISION
OF
WESTERN AUSTRALIA
1960–61 FIRE SEASON
SCALE: 1 INCH = 40 MILES

Figure 1. *Report of Royal Commission upon the Bush Fires of December 1960 and January, February and March 1961 in Western Australia*, 61. Western Australian Crown copyright materials are reproduced by permission of the copyright owner, the State of Western Australia.

lined up to say that Goldman had admitted that there had been a fire in the redgum and that he had said that he thought he had done enough to prevent its spread.[22] Some witnesses recounted that Goldman had told them that he had reported the fire to the police and the fire officers but that they had told him they would do nothing 'and neither would he'.[23] Later evidence from those involved directly contradicted Goldman's story to police on 2 March that he had been offered no help.[24] Other evidence suggested that Goldman's response to the threat was inadequate; one witness indicated he had requested Goldman to put water on the original fire when the tree was first lopped but that he had refused, and suggested that there were fires outside the stockrace even on 26 February.[25] When Goldman returned to the stockrace on 1 March after the fire had flared up, one witness said that he and his wife had tried to put out burning fenceposts whereas Goldman kicked one against a dead tree. 'That will burn down the tree' his wife told Goldman.[26] A Gidgegannup fire control officer gave evidence that on 2 March Goldman had attempted to push some burning trees with a bulldozer into a dry creek bed filled with inflammable leaves; when he told Goldman to push them into a pond, Goldman became abusive and told him to push the branches into the pool himself.[27]

Some evidence to the inquiry went beyond portraying Goldman as careless. The police detective who interviewed him described him as 'one of the most difficult persons to interrogate. I might say he was the most difficult in my police career.'[28] He noted that Goldman would not answer questions, would always evade a pertinent issue, and was abusive and used extensive obscene language, and that Goldman went into a tirade of abuse and attempted to threaten and stand over him when warned about his obscene language.[29] More sinister motives were suggested in the evidence of Coombes, the tree-feller, who stated that at 2.00 am on 2 March he and a colleague were on patrol on the northern boundary of Goldman's property when they saw the headlights of a vehicle. Shortly afterwards a line of fires started behind them, in an area they had just patrolled, and they put them out. Coombes thought that they had been deliberately lit.[30] The most obvious attempt to discredit Goldman was by a witness who said he was a frequent visitor to Goldman's property. In January 1961 Goldman had told him 'he had something more than an atomic bomb, up his sleeve. He [Goldman] said he could put fear into Gidgegannup . . . He

---

22 *The West Australian*, 2 May 1961, 14; 3 May 1961, 8; *Daily News*, 2 May 1961, 2.
23 *The West Australian*, 2 May 1961, 14.
24 *The West Australian*, 2 May 1961, 14; 3 May 1961, 8.
25 *The West Australian*, 2 May 1961, 14.
26 *Daily News*, 2 May 1961, 2.
27 *The West Australian*, 3 May 1961, 8.
28 *The West Australian*, 3 May 1961, 2.
29 Ibid.
30 *The West Australian*, 2 May 1961, 14.

could fire Gidgegannup by tying lighted motor tyres to a chain and dragging them behind his tractor.'[31] Remarkably, this evidence survived a relevancy objection by Goldman's counsel as it went to Goldman's state of mind.

In light of this evidence, it is not surprising that the Coroner's findings were damning. The Coroner accepted evidence that the fire had started from Goldman's stockrace (supported by aerial observations and contrary to Goldman's assertions in a police statement on 2 March that it started in a gully away from the tree).[32] He also found that Goldman had been driving the vehicle seen at 2.00 am on 2 March.[33] There was no positive finding that Goldman was lighting the spot fires seen at that time, but the Coroner had 'a very strong suspicion that it was he and that he was trying to establish that the fires had started outside of his own property'.[34] Goldman's culpability was also established; there had been (initially) no deliberate attempt to set fire to the property but there was 'considerable neglect' on Goldman's part in dealing with burning tree stumps near the stockrace which had resulted in the people who initiated the inquiry sustaining damage.[35] As the fire was not deliberately lit, the Coroner could not take further action against Goldman; further action would be up to 'some other person in another place'.[36]

In terms of the subsequent legal action, the results of the Coroner's inquest were twofold. First, the credibility of Goldman was severely dented. He had been revealed as, at best, a difficult character, and, at worst, a liar, impressions reinforced by his counsel's understandable refusal to allow him to give evidence to the inquest.[37] Secondly, and more importantly, the finding of 'considerable neglect' against Goldman suggested that, if fault was required to succeed in a civil action, it would not be difficult to establish.[38] The legal issue remained to be determined, but potential plaintiffs were on firm ground with the facts.

Three months after the inquest, the Royal Commission into the bushfires of 1960–61 reported. Although the Gidgegannup fire was investigated, the different purpose of the Commission meant that it did not attribute blame in the same way as the inquest. Nonetheless, the Report commented that, after the tree was cut down, 'it was not then extinguished by the landowner as required under the Bush Fires Act' and that the 'fire

31 *The West Australian*, 3 May 1961, 8.

32 *The West Australian*, 3 May 1961, 2 (evidence of Detective RC Myers). The Coroner had also flown over the area and formed the same opinion: *Daily News*, 10 May 1961, 1.

33 *Daily News*, 10 May 1961, 1; *The West Australian*, 11 May 1961, 2.

34 *The West Australian*, 11 May 1961, 2.

35 Ibid.

36 *Daily News*, 10 May 1961, 1.

37 *The West Australian*, 11 May 1961, 2.

38 It is no surprise that the witnesses in the trial were the same as those before the inquest; a list of the trial witnesses can be found in *Printed Papers in Appeals*, 1966, Vol 4, Judgments 9–12.

could undoubtedly have been avoided if the burning tree on Swan location 1317 had been extinguished when it was felled on 26 February'.[39] These comments are consistent with findings of fault against Goldman. More interesting is the comment of the Commissioner on the evidence of the witnesses:[40]

> In a few cases, strong personal animosities were revealed, which tended to dis-
> tort the picture of the true situation and reduce the value of the evidence. There
> were also instances where witnesses, due to a mistaken sense of loyalty to their
> neighbours or fear of civil action were reluctant to tell all they knew.

The reference to civil action needs explanation. Whilst an innovative lawyer might have pondered the possibility of liability for a fire commenced by lightning, more conventional actions were available for damage caused by the escape of fire. It is true that these usually required the fire to have been deliberately or negligently commenced, but, as the Report pointed out, this was the case with most bushfires. The Report noted that bush fire did the most damage in January–March and arose from burning off fires; that is, burning off to permit cultivation of pasture or grazing or the burn-ing of bush to reduce the fire hazard.[41] These fires would have been caught by actions in negligence and under the rule in *Rylands v Fletcher*,[42] and thus may explain the hesitancy of witnesses to give full explanations. Certainly such actions were known in Australia, although, given the preva-lence of burning, there were remarkably few reported cases in rural contexts where liability was imposed for the escape of a fire. Given this sparsity, the action against Goldman seems even more difficult to explain. Perhaps his views on containing bushfires were unconventional, but, as the Royal Commission Report noted, Goldman was not alone in his view of the fire authorities:[43]

> Many farmers, especially the struggling farmers, are inclined to be self-sufficient
> in their outlook. They have developed their ideas in some degree of solitude and
> often their ideas have become convictions from which it is almost impossible to
> move them, other than by practical demonstrations. The forester or the local
> authority officers seeking to enlist the support of such members of the commu-
> nity should seek their assistance and not try to dictate to them what they should
> or should not do. No matter to what extremes it may appear that their ideas
> tend, it should be remembered that they know their country and its surround-
> ings, and know better than most others what can be done to protect it from fire.
> Their ideas may not fit in with the general scheme, but it will often be found
> that the general scheme can be adapted to absorb their ideas if due credit is
> given to them.

---

[39] *Royal Commission Report*, above n 10, 13 and 15.
[40] Ibid, 5.
[41] Ibid, 38.
[42] (1868) LR 3 HL 330.
[43] *Royal Commission Report*, above n 10, 50.

Goldman's problem was that he not amenable to this kind of compromise. Moreover, he was equally obstreperous with people generally and had made enemies; given the inquest and subsequent court action, one suspects the personal animosity referred to in the Royal Commission Report is at least partly a reference to Goldman. As he confided to a reporter shortly after the inquest,[44] he berated governments, police and agricultural experts, and he had taken on board advice that to make money 'just do the opposite to everyone else . . . I've been doing it ever since and getting in a few "blues" in the process'. Moreover, Goldman was wealthy. Russian-born, he had been a rough rider before turning to cattle during the depression, and by the time of the fires he was described as a 'cattle king', previously owning Western Australia's biggest cattle station, Moola Boola, in the Kimberley region, in the 1950s. He described himself and having 'a million in money' behind him, as well as a Rolls Royce and a Mercedes in his shed.[45] In the context a major state-wide natural disaster, the wealthy Goldman provided an attractive target to those whose property had been damaged by the fire, especially once his conduct and character had been condemned in the Coroner's Inquest. All that was needed was to find the legal basis on which he could be sued.

D. NATURE, NUISANCE AND NEGLIGENCE

If Goldman had lit a fire and it had escaped and caused damage, the legal position, as noted above, would not have been controversial. There were two bases on which such an action could have been brought. If Goldman had been careless, then an action in negligence would have been available, and there were clear Australian precedents to support this view.[46] An alternative approach would have been to argue that Goldman was liable under the strict liability recognised in *Rylands v Fletcher*. Fire would have been brought onto the land, it was something which was dangerous if it escaped, and there was High Court authority that burning off, even for recognised pastoral or rural purposes, was not a natural use of land so as to avoid the applicability of the action.[47] The same case affirmed that any special strict liability rule relating to fire had been subsumed under the wider strict liability principle recognised in *Rylands v Fletcher*.[48] The problem with

---

44 *The Sunday Times* (WA) 14 May 1961, 4.

45 Ibid.

46 For a contemporary Western Australian example see *McWhirter v Emerson-Elliot (No 2)* [1962] WAR 162.

47 *Hazelwood v Webber* (1934) 52 CLR 268.

48 Ibid, 280, where Starke J commented: 'The use of fire involved at common law the strictest responsibility, and decisions in modern times have brought that responsibility into line with what Blackburn J called 'the general rule of common law . . . given in *Fletcher v Rylands*'. The same approach was implicitly adopted by other members of the court.

these actions, however, was that they required the fire to have been a fire for which Goldman was responsible, but here the fire had started from a lightning strike.

If these grounds for liability were abandoned, however, a major difficulty arose. The charge against Goldman would be that he ought to have acted to prevent either the creation or the spread of the fire. Goldman would have to have been liable for an omission, and imposing liability for omissions was rare in the common law. Moreover, the omission was in respect of an act of nature—the lightning strike—and courts had been reluctant to impose any legal duty to act to prevent damage to neighbours as a result of the natural state of the plaintiff's property. Both of these difficulties would need to be overcome before Goldman could be liable.

1. Occupiers and Liability for Omissions

Although liability for pure nonfeasance in tort was rare, it was clear that occupiers as a class did owe duties to take positive action in some circumstances to protect visitors to their land. However, as the occupier had invited or permitted the visitor to be on the land, the requirement to act could be linked to that positive action by the occupier. Any liability would not be for a pure omission but for an omission in the course of positive conduct.[49] This also explained the no-duty rule that applied to trespassers; if there was no invitation or permission, there was nothing upon which any duty to act could be founded.

Exceptions to this general position had arisen in nuisance where occupiers could be held liable for failing to act to prevent damage to non-visitors. Whilst most of the early authorities were in public nuisance, Scrutton LJ delivered an influential dissenting judgment in *Job Edwards Limited v The Company of Proprietors of the Birmingham Navigations*, where he held that an occupier might be liable for failing to prevent the spread of fire from her land to her neighbour's land:[50]

> There is a great deal to be said for the view that if a man finds a dangerous and artificial thing on his land, which he and those for whom he is responsible did not put there; if he knows that if left alone it will damage other persons; if by reasonable care he can render it harmless, as if by stamping on a fire just beginning from a trespasser's match he can extinguish it; that then if he does nothing, he has 'permitted it to continue', and become responsible for it. This would base the liability on negligence, and not on the duty of insuring damage from a dangerous thing under *Rylands v Fletcher*. I appreciate that to get negligence you must have a duty to be careful, but I think on principle that a landowner has a

49 HK Lücke, 'Negligence and Occupiers' Liability' (1960) 2 *Melbourne University Law Review* 472, 490.
50 [1924] 1 KB 341, 357–58.

duty to take reasonable care not to allow his land to remain a receptacle for a thing which may, if not rendered harmless, cause damage to his neighbours.

If the last sentence of this passage had represented the law by the time of *Hargrave v Goldman*, it would clearly have covered the situation and, given Goldman's conduct, liability would have followed as a matter of course. Apart from the fact that it was a dissenting opinion, however, it flitted between a liability based in nuisance and one in negligence. As the primary thrust of Scrutton LJ's argument was an analogy with cases in public nuisance where liability had been imposed for this kind of omission, it is not surprising that it was the liability in private nuisance that was taken up in later cases. Even before the case, moreover, there was academic support for the view that private nuisance could extend to categories of case where a nuisance was created by the act of a trespasser, or otherwise without the act, authority or permission of the occupier, if the occupier suffered it to continue without taking reasonably prompt and efficient means for its abatement.[51]

The opportunity for the House of Lords to consider the liability of an occupier for failing to abate a nuisance on his land arose in *Sedleigh-Denfield v O'Callaghan*.[52] As is well known, the occupier was there held liable for adopting and continuing a nuisance, a culvert without a protective grate, created by the act of trespasser. Two issues are noteworthy for present purposes. The first is that the House of Lords overlooked the difficulties associated with the fact that the trespasser's conduct—omitting to protect the entrance to a culvert with a grate—was not a nuisance; it was only a potential nuisance. As has been pointed out, potential nuisances are not actionable until they cause damage. All that they do is create a risk that at some later date a nuisance might be committed. To impose liability for knowledge of a risk and for failing to take steps to eliminate the risk has decided overtones of a liability in negligence.[53] Secondly, it has perhaps not been appreciated how important it was to the nuisance-based reasoning that the trespasser's intervention was intended to benefit the land by providing better drainage. This made it much easier to conform to the doctrinal limits of an action in private nuisance, in particular the requirement of some kind of user of land by the defendant. Thus Viscount Maugham based liability on continuance or adoption of the nuisance, and explained what these terms meant:[54]

---

51 JW Salmond, *The Law of Torts*, 5th edn (London, Sweet & Maxwell, 1920) 258–65.
52 [1940] AC 880.
53 On the difficulties of the 'potential nuisance' reasoning see JG Fleming, *The Law of Torts*, 2nd edn (Sydney, Law Book Co of Australia, 1961) 353 note 3; RJ Buxton, 'The Negligent Nuisance' (1966) 8 *Malaya Law Review* 1, 12; C Gearty, 'The Place of Private Nuisance in a Modern Law of Torts' [1989] *CLJ* 214, 235–37.
54 *Sedleigh-Denfield*, above n 52, 894.

> In my opinion an occupier of land 'continues' a nuisance if with knowledge or presumed knowledge of its existence he fails to take any reasonable means to bring it to an end though with ample time to do so. He 'adopts' it if he makes any use of the erection, building, bank or artificial contrivance which constitutes the nuisance.

It can plausibly be argued that by taking advantage of the culvert constructed by the trespasser to remove water the occupier had actually used the drainage system created by the trespasser. It may be wondered whether the occupier had much choice as, once it was in place, it could only have been converted to its previous state at considerable expense. No doubt their Lordships were fortified in their conclusions by the fact that the new drainage system could be made to work without causing a nuisance simply by placing the grate in its proper position, but this is not a necessary element for a finding of 'adoption'; all that is required is use. Nonetheless, there is no doubt that the culvert was intended to be of benefit to the property, and simply by continuing to occupy the property the occupier can be said to have used it; it was part and parcel of the occupation.

More difficult is the notion that the occupier continued the nuisance. Lord Atkin described it in the following way:[55]

> If a man uses on premises something which he found there, and which itself causes a nuisance by noise, vibration, smell or fumes, he is himself in continuing to bring into existence the noise, vibration, etc, causing a nuisance. Continuing in this sense and causing are the same thing. It seems to me clear that if a man permits an offensive thing on his premises to continue to offend, that is if he knows that it is operating offensively, is able to prevent it and omits to prevent it he is permitting the nuisance to continue, in other words he is continuing it.

It is important to recognise the leap in reasoning between the first and second parts of this paragraph. The first, and relatively uncontroversial, sentence bases liability on permission evidenced by use; as the occupier had used whatever he had found on the land, he had permitted its existence and could be liable for it even though he did not create it. The second paragraph moves away from use and simply equates permission with knowledge. This equation of knowledge with permission was not followed in other aspects of an occupier's liability; courts did not, for example, impute a licence to those who were on the occupier's land with his knowledge but without his consent as a matter of course.[56] Nor does it deal with the problem of the nuisance not yet being in existence. It was one thing to hold an occupier liable in nuisance for actual nuisances on her land which she had permitted by use, as existing case law had done, but quite another to require the occupier to act to prevent an actionable

---

55 Ibid, 897.
56 *Edwards v Railway Executive* [1952] AC 737.

nuisance from coming into existence.[57] The 'nuisance' could not be used so as to be continued because it did not exist.[58] But if permission could be based on knowledge of the existence of a state of affairs from which a nuisance might arise—in other words, the risk of a nuisance existing in the future—the basis of liability moved away from use of land to knowledge of risk. The failure to act to prevent a risk from materialising characterises an action in negligence, but several of their Lordships explicitly refused to see the gist of the action as negligence. Thus, for Lord Wright negligence was 'not an independent cause of action but is ancillary to the actual cause of action, which is nuisance' and for Lord Atkin 'deliberate act or negligence is not an essential ingredient but some degree of personal responsibility is required which is connoted in my definition by the word "use"'. This reluctance to view negligence as the basis of the claim may be the reason that their Lordships did not expressly endorse Scrutton LJ's dissent in *Job Edwards*.[59]

2. Occupiers and Things Naturally on Land

Apart from the limited situations in which liability could be imposed for a failure to act, *Hargrave v Goldman* raised another obstacle for the plaintiff: the alleged nuisance was not the result of any interference created by human agency but was an act of nature. There was a long-standing reluctance to impose liability on an occupier for failing to prevent damage to a neighbour as a result of an act of nature. As far as liability based on fault was concerned, the leading authority was *Giles v Walker*,[60] where, in a pithy judgment, Lord Coleridge rejected the possibility of an occupier owing a duty to an adjoining landowner to prevent the spread of thistles.[61] In Australia, similar reasoning was applied in the early High Court decision in *Spark v Osborne*,[62] where the plaintiff sued for damage caused by the spread of the weed 'prickly pear', which had destroyed the plaintiff's fence and allowed dingoes to kill his livestock. The statement of claim did not allege negligence and the High Court seems to have thought the action was

---

58 L Robertson, '*Goldman v Hargrave*: Liability of a Bad Samaritan for the Natural Condition of his Land' (1967–69) 3 *University of British Columbia Law Review* 211, 215, argues that 'continuance' was adopted precisely because it suggested some active conduct and hence did not infringe the nonfeasance rule.

59 Buxton, above n 53, 12.

59 The omission is noted in S Roberts, 'Negligence Liability—A Glimpse of New Vistas' (1967) 30 *MLR* 445, 447–8.

60 (1890) 24 QBD 656.

61 It is not clear whether the cause of action pleaded was what modern lawyers would regard as negligence. Although the formal ground for reversing the decision was that the trial judge should not have left the question of negligence to the jury, the argument of plaintiff's counsel suggests that the liability was in nuisance, albeit fault-based.

62 (1908) 7 CLR 51.

based on *Rylands v Fletcher*, although a number of nuisance cases were also cited. Applying *Giles v Walker*, the High Court rejected the claim, O'Connor J stating that liability depended upon some act by the landowner in the use of his land which had rendered the wild growth more likely to injure, or some use or adoption of it by the landowner which put it in the same position as a growth brought by him upon his land.[63] However, there were other cases where liability had been imposed for risks caused by natural occurrences on land. In *Slater v Worthington's Cash Stores (1930) Ltd*[64] the plaintiff recovered when injured by the collapse of a roof on which snow had accumulated. Oliver J expressly recognised that the risk was created by an act of nature, but nonetheless held the defendant liable for failing to take reasonable steps to eradicate the risk in both public nuisance and (obiter) in negligence.

Academic writers also took different views. Heuston's first edition of *Salmond on Torts* in 1953 placed *Giles v Walker* in the chapter on *Rylands v Fletcher*,[65] whilst Fleming placed it in his nuisance chapter under the heading 'Natural Conditions'.[66] Fleming also considered *Sedleigh-Denfield* liability in the preceding section on liability of occupiers for nonfeasance but did not suggest that the reasoning in that case could be extended generally to natural occurrences. He clearly thought there were good policy reasons for maintaining the no-liability rule for natural occurrences in rural areas,[67] although, where he thought the rule might be abrogated, liability appears to have been based on similar considerations to those in *Sedleigh-Denfield*.[68] Conversely, Goodhart had earlier argued that an occupier could be liable in nuisance for the spread of things naturally on the land.[69] He argued there had been confusion in the cases between two different questions: whether a use of land was a natural use of land for the

---

[63] Ibid.

[64] [1941] KB 488 (KBD and Court of Appeal). Oliver J's judgment was upheld in the Court of Appeal but, apart from a brief reference by Goddard LJ to there being no answer to the plaintiff's claim in negligence or nuisance, the issue of snow being the result of a natural event was not discussed.

[65] RFV Heuston, *Salmond on Torts*, 11th edn (London, Sweet & Maxwell, 1953) 623–24.

[66] Fleming, above n 53, 374.

[67] Ibid, 375. This was especially so for countries like Australia, with vast stretches of unimproved or semi-cultivated land, where he thought any duty of inspection and abatement would be unduly onerous and disproportionate to the harm usually threatened.

[68] Ibid. This assumes that their Lordships meant reasonableness to be understood as it was in negligence actions but in truth they do not discuss the reasonableness of the defendant's action in any detail; in fact, Lords Atkin and Wright suggest that the obligation on the occupier is to abate the nuisance. The lack of discussion undoubtedly reflects the fact that little was required of the occupier to abate the nuisance so on the facts reasonableness did require the nuisance to be abated: see M Lunney and K Oliphant, *Tort Law: Text and Materials*, 3rd edn (Oxford, Oxford University Press, 2008) 651. There is, however, nothing in *Sedleigh-Denfield* to suggest that reasonableness should be determined by a subjective standard in these cases (*cf* C McIvor, *Third Party Liability in Tort* (Oxford, Hart Publishing, 2006) 43–44); this was only made clear in *Goldman v Hargrave* in the Privy Council.

[69] AL Goodhart, 'Liability for Things Naturally on the Land' [1930–32] 4 *CLJ* 13.

purposes of the rule in *Rylands v Fletcher*, and whether things naturally on the land could give rise to liability in nuisance. The cases dealing with the former question were not relevant to the latter. Although there were a number of conflicting cases, he argued that an occupier could be liable for a 'natural' nuisance but the basis of the liability was unclear; in a number of places Goodhart referred to actual or constructive knowledge of the nuisance, but he also referred approvingly to the American Restatement's view that liability was based both on knowledge and on a failure to exercise reasonable care to eradicate the nuisance.[70]

One curiosity of the arguments in *Hargrave v Goldman* is that little was made of the relatively recent English case of *Davey v Harrow Corporation*,[71] where the local authority was held liable in nuisance for the spread of tree roots from its land even though it had not planted the trees. In making this finding, Lord Goddard queried whether *Giles v Walker* would be decided the same way if the case came up before the current court. This point was noted only in passing by both the counsel and courts that heard *Hargrave v Goldman*. Two tentative reasons can be suggested why the case was not seen as more important to the *Goldman* case. First, there were well-known authorities dealing with the particular problems of encroaching tree roots and the case may have been seen as limited to that class of case.[72] However, as Lord Goddard actually refers to a variety of cases outside tree roots, and expressly acknowledges the influence of Goodhart's article on liability for things naturally on land (which deals with situations beyond tree roots), it is difficult in hindsight to see why it should have been so limited. Perhaps a more convincing reason was a doubt as to whether it was consistent with *Sedleigh-Denfield* (which was not cited in the decision), in its apparent holding that liability could arise for a nuisance not created by the occupier, even if the occupier had no actual or constructive knowledge of the nuisance. On the facts, however, the occupier clearly did have knowledge of the encroaching tree roots. Moreover, Lord Goddard's acknowledgement of Goodhart suggests that he was not advocating a strict liability but rather one based on knowledge. Even after the Privy Council decision, however, a commentator still felt the need to limit the application of the decision: 'it is dangerous to draw any general conclusions from a case such as *Davey v Harrow Corporation*, in a realm of the law where, more than in most, cases seem to turn on their particular facts'.[73] Yet even this commentator thought that after the decision 'it can never be enough for the defendant to plead that the nuisance came naturally and spontaneously without his own act or

---

[70] Ibid, 19, 26 and 30.
[71] [1958] 1 QB 60.
[72] D Barker, 'Failure to Remedy a Nuisance—Part I' (1966) 116 *New Law Journal* 1560, 1561.
[73] Ibid.

fault';[74] and it is hard to see why this was thought not be more important in *Goldman* that it apparently was.

E. BRINGING IT ALL TOGETHER: PLEADING A CAUSE OF ACTION IN *HARGRAVE V GOLDMAN*

In December 1961 the first of a number of actions (that were later consolidated) were commenced against Goldman.[75] Originally, there were two different types of statement of claim in the actions, which reflected the difficulties of working out how to plead a *Sedleigh-Denfield* liability in light of the difficulties of establishing an obligation to act in respect of things naturally occurring on the land.

The first statement of claim, by the Hargraves, based liability on the escape of the fire, the negligence of the defendant and the defendant's breach of duty to the plaintiff to ensure that the fire did not escape having regard to its nature.[76] It is not clear how the first and third bases of the claim were different, but in any case they both suffered from the difficulty that it was not Goldman's fire. The only attempt to overcome this was to allege that, after the tree had been felled, Goldman pushed up the broken boughs and broken wood onto the burning fallen tree.[77] If this did not make the fire Goldman's, the statement of claim simply pleaded an action in negligence for failing to prevent the spread of a natural hazard— something that clearly contradicted the existing rule on liability for things naturally on land.

A different approach was taken in the statement of claim by the Taylors. Here the fire was divided into two fires. The first was the one started by lightning. In paragraph 4 Goldman was alleged to have 'continued and increased' this fire by adding to it material of a highly combustible nature.[78] This created a second fire, which was the one that escaped and caused damage.[79] Negligence was alleged in respect of both fires: by not extinguishing or attempting to extinguish the first fire, and by effectively creating the second fire in weather conditions conducive to its spread.[80] Although the allegation of negligence in respect of the first fire faced the same difficulties discussed above, the allegation in respect of the

---

[74] Ibid.

[75] Goldman opposed consolidation but his attempt to overturn the order was dismissed, despite counsel for one of the plaintiffs earlier arguing that it was probably in favour of the defendant: Supreme Court of Western Australia, Court File No H52 of 1961, Summons of 13 August 1962, Affidavit of Alexander Asplin.

[76] Ibid, Statement of Claim of Hargraves, 1 December 1961, para 10.

[77] Ibid, para 4.

[78] Ibid, Statement of Claim of Taylors, para 4.

[79] Ibid, para 5.

[80] Ibid, para 6, Particulars of Negligence.

second fire did not; it was an ordinary negligence action for creating an additional risk over and above that created by the natural occurrence.

In August 1962, when the actions were consolidated, the statements of claim in the various actions were amended to a standard form. Apart from adding a fresh cause of action for breach of statutory duty for infringements of the Bush Fires Act 1954 (WA),[81] the statement of claim was now clear on the various actions pleaded. One allegation was that the defendant had allowed or permitted a fire that *he had started* on his property to escape to the plaintiff's property. This cause of action was based on *Rylands v Fletcher*.[82] The alternative was that Goldman was negligent in permitting the fire (which in the previous allegation he had started) to escape to the plaintiff's property, the cause of action being negligence and nuisance.[83] However, there was an important change to what had been alleged in the Taylor's statement of claim. The fires were not broken up into a first and second fire; rather, paragraph 4 was retained in the uniform statements of claim without any reference to a first fire, and the allegations that Goldman had created a second fire caused by his own negligence and that this had caused damage were omitted.[84] Although the references to Goldman 'continuing and increasing' the fire were retained, it was not clear what their purpose was, if not to establish that these actions amounted to carelessly creating a fire, an allegation that was much more difficult to discern than in the original pleading. However, one final amendment was allowed on the second day of the trial, in November 1961, which clarified their purpose. Paragraph 4 had the following sentence added: 'And thus brought to his said premises such increased fire maintained it and permitted it to escape to the property of the said [plaintiffs].'[85] The effect was to base Goldman's liability for continuing and increasing the fire set out in paragraph 4 on the fire being one *created* by Goldman and was thus directed to the *Rylands v Fletcher* liability rather than negligence.

More confusion was created when the same conduct—continuing and increasing the original fire—was also pleaded in the Particulars of Negligence.[86] This made sense in the original Taylor pleading (from which it was taken), as there negligence was the sole cause of action pleaded. However, it needed clarification in the uniform pleading where there were other causes of action. In particular, if the primary negligence allegation

---

[81] Ibid, Amended Statements of Claim, 1 August 1962, para 5. This unsuccessful claim is not discussed in this paper as it was analysed in the conventional manner for an action for breach of statutory duty; nor, for similar reasons, is the unsuccessful defence pleaded under the Fires Prevention (Metropolis) Act 1774 (UK), s 86.

[82] Ibid, paras 7(b) and 8(b).

[83] Ibid, paras 7(c) and 8(c).

[84] Ibid, para 4.

[85] Ibid, Final Statements of Claim, para 4.

[86] Ibid, para 8, Particulars of Negligence.

was that Goldman permitted the fire to escape, it is not clear how continuing and increasing the original fire made the escape careless. It might have made the fire Goldman's, but this went to liability under *Rylands*; if it was not his fire, then his liability in negligence could only be for failing to stop its spread.

The evolution of the pleadings demonstrates the uncertainties that attached to the claims. What is striking, however, is how little the *Sedleigh-Denfield* reasoning is expressly represented. The doubts over whether to plead one fire or two seem to have related to attempts to avoid the omission argument, a clear problem in relation to things naturally on the land. Moreover, there is confusion over what role, if any, 'continuing and increasing' the original fire should play. In relation to 'continuing' the fire, it is noteworthy that the list of cases for the plaintiff does include *Sedleigh-Denfield* but nowhere in the pleadings was it alleged that nuisance was committed by continuing the nuisance as understood in *Sedleigh-Denfield*, although this does seem to have been argued at trial.

F. THE FIRE LITIGATED

At first instance, Jackson J decided in favour of Goldman. The suggestion that Goldman had adopted or used the fire as his own was summarily rejected; at all times Goldman had been attempting to put out the fire, not to use it for his own purposes. This disposed of the *Rylands v Fletcher* ground and the 'adoption' ground of *Sedleigh-Denfield*; unlike the culvert, the fire served no function that could be said to benefit the land and hence could not have been adopted by the occupier. Jackson J also rejected liability under the 'continuance' head of *Sedleigh-Denfield* as that applied only to artificial structures and only where it could be said that there had been some 'use' of the land.[87] As noted above, the difficulty with the continuance reasoning in *Sedleigh-Denfield* was that it remained formally rooted in what was seen as the core of nuisance—the use of land—rather than knowledge of a risk. Viewed in the former light, Jackson J's reasoning is impeccable as Goldman had not used the fire in any way as part of his use of land. He also rejected the negligence claim, treating it as based on a negligent failure to extinguish the fire that had begun accidentally. As noted above, whilst this may not have been the only allegation of negligence pleaded, it was certainly one of them, and Jackson J can be excused if he limited his judgment to this issue. It may also reflect his view that Goldman's conduct in bulldozing surrounding debris into the tree was 'unexceptional', a view supported by the evidence of a fire control expert

---

[87] As The Case for the Respondent in the Privy Council recognised (*Printed Papers in Appeals*, 1966, Vol 4, Judgments 9–12), Jackson J effectively treated the *Rylands v Fletcher* and nuisance claims as one, both requiring some adoption or continuance of the fire for liability to arise.

who appeared at both the inquest and the trial. Even if Goldman had continued and increased the fire by his actions, he had not done so negligently. The negligence related to failing to extinguish the fire and, as a landowner 'is under no liability for anything which happens to or spreads from his land in the natural course of affairs, if the land is used naturally', there was no liability on negligence.[88]

Later in the year, a three-judge High Court of Australia allowed an appeal. The joint judgment of Owen and Taylor JJ differed significantly from that of Windeyer J. The primary ground for decision in the joint judgment is that the case fell within the principle expounded by the House of Lords in *Sedleigh-Denfield*. They held:[89]

> [T]he effect of their Lordships' reasons was that an occupier, with knowledge of the existence of a state of affairs on his land which is a potential nuisance but which has been created by a trespasser, is, nevertheless, liable in the event of damage resulting therefrom to the lands of his neighbours if by the exercise of reasonable care the damage would have been avoided . . . [We] can see no distinction relevant to the question of liability between potential nuisances created by trespassers and potential nuisances coming into existence 'otherwise without the act, authority, or permission of the occupier'.

It is noteworthy that the joint judgment does not talk of 'continuing' the nuisance, which had been the ostensible basis for the decision in *Sedleigh-Denfield*. This is hardly surprising, as Goldman had in no way continued the nuisance, even in the *Sedleigh-Denfield* sense of knowing of its existence and taking the benefits it provided to the land. In the joint judgment, as for Lord Atkin in *Sedleigh-Denfield*, it was knowledge of the risk that was relevant. The joint judgment moves one step closer to an explicit recognition of this when it jettisons the requirement that the nuisance be continued, but the umbilical cord cannot be cut. Instead of foresight of risk, the occupier must have knowledge of 'a state of affairs on the defendant's land which is a potential nuisance'.

The leap was made in the 'outstanding'[90] judgment of Sir Victor Windeyer. After dismissing the action based on *Rylands v Fletcher* ('he did not bring the fire upon his land, nor did he keep it there for any purpose of his own. It came from the skies'[91]), Windeyer J began his consideration of the nuisance claim by noting that it was somewhat misleading to use the word 'nuisance' to describe a situation from which damage may occur if care was not exercised. He rejected an argument that private nuisance required an active use of the land to make the occupier liable as too narrow: 'An occupier of land who passively suffers a nuisance to continue

[88] [1963] WAR 102, 108.
[89] *Goldman* (HCA), above n 1, 51.
[90] Buxton, above n 53, 25.
[91] *Goldman* (HCA), above n 1, 59.

may be liable although he did not originally create it.'[92] However, in this case, Goldman was arguing he did not suffer any nuisance to continue. He did not start the fire nor increase the danger of it, nor did he do anything to make himself responsible for it; in fact, he tried to make it harmless. This led Windeyer J to consider *Sedleigh-Denfield* liability based on continuing a nuisance, but he found this difficult to apply. Goldman had actually taken steps to eradicate the potential nuisance, unlike the defendant in *Sedleigh-Denfield*, and, even if those steps proved ineffectual, could he really be said to have continued the nuisance? Nor could he see that Goldman had permitted the nuisance to continue in line with Scrutton LJ's dictum in *Job Edwards* by failing to take steps to abate it: 'But it seems artificial in the case of a man who takes steps, although in the result ineffectual, to eliminate the danger. Trying to get rid of a thing can hardly be evidence of approval of it.'[93] The problem, as Windeyer J recognised, was that the wrong question—about continuing the nuisance—was being asked because the wrong cause of action was being used. In a crucial passage, he commented:[94]

> Instead of imputing to the respondent an intention contrary to his real intent, the straightforward approach, in such a case as this, seems to me to be to ask: was he not liable in negligence? The essential question then is not: did the respondent continue the fire as a nuisance? It is: was he negligent in not rendering it harmless?

The move from nuisance to negligence as the basis of liability allowed Windeyer J to consider whether a duty of care could be owed by an occupier to take positive action to prevent the spread of bushfires from his land. Two points should be made about this analysis. The first is that he refused to see Goldman's conduct as creating a new risk separate from the original fire. It would be impossible to impose liability because the respondent did something to control the fire when no liability would have been imposed if he had failed to act. Such a position might discourage preventative action to stop the spread of bushfires, an outcome clearly thought undesirable.[95] The second point is that the duty analysis allowed

---

92 Ibid, 60.
93 Ibid, 61.
94 Ibid, 61.
95 Allan Beever attempts to explain the result in *Goldman* on this basis, i.e. that a new risk was created: Beever, above n 4, 331–33. However, although Taylor and Owen JJ did suggest this alternative basis for the decision, they clearly also approved liability based on a failure to act. The finding of Taylor and Owen JJ on Goldman creating an additional risk was expressly challenged in The Case for the Appellants (*Printed Papers in Appeals*, 1966, Vol 4, Judgments 9–12) and was not seriously argued by counsel at the hearing. In the Privy Council Lord Wilberforce did refer to Goldman's conduct as bringing a fresh risk into operation, but shortly thereafter made it clear that the case was being decided on the basis of Goldman's failure to act: *Goldman* (PC), above n 1, 656; see too Roberts, above n 59, 449. On the evidence presented to the inquest, to the Royal Commission and at trial, there is nothing to suggest that the risk from the fire in the tree was different in kind from the fallen tree.

Windeyer to consider the reasons why a duty of care might be owed. The difficulty here was that imposing a duty to act in this kind of case was potentially inconsistent with the general no duty to rescue position adopted by the common law. He did not find the distinction easy, but settled for founding the duty to act in the case before him on occupation of land. This still required him to deal with the line of cases denying any duty to act in respect of things naturally on land. In his view, these cases could establish no general principle:[96]

> Are we—by examining what courts have said in cases about thistles, prickly pear, the roots of trees and the branches of trees, trees deliberately planted and trees growing naturally, rolling rocks, rabbits, weeds in watercourse, silt in streams, seaweed, snow and surface water—to abstract some general principle, to add qualifications to it, and then to try to apply it to a fire which lightning lit? I do not think so.

Inevitably, the conclusion would be influenced by contemporary conditions; thus anyone but a lawyer would be surprised to learn that the answer to the question of whether in modern Australia a duty should be imposed on an occupier to prevent the fire spreading to become a bushfire should be sought in a case about thistledown. For Windeyer J, all of these cases represented the unsurprising conclusion that

> often the law does not hold a man at fault because he does not take any steps to arrest the consequences of such a happening although he knows that they may be harmful to other persons: but that sometimes it does.[97]

Considering bushfires in isolation, as he thought appropriate, there were good grounds for imposing a duty to act to prevent the spread of fire and that such a duty was not 'involved in any way with nuisance'.[98] Bushfires had long been a concern in Australia, but the particular context in which the bushfire at issue in *Goldman* took place, and its subsequent history, made an impressive case for extending the law: 'The grave and widespread consequences of a bushfire may make the liability of a careless individual ruinous for him; but this only emphasizes the seriousness of the duty of care.'[99] Certainly the penalties imposed for failing to comply with bushfire legislation were unlikely to stress the seriousness of the duty of care: Goldman was successfully prosecuted for breaches of the Bush Fires Act 1954 (WA) in September 1962 and fined £10.[100] Moreover, Goldman

---

96 *Goldman* (PC), above n 1, 69.
97 Ibid, 71.
98 Ibid, 72.
99 Ibid, 72–73.
100 *The Swan Express*, 26 September 1962, 1. Costs of over £30 were awarded against him, suggesting that he may not have responded to the original summons and may have been penalised in costs although he did have counsel at the hearing.

was unlucky (or targeted); the Royal Commission noted that there were very few prosecutions for breaches of the legislation.[101]

After some confusion,[102] Goldman appealed to the Privy Council,[103] where the thrust of Windeyer J's approach was affirmed. The case was considered as one of negligence, the question of any overlap with nuisance not requiring resolution.[104] It is clear, however, that nuisance would be ancillary to any action in negligence:[105]

> The fallacy of this argument [of a distinction between hazards originating in human agency and hazards created by nature] is that, as already explained, the basis of the occupier's liability lies not in the use of land: in the absence of 'adoption' there is no such use; but in the neglect of action in the face of something which may damage his neighbour.

The result was that an occupier owed a duty in relation to hazards on their land, whether man-made or not. There is no discussion of how this might fit the general 'no duty to act' rule, but presumably the Privy Council accepted occupation as the source of the obligation. There is also evidence that the bushfire context played some role in the decision: plaintiff's counsel argued that the community required the strictest measure to be taken to prevent, control and extinguish fires, not only by organised groups, such as fire brigades, but by individuals, including occupiers of

---

101 *Royal Commission Report*, above n 10, 41. *The Swan Express*, 24 October 1962, 2, noted that the Swan-Guildford Council (covering Gidgegannup) had moved to take action on property owners to help control the upcoming year's outbreak of fires.

102 Goldman had requested that fresh evidence obtained between the hearing and judgment of the High Court and relating to his conduct once the tree had been felled be admitted: *Goldman* (HCA), above n 1, 54–55. The High Court referred this back to the trial judge who ruled the evidence was not admissible in December 1963: [1964] WAR 93. Goldman attempted to challenge this ruling but became confused over whether to proceed by way of an appeal or for a motion for a new trial (both allowable under the rules of court in Western Australia). An application was, eventually, made for an extension of time in which to appeal but this was rejected in May 1964, the chamber judge holding that the application was very much out of time and had limited prospects for success. As part of a deal whereby total damages were agreed at £3,600, Goldman sought leave from the trial judge to appeal to the Privy Council. This was rejected in early June 1964 on the ground that the appeal sought was in reality from the decision of the High Court and this should be by petition for special leave from the Privy Council: Supreme Court of Western Australia, Court File No H52 of 1961.

103 Leave to appeal was granted on 10 August 1964 on payment of £400 as security for costs: *Printed Papers in Appeals*, 1966, Vol 4, Judgments 9–12.

104 *Goldman* (PC), above n 1, 657. Beever argues that negligence was not the basis of the cause of action recognised: Beever, above n 3, 326–33. Note, though, the following passage from the advice of the Privy Council, ibid, 656: 'The issue is therefore whether in such a case the occupier is guilty of legal negligence, which involves the issue whether he is under a duty of care, and, if so, what is the scope of that duty'. Whilst the Privy Council leaves open the question of concurrent liability in negligence and nuisance, it is difficult to maintain that liability was only recognised in nuisance. Moreover, the Privy Council had plenty of opportunity to comment on liability in nuisance if they had so wanted since the The Case for the Respondents in the Privy Council expressly relied on a cause of action in nuisance (*Printed Papers in Appeals*, 1966, Vol 4, Judgments 9–12) and counsel argued the point in the oral hearing (*Goldman* (PC), above n 1, 653).

105 *Goldman* (PC), above n 1, 661.

land.[106] This argument was not presented to the High Court because it was not needed: no one who was familiar with the 1960–61 bushfires could be in any doubt about the importance of preventative measures.[107] The Privy Council recognised that the High Court 'may be taken to be aware of present-day conditions as regards bush fires' and that this was one basis for the High Court's decision to prefer authorities in favour of imposing a duty.[108]

The acceptance of negligence as the cause of action also allowed the Privy Council to turn to the issue of what constituted reasonable conduct where the occupier was required to act. This had not been considered by the High Court as the evidence at trial (based on the inquest) was that Goldman's approach to containing the fire was clearly careless. Another step further removed from the facts, the Privy Council was able to fashion a subjective breach rule that balanced a requirement to act with the resources available to the occupier. The genesis of this partly subjective test is difficult to ascertain. The Privy Council cites no authority in support of it, which is not surprising as it makes no appearance in previous cases or in the academic literature. Counsel for the respondents did argue in favour of a 'measured' duty, but the academic views cited in support only went as far as suggesting that reasonable care be exercised.[109] In *Proprietors of Margate Pier and Harbour v Town Council of Margate*,[110] one of the old cases in public nuisance used to support the imposition of the duty, there was an exchange between bench and bar, cited by Goodhart in the article referred to earlier, that peripherally raised the issue:[111]

Hayes J—Suppose a dead horse were thrown by the sea on the land, would it not be the duty of the occupier to get rid of it?

---

106 Ibid, 652. Note that the Bush Fires legislation was cited in support of this argument. When arguing in support of a 'measured' duty of care, counsel cited JA Jolowicz and T Ellis Lewis, *Winfield on Tort*, 7th edn (London, Sweet & Maxwell, 1963) 179 (incorrectly referred to in the report as the 17th edn), an extract from a section on the element of policy in the negligence action.

107 *Cf* Fleming (1961), above n 53. In later editions Fleming recognised that his concerns over duties of inspection and abatement could be dealt with in the breach enquiry: eg JG Fleming, *The Law of Torts*, 6th edn (Sydney, Law Book Co, 1983) 398–99.

108 *Goldman* (PC), above n 1, 662.

109 See AL Armitage (ed), *Clerk & Lindsell on Torts*, 12th edn (London, Sweet & Maxwell, 1961) 655; Jolowicz and Ellis Lewis, above n 106, 179; RFV Heuston, *Salmond on the Law of Torts*, 13th edn (London, Sweet & Maxwell, 1961) 200; JG Fleming, *The Law of Torts*, 3rd edn (Sydney, Law Book Co, 1965) 384–85. The Case for the Appellant refers to any duty being discharged 'by taking reasonable care to extinguish and prevent the spread of fire *as first discovered by him and by reference to the circumstances then prevailing*': *Printed Papers in Appeals*, 1966, Vol 4, Judgments 9–12 (emphasis added). The 'circumstances then prevailing' might be construed as including the financial resources of the occupier but more plausibly the argument was that Goldman had discharged his duty by acting reasonably when he first came across the fire (as had been held by the trial judge).

110 (1869) 20 LT (NS) 564.

111 Goodhart, above n 69, 27.

J Browne QC—We might suppose a large whale to be thrown upon a small plot of ground of a poor man; it is doubtful if it would be his duty to remove it.

Neither Goodhart nor Noel, who wrote on a similar topic from an American perspective some years later and who also quoted the exchange,[112] made any reference to it as suggesting a subjective element to the question of reasonableness; in fact, in Goodhart's case, he thought that, despite any hardship it might impose, it was part and parcel of the benefits and burdens of occupation.[113] It seems, then, that the partly subjective standard was introduced *sui generis* by the Privy Council as the trade-off for requiring the occupier to act to prevent a risk of harm that was not his doing.[114]

The Privy Council's view on both duty and breach was broadly adopted in English law and remains the law today in respect of natural hazards on land.[115]

G. *GOLDMAN* AS A LANDMARK CASE

As the previous paragraph indicates, *Goldman v Hargrave* has made at least some impact on the law, but is this sufficient for it to be considered a landmark case? Was it so viewed when it was decided? It is true to say that contemporary academic comment on the case was limited.[116] Commenting on the High Court decision, the *Australian Law Journal* noted that the bush fire context had played some role in allowing Windeyer J to distinguish earlier cases and thought his distinction between negligence and nuisance

---

112 DW Noel, 'Nuisances from Land in its Natural Condition' (1943) 56 *Harvard Law Review* 772, 785–86.

113 Goodhart, above n 69, 27.

114 Six years afterwards a similar partly subjective standard was imposed by three members of the House of Lords in defining an occupier's duty to trespassers, another situation where a positive duty to act was imposed on the occupier: *Herrington v British Railways Board* [1972] AC 877, 899 (Lord Reid), 920–21 (Lord Wilberforce) and 942 (Lord Diplock). The other two members of the House did not expressly address the issue. Four members of the House in *Herrington* had also sat in the Privy Council in *Goldman*.

115 There remains some doubt as to whether the duty and breach were exclusively in the tort of negligence as the point was left open in *Leakey v National Trust* [1980] QB 485; see also *Holbeck Hall Hotel Ltd v Scarborough Borough Council* [2000] QB 836. For examples of post-*Goldman* case law in Australia see *Stockwell v State of Victoria* [2001] VSC 497, where the occupier was held liable in both negligence and nuisance for the failure to take steps to prevent wilds dogs on its land from causing damage to stock on neighbouring property, and *Gardner v Northern Territory of Australia* [2004] NTCA 14, where liability for the escape of a fire was decided solely as an action in negligence. The few Canadian cases to consider *Goldman* have not discussed the negligence/nuisance divide, although there are examples of *Goldman* liability being treated as negligence: *Loring v Brightwood Golf and Country Club* (1972) 7 NSR (2d) 501; *Zbarsky v Lukashuk* (1991) 8 BCAC 151 [15].

116 It was not noted at all in the *Sydney Law Review* and the *Melbourne University Law Review*, the major Australian academic journals of the time, and only the Privy Council decision was thought to merit an editor's note in the *Law Quarterly Review*: (1967) 83 *LQR* 324.

would be a valuable source for law teachers.[117] More was said about the advice of the Privy Council and the potentially wide-ranging consequences of the decision. Harris thought that the policy behind the creation of the occupier's duty was clearly expressed and that 'the case should form the basis for further progress in the modernisation of tort law'.[118] Conversely, it was argued that the novelty was not in the actual decision—which could have been reached by application of the existing law of nuisance—but by the choice to impose liability for the negligence. Such a view does not acknowledge the difficulties of using nuisance highlighted above, but it does recognise the significance of basing liability in negligence: 'the foundation of liability [is based] upon the defendant's potential for preventing or controlling the harm suffered by the plaintiff, rather than upon the former's original responsibility for the hazard from which the harm results'.[119] Some recognised that the approach of the Privy Council could pave the way for challenges to no liability cases outside of occupiers' liability: would the argument that the damage was caused by an act of nature, for example the flood in *East Suffolk Rivers Catchment Board v Kent*, be accepted after *Goldman*?[120] Others correctly saw the difficulties associated with failing to determine whether the liability was in negligence, nuisance or both. Writing in the *New Law Journal*, David Baker saw difficulty in reconciling the decision with previous authority in nuisance, such as Lord Wright's view in *Sedleigh-Denfield* that proof of negligence was not essential in an action for nuisance.[121] Whilst he could see the 'attractive simplicity' of requiring negligence to be proved, irrespective of whether the action was in negligence or nuisance, 'since it would mean the supersession of the action of nuisance in this type of case by that of negligence', the complete absence of authority cited by the Privy Council led him to doubt the existence of such a rule.[122] This forced him to a rather convoluted description of the effect of the decision on the law of private nuisance:[123]

> The decision in *Goldman v Hargrave* conflicts with much of the previous authority; it may be that where the plaintiff alleges nuisance caused by the defendant's failure to remedy a natural hazard on his land, he may succeed

---

117 (1964) 37 *Australian Law Journal* 334. Windeyer J had provided a succinct summary of the differences in his judgment: in nuisance, liability was founded upon a state of affairs, created, adopted or continued (otherwise than as a reasonable user of land), which substantially harmed another person (an owner or occupier of land) in his enjoyment of land; in negligence, liability was founded upon the negligent conduct of one person which caused foreseeable harm to the person or property of another (not necessarily an occupier of land) to whom a duty of care was owed: *Goldman* (HCA) 62.

118 DM Harris, 'Nuisance, Negligence and Dangers Arising Naturally on Land' [1967] *CLJ* 24, 27.

119 Roberts, above n 59, 450.

120 Robertson, above n 57, 229–30.

121 D Baker, 'Failure to Remedy a Nuisance—Part II' (1966) 116 *New Law Journal* 1593.

122 Ibid.

123 Ibid.

without proof of negligence. In this case, the fact that the defendant acted with reasonable care, or that the nuisance was expensive or difficult to remedy, may be relevant, but only in assessing the reasonableness of the defendant's conduct, as a defence to an action.

It took some time, but, in hindsight, these early commentators were correct to see the case as important for at least three reasons. First, it was an important step in the move away from private nuisance, and towards negligence, as the appropriate cause of action for fault-based liability for physical harm or damage to property.[124] As the quotation from Baker demonstrates, it was possible to construe *Goldman v Hargrave* as maintaining a liability in nuisance that was in theory different from that in negligence in cases where the occupier's liability was based on unreasonable conduct, but a more convincing explanation of the decision was that it recognised that fault-based liability should lie primarily in negligence. Viewed in this light, the decision required the dividing line between nuisance and negligence, and other torts, to be redefined, a process that remains incomplete.[125] For example, if liability is to be based in negligence, would this cover amenity interference with the claimant's land? Would negligence be available if the blocked culvert in *Sedleigh-Denfield* had caused a stench rather than flooded the plaintiff's land, or if the neighbours in *Goldman* were complaining about smoke blowing onto their land rather than it being burnt?[126] Secondly, and more importantly, the case created an exception to the 'no duty-to-act' rule which, on its face, applied well beyond natural occurrences on the land. In particular, it raised the question of whether the same analysis could apply where the risk of which the occupier knew was created not by the state of the land but by the things people did on the land.[127] If it did, it challenged traditional notions of causation; it might not be an answer to say that the plaintiff's damage was caused by a third party over which the occupier had no control.[128] If the occupier knew, for example, that trespassers were lighting fires on the

---

124 Buxton, above n 53, 22–31. Although written before the Privy Council decision, the author cited Windeyer J's judgment in the High Court.

125 The point was noted even before the Privy Council decision by Buxton, above n 53. For a recent example of this discussion see *Colour Quest Limited v Total Downstream UK plc* [2009] EWHC 540 (Comm) [408]–[421] and more generally M Lee, 'What is Private Nuisance?' (2003) 119 *LQR* 298.

126 See ME Stockwell, 'Recent Cases: *Goldman v Hargrave*' (1967–68) 8 *University of Western Australia Law Review* 430, 433, suggesting that a mere annoyance, such as the spread of thistledown or other weeds, would probably not give rise to a duty. This was also Goodhart's view, arguing that the result in *Giles v Walker* could be justified in this way: Goodhart, above n 69, 17; see also Noel, above n 112, 779.

127 See, eg *Modbury Triangle Shopping Centre v Anzil* (2001) 205 CLR 254.

128 Later cases have made it clear, however, that the *Goldman* reasoning does not extend to imposing a general duty on occupiers to take steps to prevent harm caused by the conduct of trespassers on their land, nor has it created a general duty to act to prevent harm to others caused by third parties: *Smith v Littlewoods Organisation Ltd* [1987] 1 AC 241; *Topp v London Country Bus* [1993] 1 WLR 498; *Modbury*, ibid.

land, would there be a requirement to take steps to prevent the fires from escaping?[129] Finally, if liability was based not on any hazard connected with the land but simply for things that happened on the land without the occupier's consent, why was the fact of occupation necessary to found the duty? Seen in this way, *Goldman* had the capacity to expand the categories of case in which a duty of care might be owed; it may have been Lord Reid who, three years later, commented that the Atkinian approach to the duty of care 'ought to apply unless there is some justification or valid explanation for its exclusion',[130] but an important step along this road had already been taken by *Goldman*.

H. CONCLUSION

The case for *Goldman v Hargrave* being seen as a landmark case is that it represents an important staging point in the staggering march of negligence to the predominant position it retains in tort law. It was particularly suited for its purpose as the 'user' reasoning of private nuisance previously adopted to impose liability on occupiers for a failure to act was inapposite for a natural condition for which the occupier bore no responsibility and which he tried to eradicate. The move away from a liability based on use to one based on knowledge of risk to create a duty to one's neighbours had implications well beyond the liability of occupiers for things on their land, whether present through the act of trespassers or there naturally. It raised the question of whether occupiers could be liable for failing to act to prevent harm to others where the risk was created by human agency and for failing to act more generally. The difficulties associated with defining the outer boundaries of these obligations remain with us.

Apart from its doctrinal importance, *Goldman* is another example of the importance of understanding legal developments in their historical context. The social, political and economic imperatives to limit the spread of bushfires were contradicted by a common law that imposed an obligation to act only in rare circumstances. It is not suggested that in these circumstances the previous common law was simply sacrificed to expediency; that is far too reductionist an approach. But it is equally implausible to deny the importance of the bushfire context to the decision. This meshing of the internal discourses of law with its wider goals was not easy to achieve and it is no surprise that Jackson J reached a different result from that of the appellate courts; there was a wide margin of appreciation in determining the correct balance between these competing drivers. Nor can the difference in outcomes be explained by proximity to

---

[129] See, eg *Smith v Littlewoods*, ibid.
[130] *Home Office v Dorset Yacht Co* [1970] AC 1004, 1027.

the scene. Jackson J, as a Western Australian judge, could hardly have been unaware of the problem of bushfires, but found in favour of Goldman.[131] It is no surprise, however, that it was Sir Victor Windeyer who most explicitly recognised the importance of context to the development of the law. His undergraduate record included a Sydney University medal for History and he lectured in legal history at Sydney Law School between 1929 and 1936, later publishing a book of the lectures.[132] His historicism was very much that of his hero, Oliver Wendall Holmes;[133] he believed that an understanding of history was integral to the common law's dynamic ability to adapt to the needs of contemporary society. Shortly after his retirement, he wrote:[134]

> Legal doctrine prevailing at particular times is often the product of happenings outside the law itself. The continuous progress of events prevents generalisations of the course of legal developments, like so called philosophies of history. They may serve their age and time but not all time and all ages.

These views, which he had held at least since his lectures on legal history,[135] illustrate his belief in the contingent nature of legal development and made it less difficult for him to consider the requirements of community in fashioning a legal rule.

Whatever the reasons for the different answers to the question of law given by the various judges, the background to the case makes it clear why this case was the one to ask the question. Depending on one's view of the case, Alan Goldman's rugged individualism played its role in the modernisation of tort law or an unprincipled extension to the law of negligence.

---

131 Note, however, that the argument of the plaintiff was not put before Jackson J in the best light by plaintiffs' counsel: see National Archives of Australia, *Goldman v Hargrave*, A10078, 1963/5 Part 2, and 'Contingency and the Common Law: *Hargrave v Goldman* at 1st Instance', 28th Australia and New Zealand Law and History Society Conference, Wellington, New Zealand, 11–13 December 2009.

132 B Debelle, 'Windeyer, (William John) Victor' in M Blackshield et al (eds), *The Oxford Companion to the High Court of Australia* (Melbourne, Oxford University Press, 2001) 717; WJV Windeyer, *Lectures on Legal History* (Sydney, Law Book Co of Australia, 1938).

133 Windeyer referred to Holmes as 'rather a hero of mine' in a Speech Day Address at his old school, Sydney Grammar, in 1970. The annotations to his copy of *The Common Law* also indicate a deep respect for Holmes. I am grateful to David Miller and to [ooo] for these references.

134 Sir Victor Windeyer 'History in Law and Law in History' (1973) 11 *Alberta Law Review* 123, 138.

135 Windeyer *Lectures*, above n 131, 3. See also Debelle, above n 131, 718, who notes that after his retirement Windeyer commented that 'the law of a people is not an aggregate of abstract concepts, it governs their lives and reflects their history'—a view, as Debelle notes, he had expressed 40 years earlier in *Lectures on Legal History*.

9

Tate & Lyle Food & Distribution Ltd v Greater London Council (1983)

JW NEYERS

A. INTRODUCTION

According to the usual standards, the House of Lords' decision in *Tate & Lyle Food & Distribution Ltd v Greater London Council*[1] would not appear to be a landmark case in the law of torts. It does not, for example, mark the beginning (or the end) of an important course of legal development.[2] Moreover, it is not recognised as a leading tort law case by either the judiciary[3] or the academy.[4] Nor has the case had any discernible impact on developments in other common law jurisdictions, certainly nothing approaching the impact of some of the other cases analyzed in this volume.[5] Finally, if we are being honest, it does not even have

---

[1] [1983] 2 AC 509.

[2] For example, this sensible standard is employed by Catherine MacMillan in justifying her essay on *Taylor v Caldwell* (1863) 3 B & S 826, 122 ER 309: C MacMillan, '*Taylor v Caldwell* (1863)' in C Mitchell and P Mitchell (eds), *Landmark Cases in the Law of Contract* (Oxford, Hart Publishing, 2008) 127, 127.

[3] For example, *Tate & Lyle* is cited only three times in subsequent House of Lords decisions, compared with 24 times for *Murphy v Brentwood DC* [1991] 1 AC 398, 17 times for *Leigh and Sillivan Ltd v Aliakmon Shipping Co Ltd, The Aliakmon* [1986] AC 785, and 78 times for *Anns v Merton LBC* [1978] 1 AC 728 (according to Westlaw).

[4] For example, in A Dugdale and M Jones (eds), *Clerk & Lindsell on Torts*, 19th edn (London, Sweet & Maxwell, 2006) *Tate & Lyle* is mentioned only once in the text in relation to the defence of statutory authority (at 230) and is not mentioned in the treatise's discussion of negligence in either the text or the footnotes. In J Murphy, *Street on Torts*, 12th edn (Oxford, Oxford University Press, 2006) the case makes appearances in only two footnotes (at 78 and 441). Even NJ McBride and R Bagshaw, *Tort Law*, 3rd edn (London, Pearson, 2008), which adopts a rights-based view of tort law, makes only one mention of *Tate & Lyle* and only on the issue of the costs of removing a public nuisance (at 802).

[5] For example, *Tate & Lyle* has only been cited once, in passing, by a Canadian appellate court, whereas *Hedley Byrne & Co Ltd v Heller & Partners Ltd* [1964] AC 465 has been cited 109 times and *Alcock v Chief Constable of South Yorkshire* [1992] 1 AC 310 has been cited 11

the literary flair of a tort judgment by a Cardozo[6] or a Denning;[7] in comparison, the judgments in *Tate & Lyle* have a workmanlike quality: solid yet not spectacular in any particular way.

So in what way could it be said that *Tate & Lyle* is a landmark case worthy of inclusion in this volume? The answer is that the decision is important from a conceptual point of view. As John Fleming noted in his highly regarded treatise, *Tate & Lyle* 'is a rare case where the [claimant's] negligence claim was defeated specifically on the ground that he lacked a legally protected interest'.[8] Thus, *Tate & Lyle* explicitly recognises what is implicit in every tort law decision—namely that the concepts of right and duty are correlative.[9] The case is therefore an exemplar of rights-based reasoning which demonstrates that tort liability requires the claimant to prove *both* the existence of a right *and* interference that is wrongful in relation to that right.[10] The argument of this essay will be that this view of tort law more easily explains the patterns of liability found in English nuisance and negligence law than do the usual explanations given by modern courts and academic commentators. Moreover, it does so in a way that is coherent and better justifies the results of the cases. In order to make this argument, the essay is divided into several parts. In parts B and C, I will set out the facts and decisions in *Tate & Lyle* itself. In the subsequent parts, I will turn to demonstrating how the reasoning process exemplified by *Tate & Lyle* simply and coherently justifies situations of no liability in the law of nuisance and negligence.

times. Moreover, the case is not even mentioned in AM Linden and B Feldthusen, *Canadian Tort Law*, 8th edn (Markham, LexisNexis Butterworths, 2006).

[6] See, eg *Palsgraf v Long Island Railway Co* 248 NY 339 (1928) 343–44 ('What the [claimant] must show is "a wrong" to herself; ie, a violation of her own right, and not merely a wrong to some one else, nor conduct "wrongful" because unsocial'); *Murphy v Steeplechase Amusement Co* 166 NE 173 (NY 1929) 174 ('The antics of the clown are not the paces of the cloistered cleric'); *Ultramares Corporation v Touche* 255 NY 170 (1931) 179–80 ('If liability for negligence exists, a thoughtless slip or blunder . . . may expose accountants to a liability in an indeterminate amount for an indeterminate time to an indeterminate class').

[7] See, eg *Miller v Jackson* [1977] 1 QB 966 (CA) 796 ('In summertime village cricket is the delight of everyone. Nearly every village has its own cricket field where the young men play and the old men watch'); *Hinz v Berry* [1970] 2 QB 40 (CA) 40 ('It happened on April 19, 1964. It was bluebell time in Kent').

[8] See J G Fleming *The Law of Torts*, 9th edn (Sydney, Law Book Co, 1998) 150 note 6.

[9] For the clearest enunciation of this, see WN Hohfeld, 'Some Fundamental Legal Conceptions as Applied in Judicial Reasoning' (1913) 23 *Yale Law Journal* 16.

[10] EJ Weinrib, 'Corrective Justice in a Nutshell' (2002) 52 *University of Toronto Law Journal* 349, 352: 'it is not enough that the defendant's . . . act resulted in harm to the [claimant]. The harm has to be to an interest that has the status of a right, and the defendant's action has to be wrongful with respect to that right'.

B. THE FACTS AND DECISIONS OF THE LOWER COURTS

Although the facts of *Tate & Lyle* were complicated, they can be summarised as follows.[11] For many years,[12] Tate & Lyle Industries Ltd operated a sugar refinery approximately 1,000 yards upstream of the Woolwich ferry terminals on the River Thames. In 1922, the Port of London Authority (PLA), who were, by statute,[13] the owners of the riverbed, authorised Tate & Lyle to construct a refined sugar jetty on the river. This jetty was used by the company to load small vessels with refined sugar intended for export. The raw sugar that Tate & Lyle needed for its operations, however, arrived in large vessels which, due to their size and depth requirements, were unable to travel up the main shipping channel or to unload at Tate & Lyle's wharves. For many years, these vessels were therefore unloaded downstream and the raw sugar barged to Tate & Lyle's property. In 1964, Tate & Lyle approached the PLA to get permission to take three actions. The first action was to construct a new jetty, called the raw sugar jetty, at which these larger vessels might be unloaded. The second action was to dredge the main shipping channel six feet deeper than it had been previously to accommodate these larger vessels. The third action was to dredge a D-shaped path from the shipping channel to the raw sugar jetty (and back) at that same depth. Permission for all three actions was given by the PLA by the spring of 1965 and the construction completed by 1966.

Between 1964 and 1966, the Greater London Council (GLC) built two new ferry terminals for the Woolwich Ferry in the Thames. This construction was done with the approval of the PLA and in the exercise of powers conferred on the GLC by statute.[14] Due to faulty design, the terminals unduly obstructed the flow of the river.[15] This is turn caused siltation, which materially reduced the depth of the river upstream and in front of both the refined sugar and raw sugar jetties. As a result of this siltation, vessels which had previously loaded and departed from the jetties were unable to do so. Between 1967 and 1974, Tate & Lyle (with the consent of the PLA) incurred substantial dredging costs of £540,000 above what would normally have been expected in order to continue to use the

---

11 The facts are summarised at *Tate & Lyle* (HL), above n 1, 527–29 and *Tate & Lyle Food & Distribution Ltd v GLC* (1982) 80 LGR 753 (CA) 758–63. There was a second claimant, Silvertown Services Lighterage Ltd. It was a subsidiary company of the first claimant that provided lighterage and barge facilities for the refinery. Its claims are ignored in the summary given here.

12 For a history of the firm, see A Hugill, *Sugar and All That* (London, Gentry Books, 1978) and the company's website, http://www.tateandlyle.com/TateAndLyle/our_business/history/history_timeline.htm. (last accessed on 8 June 2009). The litigation herein described is not mentioned in either source.

13 Port of London (Consolidation) Act 1920.

14 London County Council (Improvements) Act 1962.

15 An alternative design of the terminals would have reduced this siltation by 75%: *Tate & Lyle* (HL), above n 1, 528; *Tate & Lyle* (CA), above n 11, 761.

jetties. In 1975, the PLA made major alterations to the main shipping channel of the Thames that put an end to the siltation problem and obviated the need for dredging.

In order to recoup its losses, Tate & Lyle sued both the GLC and the PLA for negligence, private nuisance and public nuisance, on the theory that the GLC had caused the siltation and the PLA had approved it. It also sued the PLA for breach of contract on the basis that there was an implied term in its licence to the effect that the PLA would permit nothing to be done in the river that would interfere with Tate & Lyle's use of its jetties. At trial,[16] the claimant was largely unsuccessful on its claims of nuisance and breach of contract but successful against both defendants in negligence.[17] Applying the *Anns* test,[18] the learned judge found that, since some siltation was reasonably foreseeable upstream, the defendants owed Tate & Lyle a prima facie duty of care. This duty of care was not dependent on the claimant being able to assert a property right nor was it negated, since the acts of the GLC and the PLA were not policy decisions but rather taken in the operational field.[19]

In the Court of Appeal, Tate & Lyle's claims against the GLC and the PLA were dismissed entirely. Neither the GLC nor the PLA was liable in public nuisance because the statutes that authorised the GLC to build the ferry terminals, and empowered the PLA to approve them, also authorised the interference with the public right of navigation that the siltation had created. Thus the defendants were able to rely on the defence of statutory authority.[20] The negligence and private nuisance actions were also dismissed since they depended on Tate & Lyle demonstrating that their riparian rights included the right to a particular depth of water in front of the jetties and this it could not do since the bed of the river was owned by the PLA. The Court of Appeal found that the only rights that riparian owners enjoy are (i) a right of access to the water and (ii) a right to a flow of water in its natural state in regard to quality and quantity. The court determined that neither of these rights was violated by the siltation that had occurred.[21] As Oliver LJ noted in giving the judgment of the court:[22]

---

[16] The full text of the trial decision is unreported (Forbes J, 15 May 1980, QBD). It is however digested in the *New Law Journal*, 11 September 1980, 829. Interestingly, Forbes J's decision on damages, which contains discussion of whether lost managerial time is compensable, is reported: [1982] 1 WLR 149.

[17] A summary of the trial judge's decision can be found at *Tate & Lyle* (CA), above n 11, 769–71.

[18] *Anns*, above n 3.

[19] See also *Tate & Lyle* (QBD), above n 16, 830.

[20] *Tate & Lyle* (CA), above n 11, 779.

[21] Ibid, 784–85.

[22] Ibid, 784.

it is in general necessary for a [claimant] to show that some right to which he is entitled and which the law will protect has been invaded and it is not suffi-cient . . . for a man merely to say . . . that he has been prevented from doing something which previously he was lawfully (that is to say not illegally) doing. There are many things that people may do de facto and without complaint but it by no means follows that the law will give them a remedy if they are pre-vented from doing so.

The claimant's breach of contract claim against the PLA was also dismissed since the term to be implied into the grant was inconsistent with the PLA's statutory right[23] to request Tate & Lyle to remove both the raw sugar and refined sugar jetty on seven days' notice and therefore would not pass the 'officious bystander' test for implied terms.[24] Tate & Lyle then appealed to the House of Lords.

C. IN THE HOUSE OF LORDS

The majority decision at the House of Lords was delivered by Lord Templeman.[25] In it he rejected the argument 'put with engaging simplicity' by counsel for Tate & Lyle that the GLC and the PLA should be liable since Tate & Lyle's loss was the reasonably foreseeable consequence of constructing and authorising faulty terminals.[26] For Lord Templeman, the foreseeability of the damage was not the key issue on the facts of the case. Instead, the key issue was whether Tate & Lyle had a pre-existing primary right that could negligently be interfered with. As his Lordship explained in the crucial passage:[27]

> The question is whether Tate & Lyle possess any right to any particular depth of water. If they have any such right then they will have a remedy for interfer-ence with that right. But if they have no such right then interference with the depth of water causing damage to Tate & Lyle's business constitutes an injury for which Tate & Lyle have no remedy.

In the passages that followed, Lord Templeman examined whether Tate & Lyle had the requisite right as (i) a riparian land owner; (ii) through its licence with the PLA; or (iii) as a member of the public suffering particular damage from an interference with the public right of navigation on the Thames.

In respect to its riparian rights, his Lordship held that riparian owners are merely entitled 'to access to the water in contact with their frontage, and to have the water flow to them in its natural state in flow, quality and

23 Port of London (Consolidation) Act 1920, s 243.
24 *Tate & Lyle* (CA), above n 11, 790–91.
25 Lords Keith, Roskill and Bridge concurring.
26 *Tate & Lyle* (HL), above n 1, 529.
27 Ibid, 530–31.

quantity'.[28] Thus the riparian landowner only has a power to object to siltation if it causes or threatens damage to her land, interferes with the exercise of her recognised riparian rights or creates an actionable nuisance on her land (for example, through emitting a noxious odour).[29] Since the siltation had done none of these things on the facts, Tate & Lyle could not complain. Moreover, his Lordship held that riparian rights could not attach to the jetties (as opposed to Tate & Lyle's wharf) since riparian rights attach to the fee simple of the land *ex jure naturae* and not to a licensed chattel.[30] Thus, Tate & Lyle's claims in negligence and private nuisance failed against both the GLC and the PLA.[31]

With regard to its licence with the PLA, Lord Templeman held that the terms of the licence, when properly interpreted in light of the relevant statutes, did not give Tate & Lyle a right vis-à-vis the PLA to a particular depth of water (as opposed to a right to have its jetties rest on the river bed).[32] In response to the claimant's 'faintly argued' claim to an implied term for their benefit, his Lordship stated that the PLA had no statutory power to expressly or impliedly agree 'that no works would be allowed which affected the depth of water in the Thames between the jetties and the main shipping channel'.[33]

Having dispensed with the claims in private nuisance, negligence and contract, Lord Templeman next turned his attention to Tate & Lyle's public nuisance claim. His Lordship held that each member of the public has a right to pass and repass over the whole width and depth of the Thames and that the siltation caused by the GLC had interfered with this public right of navigation.[34] He further held that Tate & Lyle had suffered the requisite special damage necessary to bring a public nuisance claim since its vessels had been unable to pass and repass over the riverbed between the main shipping channel and its two jetties.[35] The only questions remaining were: (i) whether the GLC could avail itself of the defence of statutory authority; and (ii) whether the PLA could have been said to have continued or adopted the nuisance.

---

[28] Ibid, 531.

[29] See, eg *Booth v Ratté* (1890) 15 App Cas 188 (PC).

[30] *Tate & Lyle* (HL), above n 1, 534, agreeing with *Tate & Lyle* (CA), above n 11, 787.

[31] Ibid, 536, stating that 'An action in private nuisance must also fail if Tate & Lyle have no private rights in connection with the depth of the river Thames'.

[32] Strangely, Lord Templeman does not make it clear that, even if the PLA had granted a licence to Tate & Lyle that guaranteed them a particular depth of the river, this could not have caused the GLC to be liable for its negligent interference, since a contractual licence creates only a personal right that is opposable against the parties to the contract and not a proprietary right opposable against the world: *King v David Allen & Sons, Billposting, Ltd* [1916] 2 AC 54; B McFarlane, *The Structure of Property Law* (Oxford, Hart, 2008) 504–22.

[33] *Tate & Lyle* (HL), above n 1, 536.

[34] Ibid, 537. Later in his judgment, Lord Templeman made clear that the depth of the river was not its natural depth but rather its depth after all licenced works had been completed: ibid, 543.

[35] Ibid, 537.

With regard to the defence of statutory authority, Lord Templeman concluded, on the authority of *Allen v Gulf Oil Refining Ltd*,[36] that the GLC could only invoke the defence if it could prove that it had paid 'all reasonable regard and care for the interests of other persons'.[37] Since the GLC had failed to consider the effect that the chosen design would have on river users upstream, and had failed to take advice from experts that would have led to the adoption of a different design, Lord Templeman concluded that the GLC was partially barred from relying on the defence. Thus, the GLC was entitled to rely on the defence in respect of the siltation which would inevitably have been caused by reasonably designed ferry terminals. It was not, however, entitled to the defence in respect of the rest of the siltation.[38] In light of the trial judge's factual finding that 25% of the siltation was inevitable, Tate & Lyle's damages were reduced from £540,000 to £405,000.[39]

Finally, his Lordship concluded that the mere act of approving the plans did not mean that the PLA had adopted or continued the public nuisance as those terms were traditionally understood.[40] Thus, Tate & Lyle succeeded against the GLC on public nuisance but failed in all its claims against the PLA.

Lord Diplock dissented. While his Lordship agreed that Tate & Lyle's claims for negligence, nuisance and breach of contract failed against both the GLC and the PLA, he denied that there was any liability for public nuisance in relation to access to the raw sugar jetty. His reasoning was twofold. First, his Lordship argued that, since the raw sugar jetty had been completed after the plans for the ferry terminals had been approved, the public was entitled to only the depth of water in front of the raw sugar jetty that would have pertained absent the dredging. Therefore, as the natural depth of the river was 'insufficient to permit of navigation by vessels of the draught that the raw sugar jetty was intended to accommodate . . . there could be no public right to navigate there in vessels of that draught'.[41] Thus, even Tate & Lyle's public right was not violated since it was not entitled to the depth of water required for its operations.

Secondly, his Lordship argued that, even if one assumed that the siltation did create a public nuisance by interfering with the public right of navigation at a particular depth, it was Tate & Lyle's use of the river in this particular way which caused its special damage. As he argued:

---

[36] [1981] AC 1001.
[37] *Tate & Lyle* (HL), above n 1, 538.
[38] Ibid, 539.
[39] Ibid, 543–44.
[40] Ibid, 542, citing *Sedleigh-Denfield v O'Callaghan* [1940] AC 880.
[41] Ibid, 546.

I do not think that particular damage arising from the choice of a person as to how he uses his public as distinguished from his proprietary rights can, in principle, give rise to a civil cause of action in damages against the creator of the public nuisance.[42]

D. SIGNIFICANCE OF THE DECISION

As mentioned in the introduction, the significance of the House of Lords' decision in *Tate & Lyle* is that it recognises that the torts of nuisance and negligence require a particular two-step analysis. At the first step, one must determine if the claimant holds a primary right[43] that has been interfered with—without a right there cannot possibly be a duty of any kind. While this is not always an easy task, as demonstrated by the disagreement between Lord Templeman and Lord Diplock as to the public right of navigation, it is nonetheless conceptually prior to any other question. Only after one has determined whether the claimant has a primary right does one turn to the question of whether the defendant has behaved wrongfully in relation to that right.[44] For the purposes of this essay, I will call this the *Tate & Lyle* or rights-based approach.

The argument of this essay is that the *Tate & Lyle* approach is superior to the standard process employed by academics and modern courts. This process is as follows.[45] First, one determines if, according to the generalised legal rules, the behaviour of the defendant was wrongful and caused loss (ie if there was fault plus causation of loss). In the case of negligence, this would mean determining whether the defendant behaved negligently and thereby caused reasonably foreseeable injury to the claimant; in the case of nuisance, it would mean determining whether the defendant caused an unreasonable interference with the claimant's use and enjoyment of her land and thereby caused the claimant a reasonably foreseeable injury. If

---

[42] Ibid, 547.

[43] A primary right is a right that is recognised by the substantive law and that pre-exists the wrongful interference. A primary right is contrasted with secondary rights which arise when a primary right has been infringed (ie the right to damages). For discussion, see P Birks, 'The Concept of a Civil Wrong' in D Owen (ed), *Philosophical Foundations of Tort Law* (Oxford, Oxford University Press, 1995) 29, 38ff; A Beever, *Rediscovering the Law of Negligence* (Oxford, Hart, 2007) 212ff.

[44] For detailed book-length accounts of how this primary right analysis applies to negligence and the whole of tort law see, respectively, Beever, above n 43, and R Stevens *Torts and Rights* (Oxford, Oxford University Press, 2007). The discussion in this essay has benefited greatly from these works.

[45] For a similar view see A Beever, 'Justice and Punishment in Tort: A Comparative and Theoretical Analysis' in C Rickett (ed), *Justifying Private Law Remedies* (Oxford, Hart, 2008) 249, 272: 'There are two parts to this [modern] conception. The first part consists of a general principle, according to which persons are responsible for the injuries they cause others. The second part holds that the strict application of this principle would lead to overly extensive liability and so the principle must, for reasons of broad social and economic policy, be accompanied by a long list of exceptions.'

one reaches a positive conclusion on the first step, then at the second step one asks whether there are any policy reasons 'which ought to negative, or to reduce or limit' this liability.[46] For the purposes of this essay, I will call this the modern approach.[47]

The claim that the rights-based approach is superior to the modern approach is based on the fact that it is the better interpretative theory of nuisance and negligence.[48] I say this for four reasons. First, it fits the outcomes of the English cases quite tightly. Secondly, the rights-based view is coherent.[49] It is coherent in the sense that: (i) the reason for limiting liability is the same reason for thinking that liability ought to be imposed in the first place—the presence or absence of a primary right; and (ii) it does not cause conflict with determinations of entitlement made by other areas of private law, such as the law of property or persons. Thirdly, in comparison to the modern approach, which requires the judge to take into account literally everything that might be relevant in considering whether to limit liability,[50] the rights-based view is comparatively simple to employ. Finally, the rights-based approach puts these areas of the law in their best light since it: (i) shows that the results of the cases are demanded by justice; and (ii) is more consistent than the modern approach with the rule-of-law[51] and with the traditional understanding of the role of the

---

46 *Anns*, above n 3, 752. As pointed out by Stevens, above n 44, 1–2, while commentators and the courts have made a 'great deal of [the] abandonment of Lord Wilberforce's two stage test', the underlying approach in the new three stage test deployed in *Caparo Industries plc v Dickman* [1990] 2 AC 605 (HL) 'is essentially the same'. The truth of Stevens' statement is probably best proven by the fact that the Supreme Court of Canada arrived at essentially the same three step process while claiming to keep the *Anns* test intact: *Cooper v Hobart* [2001] 3 SCR 537; *Odhavji Estate v Woodhouse* [2003] 3 SCR 263.

47 I take this usage from McBride and Bagshaw, above n 4, xiii.

48 On the requirements of interpretative theory (fit, coherence, best light, etc), see SA Smith, *Contract Theory* (Oxford, Oxford University Press, 2004) 36; A Beever and C Rickett, 'Interpretive Legal Theory and the Academic Lawyer' (2005) 68 *Modern Law Review* 320.

49 As used in this essay, coherence means more than non-contradiction. It also demands that the internal components of a theory 'exemplify a single theme' and constitute a unitary whole, rather than merely being 'an aggregate of conceptually disjunct or inconsistent elements that . . . happen to be juxtaposed': EJ Weinrib, 'Legal Formalism: On the Immanent Rationality of the Law' (1988) 97 *Yale Law Journal* 949, 968–69.

50 See Stevens, above n 44, 1, who states: 'The second limb [of the modern approach] enables any considerations which ought to negative the duty to be taken into account. This could encompass every reason imaginable for denying liability.'

51 See JCP Goldberg and BC Zipursky, 'The Restatement (Third) and the Place of Duty in Negligence Law' (2001) 54 *Vanderbilt Law Review* 657, 723: 'As numerous scholars from across the jurisprudential and political spectrums have argued, all-considered policy judgments lack features that are critical to rule-of-law values. They do not engender predictability or stability. They undercut the capacity of the law to guide. They open up courts to various political pressures, both at an individual level and on a broader level. There is little distinction between decisions of this nature and decisions that are mere exercises of discretion by those who have power. In all of these respects, a general duty-as-policy exemption provision, such as [stage 2 of the modern approach], disables negligence law from functioning as law.'

judge as a neutral apolitical adjudicator.[52] In the parts that follow, I seek to show how this is the case in relation to private nuisance and negligence.

E. NUISANCE

Let us begin with nuisance. The generalised test for liability in nuisance—whether the defendant has unreasonably interfered with the claimant's use and enjoyment of her land—has a difficult time explaining the lack of liability found in three well-known common law decisions, namely *Mayor of Bradford v Pickles*,[53] *Fontainebleau Hotel Corp v Forty-Five Twenty Five Inc*[54] and *Hunter v Canary Wharf Ltd*.[55] The argument of this section is that they are rather simple to understand using the reasoning process exemplified in *Tate & Lyle*.

In *Mayor of Bradford v Pickles*, the claimant owned a piece of property that was used to supply the town of Bradford with water. The claimant's property was located at the bottom of a large, steep hill and the defendant's property was at the top. Through force of gravity, percolating subterranean water made its way from the defendant's property to the claimant's. The defendant then purposefully drained the percolating water from his property, which caused the amount and quality of the water on the claimant's land to substantially decline. The defendant claimed that he had done this drainage in order to work the minerals on his land. The Mayor of Bradford claimed that the defendant had done so maliciously in order to induce the borough to purchase his land and asked for an injunction. The House of Lords, proceeding on the basis that the Mayor's view of the defendant's actions was correct, unanimously found for the defendant. If one applies the modern approach, however, it is not clear why this should be the case.[56] Depriving a landowner of water on her land

---

[52] As noted in P Birks, 'Equity in Modern Law: An Exercise in Taxonomy' (1996) 26 *Western Australia Law Review* 3, 97, this is part of the 'democratic bargain'. 'The terms of that bargain are, on the part of the demos, that some of its power shall be ceded to unrepresentative experts whose expertise consists in the interpretation of the law, and on the part of those experts that they will not usurp the functions of the representative legislature. The difficulty in drawing the line is great, but not so great as to render the bargain void for uncertainty.' He continues (at 98): 'The legitimacy of expert law-making in a sophisticated democracy depends on the truth of the assertion that the interpreters are and must be both masters and servants of a complex system of reasoning. Why are they not elected? The answer must be that they are doing something different from the legislator and something that cannot be done by just anybody on the Clapham bus. They are restrained in their creativity by the system of reasoning which they serve, and they are qualified for the work which they do, not as chosen representatives but by hard-won mastery of the specialized rationality.'

[53] [1895] AC 587.

[54] 114 So 2d 357 (Fla CA 1959).

[55] [1997] AC 655.

[56] As pointed out in J Fleming, 'Negligence and Property Rights' (1988) 104 *LQR* 183, 183. See also the arguments of claimant's counsel in *Stephens v Anglian Water Authority* [1987] 1 WLR 1381 (CA) 1386–87.

must surely constitute an unreasonable interference with her use and enjoyment of it. While the result might be rationalised by invoking policy considerations, the problem is that it is not clear what the policy invoked might be—the court certainly did not offer any—nor how such a policy might be balanced by the city's need for clean and salubrious water. Why, then, did the claimant's action fail? According to the court, it failed for the same reason that Tate & Lyle's claim in nuisance had failed—namely, because the claimant could not prove that it had a primary right to percolating water not yet on its property.[57]

In *Fontainebleau*, the claimant owned a hotel that was adjacent to property owned by the defendant. The defendant began construction of a 14-storey addition to its hotel. Once completed, the addition would have cast a shadow over the outdoor bar and the entire swimming and sunbathing areas of the claimant's hotel from 2 pm onwards. The claimant sought, and was granted, a temporary injunction ordering a halt to the construction on the basis that the size of the shadow would create an unreasonable interference with the claimant's use and enjoyment of its land as a hotel. The defendant appealed and the appellate court unanimously dissolved the injunction. If one thinks only in terms of the general test for nuisance, then the result seems strange and could only be justified on policy grounds which a later court might re-evaluate;[58] however, this was not the reasoning of the court. According to the justices, the claim failed, just as it had in *Tate & Lyle*, because the law did not recognise a primary right to sunlight that was not yet on the claimant's property; nor, under Florida law, was there a way for the claimant to acquire such a property right, since the English doctrine of 'ancient lights' had been repudiated.[59] To find in the claimant's favour in nuisance would therefore create an inconsistency or incoherence in the law by conferring 'upon an

---

[57] See *Pickles*, above n 53, 592, where Lord Halsbury states: 'But although it does deprive them of water which they would otherwise get, it is necessary for the [claimants] to establish that they have a right to the flow of water'—which they could not do since previous case law had decided that such a right did not exist, see *Chasemore v Richards* (1859) 7 HL Cas 349. Moreover, as his Lordship pointed out at 593, at a conceptual level it would be hard to envisage how such a primary right might come into existence ('You may have a right to a flow of water; you may have property in the water when it is collected and appropriated but' not before).

[58] See, eg *Prah v Maretti* 321 NW 2d 182 (Wisc SC 1982) 189–90, where the court states: 'This court's reluctance in the nineteenth and early part of the twentieth century to provide broader protection for a landowner's access to sunlight was premised on . . . policy considerations . . . These . . . policies are no longer fully accepted or applicable. They reflect factual circumstances and social priorities that are now obsolete. First, society has increasingly regulated the use of land by the landowner for the general welfare. Second, access to sunlight has taken on a new significance in recent years. In this case the [claimant] seeks to protect access to sunlight, not for aesthetic reasons or as a source of illumination but as a source of energy . . . Third, the policy of favoring unhindered private development in an expanding economy is no longer in harmony with the realities of our society.'

[59] *Fontainebleau*, above n 54, 359.

adjacent property owner incorporeal rights incidental to his ownership of land which the law does not sanction'.[60]

In *Hunter v Canary Wharf*, one of the important issues to be decided was whether the claimants could recover in nuisance for the defendant's interference with their reception of television signals.[61] The interference was caused by the defendant's construction of a large commercial building between the claimants' homes and the relevant broadcast towers. In the end, their Lordships unanimously found that there was no nuisance. Once again, this lack of liability is difficult to understand using the modern approach since most people would agree that being denied access to television in the modern age is a substantial and unreasonable interference with their use of land and that any such interference would require a strong reason based in policy to trump it.[62] As Lord Cooke noted: 'Television has become a significant and, to many, almost an indispensable amenity of domestic life.'[63] What, then, were the policy reasons given? Lord Cooke and Lord Goff thought that there could be no nuisance since the general principle was limited to include only things emanating from another's land and not the mere building of a structure,[64] which from a policy perspective seems a fairly weak justification.[65] Lord Lloyd and Lord Hoffmann can be read as positing a floodgates-cum-economic objection. As Lord Hoffmann stated: '[i]f an exception were to be created . . . the developers would be exposed to legal action by an indeterminate number of [claimants], each claiming compensation in a relatively modest amount. Defending such actions . . . would hardly be cost-effective.'[66] While the invocation of 'floodgates' can explain the result in *Hunter v Canary Wharf*, it does so at the expense of coherence. This is due to the fact that liability was arbitrarily cut off by reasons that have nothing conceptually to do with the underlying wrong complained of in nuisance, namely the

---

[60] Ibid, 360, citing *Musumeci v Leonardo* 75 A 2d 175 (RI 1950).

[61] The other important issue decided by the court was who has standing to maintain a suit in nuisance. By a majority of 4–1 (Lord Cooke dissenting), their Lordships decided that only a person with an interest in the land affected might sue. Although not discussed in the text, this conclusion is also consistent with the *Tate & Lyle* approach.

[62] PV Baker, 'Note' (1965) 81 *LQR* 181; J O'Sullivan, 'A Poor Reception for Television Nuisance' [1996] *CLJ* 184; J O'Sullivan, 'Nuisance in the House of Lords—Normal Service Resumed' [1997] *CLJ* 483. In fact, in *Nor-Video Services Ltd v Ontario Hydro* (1978) 84 DLR (3d) 221 (Ont HCJ), the court, using the modern approach, found liability for depriving a land-owner of television reception.

[63] *Hunter*, above n 55, 719. See also Lord Goff at 684: 'it can be asserted with force that for many people television transcends the function of mere entertainment'.

[64] Lord Cooke was willing to make an exception where the building constructed did not conform to local planning restrictions or where the defendant maliciously built the structure with the purpose of blocking television reception, see *Hunter*, above n 55, 721.

[65] 'Faintly absurd' (from a policy perspective) according to E Reid, 'Eastenders and Neighbours' (1998) 2 *Edinburgh Law Review* 94, 96.

[66] *Hunter*, above n 55, 710.

causing of an unreasonable interference with the use and enjoyment of one's property.

From the rights-based perspective, however, the result in *Hunter v Canary Wharf* makes sense. The claim in nuisance should fail unless the claimants could prove that they had a primary right to receive television signals. Since, in general,[67] there can be no negative easements acquired by prescription (as evidenced by the lack of a right to a view[68] or the free flow of air[69]), the claim was destined to fail. As Lord Hope made clear, to recognise such an easement would unduly interfere with the building owner's property rights:

> I do not think that it would be consistent with principle for such a wide and novel restriction to be recognized. If that is so for easements, then the same result must follow so far as a remedy in nuisance is concerned.[70]

Or, as Lord Lloyd put it, the case was simply an example of *damnum absque injuria*.[71]

Thus, as opposed to the modern approach, the rights-based view can explain the lack of liability in nuisance for depriving a claimant of percolating water, sunlight and television reception in a way that is both simple and coherent. To reiterate, the actions in *Mayor of Bradford v Pickles*, *Fontainebleau* and *Hunter* failed even though the claimants had a primary right to their land because they also needed a primary right to another good to complete their claims (to percolating water, to light or to television signals not yet on their land)—a primary right that the private law does not recognise.

Perhaps now is the appropriate time to deal with one possible objection to the *Tate & Lyle* approach to nuisance and negligence. This objection is that this way of viewing the law is no better than the modern approach since the policy reasons that are utilised at step two are the very same policy reasons that the courts would be forced to examine in any event when trying to determine the scope of our primary rights. So, the argument goes, since these primary rights are ultimately based on policy, some policy analysis is unavoidable.[72] There are two answers to this objection.

---

[67] The exceptions being to light, to air through a defined channel and to support: *Dalton v Angus* (1881) 6 App Cas 740. The judgments of Lord Hoffmann, Lord Lloyd and Lord Hope are most plausibly read as trying to give cogent reasons as to why a primary right to receive television signals should not be recognised as a rational extension of the rights enumerated in *Dalton*. Lord Hoffmann's reasoning is more policy-based whereas Lord Hope's is more conceptual.

[68] See *A-G v Doughty* (1752) 2 Ven Sen 453, 28 ER 290; *Fishmongers' Co v East India Co* (1752) 1 Dick 163, 21 ER 232.

[69] See *Chastey v Ackland* [1895] 2 Ch 389 (CA).

[70] *Hunter*, above n 55, 727.

[71] Ibid, 699.

[72] See, eg P Cane, 'Distributive Justice and Tort Law' [2001] *New Zealand Law Review* 401.

The first is that, even if it is true that the 'rights base' of nuisance and negligence is the result of policy analysis,[73] it does not follow that policy analysis should also take place at step two of the modern approach (ie the time when the court is to determine whether a secondary right to damages should be available). The reason why this does not follow is a concern for coherence. If courts were attempting to discern what our primary rights were in two (conceptually) distinct venues, there would be a danger that they would end up with inconsistent answers. And this is a very real danger, as *Hunter* and *Fontainebleau* illustrate, given the open-ended analysis required. For example, what is the law to do when the law of easements says that there is no right to receive television signals or light and the law of nuisance says that there is? A similar problem was created by Justice McLachlin's (in)famous decision in *CNR Co v Norsk Pacific Steamship Co*,[74] which in essence argued that the claimant should be treated as a joint owner of a bridge in the eyes of tort law despite the fact that the law of property said that no joint ownership existed.[75] The traditional law relating to prenatal injury also displayed this tension, with some tort law decisions suggesting that a foetus is a legal person[76] and the law of persons holding that legal personality begins at birth.[77] The surest way to avoid these inconsistent and incoherent results is for the law of nuisance and negligence, which deals with the remediation of violations of primary rights, to leave the elucidation of primary rights to those areas of the law whose function this is (ie the law of persons and property, amongst others).

The second answer to the everything-is-policy argument is that it is not at all clear that the only plausible justification for the law's current rights base is one based on policy. For example, legal philosophers and lawyers working in the corrective justice and natural law traditions have attempted

---

73 I take this term from Beever, above n 43.

74 [1992] 1 SCR 1021.

75 A point made in Beever, above n 43, 229; J Fleming, 'Economic Loss in Canada' (1993) *Tort Law Review* 68, 70; N Rafferty, 'Developments in Contract and Tort Law: The 1992–93 Term' (1994) 5 *Supreme Court Law Review (Second Series)* 367, 375.

76 Cases such as *Burton v Islington Health Authority* [1993] QB 204 (CA) and *Montreal Tramways Co v Léveillé*, [1933] SCR 456, which hold that a born alive child may sue for injuries sustained as a foetus seemingly imply that legal personality, for the purposes of tort law, begins at conception. If we accepted that legal personality begins at birth then the child should have no claim since 'the subject matter of the right, here the child's body, is never free from the defect from the moment of acquisition of the right, just as with someone who acquires a defective thing': see Stevens, above n 44, 186. In fact the majority's reasoning in *Dobson (Litigation Guardian of) v Dobson* [1999] 2 SCR 753 which denied the liability, on policy grounds, of a mother for injuries done to her foetus really only makes sense if one assumes that legal personality begins at conception. As Cory J argued at [20]: 'it is appropriate in the present case to assume, without deciding, that a pregnant woman and her foetus can be treated as separate legal entities. Based on this assumption, a pregnant woman and her foetus are within the closest possible physical proximity that two "legal persons" could be.'

77 *Paton v British Pregnancy Advisory Services* [1979] 1 QB 276; *C v S* [1988] 1 QB 135 (CA); *Winnipeg Child and Family Services (Northwest Area) v G (DF)* [1997] 3 SCR 925.

to justify why we have the rights we have for centuries. Recent examples of non-policy-based justifications for the existence of our primary rights, which also happen to tightly fit the law's current rights base, can be found in the works of Robert Stevens,[78] Arthur Ripstein,[79] Peter Benson[80] and Ernest Weinrib.[81] In Weinrib's view, for example, the rights base of the private law is justified and explained by the concept of personality:[82]

> Personality, in this context, is not a psychological but a normative idea: It refers not to the pattern of an individual's behavioural characteristics, but to a presupposition about imputability and entitlement that is implicit in the rights and duties of private law. This presupposition is that, as participants in a regime of liability, the parties are viewed as purposive beings who are not subject to a duty to act for any particular purpose, no matter how meritorious . . . personality signifies the capacity for purposiveness without regard to particular purposes . . . Among these rights [created by personality] are the right to the integrity of one's body's as the organ of purposive activity, the right to property in things appropriately connected to an external manifestation of the proprietor's volition, and the right to contractual performance in accordance with the mutually consensual exercises of the parties' purposiveness.

Thus, due to the facts that (i) there are real dangers of incoherence in dealing with the existence of primary rights at two conceptual levels and (ii) it is entirely plausible that the rights-base of tort law is not dependent on policy, the *Tate & Lyle* approach is to be preferred since it leaves the elucidation of primary rights to other areas of the law and eschews the use of policy itself. Having dealt with this potential objection, I will now turn to an examination of negligence.

F. NEGLIGENCE

As is the case with nuisance, the modern approach has problems coherently explaining the lack of liability in negligence in a litany of common

---

78 Stevens, above n 44, ch 15, on 'Justice'.

79 Eg A Ripstein, 'Authority and Coercion' (2004) 32 *Philosophy and Public Affairs* 2.

80 Eg P Benson, 'The Basis of Corrective Justice and Its Relation to Distributive Justice' (1992) 77 *Iowa Law Review* 515; P Benson, 'The Unity of Contract Law' in P Benson (ed), *The Theory of Contract Law: New Essays* (Cambridge, Cambridge University Press, 2001); P Benson, 'Misfeasance as an Organizing Normative Idea in Private Law' (2010) *University of Toronto Law Journal* (forthcoming).

81 EJ Weinrib, *The Idea of Private Law* (Cambridge, MA, Harvard University Press, 1995) ch 4.

82 Weinrib, above n 10, 353–54. See also E Weinrib, 'Correlativity, Personality, and the Emerging Consensus on Corrective Justice' (2001) 2 *Theoretical Inquiries in Law* 107, 147: 'Each person has a right to bodily integrity because the body is the organ through which purposive action occurs. Property rights in things (ie, in whatever lacks personality) are also available, because purposive beings cannot—consistently with their personality — be denied access to what is both unstamped with another's right and necessary for the exercise of their purposive capacity.'

factual situations. As Lord Diplock explained in *Home Office v Dorset Yacht Co*:[83]

> The branch of English law which deals with civil wrongs abounds with instances of acts, and, more particularly, of omissions which give rise to no legal liability in the doer or omitter for loss or damage sustained by others as a consequence of the act or omission, however reasonably or probably that loss or damage might have been anticipated . . . Examples could be multiplied. You may cause loss to a tradesman by withdrawing your custom though the goods which he supplies are entirely satisfactory . . . you need not warn him of a risk of physical danger to which he is about to expose himself unless there is some special relationship between the two of you such as that of occupier of land and visitor; you may watch your neighbour's goods being ruined by a thunderstorm though the slightest effort on your part could protect them from the rain and you may do so with impunity unless there is some special relationship between you . . .

In this portion of the essay, I propose to deal with two situations—that of rescue and that of pure economic loss—in order to demonstrate the relative superiority of the rights-based view.

1. Rescue

As noted by Lord Diplock, it has long been recognised that there is no liability for a failure to rescue in English law provided: (i) there exists no special relationship between the parties; and (ii) the defendant has not contributed to the risk of the injury.[84] If one accepts the modern approach, however, this result is difficult to justify.[85] As Lord Hoffmann noted in *Stovin v Wise*, '[o]missions, like economic loss, are notoriously a category of conduct in which Lord Atkin's generalization in *Donoghue v Stevenson* . . . offers limited help'.[86] While the lack of a general duty to rescue might be explicable on grounds of indeterminacy, the lack of a duty in cases of easy rescue, such as a baby drowning in a shallow pool,[87] is

---

[83] [1970] AC 1004, 1060.

[84] *Mitchell v Glasgow City Council* [2009] UKHL 11, [2009] 2 WLR 481 [40] (Lord Scott) where the rule and its 'exceptions' are stated: 'The requisite additional feature that transforms what would otherwise be a mere omission, a breach at most of a moral obligation, into a breach of a legal duty . . . may take a wide variety of forms. Sometimes the additional feature may be found in the manner in which the victim came to be at risk of harm or injury. If a defendant has played some causative part in the train of events that have led to the risk of injury, a duty to take reasonable steps to avert or lessen the risk may arise. Sometimes the additional feature may be found in the relationship between the victim and the defendant: (eg. employee/employer or child/parent) or . . . [s]ometimes the additional feature may be found in the assumption by the defendant of responsibility for the person at risk of injury.' The justification for liability on the rights-based perspective when there is an assumption of responsibility is discussed below.

[85] Beever, above n 43, 210.

[86] *Stovin v Wise* [1996] AC 923 (HL) 943.

[87] The classic example, given by their Lordships in *Mitchell*, above n 84, [55].

much harder to explain. In such a situation, a comparison of the interests at stake clearly points to liability. As Weinrib notes:[88]

> Obviously the drowning person's interest in life is more important for the drowning person than the non-rescuer's liberty interest in not bestirring himself to toss the rope: the autonomy of the drowning person will be wholly extinguished by death, whereas a duty of easy rescue would amount only to sporadic, transient, and non-onerous diminution of the potential rescuer's interest in liberty.

Moreover, recognising a duty and imposing liability seems to accord with commonsense notions of responsibility and therefore would not pose policy problems in the sense of conflicting with the will of the populace.[89]

In contrast to this somewhat unsatisfactory conclusion, the *Tate & Lyle* approach can account for the non-existence of a duty in situations of both easy and difficult rescue. The reason why there is no liability is that the claimant does not have a primary right to demand the assistance of others.[90] While the claimant does have a right to bodily integrity, this right is a negative right to exclude others from interference. As Peter Benson explains:[91]

> what the [claimant] can assert to the exclusion of the defendant is *just* her bodily existence or property *in this condition of danger*. This is what belongs to the [claimant] as her protected interest relative to the defendant. And it is this 'asset' which the defendant must not injure or otherwise affect without the [claimant's] consent. But this is precisely what the defendant's decision not to rescue does: it simply leaves the [claimant's] condition untouched, as is. Holding the defendant liable would therefore compel the gratuitous conferral upon the [claimant] of a benefit over and above what belongs to her exclusively as against the defendant. The parties' merely exclusionary rights cannot require this of the defendant. Even though it may be true that the defendant's failure to rescue represents a possible choice and decision and so a course of conduct, it is not conduct that can possibly affect whatever rights the [claimant] has as against the defendant.

Thus, the action fails in a duty to rescue situation for the same reason that it failed in the nuisance situations detailed above—the lack of the requisite primary right. Phrased differently, although the claimant had a primary right in each of the cases (to land, to bodily integrity), she also needed a primary right to another good to complete her claim (to

---

88 Weinrib 'Emerging Consensus', above n 82, 142.
89 JCP Goldberg and BC Zipursky, 'The Moral Of Macpherson' (1998) 146 *University of Pennsylvania Law Review* 1733, 1836. Although discussing America, one assumes a similar view persists in England.
90 See *Mitchell*, above n 84; *Deyong v Shenburn* [1946] KB 227 (CA).
91 Benson, 'Misfeasance', above n 80, at text surrounding note 8 (original emphasis).

water, to light, to assistance), a primary right that the private law does not recognise.[92]

2. Pure Economic Loss

Much like situations of rescue, it has long been English law that there is no liability for the infliction of pure economic loss. Thus, absent a special relationship, the claimant cannot succeed in an action for negligence for economic loss unless she can prove that there has been an interference with her bodily integrity, her property or another recognised primary right.[93] From the perspective of the modern approach, this is hard to explain, but it is usually accomplished by relying on concerns of floodgates or indeterminate liability.[94] Although this view suffers from incoherence,[95] it can at least explain the general pattern of liability found in the law.

Like situations involving rescue, however, this policy is unhelpful in cases where there are few concerns of indeterminate liability. Take, for example, the House of Lords decision in *The Aliakmon*. In that case, the claimants were buyers of goods carried on the defendant's ship. Due to the unique nature of the contractual arrangements between the claimant buyer and the seller of the goods,[96] the risk (of the goods being damaged) passed immediately upon shipment, but title to the goods did not pass until they were released from the port warehouse.[97] Due to negligent stowage by the shipowner, the goods were damaged; due to the terms of the sale contract, the claimant could not refuse payment to the seller on account of this damage. The claimant then sued the shipowner in negligence for damage to the goods. The House of Lords unanimously dismissed the claimant's action on the basis that the claimant did not have legal ownership or possessory title to the goods at the time they were damaged.

---

[92] See also the explanation given in EJ Weinrib, 'The Passing of Palsgraph' (2001) 54 *Vanderbilt Law Review* 803, 807: 'In circumstances of nonfeasance, the entitlement claimed is not merely to one's own physical integrity—which *ex hypothesi* the defendant has not endangered—but to the defendant's positive assistance. Under the common law, however, one has no general right to be benefitted by another.'

[93] See, eg *Cattle v Stockton Waterworks Co* (1875) LR 10 QB 453, *Société Anonyme de Remorquage A Hélice v Bennetts* [1911] 1 KB 243; *Murphy*, above n 3.

[94] See *Candlewood Navigation Corporation Ltd v Mitsui OSK Lines Ltd, The Mineral Transporter* [1986] AC 1, 25; *The Aliakmon*, above n 3, 914. See also the classic argument in F James, Jr, 'Limitations on Liability for Economic Loss Caused by Negligence: A Pragmatic Appraisal' (1972) 25 *Vanderbilt Law Review* 43.

[95] In the sense that liability is arbitrarily being cut off by reasons that have nothing conceptually to do with the underlying wrong complained of, see the discussion at text surrounding nn 66–67.

[96] Which were described in *The Aliakmon*, above n 3, 916, as being of 'an extremely unusual character'.

[97] See *The Aliakmon*, ibid, 907, where the contract is described in detail.

As counsel for the claimant argued, on the facts of *The Aliakmon* and other similar cases, this result makes little sense.[98] The defendant owed a prima facie duty because this loss to the claimant was reasonably foreseeable and proximate.[99] Moreover, counsel argued that indeterminate liability is not a concern at step two since:[100]

> recognition by law of a duty of care by shipowners to a cif or c and f buyer . . . would not of itself open any floodgates . . . It would . . . only create a strictly limited exception to the general rule, based on the circumstance that the consideration of policy on which the general rule was founded did not apply to that particular case.

Their Lordships rejected this line of reasoning on two bases. The first basis was that to allow claimants to argue for exceptions, even where the policy reason for negating a duty did not apply, would undermine legal certainty and 'certainty of the law is of utmost importance'.[101] The second basis was that their Lordships did not feel sympathy for the plight of the claimant since it could have protected itself by taking an assignment of the seller's contractual rights or by organising its affairs differently so as to have the benefit of the remedial sections of the Bills of Lading Act 1855.[102]

As others have pointed out, this reasoning is far from ideal.[103] For example, should we apply an unjust rule merely because it is simple to understand, easy to apply and thereby conducive of legal certainty?[104] The intuitive answer is obviously no (at least if we think that the law should also consider concerns of coherence and justice between the parties). In

---

[98] The counsel was Anthony Clarke, who was also counsel for the claimant in *Tate & Lyle* and who is now Lord Clarke of Stone-cum-Ebony.

[99] *The Aliakmon*, above n 3, 911.

[100] Ibid, 914. See also Goff LJ's comments in the Court of Appeal, [1985] QB 350 (CA) 399: 'In my judgment, there is no good reason in principle or in policy, why the c. and f. buyer should not have . . . a direct cause of action. The factors which I have already listed point strongly towards liability. I am particularly influenced by the fact that the loss in question is of a character which will ordinarily fall on the goods owner who will have a good claim against the shipowner, but in a case such as the present the loss may, in practical terms, fall on the buyer. It seems to me that the policy reasons pointing towards a direct right of action by the buyer against the shipowner in a case of this kind outweigh the policy reasons which generally preclude recovery for purely economic loss.'

[101] Ibid, 915.

[102] Where property passes to the purchaser as a result of the endorsement of the bill of lading, by virtue of s 1 of the Act, the claimant is vested with all rights of suit, and is subject to the same liabilities in respect of the goods, as if the contract had been made with the claimant. See the descriptions of the act given by Lord Brandon, ibid, 907 and 916–17.

[103] Eg BS Markesinis, 'The Imaginative Versus the Faint-Hearted: Economic Loss Still in a State of Chaos' [1986] *CLJ* 384, 386. See also M Clarke, 'Buyer Fails to Recover Economic Loss from the Negligent Carrier' [1986] *CLJ* 382, 383, who points out that (i) since insurance law allows the CIF buyer to purchase insurance and (ii) since both the insurance rule and the rule prohibiting recovery of pure economic loss are 'rules of public policy designed to draw clear lines between interests that merit protection by law and interests that do not', then (iii) it is incoherent from a policy perspective that the economic interest of the buyer would be protected by one area of the law and not the other.

[104] Markesinis, above n 103, 386.

regard to the second reason given by Lord Brandon, if it is correct, then we should not even allow recovery for negligent injury to person or property since, given modern conditions, claimants can protect themselves from these losses via insurance.

In contrast to this convoluted and unsatisfactory (even on its own terms) reasoning, the analysis utilised in *Tate & Lyle* can explain the result in *The Aliakmon* in a way that is simple, coherent and just. In *The Aliakmon*, the reason why the claimant's action failed was because the claimant possessed no primary right to the goods at the time the goods were injured. Without a right, there could conceptually be no duty, since the two concepts are correlative. The reason why the claimant could not sue after the goods were received, ie after it acquired the primary right to the goods, was that the goods did not suffer any fresh damage at that time. Phrased differently, from the very moment that the claimant acquired those goods, they were damaged goods. So, although the claimant subsequently had a right to the goods (in the state that they were acquired), this right was not infringed by the shipowner's negligence. Beyond the facts of *The Aliakmon*, this reasoning explains the lack of liability in the major economic loss cases since they for the most part share the same pattern of a lack of a primary right.[105]

At this point, two major objections might be raised in relation to the *Tate & Lyle* approach as a universal explanation of economic loss in negligence. The first is that it cannot explain why the common law makes an exception for pure economic loss that flows from a special relationship. The second is that it cannot explain the lack of liability in negligence in situations where a primary right, such as that created by contract, exists and has been interfered with. I propose to deal with these in turn.

The answer to the first objection is that the line of cases epitomised by *Hedley Byrne*[106] is not an example of pure economic loss since there is a primary right that is infringed in those cases. What sort of primary right is it? Broadly speaking, there are three theories of what the primary right might be. The first theory, which is offered by Allan Beever, is that the primary right created by the assumption of responsibility is one that is in all material respects equivalent to the primary right created through contract.[107] The reason why negligence and detrimental reliance seem to be at issue is that the assumed responsibility in many of the leading cases was to use reasonable care to protect the claimant from loss.[108] The

---

[105] See, eg *Murphy*, above n 3, which is the real estate equivalent of *The Aliakmon*. In that case, there could be no liability since, at the time of the negligence, the claimant was not the owner of the building and, at the moment he became owner, the building was already defective. For a thorough discussion of the pure economic loss cases, see Beever, above n 43, ch 7; Stevens, above n 44, 20ff.

[106] *Hedley Byrne & Co Ltd v Heller & Partners Ltd* [1964] AC 465.

[107] Beever, above n 43, ch 8.

[108] Ibid, 300–02.

second theory, which is offered by Robert Stevens, is that the primary right created is one that is most similar to that created by express trusts, bare promises in deeds and bailments.[109] It is different than the primary right created by contract since breach of this type of undertaking is not actionable per se but rather only if the claimant suffers consequential loss.[110] For Stevens, the fact that the undertaking is usually to see that care is taken combined with the requirement for consequential loss explains the focus that the courts have put on negligence and reliance in this line of cases.[111] The third theory, which is offered by Peter Benson,[112] is that the primary right is one that is *sui generis* and is created by the special inter-action between the claimant and the defendant.[113] In essence, the assumption of liability and the reasonable reliance creates a baseline or right as between these two parties, one which is different from our rights against the world and more limited than our rights created by contract or trust law. Hence the law's requirement of proving negligence and detri-mental reliance.[114] While I have argued before that Benson's theory is the most compelling justification,[115] the important point for the purpose of this essay is not which of these theories is best; the important point is that they all give plausible reasons as to why the assumption of responsibility envisaged by *Hedley Byrne* creates some type of primary right. If this is possible, then one can explain how liability for economic loss in special relationships can sit coherently with non-liability in other situations such as those epitomised by *The Aliakmon*. This reason is that the economic loss in a *Hedley Byrne*-type case is *impure* since it flows from the violation of a primary right (it is *damnum cum injuria*), whereas the economic loss in cases like *The Aliakmon* is *pure* since no primary right of the claimant's has been violated by the defendant's negligence (it is *damnum absque injuria*).

The second possible objection is that the *Tate & Lyle* approach cannot account for the lack of liability in situations where the claimant has a recognised primary right, such as that created by contract, unless it too employs the policy-based reasoning used in the modern approach. The classic example of such a problematic situation is provided again by the

---

109 Stevens, above n 44, 10. See also N McBride and A Hughes, 'Hedley Byrne in the House of Lords: An Interpretation' (1995) 15 *Legal Studies* 376.

110 Ibid, 11.

111 Ibid, 14.

112 P Benson, 'The Basis for Excluding Liability for Economic Loss in Tort Law' in D Owen (ed), *Philosophical Foundations of Tort Law* (Oxford, Oxford University Press, 1995) 427, 450–54.

113 For a similar view, see S Perry, 'Protected Interests and Undertakings in the Law of Negligence' (1992) 42 *University of Toronto Law Journal* 247; R Brown, 'Assumption of Responsibility and Loss of Bargain in Tort Law' (2007) 29 *Dalhousie Law Journal* 345.

114 Benson 'Excluding', above n 112, 454.

115 JW Neyers, 'On the Right(s) Path' (2008) 19 *King's College Journal* 413, 419–20.

facts of the Supreme Court of Canada's decision in *Norsk*.[116] In *Norsk*, the claimant had a contractual right to use a bridge owned by PWC. The defendant negligently collided with the bridge, thereby rendering it unusable for several weeks. This caused the claimant to suffer economic losses in the form of additional costs for re-routing traffic to avoid the bridge. It is now well accepted in England[117] (and Canada[118]) that, for reasons of policy, the claimant will not be able to recover these economic losses. How could such a result be explained using *Tate & Lyle*, given that the claimant had a primary right (one created by contract) and that the defendant was negligent in relation to that right? If this lack of liability cannot be explained in a principled fashion, so the argument goes, then the *Tate & Lyle* approach is just the modern approach in disguise.

While the issue might appear perplexing at first, the answer to this question is straightforward if one recognises that the primary right created by contract is special in that the right/duty created by contract is personal and therefore binds only the parties to the contract.[119] Thus, the reason why the claimant's action fails in a case like *Norsk* is the absence of a primary right of the correct type. Phrased differently, although the claimant has a primary right to use the bridge opposable against its owner (PWC), this primary right (being only personal in nature) is not good against the negligent defendant. The only person with a primary right good against the world is the bridge's owner (whom the law says can sue), but the owner did not suffer the losses complained of.[120] From the perspective of rights, as against anyone other than its co-contracting party, the claimant is no different than one who merely has a liberty or privilege to use the bridge (which by definition entails no right against anyone).[121] Thus, the logic of *Tate & Lyle* can explain the lack of negligence-based liability found in relational economic loss cases even though a primary right is present.[122]

---

116 *Norsk*, above n 74.

117 See, eg *Spartan Steel & Alloys Ltd v Martin & Co (Contractors) Ltd* [1973] QB 27 (CA).

118 Although the court allowed recovery in *Norsk*, the Supreme Court subsequently retreated from liability and adopted the reasoning of the dissent which in result is consistent with the *Tate & Lyle* approach: *Bow Valley Huskey (Bermuda) Ltd v Saint John Shipbuilding Ltd* [1997] 3 SCR 1210.

119 For a reiteration of this fundamental principle, see *Dunlop Pneumatic Tyre Co Ltd v Selfridge & Co Ltd* [1915] AC 847.

120 See Benson, above n 112, 434–45.

121 See Benson, 'Misfeasance', above n 80, at text surrounding note 14.

122 For reasons why *Lumley v Gye* liability (ie intentional interference with contract) might be justified on the rights-based grounds, see Benson, above n 112; 455–57; Stevens, above n 44, 281–82; JW Neyers, 'The Economic Torts as Corrective Justice' (2009) 17 *Torts Law Journal* 162.

G. CONCLUSION

The argument of this essay is that *Tate & Lyle* deserves to be recognised as a landmark case in the law of torts. It deserves this status not because it marks a historical turning point, or because it is beautifully written or commonly cited; instead, it deserves this status because it is conceptually important. It is one of the few cases in English law that explicitly makes clear that liability in nuisance and negligence requires both an interference with a primary right and an interference that is wrongful in relation to that right. The argument of this essay is that, once the truth of *Tate & Lyle* is recognised, the law's isolated islands of liability and oceans of non-liability in nuisance and negligence can be simply and coherently explained. The reason why liability is denied for factually depriving someone of percolating water, light or television signals is the same reason why liability is denied when a claimant sues for pure economic loss or for a failure to rescue—the lack of a recognised primary right. Similarly, the reason why liability is recognised in other cases (ie in situations of economic loss in special relationships) is that a primary right has been wrongfully interfered with. If I am correct, however, an obvious question arises. If *Tate & Lyle* is such an important case conceptually, why has it not been more universally recognised as such? I would suggest that there are two reasons for this. The first reason is practical: namely, that the facts and statutory regimes at issue in the case are so complicated that a reader would have to go through much relative dross in order to find the gold hidden at the centre.[123] The second reason is conceptual: namely, given the dominance of the modern approach in the courts and in the academy, the insight offered by their Lordships in *Tate & Lyle* has not been well understood.[124] Hopefully, this essay has remedied both these deficiencies so that *Tate & Lyle* can rightfully take its place amongst the landmark cases in the law of tort.

---

123 *Cf* S Tromans, 'A Tale of Sugar and Silt, Or, Muddy Waters in the House of Lords' [1984] *CLJ* 21, 22: 'A large part of the judgment of the House is taken up with arcane questions on the construction of statutory material which is of interest to comparatively few people.'

124 See, eg Tromans, above n 123, who comments that the decision in *Tate & Lyle* is 'a rejection of negligence in favour of a property based approach' and criticises their Lordships for being 'over-subtle in denying liability for private nuisance' since the facts of the case cannot be distinguished 'from extreme pollution of a river engendering smells which render adjacent land unusable, which would clearly be a nuisance'. From the rights-based perspective this criticism is misguided since there is a world of difference between the two situations. The reason why the action succeeds in the 'smells' example is that the claimant only needs to rely on its property right—its claim is to exclude the smells from entering the area protected by this right. No other right is necessary to found the claim. In contrast, in *Tate & Lyle* the claimant needs both a right to use the jetties and a right to a depth of water on land it does not own. Since the second of these rights is not recognised by the law, there can be no claim in nuisance.

10

Smith v Littlewoods Organisation Ltd (1985)

ELSPETH REID*

A. *DONOGHUE V STEVENSON* AND SCOTS AND ENGLISH DIFFERENCE

The most famous of all landmark cases in the law of tort, *Donoghue v Stevenson*, came from Scotland. Much has been written about *Donoghue* and its role in establishing 'one law for Britain' for negligently inflicted harm.[1] One particularly fascinating study, by Lord Rodger of Earlsferry, examined Lord Macmillan's speech in *Donoghue*. Lord Rodger compared the final version of that text against the version first composed to show that:[2]

> The earlier version contains quite a bit about Scots law—indeed it professes to decide the case on Scots law. By contrast in May [the final version of] the speech proceeds, like all the other speeches, on the basis adopted by counsel at the hearing that there was no material difference between Scots and English law and so the case could and should be decided on the English authorities.

As Lord Rodger uncovered, one of the discarded passages in Lord Macmillan's earlier version distinguished Scots and English law to the extent that 'the law of Scotland has never recognised the English distinction between misfeasance and non-feasance, which has had considerable influence on the development of the English law of negligence'.[3] In this connection, Lord Macmillan had cited the Scots Institutional writers, Stair,

---

* The author expresses her thanks to Professor Douglas Brodie for comments on a draft of this chapter.

1 R Evans-Jones, 'Roman Law in Scotland and England and the Development of One Law for Britain'(1999) 115 *LQR* 605, 628; for a Scots perspective see HL MacQueen and WDH Sellar, 'Negligence' in K Reid and R Zimmermann (eds), *A History of Private Law in Scotland* (Oxford, Oxford University Press, 2000) vol 2, 517; see also A Rodger, 'Mrs Donoghue and Alfenus Varus' (1988) 41 *Current Legal Problems* 1.

2 A Rodger, 'Lord MacMillan's Speech in *Donoghue v Stevenson*' (1992) 108 *LQR* 236, 238.

3 Ibid, 249.

Erskine and Bell, and in particular Erskine's statement that 'Wrong may arise not only from positive acts of trespass or injury, but from blameable omission or neglect of duty'.[4] In the specific 'practical problem of everyday life' presented in *Donoghue*, Lord Macmillan had concluded that Scots and English law were 'not really in variance in principle'.[5] However, even though these references were excised from the final version of his speech, the notion of Scots and English divergence on the question of liability for non-feasance never completely disappeared and has reasserted itself in the Scots case law of more recent decades.[6] Against that background, this chapter considers *Smith v Littlewoods* (or *Maloco v Littlewoods* as it is known to Scots lawyers),[7] a leading Scots case of the 1980s, and its role in establishing 'one law for Britain' with regard to negligent omissions.

B. MISFEASANCE AND NON-FEASANCE

The precise extent to which English and Scots law at the time of *Donoghue* did indeed differ in their treatment of misfeasance and non-feasance is unclear. One of the leading Scots treatises of the pre-*Donoghue* era, J Guthrie Smith's *Treatise on the Law of Reparation*, first published in 1864, certainly allowed that negligence could be 'active' or 'passive'—'either in doing these things which we ought not to have done (*culpa in faciendo*), or in leaving undone these things which we ought to have done (*culpa in non faciendo*)'[8] (with echoes perhaps of the *Book of Common Prayer*). That was not to say, however, that both types were treated in exactly the same way. Liability for omission arose only where there was 'breach of a pre-existing obligation to act otherwise'. Guthrie Smith's discussion of the circumstances in which such an obligation arose was non-exhaustive and included, in particular, examples of landowners failing to take precautionary measures against risks of their creation.[9] His second edition, of 1889, drew a sharper distinction between faults of commission and those of omission, and cited English authority to

---

[4] *Institute* 3.1.13, appears in the version of the speech reproduced in Rodger, above n 2, 249.

[5] In Rodger, above n 2, 249.

[6] Eg *RHM Bakeries v Strathclyde Regional Council* 1985 SLT 3, 11–12 (Lord Dunpark), rev'd 1985 SC (HL) 17; *Duff v Highland and Islands Fire Board* 1995 SLT 1362, 1363 (Lord Macfadyen); *Burnett v Grampian Fire and Rescue Services* 2007 SLT 61, [34] (Lord Macphail).

[7] *Smith v Littlewoods Organisation Ltd*, reported in the Scots reports as *Maloco v Littlewoods Organisation Ltd*, 1987 SC (HL) 37; [1987] AC 241 (HL). Page references are to the AC report throughout (pace WW McBryde, 'The Citation of Cases in Court' in HL MacQueen (ed), *Scots Law into the 21st Century* (Edinburgh, W Green, 1996) 171, 174).

[8] J Guthrie Smith, *A Treatise on the Law of Reparation* (Edinburgh, T & T Clark, 1864) 63–64. This formulation disappeared from the second edition, published in 1889.

[9] Ibid, 65.

vouch for the restricted circumstances in which liability might arise for the latter.[10]

Where the defender was alleged to be at fault for failing to avert wrongdoing by a third party, liability was yet more restricted. The leading late-nineteenth-century authority on liability for the misdeeds of others, often cited in this connection, is *Scott's Trs v Moss*.[11] In that case an Edinburgh impresario arranged a balloon flight by a 'world-renowned scientific aeronaut', advertising that this personage would descend from the air at a designated spot, landing on ground rented by him. In the event, the balloon overshot and landed in a turnip (swede) field owned by the pursuers. Fences and turnips were trampled by the crowd rushing to the scene, and a claim was brought against the impresario for the damage caused. However, a close reading of that case suggests that the court regarded the defender's alleged fault as one of commission rather than omission. A proof was allowed to determine whether 'the defender was the proximate cause of the damage, that it was owing to his *action* that the crowds assembled'.[12] Other cases indicate that inaction of itself did not ground liability. Even before *Donoghue*, the Scots courts sought some kind of pre-existing nexus between the parties, such as a relationship of responsibility between the defender and the persons who caused the damage.[13] Further examples involved liability of transport authorities for injuries suffered due to the authority's failure to control crowds, where the defenders might be regarded as having assumed a level of responsibility for their passengers.[14]

If, therefore, Guthrie Smith's account can be accepted as stating the general Scots law position, there seems to be little to separate this from comparable statements of English law from the same period. Underhill's

---

10 Ibid, 27. Liability for omissions turned upon whether the thing omitted to be done: was clearly within the defender's power; would in all probability have prevented the accident; and would have occurred to any person of competent skill and experience in the position of the defender. The authority cited was an English shipping case, *Inman v Reck* (1867–69) LR 2 PC 25.

11 (1889) 17 R 32, cited, eg in *Home Office v Dorset Yacht* [1970] AC 1004 (HL) 1028 (Lord Reid).

12 Ibid, 37 (emphasis added).

13 See, eg *Buchanan v Alexandra Golf Club* 1916 1 SLT 353 in which a golf club was held liable for the depredations of its members who trampled the pursuer's land adjacent to the 14th green in search of misdirected golf balls; see also *Marshall v Caledonian Railway Co* (1899) 1 F 1060, in which the defenders were found liable after leaving a small gap in a wall when rebuilding a tunnel. This had allowed one of their employees the opportunity to squeeze through and steal from the adjacent shop.

14 *Fraser v Caledonian Railway Company* (1902) 5 F 41; *Buchanan v Glasgow Corporation* 1919 SC 515; but see *Degan v Dundee Corporation* 1940 SC 457, doubting that such cases should be interpreted as imposing responsibility for the actions of a crowd (and *cf Cobb v Great Western Railway Co* [1894] AC 419; *M'Dowall v Great Western Railway Co* [1903] 2 KB 331). In connection with possible liability of carriers see also *Bullock v Tamiami Trail Tours Inc* (1959) 266 F 2d 326, cited by Lord Rodger in *Mitchell v Glasgow City Council* [2009] UKHL 11, 2009 SLT 247, and his Lordship's comments at [61].

definition of 'negligence' in his 1881 edition, for example, drew on the well-known dictum of Alderson B in *Blyth v Birmingham Waterworks* to the effect that it constituted 'the omission to do something which a reasonable man, guided upon those considerations which ordinarily regulate the conduct of human affairs, would do, or doing something which a prudent and reasonable man would not do.'[15] Whether negligence lay in omission or commission, liability was contingent upon some kind of antecedent duty between plaintiff and defendant, but while failure to act might be found actionable only in limited circumstances, those circumstances did not at this stage appear to derive from a fixed list.

1. *Squires v Perth and Kinross DC*

In the middle years of the twentieth century there was relatively little Scots case law to indicate how the Atkin dictum was to be related to omissions. In his *Short Commentary on the Law of Scotland*,[16] a work which set out to reassert 'Scotland's European tradition',[17] Sir Thomas Smith had instanced liability for omissions as an area in which the law of Scotland had greater affinity with the law of South Africa than that of England. In support Smith cited a recent South African case concerning duty to rescue,[18] but offered no Scots authorities for comparative purposes. However, the possibility of cross-border difference came to the fore once more in a cluster of cases in Scotland and England during the 1980s. One of the most notable of these cases north of the border was *Squires v Perth and Kinross DC*,[19] later to be reviewed in detail in *Smith v Littlewoods*.

In *Squires* the tenants of a ground-floor jewellery shop brought a claim against building contractors working in the unoccupied first-floor flat above their premises. Although the pursuers had given notice to the defenders that lax security might make it easy for a burglar to obtain access to the pursuers' premises, no action had been taken. Eventually the shop had indeed been broken into by a thief gaining easy entry upstairs and making a hole in the floor. Unusually for such cases, where the

---

[15] (1856) 11 Ex 781, 784; 156 ER 1047, 1049 (discussed, notably, by Viscount Simonds in *Overseas Tankship (UK) Ltd v Morts Dock & Engineering Co Ltd (The Wagon Mound)* [1961] AC 388 (PC) 426), cited in A Underhill, *A Summary of the Law of Torts*, 3rd edn (London, Butterworths, 1881) 163. See also R Campbell, *The Laws of Negligence* (London, Stevens & Haynes, 1871). In setting out the principles 'substantially common to all parts of the United Kingdom' (at 1), Campbell, who was dual-qualified at the Scots and English bars, drew no distinction in thetreatment of omissions.

[16] (Edinburgh, W Green, 1962).

[17] Ibid, vii.

[18] *Silva's Fishing Corp Ltd v Maweza* 1957 (2) SA 256 (AD). This case was cited to the House of Lords half a century later in *Mitchell v Glasgow City Council*, above n 14, discussed below, and commented upon by Lord Scott at [43]–[44].

[19] 1986 SLT 30.

third-party wrongdoer is typically unknown and unaccounted for, the thief, one Ian Sneddon, himself gave evidence (having been released after serving two years of imprisonment for the offence) to the effect that the unglazed windows of the first floor flat had drawn his attention to the possibility of theft by breaking through to the premises below.

The facts of *Squires* closely paralleled an English case decided only a short time previously in the Court of Appeal, *P Perl (Exporters) Ltd v Camden LBC*.[20] In *Perl* the plaintiffs claimed against their landlords as occupiers of the premises next door when burglars took advantage of a broken lock on the door of the landlords' flat to enter, break a hole in the adjoining wall and steal the plaintiffs' goods. Complaints had been made about lack of security and earlier break-ins, but, in the absence of any relationship between the defendants and the wrongdoers, it was held that a duty to prevent third parties causing damage required more than the fact that such wrongdoing was a foreseeable possibility. Robert Goff LJ, as he then was, had 'no hesitation in rejecting the suggestion that there is a duty of care upon occupiers of property to prevent persons from entering their property who might thereby obtain access to neighbouring property'.[21]

At first instance in *Squires*, the sheriff, to whom counsel had presented *Perl* 'hot off the press',[22] found no duty of care to be established. His decision was, however, overturned on appeal to the Inner House. The defenders attempted to found not only upon *Perl* but also on *Home Office v Dorset Yacht* to argue that, unless there was a special relationship between the defenders and the third-party perpetrator of the wrong, there could be no duty. However, the court distinguished *Perl* on a number of counts, the most fundamental of which was their rejection of a relationship between the parties as a 'sine qua non' of duty. Indeed, the sheriff was regarded as having been unduly 'impressed' by the element of special relationship emphasised in the English case.

The central authorities relied upon by the Inner House were therefore the classic Scots trilogy of *Donoghue*,[23] *Muir v Glasgow Corporation*[24] and *Bourhill v Young*,[25] as well as dicta by Lord Reid in *Home Office v Dorset Yacht*.[26] The primary 'test' was foreseeability, which was 'two-fold

---

20 [1984] QB 342 (CA).
21 Ibid, 361.
22 *Squires*, above n 19, 32 (Lord Justice Clerk Wheatley).
23 [1932] AC 562 (HL).
24 [1943] AC 448 (HL).
25 [1943] AC 92 (HL).
26 [1970] AC 1004 (HL), in particular at 1030: 'where human action forms one of the links between the original wrongdoing of the defendant and the loss suffered by the plaintiff, that action must at least have been something very likely to happen if it is not to be regarded as novus actus interveniens breaking the chain of causation. I do not think that a mere foreseeable possibility is or should be sufficient, for then the intervening human action can more properly be regarded as a new cause than as a consequence of the original wrongdoing. But if the intervening action was likely to happen I do not think that it can matter whether that action was innocent or

in regard to (a) whether the act or omission is likely to injure a neighbour and (b) which persons are likely to be injuriously affected by the act or omission'.[27] Stages (a) and (b) were 'interlinked'[28] to the extent that it is difficult to disentangle the different strands of foreseeability in the reasoning applied by the court. However, it is evident that the focus was upon standard of care rather than upon establishing a pre-existing relationship upon which duty could be predicated. Finding grounds of fault to be clearly established and, noting in particular that notice of the specific risk had been given by the pursuers to the defenders, the court found for the Squires.[29]

The Scots legal community gave a mixed reception to *Squires*, and some commentators saw it as opening up a disconcerting gap between the reasoning of the Scots and English courts.[30] *Smith v Littlewoods*, which came before the Scottish courts only a short time later, did little to allay those concerns.

C. SMITH V LITTLEWOODS

Writing in the LQR a year or two after *Smith*, Markesinis described the case as promising 'a significant new process in the tort of negligence' which was the 'logical concluding phase' of a series of English decisions.[31] North of the border, however, the reading of the decision was less straightforward. A case note published in the *Juridical Review* declared that 'The inconsistencies apparent as between Scottish and English cases pre-Smith have now become inconsistencies inherent in Scots law with, as yet, no definitive resolution'.[32] So what was it about *Smith* that merited this divided response?

tortious or criminal. Unfortunately, tortious or criminal action by a third party is often the "very kind of thing" which is likely to happen as a result of the wrongful or careless act of the defendant.'

[27] *Squires*, above n 19, 33 (Lord Justice Clerk Wheatley).

[28] Ibid.

[29] Ibid, 34 (Lord Justice Clerk Wheatley).

[30] S Stuart, 'Bad Neighbours' [1984] *SLT (News)* 45 argued that the sheriff was wrong to have followed *Perl*, which did not represent Scots law. However, an anonymous case note in the *Journal of the Law Society of Scotland* dismissed the decision of the Second Division as 'theoretical nonsense' and looked forward to an appeal to the House of Lords (which did not happen) and the 'imposition of the [more sensible] English doctrine on Scots law' (1986) 31(10) *Journal of the Law Society of Scotland* 406, 408.

[31] B Markesinis, 'Negligence, Nuisance and Affirmative Duties of Action' (1989) 105 *LQR* 104, 104.

[32] J Logie, 'Special Relationships, Reasonable Foreseeabilities and Distinct Probabilities: The Duty to Prevent Damage to the Property of Others' (1988) *Juridical Review* 77, 89.

1. The Facts of *Smith*

The Regal Cinema in the centre of Dunfermline opened in December 1931. Built on a sloping site, it was by all accounts a grand institution, with a floodlit façade, 1,800 seats and a marble staircase between balcony and stalls.[33] By 1976, however, it had fallen upon hard times. The last film was screened on 29 May 1976 (*Hustle*, starring Burt Reynolds and Catherine Deneuve), and the building was sold immediately thereafter to the defenders, the Littlewoods organisation, for redevelopment into a super-market. After the cinema's closure, local youngsters quickly discovered the potential of this 'well kent'[34] building. When the contractors working there had left the premises at the end of the day, unknown individuals forced entry in the evenings. The contractors completed work at the site on 18 June, a time which unfortunately coincided with the beginning of the Scottish school holidays in what was an unusually warm summer. There-after it seems that gangs of local teenagers broke open the fire doors and turned the cinema into an exotic adventure playground. Some were content to play 'cowboys and Indians' in the dark of the auditorium,[35] but others were more destructive, tearing radiators off the walls and effectively running amok. On one occasion there were signs of a fire having been started with debris from the cinema in the lane outside. On another, one of the church officers, who also happened to live next door, extinguished a fire which he found smouldering inside the cinema itself. He did not, however, report the incident to the police or to Littlewoods, although he did mention it to an individual whom he believed to be a surveyor working in the premises (not a Littlewoods employee). It was plainly common knowledge in the area, and was not disputed by the defenders, that the cinema building was not lockfast and was being frequented by young intruders. Somewhat surprisingly, however, the pursuers were not able to prove that the build-ing's inadequate security had been drawn to the attention of either Littlewoods or the police during this time. On the evening of 5 July, police were called to the cinema to deal with a group of boys who were throwing large objects from the building onto the property next door. Two or three hours later, smoke was seen coming from the building and a group of boys were spotted running away. A fire was discovered which took hold very quickly. The building was subsumed by a fire so fierce that the flames leapt 80 feet into the air and caused substantial damage to the neighbouring properties on two sides of the building, St Paul's Church and a café and billiard saloon owned by Angelo Maloco. It took 13 fire engines and over 70 firemen more than six hours to bring the blaze under control.[36] Actions

---

33 See http://cinematreasures.org/theater/2487/ (accessed on 2 November 2009).

34 1986 SLT 272, 279 (Lord Grieve).

35 Evidence given by Alexander Scott, church officer.

36 See http://www.kinemagigz.com/cinemas.htm#The_Regal_Picture_House (accessed on 2 November 2009).

for damages were thereafter brought against Littlewoods by the Reverend Frank Smith and his church officers and by Maloco. Those actions were successful at first instance in the Outer House of the Court of Session, but the decision of the Lord Ordinary, Lord Cowie, was overturned on being reclaimed to the Inner House. Smith's and Maloco's conjoined appeals to the House of Lords[37] were unsuccessful.

2. First Instance

At proof, counsel for the defenders conceded that the fire had been started deliberately and Lord Cowie concluded that the likely culprits were unidentified local teenagers, but he rejected the defenders' argument that the defenders were under a duty to prevent such wrongdoing only if there was a special relationship between them and the third-party intruders. The appeal in *Squires* had not yet been heard, but Lord Cowie's discussion of the authorities included *Donoghue* and *Bourhill*, as well as *Dorset Yacht v Home Office*, and he gave particular attention to two other English cases decided not long previously in the Court of Appeal—*Lamb v Camden LBC*,[38] and *Perl* (noted above). In *Lamb* the defendants had been responsible for substantial flood damage to the plaintiff's house. As a result, the house became structurally unsafe and was left unoccupied for a long period, during which squatters occupied the property and looted or destroyed fittings and fixtures. Liability was accepted for nuisance, but the plaintiffs were unsuccessful in recovering compensation for the damage done by the squatters on the basis that this was too remote. However, Lord Cowie focused in particular upon a comment by Oliver LJ in *Lamb* that, even where the defendant had no pre-existing connection with the tortfeasor, liability might be found if the wrongdoing were 'such as would, viewed objectively, be very likely to occur'.[39] In similar vein, his Lordship drew also on remarks by Waller LJ in *Perl* that 'in circumstances in which it is sought to make somebody liable for the actions of a third party it would appear to require a fairly high degree of foreseeability'.[40] In the present case, Lord Cowie considered it 'very likely indeed' that if the defenders failed to secure the building and make regular inspections, children would break in and cause damage. It was also 'reasonably foreseeable' that they

---

37 Although the Court of Session is the supreme court in Scotland in civil matters, since the Union of the Scots and English Parliaments in 1707 a final appeal may be taken to the House of Lords in London. See AJ MacLean, 'The 1707 Union: Scots Law and the House of Lords' in A Kiralfy and HL MacQueen (eds), *New Perspectives in Scottish Legal History* (London, Cass, 1984) 50.

38 [1981] QB 625 (CA).

39 Ibid, 642.

40 [1984] QB 342 (CA) 351.

would start a fire there.[41] Although his Lordship conceded that the dividing line between 'bare' and 'reasonable' foreseeability was a 'very narrow' one, he found it to have been crossed in this case and accordingly found the defenders liable. Since the café Maloco and the church were both very close, he ruled, without detailed analysis, that the damage to their premises was not too remote.

A third-party notice had been served by the defenders upon the Fife Constabulary, but the case against them fell because evidence could not be obtained to show that the police knew of the state of the building or of the presence there of the young trespassers in the period leading up to the fire.

3. The Inner House

On the case being reclaimed, the authorities relied upon by the Inner House were primarily Scots, and the test of reasonable foreseeability was similarly central to its deliberations. Lord Grieve's starting point, 'which never grows stale', was Lord Macmillan's dictum in *Bourhill v Young*:

> The duty to take care is the duty to avoid doing or omitting to do anything the doing or omitting to do which may have as its reasonable and probable consequence injury to others, and the duty is owed to those to whom injury may reasonably and probably be anticipated if the duty is not observed.[42]

Liability depended 'solely on the law of neighbourhood as enunciated in *Donoghue v Stevenson*' and had 'nothing to do with the question of any special relationship between those who caused the fire and the reclaimers'.[43] No reference was made in the Inner House judgments to Lord Wilberforce's two-stage test for duty of care as stated in *Anns v Merton London Borough Council*[44] (applied in English cases of the period such as *Perl*), although brief reference was made to Lord Reid's speech in *Home Office v Dorset Yacht*, as noted below. In short, a special relationship between defender and wrongdoer was rejected as a prerequisite of liability, just as it had been in *Squires*. Since the existence of duty between neigh-

41 The Lord Ordinary's judgment of 23 March 1984 is unreported, but this passage is reproduced in the judgment of Lord President Emslie in 1986 SLT 272 at 274 (the full text may be found in the process, CS258/1985/8781).

42 1986 SLT 272, 278, citing [1943] AC 92 (HL) 104.

43 1986 SLT 272, 281 (Lord Brand).

44 [1978] AC 728, 751–52: 'First one has to ask whether, as between the alleged wrongdoer and the person who has suffered damage there is a sufficient relationship of proximity or neighbourhood such that, in the reasonable contemplation of the former, carelessness on his part may be likely to cause damage to the latter—in which case a prima facie duty of care arises. Secondly, if the first question is answered affirmatively, it is necessary to consider whether there are any considerations which ought to negative, or to reduce or limit the scope of the duty or the class of person to whom it is owed or the damages to which a breach of it may give rise . . .'

bouring proprietors could be assumed, the main focus was upon the question of fault, or standard of care.

The Second Division's conflation in *Squires* of what was 'reasonably foreseeable' with what was 'likely or even very likely' was commented upon to the extent that:[45]

> the true test merely requires that it was reasonably foreseeable that the event which caused the damage was, in the absence of precautions, 'likely' to occur. The words 'very likely' were first used by Lord Reid in a passage in his speech in *Dorset Yacht Co Ltd v Home Office* but when the passage is read as a whole I do not consider that his Lordship intended to make the test a more stringent one than it had previously been understood to be, and that he recognised that the critical question was that of likelihood. As Lord Thankerton said in *Muir v Glasgow Corporation* 1943 SC (HL) 3 at 8 '[I]t has long been held in Scotland that all that a person can be held bound to foresee are the reasonable and probable consequences of the failure to take care, judged by the standard of the ordinary reasonable man'.

However, this combined test of reasonable foreseeability and likelihood was applied to overturn the decision of the Lord Ordinary, who, it was said, had erred in applying it only to the possibility of the young vandals entering the premises and lighting a fire. The 'real question', which he had failed to ask, was 'whether it was likely or "very likely" that they would deliberately set fire to the building itself, or light such a fire as would be likely to set the whole building ablaze'.[46] Since this specific outcome was judged not to be foreseeable/likely, liability was held not to be established.

A recent Outer House decision, *Playtex (UK) Ltd v Kelman*,[47] was referred to with approval. In that case, a fire started by children playing beside a group of storage sheds engulfed the sheds and caused an explosion when sodium chlorate stored in one of them was ignited. The Lord Ordinary in that case, Lord Mackay, had rejected the claim against the shed owner by the proprietors of buildings damaged by the blast since they could not show that the defender had 'failed to take reasonable care in respect of any risk which he should have anticipated as likely to affect the premises he occupied'.

Counsel for Littlewoods had made further submissions regarding the practicability of preventive measures, arguing that it would have required a 24-hour caretaker to deter the fire-raisers. However, although the Inner House accepted the Lord Ordinary's assessment that precautions of this nature might have prevented the events from unfolding, it was not regarded as necessary to consider such arguments further since the first

---

[45] 1986 SLT 272, 275–76.
[46] 1986 SLT 272, 275 (Lord President Emslie).
[47] Unreported, OH, Lord Mackay of Clashfern, 12 February 1985.

and main question—whether a conflagration of this kind was fore-seeable—had been answered in the defenders' favour.[48]

4. The House of Lords

The appeal by Maloco and Smith was heard in the House of Lords by Lords Keith, Brandon, Griffiths, Mackay and Goff. By far the longest speeches were by Lords Mackay and Goff, but, while both were for refusing the appeal, the reasoning they applied was significantly different. Lord Keith, along with Lord Mackay, the other Scots member of the court, delivered a cryptic one-sentence speech agreeing, without explanation, with both Lord Mackay and Lord Goff.[49] Lord Brandon offered only a few lines, concurring with, and not distinguishing between, the reasoning of his brother judges, but indicating, as did Lord Mackay, that reasonable foreseeability was of the essence.[50] Lord Griffiths, on the other hand, expressly declared himself to be in agreement with the 'statement and evaluation of the facts' by Lord Mackay, but 'agreed' that 'foreseeability of damage is certainly not a sufficient basis to found liability', doubting

> that more can be done than to leave it to the good sense of the judges to apply realistic standards in conformity with generally accepted patterns of behaviour to determine whether in the particular circumstances of a given case there has been a breach of duty sounding in negligence.[51]

While the decision was itself unanimous therefore, the majority, on balance, gave greater support to Lord Mackay's reasoning than to Lord Goff's. As discussed below, however, Lord Goff's speech has been more often cited in subsequent case law.

(a) Lord Mackay's Speech

As the courts in Scotland had done, and as in his earlier Outer House judgment in *Playtex*, Lord Mackay focused upon reasonable foreseeability as the overarching test for liability. The case of *Home Office v Dorset Yacht*[52] was cited as providing an example of a 'clear basis' upon which foreseeability might be established, but, as in the Inner House, he plainly did not regard the existence of a relationship of responsibility between defendants and wrongdoers as the prerequisite of liability.

---

[48] See Lord President Emslie, 277.
[49] [1987] AC 241 (HL) 249.
[50] Ibid, 249–50.
[51] Ibid, 250.
[52] [1970] AC 1004 (HL).

Lord Mackay cited Lord Reid's statement of the general principle in *Overseas Tankship (UK) Ltd v Miller Steamship Co Pty (The 'Wagon Mound' No 2)*[53] that

> a person must be regarded as negligent if he does not take steps to eliminate a risk which he knows or ought to know is a real risk and not a mere possibility which would never influence the mind of a reasonable man.[54]

The difficulty was how exactly reasonable foreseeability should be measured in cases involving inherently unpredictable actions by third parties for whom the defenders had no responsibility. The test which he formulated to deal with this seemed to combine assessment of fault with a *Wagon Mound*-type test for remoteness:[55]

> The more unpredictable the conduct in question, the less easy to affirm that any particular result from it is probable and in many circumstances the only way in which a judge could properly be persuaded to come to the conclusion that the result was not only possible but reasonably foreseeable as probable would be to convince him that, in the circumstances, it was highly likely. In this type of case a finding that the reasonable man should have anticipated the consequence of human action as just probable may not be a very frequent option. Unless the judge can be satisfied that the result of the human action is highly probable or very likely he may have to conclude that all that the reasonable man could say was that it was a mere possibility. Unless the needle that measures the probability of a particular result flowing from the conduct of a human agent is near the top of the scale it may be hard to conclude that it has risen sufficiently from the bottom to create the duty reasonably to foresee it.
>
> In summary . . . what the reasonable man is bound to foresee in a case involving injury or damage by independent human agency, just as in cases where such agency plays no part, is the probable consequences of his own act or omission, but that, in such a case, a clear basis will be required on which to assert that the injury or damage is more than a mere possibility.

Lord Mackay contrasted a similar Scots Sheriff Court case, *Thomas Graham & Co Ltd v Church of Scotland General Trs*,[56] in which the needle had pointed to liability. There the defenders had been given notice about the likelihood of fire being started by vandals on their property and straightforward security measures had been identified. Similarly, he noted Lord Wylie's statement in the Outer House case of *Evans v Glasgow DC* of

> a general duty on owners or occupiers of property . . . where they chose to leave it vacant for any material length of time, to take reasonable care to see that it

---

53 [1967] 1 AC 617 (PC).
54 [1987] AC 241 (HL) 268, citing Lord Reid in *The Wagon Mound*, 642, who was in turn commenting upon *Bolton v Stone* [1951] AC 850 (HL).
55 Ibid, 261.
56 1982 SLT (Sh Ct) 26.

was proof against the kind of vandalism which was calculated to affect adjoining property.[57]

However, in his assessment, the 'needle' of probability remained at the bottom of the scale in relation to the conflagration in Dunfermline, and his gloss on *P Perl (Exporters) Ltd v Camden LBC* and *Lamb v Camden LBC* was that the 'needle' had moved insufficiently in those cases also.[58]

The practicability of preventive measures was also considered, and Lord Mackay gave this issue greater emphasis than the Inner House had done: the assessment of risk required to factor in the difficulty of eliminating it,[59] as well as the resources of the defender to do so.[60] However, this part of his analysis was brief since the question as to foreseeability had be answered in Littlewoods' favour, and by this stage counsel for Smith and Maloco had conceded that the only precaution likely to have been effective in preventing the entry of the young marauders was a 24-hour watch over the premises.

In summary, therefore, Lord Mackay drew upon substantially the same framework as the Inner House. Underlying his analysis of the case law seemed to have been an assumption that duty of care might readily be established between neighbouring proprietors, even in relation to risk which was not of their own creation.[61] Liability for omission to avert harm by a third party was not restricted to those circumstances where there was a specific relationship between the parties. It could only arise, however, where the risk caused the needle of probability to register high on the scale.

(b) Lord Goff's Speech

Lord Goff"s speech began from the general premise, substantiated by English and Commonwealth authority, that the 'common law does not impose liability for what are called pure omissions'.[62] Although he acknowledged that there were 'special circumstances in which a defender may be held responsible in law for injuries suffered by the pursuer through a third party's deliberate wrongdoing',[63] he indicated unequivocally that he did not agree with the reasoning applied by the majority:[64]

---

57 1978 SLT 17, 19. This case had also been cited by the Lord Ordinary, Lord Cowie.

58 [1987] AC 241 (HL) 265–66.

59 Ibid, 268 (noting Lord Reid's speech in *Overseas Tankship (UK) Ltd v Miller Steamship Co Pty (The Wagon Mound No 2)* [1967] 1 AC 617 (PC) 642).

60 Ibid, 269, citing Lord Wilberforce's speech in *Goldman v Hargrave* [1967] 1 AC 645 (PC) 663.

61 In this connection reference was made, at 265, to the law of nuisance and in particular *Sedleigh-Denfield v O'Callaghan* [1940] AC 880 (HL).

62 [1987] AC 241 (HL) 271.

63 Ibid, 272.

64 Ibid.

one thing is clear, and that is that liability in negligence for harm caused by the deliberate wrongdoing of others cannot be founded simply upon foreseeability that the pursuer will suffer loss or damage by reason of such wrongdoing. There is no such general principle. We have therefore to identify the circumstances in which such liability may be imposed.

He went on to specify those 'circumstances' as being: (i) where a duty of care arose from a relationship between the parties, by which the defender assumed responsibility for the pursuer or the pursuer's property;[65] (ii) where a duty arose from a special relationship between the defender and the third party, by virtue of which the defender is responsible for controlling the third party;[66] (iii) where the defender negligently caused or permitted to be created a source of danger and it is reasonably foreseeable that third parties might 'spark off' that danger, causing damage to persons such as the pursuer;[67] or (iv) where the defender knew that a third party had created a risk of fire, or started a fire, on his premises, and then failed to take such steps as were reasonably open to him to prevent that fire from damaging neighbouring property.[68] Attention was therefore to be directed at identifying special circumstances in the case in hand which might allow duty of care to be established:[69]

> Problems such as these are solved in Scotland, as in England, by means of the mechanism of the duty of care; though we have nowadays to appreciate that the broad general principle of liability for foreseeable damage is so widely applicable that the function of the duty of care is not so much to identify cases where liability is imposed as to identify those where it is not.

On applying this framework to the Scots authorities, Lord Goff found *Thomas Graham & Co Ltd v Church of Scotland General Trs* to have been correctly decided since it could be brought within head (iv) above. However, he considered *Squires v Perth and Kinross DC* to be wrongly decided on a number of counts, but primarily because it could not readily be brought within one of the heads above and there was no

> general duty to *prevent* third parties from causing damage to others, even though there is a high degree of foresight that they may do so. The practical effect is that everybody has to take such steps as he thinks fit to protect his own property . . . against thieves. He is able to take his own precautions.[70]

---

65 Ibid.
66 Ibid.
67 Ibid, 272–73.
68 Ibid, 274.
69 Ibid, 280 (under reference to *Anns*).
70 Ibid, 278.

In this respect, Lord Goff appeared to gloss over the considerable practical differences acknowledged by Lord Mackay[71] between the feasibility of precautions against fire as opposed to burglary. Perhaps most notably, Lord Goff criticised his brother judges in 'your Lordships' House' for succumbing in the recent Scots case of *Junior Books v Veitchi*[72] 'perhaps too easily, to the temptation to adopt a solution based simply upon proximity'. A 'simple criterion of foreseeability would impose an intolerable risk upon defendants [*sic*]', and to that extent 'generalised principle' was to be rejected and 'special cases' identified in which liability could 'properly' be imposed.[73]

Since none of the special circumstances which Lord Goff enumerated could be said to apply to the facts of *Smith*—in particular, the empty cinema had not been found to represent a particular fire hazard—duty was not established and liability did not arise.

(c) The Speeches of Lord Mackay and Lord Goff: Cross-border Difference?

The significant differences in the reasoning applied by Lord Mackay and by Lord Goff have not escaped academic comment in the intervening years. Lord Mackay's sternest critics have dismissed the open-endedness of his approach as 'intellectually incoherent',[74] complaining that it is impossible to predict exactly when his needle of probability will register that an outcome is 'reasonably foreseeable as probable' or why this should be ascertained by reference to what is 'highly likely'. Indeed, if reasonable foreseeability/probability/high likelihood is the only measure applied to the facts of *Smith*, its outcome seems in some ways anomalous. Was the risk of fire started by vandals so highly improbable,[75] given that 'anyone with half an eye . . . could have seen that the main building of the cinema was no longer lockfast and was being regularly entered by unauthorised persons',[76] the Lord Ordinary had found it very likely that the empty cinema would be a 'magnet'[77] for adventure-seeking youngsters and, as earlier cases had indicated, fire was a not infrequent consequence of vandals targeting derelict property? And why should the test have been based upon what Littlewoods actually knew rather that what prudent proprietors in their

---

71 Ibid, 267–68. Lord Mackay also distinguished between fire and theft since, in practical terms, neighbours can protect themselves more effectively against the risk of theft than the risk of eighty-foot flames spreading from a next-door building.

72 [1983] 1 AC 520 (HL).

73 [1987] AC 241 (HL) 280.

74 A Beever, *Rediscovering the Law of Negligence* (Oxford, Hart Publishing, 2007) 152.

75 See Logie, above n 32, 84–85.

76 1986 SLT 272, 274 (the Lord Ordinary, Lord Cowie's, judgment as noted by Lord President Emslie).

77 1986 SLT 272, as noted by Lord President Emslie at 276.

position should have known—a device which results in a higher standard of care being imposed upon the vigilant than the lackadaisical who do not bother to watch out for the presence of trespassers?

Lord Goff's approach, on the other hand, offers far greater certainty and clarity, but seems to constrain the law's development in an area where the fact patterns are inherently unpredictable. His speech has been criticized as imposing 'rigid conceptualism'[78] which 'freezes' the law 'so that it cannot easily recognise any more social democratic mutual obligations'. This plainly contrasts with the flexibility of Lord Mackay's approach allowing the courts to 'strike a new balance between the specific utility of preventing harm and the general utility of leaving people alone to make their own decisions'.[79]

For some, the dissimilarities between the two speeches were attributable not just to Lord Goff's apparent reliance on English cases and neglect of Scots authority,[80] but also to deeper-rooted difference in modes of reasoning on the different sides of the Tweed. For Whitty, for example, the contrast between Lord Mackay's emphasis on a broad criterion of fault and Lord Goff's incremental approach helped to illustrate 'the idea that Scots law is based on precedent and "restrictive categories" less, and depends on generalised rights more, than English law'.[81] (In this respect, a parallel might perhaps be drawn with cross-border debates over the law of unjustified enrichment, with the Scots emphasis on an overarching principle of enrichment as contrasted with the English focus on unjust factors.[82])

But, although academic commentators have continued to cite *Smith* as raising the possibility of 'national divisions' and a generation of Scots law students has been instructed to this effect,[83] the issue has, until recently, received little direct judicial consideration. *Smith* has been cited frequently over the years in both the English and Scots courts, but even the Scots courts often preferred to consider Lord Goff's list of categories rather than to operate Lord Mackay's needle of probability.[84] The recent case of

---

78 Logie, above n 32, 86.

79 D Howarth, 'My Brother's Keeper? Liability for Acts of Third Parties' (1994) 14 *Legal Studies* 88, 95.

80 A charge made in Logie, above n 32, 86.

81 NR Whitty, 'The Civilian Tradition and Debates on Scots Law (Part 1)' (1996) *Journal of South African Law* 227, 234. See also NR Whitty, 'Nuisance', in *The Laws of Scotland: Stair Memorial Encyclopaedia*, reissue (Edinburgh, Law Society of Scotland and Butterworths, 2001) [141], noting the Scots judges' preference for the 'broad principles of foreseeability' rather than the English particularised approach to duty of care.

82 On cross-border difference in this area see, eg the discussion in *Deutsche Morgan Grenfell Group plc v Inland Revenue Commissioners* [2006] UKHL 49, [2007] 1 AC 558.

83 See WJ Stewart, *Delict*, 4th edn (Edinburgh, W Green, 2004) 164.

84 See, eg *Fearns v Scottish Homes* 2007 SCLR 632, [48] (Sheriff Principal Lockhart); *West v Castlehill LLP* [2008] CSOH 182; 2009 GWD 1–4 (in which the Lord Ordinary, Lord Brodie, at [23] rejected 'an analysis based simply on foreseeability'), although the Mackay test was apparently preferred, for example, in *Fry's Metals v Durastic* 1991 SLT 689. Even in *Topp v*

Mitchell v Glasgow CC[85] has now, however, given extended consideration both to differences between Lord Goff's and Lord Mackay's speeches in *Smith* and to the wider issues of Scots and English difference.

D. *MITCHELL V GLASGOW CITY COUNCIL*

In *Mitchell* the relatives of a tenant who died as a result of an assault by his neighbour sought damages from the landlords, a local authority. There had been a long history of threatening behaviour by the assailant towards the deceased and others. After a series of warnings, the landlords arranged a meeting with the assailant at which repossession of his house was discussed. The fatal assault took place after that meeting, and appeared to have been provoked by it. The pursuers alleged that, in omitting to warn the victim about the meeting and thus failing to avert the risk of harm, the landlords had been in breach of a common law duty of care towards their tenant. The Mitchells also argued that this failure to act contravened Article 2 of the European Convention on Human Rights, protecting the right to life, and that, as a public authority, the defenders had thus contravened section 6(1) of the Human Rights Act 1998. The action was dismissed at first instance, but on appeal to the Extra Division of the Inner House the claim at common law was permitted to proceed to proof. The defenders then appealed to the House of Lords against the allowance of a proof and the pursuers cross appealed against the exclusion of their claim under Article 2. The appeal was successful and the cross appeal unsuccessful; in short, the Mitchell family's claim was ultimately unsuccessful on both counts. It is, however, the common law claim which is of principal interest for present purposes.

At first instance the Lord Ordinary, Lord Bracadale, attempted a reading on Lord Mackay's needle of probability scale and on that basis alone would have allowed a proof. However, without making reference to Lord Goff's speech in *Smith*, he ruled that foreseeability was not 'the only live issue', and that it would not be 'fair, just and reasonable' to impose a duty of care upon landlords, local authority or private, to warn tenants about the anti-social tendencies of neighbours.[86]

London Country Bus South West (Ltd) [1992] RTR 254 (CA), for example, one of the few English cases where Lord Mackay's needle of probability test (or 'swingometer') is mentioned, May J described the relevant passages of his speech as 'obiter dicta', at 261, before proceeding to apply Lord Goff's analysis.

[85] [2009] UKHL 11, 2009 SLT 247.
[86] 2005 SLT 1100, [56]–[57].

1. The Inner House

In a lengthy and detailed opinion in the Inner House,[87] Lord Reed addressed both the spectre of cross-border difference in the treatment of omissions and the ratio to be drawn from *Smith*. With regard to the former, he queried the view that 'the law of Scotland does not draw a distinction between acts and omissions comparable to that which appears to exist in the English law of tort'.[88] On his interpretation of the authorities, the distinction was 'determinative' in neither jurisdiction, but was clearly relevant in both.[89] In Scots law, as in English law, liability did not ordinarily attach to 'pure' omissions.[90] More particularly, Lord Reed explicitly rejected the idea underlying Lord Mackay's speech in *Smith* that 'reasonable foreseeability' could of itself be used as 'normative concept' expanding or restricting the scope of liability for failure to avert wrong-doing by third parties. Previous case law indicated that duty had to be rooted in some special circumstance, such as assumption of responsibility, and therefore Lord Goff's approach in *Smith* was to be preferred.[91] Lord Goff's listing of special circumstances in *Smith* should not be regarded as exhaustive, however, and the jurisprudence which flowed from *Caparo Industries v Dickman*[92] was now germane in determining how that list should be formulated. It might be fair, just and reasonable to impose a duty to take action where the defender stood in a 'special' relationship to the pursuer, notably where he or she had undertaken an activity 'which carried a risk of such harm which would not otherwise have existed' or had 'acted in such a way as to induce the pursuer to rely upon him for protection against the risk of such harm, and [had] then failed to take reasonable care to afford such protection'.[93]

Applying this framework to the facts of *Mitchell*, Lord Reed found there to have been no common law duty to secure Mr Mitchell's safety against attack by his neighbour and was for dismissing the action. The other judges in the Extra Division, Lady Paton and Lord Penrose, did not discuss the issues raised by *Smith*, but did not dissent from Lord Reed's analysis of the relevant law. However, they were not persuaded that on this reasoning the Mitchells would necessarily fail in their claim, and they were therefore for allowing proof. (The court also ruled, this time with Lady Paton dissenting, that the Article 2 claim should be dismissed.)

---

[87] 2008 SC 351.

[88] *Burnett v Grampian Fire and Rescue Services* 2007 SLT 61 [34] (Lord Macphail), cited by Lord Reed at 2008 SC 351, [87].

[89] 2008 SC 351, [87]–[89], referring to T Honoré, *Responsibility and Fault* (Oxford, Hart Publishing, 1999) ch 3.

[90] Ibid, [93] and [116].

[91] Ibid, [93]–[94].

[92] [1990] 2 AC 605 (HL).

[93] 2008 SC 351, [99].

2. The House of Lords

In the House of Lords the decision to allow the City Council's appeal was unanimous. Lord Hope stated at the outset that the case was to be judged in the light of three basic principles: (i) that 'foreseeability of harm is not of itself enough for the imposition of a duty of care'; (ii) that 'the law does not normally impose a positive duty on a person to protect others'; and (iii) that 'the law does not impose a duty to prevent a person from being harmed by the criminal act of a third party based simply upon foreseeability'.[94] The authority cited for this last point was *Smith* and, very specifically, the speech of Lord Goff. Indeed, both Scots members of the court, Lord Hope and Lord Rodger, expressly declared their agreement with Lord Goff's approach in *Smith*, rejecting Lord Mackay's needle of foreseeability, and Lord Hope referred in this connection to the analysis of Lord Reed in the Inner House.[95] Lord Goff's list of circumstances in which duty might be found was not closed, however, and the threefold test for duty formulated in *Caparo* was now a 'general guide to what is required'[96] in Scots law as in English law. Their Lordships cited with approval foreign authorities in which the existence of duty had been supported, for example, by the defendant's assumption of responsibility for the plaintiff's safety,[97] or by reckless conduct increasing the danger to the plaintiff.[98]

Of course, the facts of *Smith* were very different from those of *Mitchell*. Unlike in *Smith*, the identity of the third-party wrongdoer was well known to the defenders, as was his past propensity for physical aggression. Nonetheless, the court was much persuaded by the excessive nature of the burden placed upon local authority landlords if they were to be required 'to determine, step by step at each stage, whether or not the actions that they proposed to take in fulfilment of their responsibilities as landlords required a warning to be given, and to whom'.[99] This might bring the constant threat of legal proceedings, taking up 'time, trouble and expense' which could be more usefully devoted to the 'primary functions' of providing services to tenants.[100] There is likely to be continuing debate on whether such public interest arguments are adequately supported,[101] although there is no serious suggestion that the arguments themselves are

---

94 [2009] UKHL 11, 2009 SLT 247, [15].

95 Ibid, [20] (Lord Hope), [56] (Lord Rodger).

96 Ibid, [25] (Lord Hope).

97 *Silva's Fishing Corp Ltd v Maweza* 1957 (2) SA 256 (AD), discussed by Lord Scott at [43]–[44]. See also text at n 18 above.

98 *Bullock v Tamiami Trail Tours Inc* (1959) 266 F 2d 326, discussed by Lord Rodger at [59]–[61].

99 [2009] UKHL 11, 2009 SLT 247, [27] (Lord Hope).

100 Ibid, [28] (Lord Hope), under reference to *Van Colle v Chief Constable of the Hertfordshire Police* [2008] UKHL 50, [2009] 1 AC 225, [133] (Lord Brown).

101 See, eg J Morgan, 'Policy Reasoning in Tort Law: The Courts, the Law Commission and the Critics' (2009) 125 *LQR* 215.

to be run differently north and south of the border. On the other hand, where the parties are occupiers of adjacent land, it does not appear unfair, unjust or unreasonable to impose a positive duty to prevent the spread from one property to another of a hazard which the defender either knew or ought to have known about.[102] To that extent, the *Mitchell* court's more flexible recasting of the framework by which duty is established may mean that, were a case like *Smith* to arise in future, the enquiry may switch from the existence of duty to whether duty has been breached in the circumstances.[103]

So, if in *Smith* the Inner House of the Court of Session and the House of Lords had been in agreement as to the outcome of the case but in disagreement over the analysis of negligence, in *Mitchell* there was agreement over the framework of analysis although there had been disagreement in the Inner House over how that analysis should be applied to the facts. All three judges in the Inner House and both Lord Hope and Lord Rodger accepted that liability for omission to avert wrongdoing by third parties depended upon more than a broad test of foreseeability. All accepted that liability should be restricted to situations where duty of care could be clearly established, and the application of the *Caparo* test of fair, just and reasonable was endorsed. The question of how that test may evolve in this context is not straightforward, but this is perhaps best left to the story of *Caparo*—another landmark case.

E. POSTSCRIPT

Not long after judgment was delivered in *Mitchell* a perceptive Scots law 'blogger'[104] drew attention to one particular passage in Lord Brown's speech:[105]

> There was some suggestion in argument that the test for liability was different (and more exacting) in England than in Scotland but that cannot be. That would be bizarre indeed, not least given that much of England's negligence law was forged in Scottish appeals.

102 As in the law of nuisance. The authority of the English case, *Sedleigh-Denfield v O'Callaghan* [1940] AC 880 (HL) (on the liability of proprietors who 'continue' or 'adopt' a nuisance caused by force of nature or the actions of third parties), has long been accepted in leading Scots cases such as *Watt v Jamieson* 1954 SC 56; *RHM Bakeries v Strathclyde Regional Council* 1985 SC (HL) 17; *Plean Precast Ltd v National Coal Board* 1985 SC 77; *Kennedy v Glenbelle* 1996 SC 95.

103 See comments on *Smith* by T Weir, *Introduction to Tort Law*, 2nd edn (Oxford, Oxford University Press, 2006) 54.

104 S Wortley, *Scots Law News*, 19 February 2009, available at http://www.law.ed.ac.uk/sln/blogentry.aspx?blogentryref=7699 (accessed on 2 November 2009).

105 2009 SLT 247 [80].

The blog comments wryly that this remark prefaces a speech in which no Scots decision is mentioned whatsoever. No doubt Lord Brown's observation would have been more persuasive if Scots authority had also been applied. However, in his Lordship's defence, his words echo those used nearly 40 years previously by that most distinguished Scots lawyer, Lord Reid, introducing Scots authority in an English case, *Home Office v Dorset Yacht*, 'because the Scots and English laws of negligence are the same'.[106] Some may argue that Lord Reid had been right all along but, to the extent that differences had remained in the late twentieth century, *Mitchell* now indicates convergence—at least in relation to liability for omissions. Moreover, this is not 'law from over the border',[107] since the reasoning applied in *Mitchell* was supported by the Scots judges in both Edinburgh and London. That is not to say that the 'intellectual superstructure'[108] of the law of delict is the same as that of the law of tort, or that there are no differences in the way that Scots and English lawyers reason, as was perhaps illustrated by the different approaches of Lord Mackay and Lord Goff in *Smith*. However, attention may now usefully be focused upon areas of delictual liability where differences are real and substantial rather than marginal or even illusory.

Meanwhile, in Dunfermline, it was a sign of the times that, although Maloco's billiard saloon was refurbished and reopened in 1978, St Paul's Church did not rise from the ashes but was eventually demolished. A decade later, Maloco's too disappeared, making way for a Co-op supermarket. The Co-op has now also closed down, and a local councillor has recently called for that site to be redeveloped in the style of the Spanish steps in Rome, an ambitious development which would apparently ensure Dunfermline's enduring superiority over 'Coatbridge, Dumbarton and Airdrie'.[109] As for the store that Littlewoods eventually built on the adjacent site, in 2006 it became a branch of Primark.

---

106 [1970] AC 1004 (HL) 1028 (before discussion of *Scott's Trustees v Moss* (1889) 17 R 32).

107 A reference to those House of Lords decisions in Scots cases of an earlier era where English judges appeared mistakenly to have assumed uniformity of Scots and English law or, more rarely, to have assumed that any divergence between Scots and English law was the result of underdevelopment on the part of the former (see A Dewar Gibb, *Law from over the Border* (Edinburgh, W Green, 1950)).

108 See HL MacQueen and WDH Sellar, 'Negligence' in K Reid and R Zimmermann (eds), *A History of Private Law in Scotland* (Oxford, Oxford University Press, 2000), vol 2, 517, 547.

109 A McRoberts, 'Councillor Calls for Dunfermline's own Spanish Steps', *Dunfermline Press*, 19 March 2009. The proposal came from Councillor Joe Rosiejak, and the favourable comparison with other Scots towns was drawn by Councillor Tony Martin.

11

Alcock v Chief Constable of South Yorkshire Police (1991)

DONAL NOLAN

A. INTRODUCTION

At the time of writing, it is almost exactly 20 years since the day of the Hillsborough disaster, 15 April 1989, when 96 Liverpool foot-ball fans lost their lives in a human crush at an FA Cup semi-final at the Hillsborough stadium in Sheffield. The media coverage of the anniversary of the disaster has inevitably focused on the terrible human cost of the events at Hillsborough, and on the very considerable impact which the disaster had on the game of football itself. However, the disaster also had significant consequences for English tort law, and in particular for that corner of negligence law dealing with liability for psychiatric injury, or 'nervous shock'. No less than three negligence cases arising out of the disaster reached the House of Lords, two of which, *Alcock v Chief Constable of South Yorkshire Police*[1] and *White v Chief Constable of South Yorkshire Police*,[2] concerned nervous shock.[3] Of the two, it is undoubtedly the *Alcock* decision which is the most significant. Indeed, even after nearly two decades, *Alcock* remains the single most important English authority on liability for nervous shock since, although its implications for so-called 'primary victims' and rescuers may have been diluted by the later cases of *Page v Smith*[4] and *White*, as far as 'secondary victims' are concerned, it remains—in the words of Lord Steyn in *White*—'the controlling decision'.[5] Since I do not believe that *Alcock*'s landmark status is really in doubt, the focus of my analysis lies elsewhere. First and foremost, I hope to demon-

---

[1] [1992] 1 AC 310 (HL).
[2] [1999] 2 AC 455 (HL).
[3] The third case was *Hicks v Chief Constable of South Yorkshire Police* [1992] 2 All ER 65 (HL), in which claims by the estates of two young sisters who died at Hillsborough for their pre-death pain and suffering were dismissed on the grounds that they had suffered no physical injury prior to the crushing injury which caused their deaths.
[4] [1996] AC 155 (HL).
[5] *White v Chief Constable of South Yorkshire Police* [1999] 2 AC 455 (HL) 496.

strate that *Alcock* was an essentially conservative decision, rather than the reactionary one which it is often assumed to have been, and hence that it is a landmark case, not so much because it represented a significant change in the law's direction, but because it codified or systematised what had come before. I also hope to show that the conservatism of *Alcock* was likely to have been influenced not only by the facts of the case itself, but also by the large number of other man-made disasters that occurred in the UK in the late 1980s, by developments in Australia and the US, and by broader trends in English tort law. Seen in this light, the *Alcock* decision seems almost to have been inevitable. Finally, I will explore the claim that in *Alcock* the House of Lords overstepped the proper limits of adjudication and engaged in 'judicial legislation'. The structure of my analysis is largely chronological. I begin with the development of the English law relating to nervous shock up until *Alcock*, and then look at some important cases in Australia and the US, before considering the wider context in which *Alcock* was decided. There follows a detailed analysis of the *Alcock* litigation itself. I conclude by making some general observations about the House of Lords' decision. I do not at any stage pass judgment on the merits of the limits on nervous shock recovery which were recognised in *Alcock*, the evaluation of which falls outside the scope of this paper.

B. DEVELOPMENTS IN ENGLISH LAW BEFORE *McLOUGHLIN V O'BRIAN*

It is customary to begin discussions of the development of liability for nervous shock with the late-nineteenth-century decision of the Privy Council in *Victorian Railways Commissioners v Coultas*.[6] The plaintiff in *Coultas* was a passenger in a buggy which had narrowly missed being hit by a train at a level crossing through the negligence of a gatekeeper employed by the defendants. The Victorian jury had awarded the plaintiff damages for physical and mental injuries which she had suffered as a result of the fright, but the Privy Council allowed the defendants' appeal on the ground that the plaintiff's injuries had been too remote. The test of remoteness at the time was whether the consequence was one which 'in the ordinary course of things would flow from the act'[7], and, according to Sir Richard Couch, 'damages arising from mere sudden terror unaccompanied by any actual physical injury but occasioning a nervous or mental shock' could not be considered a consequence which, in the ordinary course of things, would flow from the gatekeeper's negligence.[8] Although we might now interpret this reasoning as meaning only that the plaintiff's injury was

---

[6] (1888) 13 App Cas 222 (PC).
[7] Ibid, 225 (Sir Richard Couch).
[8] Ibid.

not sufficiently foreseeable as a matter of fact, it seems clear that at the time the Privy Council's decision was understood to mean that, as a matter of law, trauma not flowing from physical harm was not actionable in negligence, even if the trauma itself triggered physical injury.

However, this complete bar on nervous shock actions was relatively short-lived, as, just after the turn of the century, a Divisional Court refused to follow *Coultas* in *Dulieu v White*,[9] a case brought by a woman who had given birth prematurely after the defendants' carriage had smashed through the front door of the pub where she was working. The defendants' argument that the harm the plaintiff had suffered was too remote as a matter of law was rejected. According to Kennedy J, damages could be recovered for nervous shock, although only if the shock produced physical injury and arose out of a 'reasonable fear of immediate personal injury to oneself';[10] there was no legal duty not to shock another's nerves by negligence towards a third party. The language used by Kennedy J indicated that, for him, the issue was one of duty, as opposed to remoteness, and this was confirmed in the judgment of Phillimore J,[11] who said that there might be cases in which one person owed a duty not to inflict a mental shock on another and where, if such a shock was inflicted and physical damage then ensued, the victim might have an action for the physical damage.

The next landmark in the development of the law was *Hambrook v Stokes Bros*,[12] the first case allowing recovery by a 'secondary victim' (a person who suffers nervous shock because of what happens to someone else). An employee of the defendants had carelessly left a lorry at the top of a steep and narrow street without making it secure. The lorry started off down the hill at great speed, and a pregnant woman who saw it became frightened for the safety of her children, who were out of sight round a bend in the road. She suffered shock when she found out that the lorry had seriously injured her daughter, and two days later she had a severe haemorrhage, which eventually killed her. A loss of dependency action was brought by her widower, and the Court of Appeal (Sargant LJ dissenting) refused to apply the bar on secondary victim claims laid down in *Dulieu v White*. Bankes LJ argued that the defendant's duty was based on what he ought to have anticipated and that, from that point of view, no real distinction could be drawn between a woman who feared for herself on the facts of *Hambrook* and a woman who feared for her children. However, he also made it clear that this departure from *Dulieu* was limited to cases where the shock resulted from what the secondary victim 'either

9 [1901] 2 KB 669 (DC).
10 Ibid, 675 (Kennedy J).
11 Ibid, 685 ('The difficulty in these cases is to my mind not one as to the remoteness of the damage, but as to the uncertainty of there being any duty').
12 [1925] 1 KB 141 (CA).

saw or realized by her own unaided senses' and was due to a 'reasonable fear of immediate personal injury either to herself or to her children'.[13]

The first nervous shock case to reach the House of Lords was a Scottish appeal, *Bourhill v Young*.[14] The pursuer was an Edinburgh woman who had suffered severe nervous shock and a miscarriage after witnessing a fatal road accident. The accident was the fault of a speeding motorcyclist, who died after colliding with a car. The pursuer's view of the crash was obscured by a tram, but she heard it, and later saw blood on the road. It was accepted by the pursuer that her shock had not been caused by any reasonable fear of immediate bodily injury to herself. Their Lordships dismissed her action against the motorcyclist's estate on the ground that he had owed a duty only to those whom he could foresee might be harmed by his negligence, and that the pursuer had not been in the area of foreseeable risk. Although one way of interpreting *Bourhill* would be that it laid down a simple test of reasonable foreseeability for the determination of nervous shock cases, this seems not to have been the intention of at least three of their Lordships. Lord Thankerton, for example, specifically limited his analysis to the question of a motorcyclist's duty towards 'other passengers on the road',[15] and said that there were certain obiter dicta in *Hambrook* on the duty issue 'which might be considered too wide',[16] while Lord Macmillan preferred to reserve his opinion on whether it had been right for the majority in *Hambrook* to depart from the limitation Kennedy J had laid down in *Dulieu v White*. Lord Russell was even more forthright, saying that he preferred the dissenting judgment of Sargant LJ to the decision of the majority in *Hambrook*.[17]

Even Lord Wright, who took a more liberal line, made it clear that the finding that injury to the pursuer had not been a reasonably foreseeable consequence of the motorcyclist's negligence was enough to dispose of the appeal, and while he expressed tentative agreement with the decision in *Hambrook*, he refused to express a final opinion on the matter. His Lordship also reiterated that what was at issue in such cases was not mental harm unaccompanied by physical injury, but 'physical injury due to nervous shock'.[18] Finally, although Lord Porter seemed closest to accepting an overarching test of reasonable foreseeability in this context, even he conceded that 'whether illness due to shock which might reasonably have been anticipated as the result of injury to others can or cannot form the basis of a successful claim need not now be considered'.[19] To sum up,

---

13 Ibid, 152.
14 [1943] AC 92 (HL).
15 Ibid, 98.
16 Ibid, 100.
17 Ibid, 103.
18 Ibid, 112.
19 Ibid, 120.

Bourhill decided only that reasonable foreseeability of injury by shock to the plaintiff was necessary to establish liability for nervous shock, not that it was sufficient to do so, and the House deliberately left open the question of whether in such cases recovery by secondary victims should be permitted at all. Furthermore, at this time what the courts meant by liability for 'nervous shock' was not liability for psychiatric injury, but liability for the physical consequences of mental trauma, such as the haemorrhage in *Hambrook* or the miscarriage in *Bourhill*.[20] It would therefore be a mistake to associate *Bourhill v Young* with a straight-forward test of reasonable foreseeability in psychiatric injury cases.

The 40-year period from *Bourhill v Young* to *McLoughlin v O'Brian*,[21] the next nervous shock case to reach the House of Lords, was marked by a series of rather ad hoc decisions at first instance and in the Court of Appeal. The first of these was *Dooley v Cammell Laird & Co Ltd*,[22] where the plaintiff was the driver of a crane which had been used to load insulating materials into the hold of a ship that was being fitted out at a shipbuilding yard in Birkenhead. The rope from which the crane's load was suspended had snapped, with the result that the load had dropped into the hold of the ship, where the plaintiff's colleagues were working. Although no one was in fact hurt, the plaintiff suffered a severe nervous shock which aggravated his pre-existing neurasthenia, permanently incapacitating him. Donovan J held that the plaintiff was entitled to damages from those responsible for the snapping of the rope,[23] but his unreserved judgment is less than satisfactory. His reasoning was essentially that *Hambrook v Stokes* had survived *Bourhill*, and that the only restriction on nervous shock recovery was the foreseeability of the injury, a test he considered to be satisfied on the facts. The limited ratio of *Bourhill*, and the fact that all the earlier authorities concerned physical conse-quences of shock, went unremarked.

Two years later, another nervous shock case, *King v Phillips*,[24] reached the Court of Appeal. A taxi driver had negligently backed his cab into a small boy on a tricycle. The damage to the boy was slight, but his mother, who was looking out of an upstairs window some 70 or 80 yards away, heard him scream, and saw his tricycle under the cab. The experience had

---

20 See J Havard, 'Reasonable Foresight of Nervous Shock' (1956) 19 *MLR* 478, 479 ('the courts have restricted recovery for nervous shock to that resulting in physical illness; in other words mental distress unaccompanied by such illness will not be actionable').

21 [1983] AC 410 (HL).

22 [1951] 1 Lloyd's Rep 271.

23 There were two defendants in *Dooley*, the plaintiff's employer (Cammell Laird) and the Mersey Insulation Co. While Cammell Laird were found liable for breach of statutory duty, it was the Mersey Insulation Co who were held liable in negligence. It is therefore a mistake to describe *Dooley* as a case of employer's liability, as is commonly done. See, eg *Frost v Chief Constable of South Yorkshire Police* [1997] 1 All ER 540 (CA) 545 (Rose LJ), 560 (Henry LJ), 575 (Judge LJ).

24 [1953] 1 QB 429 (CA).

caused her nervous shock. At first instance,[25] McNair J had dismissed the claim on the grounds that the taxi driver could not reasonably have anticipated that his actions would cause any injury to the mother. The Court of Appeal agreed that the mother's injury had not been reasonably foreseeable, and dismissed her appeal. While it is difficult to extract more general propositions from the decision in *King v Phillips*, the overall tenor of the judgments is restrictive. Singleton LJ and Denning LJ do appear to have accepted that in such cases recovery depended on the application of a reasonable foreseeability test,[26] but they applied that test in a very strict way, at least by modern standards.[27] For example, Denning LJ appeared to exclude certain categories of case from the ambit of reasonable foreseeability altogether, saying that there could be no recovery where a wife or mother suffered shock on being told of an accident to a loved one, nor where a bystander suffered shock by witnessing an accident from a safe distance. *Hambrook* had been different, he said, because there the bystander had been a mother who suffered shock by 'hearing or seeing, with her own unaided senses' that her child was in danger.[28] Indeed, Hodson LJ went so far as to question whether secondary victims could recover at all, pointing out that several of the opinions in *Bourhill* had cast doubt on the correctness of the decision in *Hambrook*, where, in any case, the existence of a duty of care had been conceded by the defendant.

The test of reasonable foreseeability was also applied in *Boardman v Sanderson*,[29] but this time the Court of Appeal held that it was satisfied. The defendant had negligently driven over a young boy's foot within earshot of the boy's father, who had then run to the scene and seen what had happened. He subsequently suffered nervous shock. The reasonable foreseeability test was fairly easily satisfied on the facts, since the accident took place in a garage to which the plaintiff and his son had gone with the defendant, so that the defendant had known that the plaintiff was close at hand. The more general significance of the case is limited, though it clearly established that fear of injury to oneself was not a prerequisite of recovery for nervous shock, and that damages could be awarded to a secondary victim out of sight of the accident but within earshot.

There are only three other reported cases on the issue before the major review of the area by the House of Lords in *McLoughlin*. The first was the

---

[25] [1952] 2 All ER 459 (QB).

[26] See [1953] 1 QB 429 (CA) 437 (Singleton LJ) (referring to the foreseeability of 'any damage' to the plaintiff), 441 (Denning LJ) ('the test of liability for shock is foreseeability of injury by shock').

[27] See *White*, above n 5, 501 (Lord Hoffmann) ('a highly restrictive view'). For contemporary criticism of the Court of Appeal's reasoning, see AL Goodhart, 'Emotional Shock and the Unimaginative Taxicab Driver' (1953) 69 *LQR* 347.

[28] [1953] 1 QB 429 (CA) 441.

[29] [1964] 1 WLR 1317 (CA).

'rescuer' case, *Chadwick v British Transport Commission*,[30] in which damages were awarded to the estate of a man who had suffered nervous shock after going to the aid of the victims of the Lewisham rail disaster, in which 90 people were killed and numerous others injured. Waller J held that nervous shock could be actionable even if it was not caused by the plaintiff's fear for his own safety or for the safety of his children, that it had been foreseeable that someone such as the deceased might come to the aid of the passengers and suffer injury as a result, and that there was no evidence that the deceased had been unusually susceptible to mental illness, so as to take him outside the defendants' reasonable contemplation. The other two cases, *Carlin v Helical Bar Ltd*[31] and *Hinz v Berry*,[32] both concerned quantum. They are of little general significance, except for the fact that in *Hinz* Lord Denning MR made it clear that damages were not recoverable for grief and sorrow caused by another's death, but only for 'nervous shock, or, to put it in medical terms, for any recognizable psychiatric illness caused by the breach of duty by the defendant'.[33] It is also noteworthy that when his Lordship said that it was now beyond doubt that damages could be given for nervous shock caused by the sight of an accident, he added afterwards, 'at any rate to a close relative'.[34]

The absence of expressions of general principle in these cases makes it difficult to sum up the law on nervous shock before *McLoughlin v O'Brian*.[35] Recovery by those not endangered by the defendant's negligence was clearly permitted, and after *Hinz v Berry* a recognisable psychiatric illness was clearly required. Beyond that, the precise limits of recovery are difficult to identify. According to the eleventh edition of *Winfield & Jolowicz on Tort*, published in 1979, the *Dooley* case (plus possibly *Chadwick*) meant that liability could not be 'based upon the existence of any special relationship between the plaintiff and the direct victim of the defendant's negligence', in which case the 'apparently simple rule' was that 'subject to the requirement that the plaintiff must have apprehended the accident by his own senses, everything depends upon what is foreseeable on the facts of the particular case'.[36] However, it is noticeable that even on this relatively liberal view, the test of factual foreseeability was subject to a strict requirement of spatial proximity, and it is by no means clear that that was the only additional limitation. After all, in every secondary victim case apart from the first instance decisions in *Dooley* and *Chadwick*, the plaintiff had been either the parent or the

---

30 [1967] 1 WLR 912 (QB).
31 (1970) 9 KIR 154 (Nottingham Assizes).
32 [1970] 2 QB 40 (CA).
33 Ibid, 42.
34 Ibid.
35 Above n 21.
36 WVH Rogers, *Winfield & Jolowicz on Tort*, 11th edn (London, Sweet & Maxwell, 1979) 151.

spouse of the direct victim, and in *King v Phillips* Denning LJ had categorically ruled out recovery by a mere bystander. Whatever the exact position was, there is therefore a good deal of truth in Harvey Teff's claim that until *McLoughlin* 'the most distinctive feature of the English case law on nervous shock was its resolute adherence to restrictive devices'.[37]

C. McLOUGHLIN V O'BRIAN

The House of Lords was given the opportunity to clarify matters in *McLoughlin v O'Brian*,[38] but unfortunately they failed to do so. The husband and children of the plaintiff were in a car which collided with a lorry as a result of the defendants' negligence. The plaintiff was at home two miles away when the accident took place, and was told about it two hours later by a neighbour, who then drove her to the hospital where her family had been taken. At the hospital, the plaintiff found out that her youngest daughter had been killed, and she saw her husband and her other three children, one of whom had suffered quite serious injuries and all of whom were in a very distressed state. She subsequently brought an action for damages for psychiatric injury. At first instance, Boreham J dismissed her claim on the grounds that the alleged injury to the plaintiff had not been a reasonably foreseeable consequence of the defendants' negligence. An appeal from that decision was dismissed by the Court of Appeal.[39]

Although there were differences of emphasis in the judgments of Stephenson LJ and Griffiths LJ (with both of which Cumming-Bruce LJ agreed), they agreed that, while in the circumstances nervous shock to the plaintiff *had* been reasonably foreseeable, her claim ought nonetheless to fail for policy reasons. Stephenson LJ said that, while it was clear that the plaintiff had the necessary 'natural or social bond' with the direct victims, as the cases stood,[40] there was no reported decision 'of any person recovering damages for injury by shock who has not been at or near the scene of the accident at the time or shortly afterwards' and there were strong indications that such a person would be 'outside the scope of the wrongdoer's responsibility'.[41] Moreover, policy considerations—principally 'floodgates' concerns—required that the scope of the duty in such cases be

---

[37] H Teff, *Causing Psychiatric and Emotional Harm: Reshaping the Boundaries of Legal Liability* (Oxford, Hart Publishing, 2009) 56. See also M Brazier *Street on Torts*, 8th edn (London, Butterworths, 1988) 179 ('The limits on liability established by analysis of the case-law up to 1982 appeared to be that the plaintiff should be present at the scene of the accident, or very near to it . . . and that generally he must be very closely related to the person suffering physical injury').

[38] Above n 21.

[39] [1981] QB 599 (CA).

[40] '[D]ecisions in English, Scottish, Canadian, Australian and American cases' (ibid, 606).

[41] Ibid, 606.

limited 'to those on or near the highway at or near the time of the accident'.[42] According to Griffiths LJ, the common thread running through all the judgments in the nervous shock cases was 'the concept of physical proximity to the accident',[43] and the decided cases established that the duty of care of a driver was limited 'to persons and owners of the property on the road or near to it who may be directly affected by the bad driving'; it was not owed to those who were 'nowhere near the scene'.[44] Both of their Lordships indicated that in their view any extension of liability for nervous shock beyond these limits was a matter for Parliament.[45]

The judgments in the Court of Appeal in *McLoughlin* are instructive because they suggest that, even in the relatively liberal atmosphere of the early 1980s, the weight of judicial opinion was firmly opposed to a straightforward test of reasonable foreseeability in nervous shock cases, preferring instead to apply strict temporal and spatial limits to secondary victim recovery. Furthermore, this approach was clearly felt to be consistent with, if not actually dictated by, the existing authorities (both in England and elsewhere). Seen in this light, the unanimous decision of the House of Lords in *McLoughlin* to allow the plaintiff's appeal was unquestionably a liberal one, extending the boundaries of liability as it did to a secondary victim who had not been in close proximity to the accident, and who had subsequently gone, not to the accident scene itself, but to a hospital to which the victims had been brought. Quite how liberal the implications of the decision were is, however, open to question, since only Lord Wilberforce and Lord Bridge made any real attempt to lay down the general guidelines for nervous shock cases which were so obviously required.

Lord Wilberforce, who gave the first opinion, was prepared to accept an extension of *Hambrook v Stokes*[46] to cases where a secondary victim had not seen or heard the incident, but where (as on the facts) he or she had come upon its immediate aftermath. More generally, however, Lord Wilberforce made it clear that recovery for nervous shock should not depend on foreseeability alone; since shock was capable of affecting so wide a range of people, there was 'a real need for the law to place some limitation upon the extent of admissible claims'.[47] It was necessary to consider three elements inherent in any claim: the class of persons whose claims should be recognised; the proximity of such persons to the accident; and the means by which the shock was caused. As for the first of these, ordinary bystanders should be excluded, and any extension beyond

---

42 Ibid, 614.
43 Ibid, 619.
44 Ibid, 623.
45 Ibid, 616 (Stephenson LJ), 624 (Griffiths LJ).
46 [1925] 1 KB 141 (CA).
47 Above n 21, 421–22.

spousal or parental relationships should be 'very carefully scrutinized'.[48] As regards proximity, 'this must be close in both time and space',[49] though it extended to one who, from close proximity, came very soon upon the scene. Finally, as regards communication, the 'shock must come about through sight or hearing of the event or of its immediate aftermath'.[50] There could therefore be no claim for shock brought about by third-party communication; whether an equivalent of sight or hearing—such as simultaneous television pictures—would suffice might have to be considered. It is noteworthy that his Lordship was of the view that these restrictions did not introduce a new principle, but represented either the existing law or 'the existing law with only such circumstantial extension as the common law process' could legitimately make.[51]

Lord Bridge's analysis was equally clear, but to very different effect. Once the plaintiff had established that he was suffering from a positive psychiatric illness attributable to the death, injury or imperilment of a third party negligently caused by the defendant, the test of liability was simply whether the psychiatric illness had been a reasonably foreseeable consequence of the defendant's act or omission, as judged by the 'consensus of informed judicial opinion'.[52] His Lordship lent heavily on the authority of *Dillon v Legg*[53], where a majority of the Supreme Court of California had laid down a reasonable foreseeability test for nervous shock cases, while making it clear that the three elements which Lord Wilberforce had identified would be taken into account in deciding whether on the facts the shock had been reasonably foreseeable. The opinions of the other three Law Lords were more opaque, but in broad terms, it seems that Lord Edmund-Davies agreed with Lord Wilberforce, that Lord Scarman agreed with Lord Bridge and that Lord Russell chose to remain on the fence, with the result that no clear ratio emerged from the decision.

The opinion of Lord Edmund-Davies was principally focused, not on the law of nervous shock, but on the legitimate role of public policy arguments in common law adjudication. Nevertheless, his Lordship clearly rejected Lord Bridge's approach of basing liability on reasonable foreseeability alone.[54] Lord Scarman equally clearly accepted Lord Bridge's approach to the law, although this was not because his Lordship did not share the policy concerns of the Court of Appeal, but because he did not think that such concerns were justiciable; setting such policy limits on the law's development was the province of Parliament. Indeed, his Lordship

---

[48] Ibid, 422.
[49] Ibid.
[50] Ibid, 423.
[51] Ibid.
[52] Ibid, 432.
[53] 441 P 2d 912 (Cal 1968).
[54] Above n 21, 426.

went so far as to doubt whether the application of a test of reasonable foreseeability untrammelled by spatial, physical or temporal limits was socially desirable, and wished to put on record his view that there was a case for legislation to deal with the issue. The short opinion of Lord Russell was singularly unhelpful. In this case, he said, there was no policy reason to deny the plaintiff damages, and he made it clear that he was not impressed by the fear of the floodgates opening — 'certainly not sufficiently to deprive this plaintiff of just compensation for the reasonably foreseeable damage done to her'.[55] However, it is by no means clear that his Lordship was ruling out limits additional to reasonable foreseeability altogether; rather, he felt that in this area it might do more harm than good to 'attempt in advance solutions, or even guidelines, in hypothetical cases'.[56] The most plausible interpretation of Lord Russell's opinion seems to be that he was taking a *via media* between Lord Wilberforce and Lord Bridge, rejecting the former's attempt to lay down general limits on recovery while not ruling out the possibility of dismissing future claims on an ad hoc basis for policy reasons despite satisfaction of the reasonable foreseeability test.

My justification for looking so closely at the opinions in *McLoughlin* is that the later decision of the House of Lords in *Alcock* broadly to follow Lord Wilberforce's approach is sometimes considered to have been a retrograde step,[57] presumably on the basis that following *McLoughlin* a simple test of reasonable foreseeability applied in nervous shock cases. Close consideration of the reasoning in *McLoughlin* reveals any such assumption to be highly questionable, an assessment which is reinforced by the contradictory judicial and academic commentary on the position in the nine years between the two House of Lords decisions. In *Attia v British Gas plc*, for example, Bingham LJ referred to Lord Bridge and Lord Scarman as 'a minority of the House' requiring only that the reasonable foreseeability of the shock be established; in his view, 'the majority ratio of the decision' was that, even where reasonable foreseeability of psychiatric damage was shown, the right to recover could still be denied on policy grounds.[58] By contrast, in a leading Australian case decided the year after *McLoughlin*, Deane J clearly took the view that *McLoughlin* represented a significant departure from the previous authorities,[59] an assessment only really consistent with the view that Lord Bridge's more radical approach had carried the day. Similarly, two textbooks published in 1989, a couple of

55 Ibid, 429.
56 Ibid.
57 See, eg K Wheat, 'Proximity and Nervous Shock' (2003) 32 *Common Law World Review* 313, 316 (comparing *Alcock* with 'the more flexible and open views' of the majority of the House of Lords in *McLoughlin*).
58 [1988] 1 QB 304 (CA) 319–20. See also Stocker LJ in the Court of Appeal in *Alcock*: *Jones v Wright* [1991] 3 All ER 88 (CA) 108, 111. Cf [1991] 3 All ER 88 (CA) 97, where Parker LJ seems to assume that Lord Bridge spoke for the majority in *McLoughlin*.
59 *Jaensch v Coffey* (1984) 155 CLR 549 (HCA) 600.

years before *Alcock*, came to quite different conclusions about the state of the law at that time. According to the sixteenth edition of *Clerk & Lindsell on Torts*, in nervous shock cases the foreseeability test had 'to be applied subject to certain arbitrary limitations',[60] a clear rejection of Lord Bridge's approach. On the other hand, the author of the thirteenth edition of *Winfield & Jolowicz on Tort*, while acknowledging that it was not easy to discern a clear ratio in *McLoughlin*, nevertheless took the view that lower courts were likely to follow the principles set out by Lord Bridge.[61]

D. DEVELOPMENTS IN OTHER JURISDICTIONS

1. Australia

By the time that *Alcock* was decided, the High Court of Australia had considered the nervous shock issue three times. The first of the three cases was *Chester v Waverley Corporation*,[62] where the plaintiff was a mother who had suffered shock after seeing the body of her seven-year-old son being recovered from a flooded trench inadequately fenced by the defendant. The majority of the High Court (Evatt J dissenting) had rather harshly dismissed the claim on the grounds that the mother's injury had not been a reasonably foreseeable consequence of the defendant's carelessness. The second case was *Mount Isa Mines v Pusey*.[63] Even by the standards of nervous shock cases, the facts were gruesome. The plaintiff had been working in the defendant's powerhouse when two fellow employees who were testing a switchboard on the floor above had suffered very severe burns as a result of the employer's negligence. After hearing explosions, the plaintiff had rushed to the scene, where he saw one of the badly burnt men. The plaintiff had helped this man to the ground floor and from there to an ambulance. The plaintiff subsequently suffered a severe schizophrenic reaction, in respect of which he sued the defendant. The trial judge found

---

[60] *Clerk & Lindsell on Torts*, 16th edn (London, Sweet & Maxwell, 1989) paras 10–12. See also FA Trindade, 'The Principles Governing the Recovery of Damages for Negligently Caused Nervous Shock' [1986] CLJ 476, 484–85 ('reasonable foreseeability by the defendant . . . is not the sole determinant in establishing a duty of care in these cases').

[61] WVH Rogers, *Winfield & Jolowicz on Tort*, 13th edn (London, Sweet & Maxwell, 1989) 109. Aside from the dictum of Bingham LJ in *Attia*, the only two fully reported decisions on nervous shock handed down by the English courts in the remainder of the 1980s, *Attia* and *Brice v Brown* [1984] 1 All ER 997 (QB), provide no guidance on the question, since in both cases the existence of a duty of care was not in doubt, with the result that the actionability of the plaintiff's psychiatric illness was dealt with as a question of remoteness of damage. In *Attia*, this was because the psychiatric injury was consequential on damage to the plaintiff's property; in *Brice v Brown*, it was because it was consequential on physical injury suffered by the plaintiff.

[62] (1939) 62 CLR 1 (HCA).

[63] (1970) 125 CLR 383 (HCA).

that the plaintiff's psychiatric illness had been reasonably foreseeable, and on that basis gave judgment for the plaintiff, a decision upheld by the High Court. It is difficult to extract general principles from the judgments in the case, although Windeyer J specifically denied that only relatives of the direct victim could recover for nervous shock, citing *Dooley v Cammell Laird* and the *Chadwick* case as authorities against such a proposition.[64] Despite the Court's approval of the trial judge's reasoning, the *Mount Isa Mines* decision is not necessarily to be interpreted as laying down a simple foreseeability test for nervous shock cases. After all, Windeyer J attached significance (how much is unclear) to the fact that the plaintiff was an employee of the defendant,[65] and his Honour also emphasised that in his opinion no damages could be recovered for nervous shock resulting simply from hearing distressing news, as opposed to 'witnessing distressing events'.[66]

The third nervous shock case to reach the High Court was *Jaensch v Coffey*,[67] a decision which undoubtedly had a major influence on the House of Lords in *Alcock*. The plaintiff in the case was the wife of a motorcyclist who had suffered serious injuries in a collision caused by the defendant's negligence. She had seen her husband in hospital shortly after the accident, where she was told that he was 'pretty bad'. The next morning she was told that he was in intensive care, and then shortly afterwards that he had taken a turn for the worse, and that she should return to the hospital as quickly as possible. Although her husband had survived, the plaintiff claimed that the experience had caused her to suffer nervous shock, and sought damages. In an echo of *McLoughlin*, the High Court agreed that her claim should succeed, but disagreed as to the relevant legal principles. Brennan J adopted a similar approach to that of Lord Bridge, and applied a test of reasonable foreseeability on the facts, subject only to the caveats that the plaintiff's psychiatric illness must have been induced by shock, and that in general the foreseeability issue was to be determined on the assumption that the plaintiff was 'of a normal standard of susceptibility'.[68] By contrast, Gibbs CJ and Deane J denied that foreseeability alone could give rise to a duty of care in such cases. Gibbs CJ considered the approach of Lord Wilberforce in *McLoughlin* to be 'realistic and correct',[69] though his Honour made it clear that, while he attached great significance to the relationship between the direct victim and the secondary victim, he also felt that Lord Wilberforce might have drawn the other restrictions on recovery too tightly.

---

64 Ibid, 403–04. See also Walsh J at 416–17 ('there is no rule of law which made it a condition of the respondent's right to recover that he should have been a close relative').

65 Ibid, 404.

66 Ibid, 407.

67 (1984) 155 CLR 549 (HCA).

68 Ibid, 568.

69 Ibid, 554.

For present purposes, the most interesting judgment in *Jaensch v Coffey* is that of Deane J, who argued that, in addition to reasonable foreseeability, there must also be a requisite degree of proximity between the two parties for a duty of care to arise. The authorities strongly supported the view

> that the requirement of a relationship of proximity operates to impose particular criteria which must be satisfied by a plaintiff before a duty of care in respect of a reasonably foreseeable injury in the form of nervous shock will be held to have arisen.[70]

It would appear, however, that his Honour saw the relationship between the plaintiff and the direct victim as an issue going to the foreseeability of the illness in the particular case, rather than 'proximity',[71] and it is also noteworthy that he took a relatively liberal approach to the issues of spatial and temporal proximity and the means of communication. Arrival at the scene in the aftermath of the accident could suffice for these purposes, and the aftermath extended to a hospital to which the direct victim was taken 'during the period of immediate post-accident treatment', for 'so long as he remained in the state produced by the accident'.[72] Indeed, Deane J went even further, by expressly leaving open the question of whether merely being told about the accident by a third party could satisfy the proximity requirement in an appropriate case.[73] Finally, Dawson J chose to leave open the question of whether the sole test of liability in nervous shock cases was reasonable foreseeability, while Murphy J said only that there were no reasons of public policy for limiting recovery on the facts.

2. The US

By English standards, American courts have tended to take a markedly restrictive approach to recovery for nervous shock (or 'emotional distress'[74]), so much so that the 1968 decision of the Supreme Court of California in *Dillon v Legg*[75] was the first case in which damages were awarded to a secondary victim who was not within the foreseeable range of physical injury (or 'zone of danger') created by the defendant's negligence. As we have seen, the majority of the court in *Dillon* were prepared to apply a test of reasonable foreseeability in such cases, while emphasising that the

---

70 Ibid, 592–93.
71 Ibid, 605–06.
72 Ibid, 607–08.
73 Ibid, 608–09.
74 Part of the explanation for the more restrictive approach may be that 'emotional distress' is a broader concept than nervous shock, in that it is not generally limited to recognisable psychiatric illnesses: See, eg *Restatement, Second, Torts* (1977), § 46, comment j.
75 441 P 2d 912 (Cal 1968).

three elements later relied on by Lord Wilberforce in *McLoughlin* would be important indicators of the foreseeability of psychiatric illness on the facts (Tobriner J commented, for example, that 'the degree of foreseeability of the third person's injury is far greater in the case of his contemporaneous observance of the accident than that in which he subsequently learns of it'[76]). Although it is doubtful whether in practice this 'guided foreseeability' approach led to especially liberal outcomes, it is noteworthy that in a number of other American jurisdictions the courts preferred to treat variations on the *Dillon* 'guidelines' as strict criteria for recovery, additional to the requirement of reasonable foreseeability.[77]

Most significantly of all, in *Thing v La Chusa*,[78] decided two years before *Alcock*, the Californian Supreme Court itself abandoned the guided foreseeability approach. According to the majority, the 'societal benefits of certainty in the law' required that bystander recovery for emotional distress be limited to cases where the plaintiff was (i) 'closely related to the injury victim'; (ii) 'present at the scene of the injury-producing event at the time' it occurred and then aware that it was causing injury to the victim; and (iii) as a result suffered 'emotional distress beyond that which would be anticipated in a disinterested witness'.[79] It was clear, the majority argued, that 'foreseeability of the injury alone' was 'not a useful "guideline" or a meaningful restriction' on the scope of the action for negligent infliction of emotional distress, and the court was under an obligation to create a clear rule under which liability could be determined.[80] Although *Thing v La Chusa* was not cited in *Alcock*, it is nonetheless possible that their Lordships were aware that the court responsible for the decision in *Dillon v Legg*—on which Lord Bridge had drawn so heavily in *McLoughlin*—had recently rejected the foreseeability test laid down there in such forceful terms. And even if this news had not reached the corridors of the House, the very fact of such a decisive move away from a factual foreseeability approach to the resolution of nervous shock cases is at the very least evidence that at the time of the *Alcock* decision the attractions of dealing with such claims by reference to additional, legal, criteria of recovery were all too obvious to courts in other common law jurisdictions.

---

76 Ibid, 921.

77 See, eg *Barnhill v Davis* 300 NW 2d 104 (Iowa 1981), where a majority of the Supreme Court of Iowa held that in order to recover for serious emotional distress a bystander would have to establish that he had been 'located near the scene of the accident'; that the emotional distress 'resulted from a direct emotional impact from the sensory and contemporaneous observance of the accident'; that 'the bystander and the victim were husband and wife or related within the second degree of consanguinity or affinity'; and that 'a reasonable person in the position of the bystander would believe, and the bystander did believe, that the direct victim of the accident would be seriously injured or killed'.

78 771 P 2d 814 (Cal 1989).

79 Ibid, 815 (Eagleson J).

80 Ibid, 826–27 (Eagleson J).

E. THE CONTEXT IN WHICH *ALCOCK* WAS DECIDED

A true appreciation of the circumstances in which the *Alcock* case was decided must take into account three further considerations, over and above the previous development of the law relating to nervous shock in England, Australia and the US. These three considerations are the so-called 'retreat from *Anns*', whereby in the late 1980s the House of Lords moved decisively towards a more restrictive approach to the imposition of duties of care in negligence; two very liberal first instance decisions on nervous shock, both of which were handed down after the first instance decision in *Alcock* itself, and before the decision of the Court of Appeal; and the spate of man-made disasters which took place in the UK in the six years between 1985 and the time that *Alcock* was decided, along with the focus on trauma-induced psychiatric illness which they brought about.

1. The 'Retreat from *Anns*'

The decision of the House of Lords in *McLoughlin* came at a time when the two-stage test for the existence of a duty of care laid down by Lord Wilberforce in *Anns v Merton London Borough*[81] still held sway in the English courts. By establishing a very broad prima facie duty of care, based on reasonable foreseeability, this test undoubtedly tended towards expansion of negligence liability in categories of case (such as nervous shock and pure economic loss) where foreseeability had not previously been regarded as the touchstone of liability. Moreover, the use of this two-stage analysis can be observed in several of the opinions in *McLoughlin*, where, by putting the onus firmly on the judge to identify specific policy reasons for imposing legal limitations on the duty of care, it provided a sound foundation for Lord Bridge's endorsement of an untrammelled test of factual foreseeability in nervous shock cases.

By the time of the *Alcock* decision, however, the *Anns* two-stage test had been abandoned and replaced with a much more conservative approach to the duty of care issue, in which emphasis was placed on a requirement of proximity between the two parties that was not necessarily coterminous with reasonable foreseeability and in which the courts were to proceed, not by reference to an overarching test of foreseeability tempered by policy considerations, but incrementally, and by analogy with previous decisions. An important landmark in this 'retreat from *Anns*' came the year before *Alcock* in *Caparo Industries plc v Dickman*,[82] where Lord Bridge effectively replaced the *Anns* test with a three-stage test that

---

[81] [1978] AC 728 (HL) 751.
[82] [1990] 2 AC 605 (HL).

required the court to consider not only reasonable foreseeability and whether it was 'fair, just and reasonable' to impose a duty of care, but in addition whether there was a relationship 'characterized by the law as one of "proximity" or "neighbourhood"' between the two parties.[83] Another feature of this period of the law's development was the revival of the floodgates argument, which had come in for some stinging criticism in *McLoughlin*.[84] Concerns that generous duty rules would give rise to indeterminate liabilities were much to the fore in a number of economic loss cases decided in the years before *Alcock*, including *Caparo* itself, where the House of Lords drew upon the floodgates argument when holding that a company's auditors generally owed no duty of care to those who invested in the company in reliance on the accounts approved by the auditors.[85] The broader legal context in which *Alcock* came to be decided was therefore radically different from the context in which the House had last considered nervous shock liability, eight years before.[86]

2. Two First Instance Decisions

The fact that no clear ratio had really emerged from the *McLoughlin* decision, and that Lord Bridge had so explicitly approved a simple test of factual foreseeability in nervous shock cases, gave judges at first instance considerable freedom to extend the boundaries of nervous shock liability well beyond the actual decisions that had been made in earlier cases. The absence of reported case law following *McLoughlin* makes it difficult to know whether or not this actually happened, but two cases which were decided shortly before *Alcock* reached the House of Lords illustrated the possibilities very clearly. The first of these cases was *Hevican v Ruane*,[87] where the plaintiff's son had been killed when the school minibus in which he was travelling collided with a lorry as a result of the minibus driver's negligence. The plaintiff was told about the accident shortly afterwards and was driven to a police station, where he was told that his son was dead. He then went to the mortuary, where he saw his son's body. The experience caused him to suffer from a reactive depression, in respect of which he sought damages from the driver's estate. Mantell J held that the plaintiff

---

83 Ibid, 617.

84 Above n 21, 421 (Lord Wilberforce), 425 (Lord Edmund-Davies), 429 (Lord Russell), 442 (Lord Bridge).

85 [1990] 2 AC 605 (HL) 643 (Lord Oliver). See also *Candlewood Navigation Corp Ltd v Mitsui OSK Lines Ltd* [1986] AC 1 (HL) 19 (Lord Fraser); *Leigh and Sillavan Ltd v Aliakmon Shipping Co Ltd* [1986] AC 785 (HL) 816 (Lord Brandon).

86 Between 1987 and 1995, plaintiffs succeeded in only 38% of negligence cases before the House of Lords, compared to an overall plaintiff/prosecution success rate of 55%: D Robertson, *Judicial Discretion in the House of Lords* (Oxford, Clarendon Press, 1998) 218.

87 [1991] 3 All ER 65 (QB).

was entitled to recover even though he had not been present at the immediate aftermath of the accident since, although the shock to the plaintiff had been administered indirectly by a third party, each link in the causal chain from the driver's negligence to the suffering of nervous shock by the plaintiff had been foreseeable. The judge was clearly aware that allowing recovery for shock brought about by third-party communication went beyond the limits laid down in the earlier cases, but relied on the opinion of Lord Bridge in *McLoughlin* as the justification for doing so.

The second, not dissimilar, case was *Ravenscroft v Rederiaktiebølaget Transatlantic*.[88] The plaintiff was the mother of a worker who had been crushed by a shuttle wagon on the cargo deck of a ship as a result of the defendant's negligence. Her son had been taken to hospital, but had died after two hours in intensive care. The plaintiff was called to the hospital, where her husband told her that their son had died. Following her son's death, the plaintiff suffered a prolonged depressive reaction, and she sought damages from the defendant for nervous shock. Ward J applied a test of reasonable foreseeability of psychiatric illness, taking into account the three elements identified by Lord Wilberforce in *McLoughlin*, and held that the plaintiff's illness had been reasonably foreseeable notwithstanding her distance in time and space from the events and the aftermath. The plaintiff was therefore entitled to recover damages.

What is striking about these two cases is the willingness of first instance judges to use the reasonable foreseeability approach to allow recovery even in the third-party communication scenario where it had generally (though not universally) been accepted in previous cases that no liability could arise, thereby opening the door to potentially very large numbers of claims for psychiatric illness triggered by relatively routine communications of bad news, as opposed to relatively rare cases of direct perception of a loved one's death or injury.[89] In so doing, Mantell J and Ward J demonstrated how broad a discretion Lord Bridge's factual foreseeability approach conferred on first instance judges in nervous shock cases. It seems plausible to suppose that these two decisions—both of which were doubted in *Alcock*[90]—played at least some part in convincing the House of Lords that legal restrictions over and above reasonable foreseeability were required.[91]

---

[88] [1991] 3 All ER 73 (QB).

[89] This latter point is emphasised by M Davie, 'Negligently Inflicted Psychiatric Illness: the Hillsborough Case in the House of Lords' (1992) 43 *Northern Ireland Legal Quarterly* 237, 251.

[90] See [1992] 1 AC 310 (HL) 398 (Lord Keith), 401 (Lord Ackner), 418 (Lord Oliver).

[91] In the Court of Appeal in *Alcock*, Parker LJ said that the two decisions had 'gone further in extending the permissible ambit of a claim for nervous shock' than had any previous cases in the Court of Appeal or House of Lords: *Jones v Wright*, above n 58, 98.

3. The 'Disaster Era' and the Topicality of Trauma

The four-year period from 1985 to 1989 is often referred to as the UK's 'disaster era' because of the large number of man-made disasters which occurred during that time. The most significant of these events were, in 1985, the Bradford football stadium fire (40 fatalities) and the Manchester Airport fire (55); in 1987, the sinking of the *Herald of Free Enterprise* car ferry (187) and the King's Cross underground station fire (31); in 1988, the Piper Alpha oil rig fire (167), the Clapham rail crash (35) and the Lockerbie plane crash (270); and in 1989, the East Midlands Kegworth air crash (47), the Hillsborough disaster (96) and the sinking of the *Marchioness* pleasure boat (51). Inevitably, many of these disasters gave rise to large-scale litigation, some of which focused on psychiatric illness suffered by those involved. Most such litigation was dealt with by means of out-of-court settlements or arbitration, so that the full picture remains unclear, but there are enough reported cases and other sources of information to leave no doubt as to the very significant liabilities which those responsible for the disasters incurred. We know, for example, that at least 200 personal injury claims were settled following the Bradford stadium fire,[92] and that survivors of the *Herald of Free Enterprise* disaster received significant damages for physical and psychiatric injury in ten test cases presided over by arbitrators.[93] The King's Cross fire gave rise to at least one reported decision on psychiatric illness (involving a rescuer),[94] as did the Kegworth air crash,[95] and the Piper Alpha disaster gave rise to at least two.[96] Finally, it appears that in 1991–92, around the time of the *Alcock* decision, a number of psychiatric illness cases arising out of the *Marchioness* sinking were being heard.[97]

One feature of this era of disasters was the spotlight it placed on trauma-induced psychiatric illness, and in particular post-traumatic stress

[92] See M Matthews, J Morgan, C O'Cinneide, *Hepple and Matthews' Tort Cases and Materials*, 6th edn (Oxford, Oxford University Press, 2009) 15.

[93] See R Ford, 'Zeebrugge 10 Share 645,000 Pounds', *The Times*, 29 April 1989; K Wheat, *Napier and Wheat's Recovering Damages for Psychiatric Injury*, 2nd edn (Oxford, Oxford University Press, 2002) 212–24. Following the decision at first instance in *Alcock*, it seems that claims were also brought on behalf of relatives of passengers on the *Herald of Free Enterprise*, who claimed to have suffered psychiatric illness after watching television pictures of the disaster (see LM Lomax, 'A Landmark in Disaster Litigation' (1990) 140 *New Law Journal* 1155), but it seems probable that these actions were discontinued following the decision of the House of Lords.

[94] *Hale v London Underground Ltd* [1993] PIQR Q30 (£27,500 awarded to a fireman for post-traumatic stress disorder of 'moderate severity'). See also *Piggott v London Underground*, *Financial Times*, 19 December 1990 (news item), where a total of £34,000 was awarded to four other firemen involved.

[95] *Pearson v British Midland Airways* [1998] CLY 1530 (QB) (£17,500 awarded to civilian rescuer for post-traumatic stress disorder).

[96] *McFarlane v EE Caledonia Ltd* [1994] 2 All ER 1 (CA); *Hegarty v EE Caledonia Ltd* [1997] 2 Lloyd's Rep 259 (CA).

[97] Wheat, above n 93, 196–97.

disorder (PTSD), a condition which had only been formally recognised by the American Psychiatric Association's *Diagnostic and Statistical Manual of Mental Disorders* in 1980.[98] PTSD would appear to have been the principal (though not, of course, the only) form of psychiatric illness suffered by those involved in these disasters, and this diagnosis dominates the reported decisions on psychiatric illness which arose out of them. There was extensive press coverage of the disorder around the time of the *Alcock* decision, and it is noteworthy that many of the most significant medical works on PTSD date from the end of the 1980s and the beginning of the 1990s,[99] as do popular accounts of the effects of trauma, such as David Muss's self-help book *The Trauma Trap*[100] and *Survivors: Lockerbie*,[101] an account of the experiences of those who survived the Lockerbie air crash. The fact that so many man-made disasters took place in the years running up to *Alcock*, coupled with the topicality of trauma-induced psychiatric injury, can only have reinforced long-standing judicial concerns about the opening of the floodgates in nervous shock litigation. And, as we shall now see, these concerns would have been raised to an even higher level by the circumstances surrounding the *Alccok* litigation itself. The contrast with the small-scale road accidents that had previously dominated the case law in the field could hardly have been starker.

F. THE FACTS OF *ALCOCK*

The events at Hillsborough on 15 April 1989 have been well documented, not least in the interim report of the Inquiry which was established into the disaster under Lord Justice Taylor.[102] There is therefore little point in going through those events in any detail here. The bare facts are that, in the run up to the match, the police officer responsible for crowd control at the stadium ordered the opening of an exit gate to relieve pressure at the entrance turnstiles at the Leppings Lane end of the ground without ensuring that access was cut off to the two central 'pens' on the Leppings

---

98 (Washington DC, American Psychiatric Association, 1980).

99 See, eg CB Scrignar, *Post-traumatic Stress Disorder* (New Orleans, Bruno Press, 1988); ME Wolfe and AD Mosnaim (eds), *Post-traumatic Stress Disorder: Etiology, Phenomenology and Treatment* (Washington DC, American Psychiatric Press, 1990); J Davidson and E Foa (eds), *Post-traumatic Stress Disorder: DSM-IV and Beyond* (Washington DC, American Psychiatric Publishers, 1993). Of the 20 articles on medical aspects of PTSD and related issues listed in the bibliography in Wheat, above n 93, 270–71, 12 date from the period 1987–93.

100 (London and New York, Doubleday, 1991).

101 G Sheridan and T Kenning, *Survivors: Lockerbie* (London, Pan Books, 1993).

102 Lord Justice Taylor, *Interim Report on the Hillsborough Stadium Disaster*, Cmnd 3878 (London, HMSO, 1989). For accounts by those involved, see R Taylor, A Ward and T Newburn, *The Day of the Hillsborough Disaster: a Narrative Account* (Liverpool, Liverpool University Press, 1995).

Lane terrace, which were already overfull. The resultant surge of supporters into those two pens led to the crushing of the supporters towards the front of the pens, who were unable to escape the crush because of the presence of a perimeter fence between the terrace and the pitch and lateral fences between the central pens and the less crowded side pens. In all, 96 fans died, and over 400 received hospital treatment for injuries they received. According to the Taylor Inquiry, the primary cause of the disaster was the failure of police control, although a number of other contributing factors were identified, including the low number of turnstiles at the Leppings Lane end, inadequate signage in the concourse behind the terrace and the poor quality of the crush barriers on the terracing.

Writs dated from 19 December 1989 to 10 April 1990 were issued against the Chief Constable of South Yorkshire Police by 16 plaintiffs, who claimed damages for nervous shock arising out of the disaster. On 14 May 1990, Rose J ordered that all 16 actions be consolidated and that the trial proceed without pleadings pursuant to RSC Order 18, rule 21. The 16 actions were representative of a large number of similar claims—Hidden J referred at first instance to about 150,[103] but press reports following the House of Lords' ruling spoke of twice that number[104]—which the parties hoped could be settled in the light of the principles which emerged from the litigation. The very fact that such a procedure was felt to be necessary is an indication of the uncertain state of the law following *McLoughlin*. The representative nature of the *Alcock* actions is noteworthy for two other reasons as well. The first is that the desirability of a clear set of governing principles emerging from the litigation must have been obvious to the Law Lords who sat in the case; the second is that it is likely that the 16 test cases were deliberately selected by the parties either because they were regarded as borderline cases or because they raised new issues that had not previously been the subject of litigation.

This is borne out by an analysis of the circumstances of the 10 plaintiffs whose cases eventually reached the House of Lords. Two of the plaintiffs had lost a son at Hillsborough, five had lost brothers, one a brother-in-law, one a fiancé and one a grandson. Two of the plaintiffs—one of whom had lost two brothers and the other a brother-in-law—had been at the match, but in a different part of the ground. Six had watched live television pictures of the emerging tragedy, and found out later that their loved one had been killed. One of these plaintiffs was Alexandra Penk, who was told at 11 pm that her fiancé had been killed; another was Stephen Jones, who found out that his brother had died when he arrived at

103 *Alcock v Chief Constable of South Yorkshire Police* [1991] 2 WLR 814 (QB) 818.
104 See F Gibb 'Hillsborough relatives lose trauma claims' *The Times* (London, 29 November 1991); and A Sage 'Hillsborough families' claims for shock rejected' *The Independent* (London, 29 November 1991).

the temporary mortuary at the stadium at 2.45 am the next day; and a third was Harold Copoc, who was told at 6 am the next day that his son had died, following which he went to the temporary mortuary, where he identified his son's body. The other two plaintiffs had listened to reports of the disaster on the radio and been told in the early hours of the morning that their loved one (a grandson and a brother, respectively) was dead. In all the reported nervous shock cases involving relatives of the direct victim, the relationship had been either parental or spousal, so that recovery by all but two of the *Alcock* plaintiffs would have broken new ground in that regard. Furthermore, the perception of the events by the two plaintiffs who were parents of a direct victim, Agnes and Harold Copoc, was through simultaneous television pictures, and—in the case of Mr Copoc—by identification of his son's body more than 15 hours after the disaster. Again, recovery by these two plaintiffs would therefore have broken new ground with regard to the secondary victim's proximity in time and space to the event that caused the shock.

Two further points can be made about the factual background. The first is that, as Hidden J pointed out in his first instance judgment, within the cases that made up the *Alcock* litigation there was 'a multiplicity of permutations of factual situations' to which the law had to be applied.[105] This made *Alcock* an ideal vehicle for judicial codification of the law on secondary victim recovery for nervous shock, since a near-complete set of rules and principles would be needed to dispose of all the individual cases, rules and principles, which would then, of course, all form part of the ratio of the decision.[106] The other point is that the very facts of *Alcock* were guaranteed to raise floodgates concerns. Whereas previous nervous shock cases had generally concerned single claims arising out of road accidents and the like, the courts were now faced with multiple claims for nervous shock arising out of a televised mass disaster, with the knowledge that the outcome of hundreds of other actions depended on their deliberations. In the words of Michael Davie:[107] 'The large scale of the Hillsborough disaster and the introduction of the television component made it very clear that an unrestrained law on the issue of negligently inflicted psychiatric illness could lead to a massive number of claims.'

---

[105] *Alcock*, above n 103, 822.

[106] See J Swanton, 'Issues in Tort Liability for Nervous Shock' (1992) 66 *Australian Law Journal* 495, 495 ('The House of Lords was thus in the unusual position of being called upon virtually to state the law comprehensively with respect to liability for nervous shock').

[107] Davie, above n 89, 249. See also Teff, above n 37, 74.

G. THE DECISION OF HIDDEN J

The speed with which the actions reached trial is impressive. The hearing of the case began before Hidden J in Liverpool on 19 June 1990, and concluded a week later. Judgment was handed down on 31 July, less than four months after the last writ had been issued and only 15 months after the disaster had taken place.[108] For the purposes of the actions, the defendant had admitted a breach of his duty of care to those who had been killed or injured in the disaster, and Hidden J proceeded on the assumption that each plaintiff had suffered a recognisable psychiatric illness (the most common diagnosis being PTSD), which he regarded as a prerequisite of recovery. The learned judge tried to tread a careful line between the competing approaches of Lord Bridge and Lord Wilberforce in *McLoughlin*. On the one hand, he said, it followed from that decision that a court of first instance was entitled to conclude that no line restricting liability had been 'firmly and inexorably drawn', but was entitled to redraw that line where the court, 'enlightened by progressive awareness of mental illness', so decided;[109] on the other hand, the licence to move the law on with changing times was 'subject to a certain degree of limitation' if the defendant who was guilty of some negligence was not to be made liable to the world at large.[110] As far as the relationship between the direct victim and the secondary victim was concerned, it was only in cases where the relationship was 'of the closest known to man' that mental illness was reasonably foreseeable.[111] However, while acknowledging that the courts had previously drawn the line at parents and spouses, Hidden J concluded that it should now be extended to include brothers and sisters. At that point, however, the limit of the process of 'logical progression' was reached, and the line should not be extended further, to encompass the other relationships at issue. Moving on to the question of proximity in time and place, Hidden J held that there had to be 'some immediacy of observation by the plaintiff of the infliction of the injury upon the loved one',[112] but went on to decide that this requirement was satisfied both by the plaintiffs who had been at the match and by those who had watched the live television broadcasts of the unfolding disaster. Applying these principles to the facts of the 16 actions, Hidden J held that 10 of the claims should succeed and that six should be dismissed.

The judgment of Hidden J is an impressive one, not least because he went out of his way to explain the law in a clear and simple manner in order to make it more easily understood by the litigants themselves. As for

108 *Alcock*, above n 103.
109 Ibid, 833.
110 Ibid.
111 Ibid, 837.
112 Ibid, 821.

his treatment of the legal issues involved, he seems to have accepted the necessity of liability limits over and above factual foreseeability, but then to have drawn those limits very generously, extending protection as he did to siblings and to television viewers. Finally, his judgment is also significant for the way in which he explained away the absence of a close family relationship between direct and secondary victim in *Dooley v Cammell Laird*.[113] The 'real basis' of the award of damages in that case, he said, was that the plaintiff had been 'the unwitting agent of the defendant's negligence', since he was the crane driver who, without any fault, was party to an accident which could have killed his fellow workers.[114] It was that involvement in the events which had given rise to the duty of care. As we shall see, this 'ex post facto rationalisation' of the outcome in *Dooley*[115]—no hint of which can be found in the case itself—was picked up by Lord Oliver in the House of Lords and used as the basis for recognition of a special category of nervous shock plaintiffs who came to be known as 'unwitting agents' or 'involuntary participants'.

H. THE DECISION OF THE COURT OF APPEAL

The defendant appealed in the case of nine of the 10 successful plaintiffs,[116] and the six unsuccessful plaintiffs also appealed. The Court of Appeal (consisting of Parker LJ, Stocker LJ and Nolan LJ) gave judgment on 3 May 1991.[117] All the appeals by the defendant were allowed and all those by the plaintiffs dismissed. Parker LJ said that for any of the plaintiffs to succeed would involve an extension of the law as it stood after *McLoughlin*,[118] and Stocker LJ made it clear that in his opinion the approach of Lord Wilberforce in *McLoughlin* was more orthodox than that of Lord Bridge: all the English decisions before 1983 had been reached by reference to an approach based on categories of relationship, subject to any limitation of proximity in time and space.[119] Stocker LJ went so far as to say that the speech of Lord Wilberforce represented the law in relation to

---

113 [1951] 1 Lloyd's Rep 271 (Liverpool Assizes).

114 *Alcock*, above n 103, 846.

115 See *White*, above n 5, 507 (Lord Hoffmann).

116 The tenth successful plaintiff was William Pemberton, who had travelled to the match with his son but then stayed in the coach with the intention of watching the game on the coach's television. He watched the disaster unfold on the television, and then went in search of his son, a search that culminated in his identifying his son's body at the mortuary some time after midnight. Presumably the defendant's legal advisers decided that the combination of a parental relationship and Mr Pemberton's close proximity to the disaster meant that in his case an appeal was unlikely to succeed.

117 *Jones v Wright*, above n 58 (also reported alongside the House of Lords decision sub nom *Alcock v Chief Constable of South Yorkshire Police* [1992] 1 AC 310, 351ff).

118 *Jones v Wright*, above n 58, 97.

119 Ibid, 104.

nervous shock,[120] and, while Parker LJ seemed to think that Lord Bridge had spoken for the majority, he cited *Caparo v Dickman*[121] as evidence that the House of Lords had 'somewhat changed direction in their approach to problems of the ascertainment of a duty of care' since *McLoughlin* had been decided.[122]

In any case, the court took a fairly conservative approach to the issues involved. As far as the relationship between the direct and secondary victims was concerned, their Lordships agreed that there was a rebuttable presumption of a sufficiently close tie in parental and spousal relationships,[123] but while Parker LJ then took a hard line, insisting that nervous shock to remoter relatives could never be reasonably foreseeable,[124] Stocker LJ and Nolan LJ were prepared (as Lord Wilberforce had been in *McLoughlin*) to subject more distant relationships to careful scrutiny to see whether they 'gave rise to similar reactions of love and affection' as those which were attributed to the spouse/parent relationship.[125] However, all agreed that in the circumstances the sibling relationships in the actions before them were not close enough to qualify.[126] As regards the other two elements identified by Lord Wilberforce, the orthodox rule that communication by a third party would not suffice was confirmed, and the decisions in *Hevican* and *Ravenscroft* therefore doubted,[127] and Parker LJ held that the identification by one of the plaintiffs of his brother's body in the mortuary at around midnight fell outside the 'immediate aftermath' doctrine.[128] Finally, their Lordships agreed that on the facts the viewing of live television pictures of the disaster did not give rise to sufficient proximity between the parties to allow recovery.[129] The reasoning of Nolan LJ on this issue was to prove influential in the House of Lords. He accepted that 'the sight or sound of an incident could be transmitted and reproduced with a vividness which could 'equal, or even exceed, that experienced by those on the spot'.[130] However, the basis of the cause of action was 'shock, in the ordinary sense of that word, resulting from the direct perception of an actual or threatened physical impact',[131] and since

---

120 Ibid, 111.

121 Above n 82.

122 [1991] 3 All ER 88 (CA) 97. His Lordship placed more reliance on *Caparo* later on in his judgment: *Jones v Wright*, above n 58, 102–103. See also 111 (Stocker LJ), 119 (Nolan LJ).

123 Ibid, 99 (Parker LJ), 113 (Stocker LJ), 121 (Nolan LJ).

124 Ibid, 100.

125 Ibid, 113 (Stocker LJ). See also 121 (Nolan LJ).

126 The *Dooley* decision, above n 113, was distinguished on the grounds that the plaintiff had been an employee of the defendant (though this was not in fact the case), and that he had been 'directly involved' in the accident: see [1991] 3 All ER 88 (CA) 98 (Parker LJ), 114–15 (Stocker LJ).

127 See [1991] 3 All ER 88 (CA) 101 (Parker LJ), 116 (Stocker LJ).

128 [1991] 3 All ER 88 (CA) 102.

129 Ibid, 101 (Parker LJ), 116 (Stocker LJ), 122 (Nolan LJ).

130 Ibid, 122.

131 Ibid.

the television pictures seen by the plaintiffs had not shown the suffering of recognisable individuals, the element of 'immediate and horrifying impact on the viewer' was not established.[132] It did not follow, though, that a duty of care could never extend to television viewers:[133]

> For example, if a publicity seeking organisation made arrangements for a party of children to go up in a balloon, and for the event to be televised so that their parents could watch, it would be hard to deny that the organisers were under a duty to avoid mental injury to the parents as well as physical injury to the children, and that there would be a breach of that duty if through some careless act or omission the balloon crashed.

I. THE DECISION OF THE HOUSE OF LORDS

Ten of the unsuccessful plaintiffs appealed to the House of Lords, which unanimously dismissed the appeals.[134] Lord Keith, Lord Ackner, Lord Oliver and Lord Jauncey gave substantive opinions; Lord Lowry simply agreed that the appeals should be dismissed. Their Lordships agreed with the Court of Appeal that the plaintiffs were seeking to extend the boundaries of recovery;[135] Lord Keith also made it clear that in his view it was Lord Wilberforce who had spoken for the majority in *McLoughlin*: his had been the 'leading speech', and the speeches of Lord Edmund-Davies and Lord Russell had not 'contained anything inconsistent' with it.[136]

Their Lordships rejected the plaintiffs' argument that the test of liability was reasonable foreseeability alone.[137] In doing so, they highlighted the fact that the plaintiffs were 'secondary' victims of the defendant's negligence, since (in Lord Keith's words) the harm they had suffered was brought about 'by the infliction of physical injury, or the risk of physical injury, upon another person'.[138] It was Lord Oliver who developed this distinction between 'secondary victims' and 'primary victims' (or 'participants') most fully. Cases of psychiatric illness inflicted directly might present greater difficulties of proof, but were not, in their essential elements, any different from cases where the damages claimed arose from direct physical injury and presented 'no very difficult problems of analysis where the plaintiff has himself been directly involved in the accident from which the injury is said to arise'.[139] He went on:[140]

---

132 Ibid.
133 Ibid.
134 *Alcock* (HL), above n 117.
135 Ibid, 399 (Lord Ackner), 419 (Lord Jauncey).
136 Ibid, 395–96.
137 Ibid, 400 (Lord Ackner), 415, 419 (Lord Oliver).
138 Ibid, 396.
139 Ibid, 407.
140 Ibid.

Broadly, [cases of liability for nervous shock] divide into two categories, that is to say, those cases in which the injured plaintiff was involved, either mediately or immediately, as a participant, and those in which the plaintiff was no more than the passive and unwilling witness of injury caused to others.

In cases of the former type, there was a directness of relationship between the two parties (and hence a duty of care) which was 'almost self-evident from a mere recital of the facts'.[141] Into this category fell cases (such as *Dulieu v White*[142]) where the plaintiff had feared for his own safety, along with the rescuer cases such as *Chadwick*,[143] it being well established that a defendant owed a duty of care not only to those directly threatened or injured by his carelessness, but also to those induced to go to their rescue who suffered injury in so doing.[144] A third category of case where the plaintiff had been 'personally involved in the incident' out of which the action arose were the 'unwilling participant' cases, such as *Dooley*,[145] where:[146]

[T]he negligent act of the defendant has put the plaintiff in the position of being, or of thinking that he is about to be or has been, the involuntary cause of another's death or injury and the illness complained of stems from the shock to the plaintiff of the consciousness of this supposed fact.

However, where, as in the present appeals, the injury complained of was 'attributable to the grief and distress of witnessing the misfortune of another person' in an event which did not personally threaten or directly involve the plaintiff, the analysis became more complex,[147] since in general the common law had declined to entertain claims for such consequential losses from third parties. The lack of a legal duty in such cases was not, in Lord Oliver's opinion, attributable to an arbitrary rule of policy, but nor did it rest on the injury being unforeseeable; rather, it was down to the fact that such persons were not 'in contemplation of law, in a relationship of sufficient proximity to or directness with the tortfeasor as to give rise to a duty of care'.[148] Lord Oliver's view that this 'essential but illusive concept of "proximity" or "directness"' was 'of critical importance in the context of the instant appeals'[149] was clearly shared by the rest of the House,[150] and his sophisticated and original exposition of the secondary victim problem can be said to have provided the intellectual ballast for the restric-

---

141 Ibid.
142 Above n 9.
143 Above n 30.
144 *Alcock* (HL), above n 117, 408. See also 420–21 (Lord Jauncey).
145 Above n 22.
146 *Alcock* (HL), above n 117, 408. See also 420 (Lord Jauncey).
147 Ibid.
148 Ibid, 410.
149 Ibid.
150 See ibid, 396 (Lord Keith), 402 (Lord Ackner), 419–20 (Lord Jauncey).

tions on secondary victim recovery which the House agreed should be imposed.

One condition of secondary victim recovery, Lord Ackner made clear, was that the plaintiff's psychiatric injury must have been induced by shock—which he defined as involving 'the sudden appreciation by sight or sound of a horrifying event, which violently agitates the mind'[151]—with the result that, for example, no duty was owed to a spouse who suffered psychiatric illness as a result of the stress of caring for a tortiously injured husband or wife.[152] As for the three elements which Lord Wilberforce had identified as inherent in any secondary victim claim, their Lordships treated the first element—the class of persons whose claims should be recognised—not as a separate 'proximity' limit on recovery, but as part and parcel of the foreseeability enquiry.[153] This represented a clear departure from Lord Wilberforce's approach, but was consistent with much of the earlier English case law, and also with the analysis of Deane J in *Jaensch v Coffey*.[154] Inevitably, it led the House to adopt a relatively flexible approach to the question (as Stocker LJ and Nolan LJ had in the Court of Appeal) and to reject hard-and-fast rules limiting recovery to particular categories of relationship.[155] As Lord Ackner put it:[156]

> Whether the degree of love and affection in any given relationship, be it that of relative or friend, is such that the defendant . . . should reasonably have foreseen the shock-induced psychiatric illness, has to be decided on a case by case basis.

Indeed, the flexibility inherent in the reasonable foreseeability approach to this issue even led their Lordships to countenance the possibility of recovery by a mere bystander, unconnected with the victims of an accident. Although psychiatric injury to such a person would not normally be foreseeable, it was possible that it would be if the circumstances of a catastrophe 'were particularly horrific',[157] as where (in Lord Ackner's example) a petrol tanker careered out of control into a school in session and burst into flames.[158] Nevertheless, because their Lordships were of the opinion that nervous shock would normally only be foreseeable in the case of the spousal and parental relationships which previously decided secondary

---

[151] Ibid, 401.

[152] See also 396 (Lord Keith).

[153] Ibid, 397 (Lord Keith), 402 (Lord Ackner), 416 (Lord Oliver), 419–20 (Lord Jauncey). Cf *McFarlane*, above n 96, 14 (Stuart-Smith LJ).

[154] Above n 67.

[155] *Alcock* (HL), above n 117, 397 (Lord Keith), 415 (Lord Oliver), 422 (Lord Jauncey) (to draw a dividing line between one degree of relationship and another would be 'arbitrary and lacking in logic').

[156] Ibid, 404.

[157] Ibid, 397 (Lord Keith). See also 416 (Lord Oliver) ('circumstances of such horror as would be likely to traumatise even the most phlegmatic spectator').

[158] Ibid, 403.

victim cases had involved, the actual application of the reasonable foreseeability approach to this question resulted in the conservative conclusion that, while a rebuttable presumption of a sufficiently close tie of love and affection would arise in the case of parents, children and spouses of the direct victim, more remote relationships would call for evidence of a particularly close emotional tie akin to a spousal or parental one.[159]

When it came to Lord Wilberforce's other two elements—proximity to the accident and the means by which the shock was caused—the House adopted a less flexible approach, laying down fairly strict limits, justified by reference not to foreseeability but to 'proximity', although even here they were careful to set the boundaries of liability in such a way as to include within them the facts of all the decided cases prior to *Hevican v Ruane*[160] and *Ravenscroft*.[161] The general position as regards these two elements was summed up by Lord Oliver as follows:[162]

> The necessary element of proximity between plaintiff and defendant is furnished, at least in part, by both physical and temporal propinquity and also by the sudden and direct visual impression on the plaintiff's mind of actually witnessing the event or its immediate aftermath.

As this summary indicates, their Lordships accepted the 'immediate aftermath' doctrine,[163] and they also made it clear that in their view the application of that doctrine on the facts of *McLoughlin* had been correct. The House was not, however, prepared to extend the immediate aftermath doctrine to encompass the identification of bodies by relatives in the temporary mortuary at Hillsborough. The obvious reason for refusing to do this was the time gap between the earliest such identification in issue and the disaster (over eight hours), and indeed Lord Ackner emphasised this, denying that this identification could be described as part of the *immediate* aftermath, and pointing out that in *McLoughlin*—where Lord Wilberforce had considered the facts to be borderline—the time gap had been much smaller.[164] Lord Jauncey was also exercised by the fact that the visits to the mortuary 'were made not for the purpose of rescuing or giving comfort to the victim but purely for the purpose of identification', and took the view that this also took them outside the immediate aftermath concept,[165] though quite why this was so was not made clear.[166]

---

159 Ibid, 403 (Lord Ackner), 422 (Lord Jauncey).

160 Above n 87.

161 Above n 88.

162 *Alcock* (HL), above n 117, 416.

163 See also 397 (Lord Keith), 404 (Lord Ackner), 423–24 (Lord Jauncey).

164 Ibid, 405. His Lordship described the time gap in *McLoughlin* as 'an hour or so', though in fact it was well over two hours.

165 Ibid, 424.

166 Though Lord Wilberforce did draw an analogy with the rescue cases in his discussion of the immediate aftermath concept in *McLoughlin*: above n 21, 419, 422.

With regard to the means of communication, their Lordships took the orthodox view that simply being informed of the event by a third party was insufficient to create the necessary degree of proximity,[167] and they also agreed that this was true of the television pictures of the disaster which many of the plaintiffs had watched. Lord Jauncey adopted a fairly sweeping approach to this latter issue, saying that the test of proximity would not be met where the plaintiff watched a normal television programme displaying events as they happened,[168] but the remainder of their Lordships took a more subtle line, which was clearly influenced by the analysis of Nolan LJ in the Court of Appeal. In essence, their reasoning seems to have been, not that the mediated viewing of the event through television pictures was inconsistent with the necessary degree of proximity being established, but that the fact that the television pictures transmitted from Hillsborough had not depicted the suffering of recognisable individuals meant that, while they would obviously have given rise to deep anxiety and distress on the part of the watching relatives, the requisite element of shock was missing, as it would have come later, when the plaintiff was told that his or her loved one had been killed.[169]

Properly understood, therefore, the refusal to extend liability to television viewers in *Alcock* was not based on a general rule barring such secondary victims from recovering, but instead on the fact that in this case the television pictures were not the true source of the 'sudden shock' which their Lordships seemed to think lay at the root of the secondary victim action. Indeed, Lord Oliver expressly agreed with Nolan LJ that the necessary element of visual perception could be provided by witnessing the actual injury to the primary victim on live television,[170] as did Lord Ackner, who thought that, in addition to Nolan LJ's balloon example, '[m]any other situations could be imagined where the impact of the simultaneous television pictures would be as great, if not greater, than the actual sight of the accident'.[171]

Be that as it may, the application of the general principles identified by the House led to the disposal of all the appeals. According to Lord Keith, in the absence of evidence of a particularly close tie of love and affection, seven of the plaintiffs (five siblings, a brother-in-law and a grandfather) had failed to establish that their psychiatric illness had been reasonably foreseeable.[172] And while his Lordship did conclude that psychiatric illness

---

[167] *Alcock* (HL), above n 117, 398 (Lord Keith), 400 (Lord Ackner).

[168] Ibid, 423.

[169] Ibid, 398 (Lord Keith), 405 (Lord Ackner). The analysis of Lord Oliver (at 417) was yet more subtle, but his conclusion was to similar effect.

[170] Ibid, 417.

[171] Ibid, 405. Lord Jauncey was less enthusiastic at 423, but still left open the position in 'the special circumstances envisaged by Nolan LJ'.

[172] Ibid, 398. See also 406 (Lord Ackner), 416 (Lord Oliver) (both referring only to the two plaintiffs present at the match, a brother and a brother-in-law) and 424 (Lord Jauncey) (referring to all the plaintiffs except for the two parents).

had been so foreseeable in the case of the other three plaintiffs (two parents and a fiancé), these three had all watched the scenes on television, and it followed that they had failed to establish the necessary degree of proximity to give rise to a duty of care.[173]

J. ANALYSIS

1. General Observations

A number of general observations can be made about the decision of the House of Lords. If we focus first on what the House actually decided, perhaps the most important aspect of the decision was the clear rejection of an untrammelled test of reasonable foreseeability in nervous shock cases. This was hardly surprising. As we have seen, it is doubtful whether there was ever a time when English law had in practice embraced this stance, even in the aftermath of the relatively liberal decision in *McLoughlin*, and at the time *Alcock* was decided, this approach had been rejected by both the High Court of Australia and the Supreme Court of California. When we factor in the retreat from *Anns*, the spate of disasters that had befallen the UK in the years running up to *Alcock* and the factual circumstances of the *Alcock* litigation, it has to be said that it would have been astonishing if the House had endorsed the ultra-liberal position taken by Lord Bridge in *McLoughlin*, which even Lord Scarman had warned could lead to 'socially undesirable' results. Indeed, arguably what is surprising about *Alcock* is not that the House of Lords rejected Lord Bridge's position, but that they did not do so more emphatically. Although clearly their Lordships' analysis was closer to that of Lord Wilberforce, one gets the distinct impression reading *Alcock* that the House considered that it was marking out a middle way between bare foreseeability on the one hand and strict limits on recovery motivated by public policy on the other.[174] After all, their Lordships accepted the import of Lord Bridge's analysis as far as the question of the relationship between the direct and secondary victims were concerned, even accepting that in an extreme case liability could extend to a mere bystander. And while arguably the House then applied the test of reasonable foreseeability rather strictly when it came to the relationships in the case itself, Lord Keith at least was prepared to include a fiancé within the range of foreseeable injury, as well as parents and spouses, and in no

---

[173] Ibid, 398.
[174] See, eg *Alcock* (HL), above n 117, 415 (Lord Oliver). This was also the view of one of the early commentators on the decision: see Davie, above n 89, 261.

previous English case had more remote relatives even brought a claim, never mind recovered damages.[175]

Even when it came to the other two elements identified by Lord Wilberforce, a degree of flexibility was apparent. While accepting that at this point limits over and above reasonable foreseeability were required, their Lordships tended to justify these by reference to a principled (if inevitably vague) notion of 'proximity' between the parties rather than explicitly by reference to policy objections to recovery, such as the floodgates argument. The House was prepared to accept the extension of the 'immediate aftermath' idea to cover the facts of *McLoughlin*, but understandably baulked at the inclusion within the 'immediate' aftermath of mortuary visits that took place more than eight hours after the disaster. (This is not to say that the House could not have countenanced a further extension of the boundaries of the requirement of proximity in time and space; my point is rather that on the existing authorities—both in England and abroad—a significant extension would have been required.) The rule against third-party communication was one of the most firmly established in the area, and its confirmation was also to be expected. Finally, the majority of their Lordships took a notably liberal approach to the question of simultaneous television pictures, with at least two members of the House making it clear that they had no objection to the idea that watching such pictures could give rise to the necessary degree of proximity, even if the very general pictures transmitted from Hillsborough did not give rise to the required element of sudden shock.

2. *Alcock* as Codification

There are several reasons why a decision can be described as a 'landmark case'. One is that it marked a very significant change of direction. Another is that it represented an authoritative consolidation and codification of the law as it then stood. Although *Alcock* is often thought to be the first type of landmark, I want to suggest that it was really the latter. After all, the effect of the decision was not so much to pull back the boundaries of liability, but by and large to confirm the law at the point in its development at which it had then arrived, and to countenance some future incremental extensions.[176] The cases that had followed *Bourhill* had left the law in something

---

[175] Commenting on this aspect of the decision shortly afterwards, Tony Weir treated it as a liberalisation of the law: see T Weir, *A Casebook on Tort*, 7th edn (London, Butterworths, 1992) 87 ('Now the House of Lords has abandoned the view that in the normal case only parents and spouses can sue'). See also *White*, above n 5, 496 (Lord Steyn) (before *Alcock* 'the general rule was that only parents and spouses could recover').

[176] The general principles which emerged from *Alcock* almost exactly replicate Francis Trindade's assessment of the state of the law in 1986: see Trindade, above n 60, 499. At times, the reasoning of their Lordships was explicitly codificatory: see, eg *Alcock* (HL), above n 117,

of a mess, and the attempt to rationalise that mess in *McLoughlin* had failed, since it was unclear whether it was Lord Wilberforce's or Lord Bridge's grand scheme that had carried the day. In *Alcock*, by contrast, there was a high degree of unanimity across the four substantive opinions, with broad agreement on all the important issues and only some minor differences of emphasis. Furthermore, their Lordships went out of their way to rationalise all the earlier case law, with Lord Oliver even developing a whole new category of 'participant' to explain away the unreserved first instance decision in *Dooley*.

The conservative spirit of the decision was also apparent in the way in which their Lordships drew heavily on earlier case law when putting together the set of principles which would in future govern secondary victim recovery. Although the sudden shock requirement had not previously been referred to expressly in an English case, it was consistent with the outcomes of all the earlier cases,[177] and had been emphasised by Brennan J in *Jaensch v Coffey*.[178] The three 'elements' were of course borrowed from Lord Wilberforce's opinion in *McLoughlin*, and the House's approach to those three elements was heavily influenced by earlier decisions. Although Lord Wilberforce had treated the close tie of love and affection question as one going to proximity, it had also been common to build this into the reasonable foreseeability enquiry,[179] and the approach of the House of Lords to this issue closely mirrored that of Stocker LJ and Nolan LJ in the Court of Appeal. The basic requirement that the plaintiff witness the event or its aftermath with his or her 'unaided senses' was certainly nothing new,[180] the treatment of the television issue was taken from Nolan LJ below, the 'involuntary participant' idea from Hidden J at first instance, and so on. The more general emphasis that Lord Oliver and Lord Jauncey put on the need for a sufficiently proximate relationship between the two parties in this type of case[181] was clearly influenced by the analysis of Deane J in *Jaensch v Coffey*,[182] and was consistent with the approach that had been taken by the House in the economic loss context.

---

406 (Lord Oliver) (refering to 'The common features of all the reported cases of this type decided in this country prior to the decision of Hidden J').

177 See H Teff, 'The Requirement of "Sudden Shock" in Liability for Negligently Inflicted Psychiatric Damage' (1996) 4 *Tort Law Review* 44, 49 ('In all the early leading English cases, sudden shock either clearly was, or was perceived to be, a central element in what happened; the successful plaintiff's medical condition was seen as induced by some instantaneous reaction to a specific occurrence'). Writing in 1986, Francis Trindade described sudden shock as a requirement of recovery: see Trindade, above n 60, 478–80.

178 Above n 59, 11–12.

179 See, eg *Jaensch v Coffey*, above n 59, 35 (Deane J).

180 See, eg *Hambrook v Stokes*, above n 12, 152 (Bankes LJ); *King v Phillips*, above n 24, 441 (Denning LJ); *McLoughlin v O'Brian*, above n 21, 418–19 (Lord Wilberforce).

181 See *Alcock*, above n 1, 406, 410, 415 (Lord Oliver), 419–20 (Lord Jauncey).

182 See also *Attia v British Gas*, above n 58, 311–12 (Dillon LJ); *Ravenscroft*, above n 88, 83 (Ward J).

Even the most original contribution that the House of Lords made to the conceptual structure it constructed, the primary/secondary victim distinction, had been adverted to by both Lord Wright in *Bourhill v Young*[183] and Stephenson LJ in the Court of Appeal in *McLoughlin v O'Brian*.[184]

3. *Alcock* as 'Judicial Legislation'

One of the claims that has been made about the *Alcock* decision is that it amounted to judicial legislation.[185] To say that a court has engaged in 'judicial legislation' is generally understood to be a criticism,[186] and here the criticism seems to be that in *Alcock* the House of Lords laid down arbitrary and unprincipled limitations on nervous shock claims for policy reasons, and by doing so exceeded the proper limits of adjudication. The second aspect of this critique lies beyond the scope of this paper, but I would like to finish by taking issue with the first aspect, which reflects an assumption that appears to be widely held about the *Alcock* case.

It is now commonplace to assert that the restrictions placed on secondary victim recovery in *Alcock* were arbitrary, and motivated by policy concerns such as the threat of indeterminate liability.[187] In the subsequent House of Lords decision in *White v Chief Constable of South Yorkshire Police*, for example, both Lord Goff and Lord Hoffmann described the *Alcock* criteria as 'arbitrary',[188] and the latter said that in *Alcock* the 'search for principle' had been called off,[189] while Lord Steyn clearly took the view that the limits were based on policy considerations.[190] Similarly, in its 2004 report on liability for psychiatric injury, the Scottish Law Commission described the criteria as 'unprincipled rules',

---

[183] [1943] AC 92 (HL) 108 ('In such cases terms like "derivative" and "original" and "primary" and "secondary" have been applied to define and distinguish the type of negligence').

[184] [1981] 2 WLR 1014 (CA) 1022 ('a secondary or derivative liability').

[185] See R Stevens, *Torts and Rights* (Oxford, Oxford University Press, 2007) 55 (in *Alcock*, the House of Lords was 'fulfilling a legislative rather than traditionally judicial function'). See also *Hunter v British Coal Corp* [1999] QB 140 (CA), 155 (Brooke LJ) ('If judges are going to don a legislative mantle in this controversial field *again*, this . . . is the proper function of the House of Lords and not of this court' (emphasis added)).

[186] See, eg *Murphy v Brentwood DC* [1991] 1 AC 398 (HL) 472 (Lord Keith), referring to the decision in *Anns v Merton London Borough*, above n 81.

[187] According to the Law Commission, the restrictions were based on 'policy grounds' and 'have been almost universally criticised as arbitrary and unfair' ('Liability for Psychiatric Illness' (Law Com No 249, 1998) paras 2.21, 6.3).

[188] [1999] 2 AC 455 (HL) 487 (Lord Goff), 502 (Lord Hoffmann).

[189] Ibid, 511. See also *Tame v New South Wales* (2002) 211 CLR 317 (HCA) [190] (Gummow and Kirby JJ) (referring to 'unprincipled distinctions and artificial mechanisms').

[190] [1999] 2 AC 455 (HL) 487, 493, 499.

which had evolved 'to limit potential liability',[191] and Robert Stevens has described the criteria as 'crude controls' and 'fixed bright line rules', imposed for reasons of 'public policy'.[192] However, close scrutiny of the opinions in *Alcock* reveals these assertions to be questionable at best. As we have seen, one of the distinguishing features of the House's approach to the limitations on secondary victim recovery was in fact a reluctance to lay down hard-and-fast rules[193] precisely because such limits would necessarily operate in an irrational and arbitrary manner,[194] and early commentators on *Alcock* praised this aspect of the decision. For example, Bernadette Lynch, who wrote a note on the case in the *Law Quarterly Review*, commented that:[195]

> The use of rebuttable presumptions for proving the requisite emotional proximity, the exceptional rules for particularly horrific events and the possibility of liability if victims are identifiable by media coverage mean that arbitrary rigidity has been avoided and scope remains for individual consideration of deserving cases.

Indeed, this element of flexibility has given rise to a very different criticism of the *Alcock* decision, namely that by not laying down bright-line rules the House of Lords failed to give future litigants a clear enough idea of whether or not a claim would succeed. According to David Robertson, for example, the House's efforts to avoid the appearance of legislating merely resulted in 'bad judicial legislation', bad because it afforded litigants inadequate guidance.[196] This criticism has often been directed in particular at the way in which their Lordships dealt with the requirement of a close tie of love affection, where the preservation of flexibility through the use of rebuttable presumptions has been castigated for forcing the courts to engage in insensitive enquiries into the extent of the claimant's emotional bond with the immediate victim.[197] It is also of note that another example of flexibility in the reasoning in *Alcock*—the possibility of bystander recovery in the case of

---

191 'Report on Damages for Psychiatric Injury' (Scot Law Com No 196, 2004) para 3.1. See also Scottish Law Commission, 'Damages for Psychiatric Injury' (Scot Law Com Discussion Paper No 120, 2002) para 4.9.

192 Stevens, above n 185, 55–56.

193 See D Robertson, 'Liability in Negligence for Nervous Shock' (1994) 57 *MLR* 649, 657 ('the speeches seemed designed to avoid appearing to draw firm lines').

194 See, eg [1992] 1 AC 310, 415 (Lord Oliver) ('So rigid an approach would, I think, work great injustice and cannot be rationally justified'); and 422 (Lord Jauncey) ('To draw such a line would necessarily be arbitrary and lacking in logic').

195 B Lynch, 'A Victory for Pragmatism? Nervous Shock Reconsidered' (1992) 108 *LQR* 367, 370. See also Davie, above n 89, 239, 254, 261.

196 Robertson, above n 193, 662.

197 See, eg 'Liability for Psychiatric Illness', above n 187, para 6.24; 'Damages for Psychiatric Injury', above n 191, para 4.16; D Nolan, 'Reforming Liability for Psychiatric Injury in Scotland: a Recipe for Uncertainty?' (2005) 68 *MLR* 983, 995; T Weir, *An Introduction to Tort Law*, 2nd edn (Oxford, Oxford University Press, 2006) 51; N McBride and R Bagshaw, *Tort Law*, 3rd edn (Harlow, Pearson Education, 2008) 100–01. Cf Department for Constitutional Affairs, 'The Law on Damages' (Consultation Paper CP 9/07, 2007) para 88.

a particularly horrific incident—was later ruled out for reasons of certainty by the Court of Appeal, which substituted a bright-line rule against recovery.[198]

As for the assumption that the *Alcock* criteria were grounded in policy concerns, in fact there is virtually no mention at all in *Alcock* of the policy objections to recovery for nervous shock which can be found in cases dating back to *Victorian Railways Commissioners v Coultas*.[199] Indeed, Lord Oliver, who delivered the most comprehensive and intellectually satisfying opinion, clearly did not think that the problem in *Alcock* was that the plaintiffs had suffered psychiatric injury at all, but rather that that injury was relational, or 'secondary' in nature, and hence at one remove from the defendant's negligence. This explains why he was so keen to distinguish between secondary victim cases of this kind and the primary victim or participant cases where he felt that the existence of a duty of care arose straightforwardly from the direct connection between the negligence and the injury.

K. CONCLUSION

Although I do not suppose that many commentators would challenge the proposition that *Alcock* is a landmark case in the law of tort, I hope to have demonstrated in this chapter that it is perhaps a misunderstood decision. A case that is often painted as retrograde and reactionary was in fact rather conservative, and even in some respects mildly progressive, not least when one takes into account the circumstances in which it was decided. Perhaps the gravest criticism that can be made of their Lordships' House is that their approach to the question of the required relationship between primary and secondary victim, although intellectually coherent, had the actual effect in most cases of adding insult to injury; as Jane Stapleton so acutely observed, was 'it not a disreputable sight to see brothers of Hillsborough victims turned away because they had *no more* than brotherly love towards the victim?'[200] It is certainly true that the contrast with the extremely sensitive judgment of Hidden J at first instance does not reflect particularly well on their Lordships, but then it would not be the first time that an appellate court has lost sight of the

---

198 *McFarlane*, above n 96.

199 Above n 6. It is true that at the end of his opinion ([1992] 1 AC 310, 418–19), Lord Oliver said that he did not regard the present state of the law as 'logically defensible' and that he referred to 'considerations of policy'; however, this was not with reference to the central limits on secondary victim recovery laid down in the case, but with reference to the requirement of a recognisable psychiatric illness and a possible bar on claims in respect of trauma caused by self-inflicted injury.

200 J Stapleton, 'In Restraint of Tort' in P Birks (ed), *The Frontiers of Liability* (Oxford, Oxford University Press, 1994) 95 (emphasis in original).

human dimension in its quest to rationalise the law, and in any case the evidence would suggest that the relatives of the Hillsborough victims were (and are) more concerned with their desire for 'justice for the 96' than with any perceived slights emanating from the House of Lords. It has often been pointed out that, when weighed up against the terrible events at Hillsborough, football is made to appear almost irrelevant. The same could perhaps also be said of the law of tort.

12

Hunter v Canary Wharf Ltd (1997)

MARIA LEE*

The development of London's Docklands since the mid-1980s has been a staggering story of physical, economic and social change. *Hunter v Canary Wharf*,[1] by any standards a significant case, sits in the context of this highly contested 'regeneration' of London Docklands. In this chapter, I argue that *Hunter* is a case about competing visions of the public interest, and that the Courts' attention to the various ways of addressing these interests is inadequate. A continued place for private nuisance in our heavily regulated world demands closer attention to regulatory context. However, there are no simple answers to the relationship between private law and regulation: an automatic preference for regulatory arrangements over ad hoc individual rearrangement through private law places too much faith in the quality of regulatory processes; but private law rights and interests are too contingent and individualised to be allowed automatically to cut across carefully considered administrative judgments of the public interest. Deciding how these arguments play out in any particular case requires a far more explicit discussion than we see in *Hunter*. Whilst *Hunter* is uncontroversially a landmark case for its conservative positioning of private nuisance as a tort against property, this wider regulatory context remains under-examined.

A. DOCKLANDS REGENERATION

The first major docks development to the east of London was in the eighteenth century, although there had been ports in the area since at least

* I am grateful to Paul Mitchell for his very helpful comments on this paper, and to Denise Leung for research assistance.
1 *Hunter and Others v Canary Wharf Ltd*; *Hunter and Others v London Docklands Development Corporation* [1997] AC 655 (CA & HL).

Roman times.[2] Parliament passed a Bill for the construction of docks on the Isle of Dogs in 1800, and London Docklands thrived through the first half of the twentieth century. The area was heavily bombed in the Second World War, after which began slow but nonetheless dramatic decline; by 1981, a House of Lords Select Committee on docklands was 'forcefully struck by the extent of that calamity'.[3] The East India dock closed in 1967, the final docks, the Royal Victoria, the Royal Albert and the King George V, in 1981. Containerisation, which meant that cargo could move from ship to truck without warehousing, and the use of ships too large for the London docks contributed to the decline, although there were arguably also more deeply rooted problems: dock space was over-provided in the nineteenth century, which had led to previous periods of economic decline and consolidation; the goods being transported were no longer those that had sustained the dockside industries; and London was no longer the trading centre of an empire.

Plans for the regeneration of Docklands had been produced from the early 1960s, and through the 1970s consultants' reports and official committees multiplied.[4] The need for regeneration was not in question, but the competing plans and proposals are indicative of the disagreement over what that regeneration should look like. Regeneration, symbolised in the *Hunter* litigation by the construction of Canary Wharf Tower, a development 'obviously of a scale totally transforming the environment',[5] always has the potential to be profoundly divisive. Conscious efforts to 'regenerate' an area, in the search for the right way to develop economically and physically, seem also to pass judgment on the right way to live. Public authority-led plans were abandoned in the 1980s in favour of a central government, market-led approach. The property-based regener-

---

[2] For some historical context (and references for this paragraph) up to the operation of the London Docklands Development Corporation see: P Ackroyd, *London: A Biography* (London, Vintage, 2001) ch 77; T Brindley, Y Rydin and G Stoker, *Remaking Planning: The Politics of Urban Change*, 2nd edn (London, Routledge, 1996) 98–99; J Foster, *Docklands: Culture in Conflict, Worlds in Collision* (London, UCL Press, 1999); R Porter, *London: A Social History* (Cambridge, MA, Harvard University Press, 1998) ch 16. For subsequent developments see M Carmona, 'The Isle of Dogs: Four Development Waves, Five Planning Models, Twelve Plans, Thirty-five Years, and a Renaissance . . . of Sorts' (2009) 71 *Progress in Planning* 87.

[3] Report from the Select Committee of the House of Lords on the London Docklands Development Corporate (Area and Constitution) Order 1980, 5 June 1981, [8.1].

[4] Starting with Report of the Rochdale Committee on the Major Ports in the United Kingdom (1962). See the discussion in House of Lords Select Committee, above n 3; London Docklands Development Corporation (LDDC), 'Initiating Urban Change' (1997), available at http://www.lddc-history.org.uk/publications/index.html#Monographs (accessed October 2009); Carmona, above n 2. Key moments include the Travers Morgan report, 'Docklands: Redevelopment Proposals for East London' (1973), which was published during the GLC elections and became highly controversial (see LDDC, ibid), and the Docklands Joint Committee's 'London Docklands Strategic Plan' (1976).

[5] *Hunter*, above n 1, 722 (Lord Cooke).

ation of the 1980s tied profound questions of economic and social direction up with disagreement over the use of land.

Whilst competing interests are often dichotomised in private litigation as public versus private interests (the general public benefit of the burning of bricks[6] or the training of pilots[7] versus the private interests of the claimant), the line between public and private interests is fuzzy. In Docklands, the public interest in physical development was tangled up in its private profit-making character;[8] equally, the private interests of the parties are tangled up with competing (public) visions for the local area. As much as public versus private interests, this case is about competing approaches to the public interest, and even competing approaches to what constitutes the relevant 'public' or 'community'. In particular, perceived national interests in economic development run against perceived local interests in the type of economic development.

The London Docklands Development Corporation (LDDC) was set up by the LDDC Area and Constitution Order 1980,[9] under the Local Government, Planning and Land Act 1980. The 1980 Act gave the Secretary of State, subject to positive parliamentary approval, powers to designate an Urban Development Area when considered 'expedient in the national interest'.[10] The LDDC was the Urban Development Corporation set up to manage the Docklands Urban Development Area. The single object of an urban development corporation was to 'secure the regeneration of its area', an object that is:

> to be achieved in particular by the following means . . . namely, by bringing land and buildings into effective use, encouraging the development of existing and new industry and commerce, creating an attractive environment and ensuring that housing and social facilities are available to encourage people to live and work in the area.[11]

Urban development corporations were described by Michael Heseltine, Secretary of State for the Environment, as 'single-minded agencies' designed to 'secure development, bring in the private sector, and secure improvements of benefit to the areas and the country as a whole'.[12] The

---

6 *Bamford v Turnley* (1860) 3 B&S 62, 122 ER 27 (Exch Ch).

7 *Dennis v Ministry of Defence* [2003] EWHC 793 (QB), [2003] 2 EGLR 121.

8 As was also the case in the nineteenth-century infrastructure development: see chapter 1, above.

9 London Docklands Development Corporation (Area and Constitution) Order 1980 SI 1980/936. The LDDC was the second urban development corporation to be set up, the first being Merseyside. The Report of the Select Committee of the House of Lords, above n 3, was a response to a challenge to the original order.

10 S 134. For analysis of the lengthy Act, including its provisions on local authority spending see M Loughlin, 'Local Government in the Welfare Corporate State' (1981) 44 *MLR* 422.

11 S 136(1) and (2).

12 Introducing the Bill for second reading in the House of Commons, Hansard, HC Deb vol 978, c 256.

statutory basis for the regeneration of London Docklands was explicitly the national interest, with the interests of local communities at best secondary.[13] Attracting private sector investment was the main purpose of the LDDC, through what has been called 'leverage planning', where public investment is used to stimulate property markets.[14] Ackroyd draws parallels between the role of commerce in shaping the Isle of Dogs at the beginning of the nineteenth century and the role of private money in the reshaping of the Isle of Dogs at the end of the twentieth.[15] The writ of the LDDC stretched over 5000 acres of London Docklands and several London boroughs, an area with nearly 40,000 residents in 1981. Land formerly held by local authorities (especially the Greater London Council and the London Ports Authority) was vested in the LDDC, which also had powers to purchase land.[16] All urban development corporations had development powers, and the LDDC was made the planning authority by statutory instrument.[17]

The same 1980 Act provided for the designation of enterprise zones.[18] Geoffrey Howe introduced the idea of enterprise zones when the Conservatives were in opposition in 1978,[19] in a speech made in Docklands. The government moved to implementation soon after the 1979 general election. The idea was originally to generate economic activity in abandoned industrial areas that did not have a significant population.[20] The various benefits available in the enterprise zone were always controversial. They included tax advantages for industrial and commercial building (but not residential building), which amounted to a considerable public subsidy during the 1980s, and the LDDC also received direct government grants at a time of general fiscal restraint. Most significant for current purposes is the supposed 'simplification' of planning regimes, to which we will return.[21] The Isle of Dogs Enterprise Zone was set up within the LDDC in 1982. This is where the Canary Wharf development took

---

13 Local Government, Planning and Land Act, s 134.

14 See the discussion in Brindley et al, above n 2, ch 6.

15 Ackroyd, above n 2, 197. Foster, above n 2, also comments on what we might call the continuity of change, ch 1.

16 Ss 141–42.

17 Ss 148–49, London Docklands Development Corporation (Planning Functions) Order 1981 SI 1981/1081.

18 S 179, sch 32. For discussion of the ideas behind enterprise zones see R Green (ed), *Enterprise Zones: New Directions in Economic Development* (London, Sage Publications, 1991).

19 S Butler, 'The Conceptual Evolution of Enterprise Zones' in Green, ibid, 27. The idea is usually attributed to Peter Hall's ideas on the 'non-plan': see P Hall, 'The British Enterprise Zones' in Green, ibid, 179; A Thornley, *Urban Planning Under Thatcherism: The Challenge of the Market* (Routledge, London 1993) ch 9.

20 Butler, above n 19.

21 On the relationship between the development of planning and the enterprise zone idea see C Jones, 'Verdict on the British Enterprise Zone Experiment' (2006) 11 *International Planning Studies* 109.

place, including Canary Wharf Tower, or One Canada Square, as it is also now known.

Loss of traditional industry, high unemployment and economic decline formed the background to the 1980 Act. Introducing the Bill to Parliament, Michael Heseltine presented it as a solution to the problem of inner city degeneration: 'the problem of the inner city areas is stark; there is tragic decay of vast areas which—as in London and Merseyside docklands—were once thriving parts of the country's prosperity'.[22] The depressed nature of Docklands is constantly emphasised in the debates on the Bill. But with hindsight, although the opposition did raise strongly the loss of local democracy implied by the wide powers being granted to the Secretary of State and the urban development corporations,[23] there was a strange silence on possible effects of regeneration on local communities. This is explained in part by the fact that Parliamentary debate on the lengthy Bill was dominated by the provisions on more general local authority powers, including spending. There was also a major focus on employment in Parliament, an agenda that allowed economics to speak across party divides, although even local unemployment was sometimes discussed as a national rather than a local problem.[24] In addition, however, the lack of specifics on what would happen in Docklands meant that there was little to which to respond. The deregulatory impulse of the government plans left the details to the market. Certainly, the intention was to make use of abandoned land (of which there were vast tracts in Docklands by the early 1980s[25]) and to create employment, but the government set out to enable the private sector to direct the regeneration.[26]

We now know what has become of the Isle of Dogs physically, even if economically things are rather open at the moment.[27] The rhetoric surrounding the designation of the Isle of Dogs Enterprise Zone, as with

---

22 Michael Heseltine, Secretary of State for the Environment, introducing the Local Government, Planning and Land Bill 1980, Hansard, HC Deb vol 978, c 256. Heseltine took urban policy very seriously: see, eg S Ward, *Planning and Urban Change* (London, Paul Chapman Publishing, 1994) ch 8 and Heseltine's own autobiography, *Life in the Jungle: My Autobiography* (London, Hodder & Stoughton, 2001). Urban development corporations were proposed at this stage for only London and Merseyside Docklands, although that is not a limitation of the Bill, a point made by Heseltine's opposite number, Roy Hattersley, Hansard, ibid.

23 Roy Hattersley, Hansard, HC Deb vol 978, cc 258–62.

24 Select Committee of the House of Lords, above n 3, [6.1].

25 Select Committee of the House of Lords, above n 3.

26 Hall, above n 19, argues that the original concept of the enterprise zone was vastly different from what was actually achieved. Michael Heseltine's autobiography, above n 22, also provides some useful insight.

27 This is not the first economic downturn affecting the new Canary Wharf—it was on its third owners by the time the pyramid went on the top of the tower in 1990, and the recession of the early 1990s hit office developments including Canary Wharf. See the discussion in Carmona, above n 2.

enterprise zones more generally, was about the incubation of new businesses. In fact, though, many enterprise zones promoted themselves as places for inward investment by large firms,[28] and the enormous capital costs of developing these run-down areas meant that large corporations rather than small businesses were always the most likely to engage.[29] A glance at the Canary Wharf website bears that out. Much Docklands development has been about extending the 'City' eastwards, in the sense of providing office space for international financial services firms, and buildings are occupied by, for example, Barclays, HSBC, Credit Suisse, Citigroup.[30] The Canary Wharf development, not coincidentally, began at a time of deregulation of financial services, becoming a symbol of the boom.

Judging the success of Docklands is difficult. The general national benefits of a large global financial sector would have been widely, although never conclusively, agreed before the banking crisis of 2008, but even that is open to question now. More specifically on the local impact, there is limited empirical evidence other than that provided by or for the government. In any event, other than at the extremes, the controversy over the performance of this particular regeneration project cannot be resolved by solely empirical information. The 'success' of property-led regeneration rests on value judgements as to what constitutes a successful economy and what constitutes a successful community. The report into LDDC performance on its winding up in 1998 was very positive:

> the LDDC has successfully tackled the widespread multiple market failure which prevailed in the London Docklands in 1981. Failures in land, housing and commercial property markets have been addressed and labour market failures have been alleviated by a combination of training projects, improvements in accessibility in and out of Docklands and the creation of new local jobs.[31]

It is, unsurprisingly, much debated how many of the jobs created are genuinely 'new' and how many would have come about anyway or were down to migration from surrounding areas.[32] The winding up report also says that 'in spite of vociferous comments to the contrary . . . the LDDC generated substantial benefits specifically for local communities and residents'.[33]

---

[28] Jones, above n 21.

[29] Butler, above n 12.

[30] http://www.canarywharfoffices.com/ (June 2009). For a view of developments from the mid-1990s see Brindley et al, above n 2.

[31] Office of the Deputy Prime Minister, 'Regenerating London Docklands', available at http://www.communities.gov.uk/archived/general-content/citiesandregions/regeneratinglondon docklands/.

[32] Hall, above n 18, argues that enterprise zones only produced a small number of truly new jobs, at considerable cost (though this is an early analysis).

[33] Office of the Deputy Prime Minister, above n 31.

Whichever way we cut the numbers, some of the wealthiest people in the country work in one of the country's most deprived boroughs. According to Department for Communities and Local Government indices of deprivation, Tower Hamlets (host to Canary Wharf) is the third most deprived borough in the country.[34] The average salary for those working in Tower Hamlets is nearly £69,000, but 18% of families in Tower Hamlets live on less than £15,000.[35] Average life expectancy at birth is low by national standards, at 75 for men (383rd of 432 local areas) and 80 for women (361st out of 432 local areas); the respective figures are 83 and 87 years in Kensington & Chelsea. Significantly, health inequalities within the borough amount to a 10 year male life expectancy differential between the St Katherine's & Wapping and Bethnal Green North wards.[36] Tower Hamlets has (or had before the latest downturn) the fastest employment growth in the country, but unemployment was also higher than both the London and national averages.[37] And increased property values are no blessing for local residents, creating pressure on social services and open spaces, as well as, more obviously, on housing;[38] indeed, the LDDC's boasts about the increase in property prices sits uncomfortably with its effort to reassure local populations of the benefits of private housing provision.[39] As Imrie and others put it of London generally:

> while in aggregate terms, urban regeneration in London seems to be successful in facilitating economic and cultural regeneration, it is faring much less well in terms of social inclusion and social sustainability, and may well be implicated in contributing to the widening of social and economic inequalities.[40]

Many argue that regeneration (and the large amounts of public money spent in 'leverage') in Docklands more specifically has not only failed to address inequalities, but has exacerbated them.[41] I do not wish to argue that the regeneration of Docklands has been a failure—in its own terms, it has been a spectacular success—and this is not the place to make the case for alternative post-industrial options for London.[42] Nor should we feel

34 Department of Communities and Local Government, 'The English Indices of Deprivation 2007; (DCLG, London 2008), available at http://www.communities.gov.uk/publications/communities/indiciesdeprivation07. The muliple indices of deprivation include health, education, employment and environment.
35 Tower Hamlets Partnership, 'Tower Hamlets Community Plan' (2009), available at http://www.towerhamlets.gov.uk/lgsl/701-750/720_community_plan.aspx.
36 Ibid, 28.
37 Ibid.
38 P Lawless, 'Urban Development Corporations and their Alternatives' (1988) 5 *Cities* 277.
39 See Brindley et al, above n 2.
40 R Imrie, L Lees and M Raco 'London's Regeneration' in R Imrie, L Lees and M Raco (eds), *Regenerating London: Governance, Sustainability and Community in a Global City* (London, Routledge, 2009) 4.
41 For example S Brownill *Developing London's Docklands: Another Great Planning Disaster?* (London, Paul Chapman Publishing, 1990).
42 Brownill, ibid, introduction.

too nostalgic for the hard and insecure labour available in the heyday of the docks,[43] or the facilities available to the local communities before regeneration.[44] But it is small wonder that regeneration on the scale of Docklands was controversial in the planning and controversial in the execution. We can look for a legal response to the controversy first in the regulatory process, then in private law.

B. THE REGULATORY PROCESS

The hundreds of plaintiffs in *Hunter v Canary Wharf*, from Limehouse and Poplar, brought two actions: against Canary Wharf Ltd for interference with television signals by the presence of Canary Wharf Tower; and against the LDDC for the deposit of dust during the construction of the Limehouse Link Road.

Canary Wharf Tower was within the Isle of Dogs Enterprise Zone. Developments that conformed with the scheme published by the LDDC[45] for the enterprise zone did not require individual planning permission. The Isle of Dogs Enterprise Zone scheme granted permission to all development, though subject to exclusions, including height limits, which meant that Canary Wharf Tower needed the agreement of the LDDC. Lord Hoffmann observes in *Hunter* that if Canary Wharf Tower had been proposed outside an enterprise zone there would have undoubtedly been a public inquiry and local people could have made representations to the inspector. In fact, permission for Canary Wharf Tower was granted very quickly by the LDDC,[46] rather than the Secretary of State or an elected local authority. The LDDC did have an obligation to consider representations, though, and there is also the somewhat unlikely possibility that the LDDC's views could have been replaced by a negative resolution of Parliament: 'In all other respects, their [local] interests were liable to be overridden by the Secretary of State's view of the national interest and the LDDC's view of the best way to achieve its statutory objectives.'[47]

The Limehouse Link Road was outside the enterprise zone, and the LDDC granted planning permission in 1988, following a public inquiry and negotiation with Tower Hamlets over rehousing of certain council tenants.[48] This is a more familiar process, although again, the decision was

---

[43] See Foster, above n 2, ch 1.

[44] Indeed, in 1970 a Universal Declaration of Independence was made in protest at the lack of facilities on the 'island': see Foster, above n 2, 55.

[45] There was a competing proposal from Tower Hamlets Borough Council: see Select Committee of the House of Lords, above n 3.

[46] Between September and October 1995; see Carmona, above n 2, 103.

[47] *Hunter*, above n 1, 701 (Lord Hoffmann).

[48] See LDDC press release, 'Planning Approval for the Limehouse Link Road', 4 July 1988. The public inquiry took place on 18 October to 16 November 1988, in respect of Compulsory Purchase Orders, a road closure order and conservation area consents.

taken by a quango rather than the local authority or Secretary of State, and again, the LDDC's ability to sideline local concerns was clear.[49]

The absence of direct local accountability and democracy that assisted development on the Isle of Dogs has been much criticised.[50] The twelve-member board of the LDDC was appointed by the Secretary of State for the Environment (although three places were reserved for Borough nominations) for a period of three years, and was responsible to the Secretary of State. Its powers have been described as 'staggering'.[51] Urban Development Areas were, as mentioned above, designated when 'expedient in the national interest'.[52] There was a clear and explicit move away from local representative democracy, alongside very limited consultation that meant there was no compensatory participatory democracy.[53] The 'partnership' envisaged between central government and the private sector sidestepped local government and local people, and even the planning of transport seems to have been as much about the needs of big developers as of local communities.[54] Usually, local planning rules at least mediate between market and local population. It is significant that the national focus was more controversial in London than in the less residential urban development areas elsewhere in the country.[55]

Although criticised, reduced local accountability was in a very major sense the whole point of the statutory schemes. The government argued that:

> the boroughs tend to look too much to the past and too exclusively to the aspirations of the existing population and too little to the possibility of regenerating docklands by the introduction of new types of industry and new types of housing.[56]

---

[49] See Brindley et al, above n 2; Thornley, above n 19, ch 8.

[50] The exclusion of local people, but also the complexity of the relationships at stake, is clear in Foster, above n 2. See also Thornley, above n 19, also discussing, and criticising, consultation arrangements; Brownill, above n 41; Docklands Consultative Committee, 'The Docklands Experiment: A Critical Review of Eight Years of the London Docklands Development Corporation' (June 1990). There was more consultation (although not local democracy) in the 1990s, reflecting a changing political context: see Foster, ibid, ch 6; M Raco, 'Assessing Community Participation in Local Economic Development—Lessons for the New Urban Policy' (2000) 19 *Political Geography* 573. From the LDDC's perspective see Judy Hillman, 'Learning to Live and Work Together' (1998), available at http://www.lddc-history.org.uk/publications/index.html#Monographs, a slightly shocking effort at self justification, albeit with some interesting observations.

[51] Lawless, above n 38, 282.

[52] Local Government, Planning and Land Act 1980 s 134 (see n 10).

[53] See n 50.

[54] A Church, 'Transport and Urban Regeneration in London Docklands: A Victim of Success or Failure to Plan?' (1990) 7 *Cities* 289.

[55] Lawless, above n 38. A point also made in the House of Commons, Mr Mikardo, Hansard, HC Deb vol 978, cc 298–305. Most enterprise zones, reflecting the decline in traditional industries, were in the north of England: Jones, above n 21, 113.

[56] Select Committee of the House of Lords, above n 3, [6.2].

The House of Lords Select Committee on Docklands said that the approach of some of the local groups opposing the LDDC was 'somewhat parochial'. It concluded that the LDDC should be brought into existence:

> The Committee are very conscious that to transfer development control over so wide an area from democratically elected councils to a body appointed by the Secretary of State is a step which is not easily to be justified, especially in an area such as docklands where the attachment to local democracy was shown to be so strong; but . . . government have made out their case.[57]

C. PRIVATE LAW: *HUNTER V CANARY WHARF*

The decision in *Hunter* needs little introduction. There were two key legal issues: whether loss of television signals can amount to a private nuisance; and whether a particular interest in property is necessary to bring a claim in private nuisance. These primary legal issues are of only incidental interest to the main purpose of this paper, but, in short, the loss of television signals in this case was not a private nuisance (although the possibility that it may be in other cases was left open). By analogy with law on loss of prospect or view, the House of Lords found the mere presence of a building to be reasonable use, regardless of the severity of the interference or (apparently) the nature of the structure. The notion of mere presence of a building reminds us of the shift of land use conflicts away from traditional 'dirty' industries. This particular land use conflict, revolving around financial services, is less obviously disruptive than an alkali works or an oil refinery, but clearly can significantly disrupt people and communities. The nature of the dispute is not so very different from the way that McLaren characterises nineteenth-century private nuisance cases: a 'clash of two very basic interests in land use disputes—the interest in conserving the land and preserving time-honoured uses on the one hand, and the interest in productive exploitation of the land and its resources on the other'.[58]

Secondly, overturning the approach of the Court of Appeal in this case and in *Khorasandjian v Bush*,[59] private nuisance was held to be a tort against property, and a proprietary interest in land was necessary to bring an action. Whilst this is not the prime focus of this paper, any potential for private nuisance to address competing public and private interests or competing understandings of the public interest depends on the nature of the interests protected by the tort. The 'land use' tort has limited responses in cases like *Hunter*, where property interests are secondary to competing visions of community. Some of the plaintiffs had a proprietary interest, so

---

[57] Ibid, [8.3], [8.8].
[58] J McLaren, 'Nuisance Law and the Industrial Revolution—Some Lessons from Social History' (1983)3 *OJLS* 155, 156.
[59] [1993] QB 727 (CA).

could in principle have continued their dust claim after the House of Lords decision. However, the housing in these areas was poor, and the property approach meant that any damages would have been correspondingly small. Any pursuit of the defendants through legal aid was no longer cost effective.[60]

Given that almost no private nuisance case is unaffected by planning law, if not other regulatory schemes, the discussion in *Hunter* of the relationship between private nuisance and planning is potentially of broad application. The distribution of burdens and benefits is a key outcome of planning decisions, sometimes requiring one group or community to bear burdens for the benefit of broader or different communities. Wind farms, waste incinerators, housing developments and even public provision of flood or coastal erosion protection involve these distributive judgments, which are more complex than simple competitions between private interests and the public good. The private law courts usually avoid directly confronting the regulatory context, but the issue was briefly raised in *Hunter* and in a handful of other cases, starting with the ambiguous High Court decision in *Gillingham v Medway Docks*.[61]

Gillingham, a case in which a local authority alleged that docks were causing a public nuisance, left open both a broad and a narrow possibility for the role of planning permission in private nuisance.[62] First, Buckley J drew an analogy between statutory authority and the grant of planning permission, arguing that, just as the defence of statutory authority arises from the fact that 'parliament is presumed to have considered the interests of those who will be affected by the undertaking or works and decided that the benefits for them should outweigh any necessary side effects',[63] so in respect of planning permission:

> Parliament has set up a statutory framework and delegated the task of balancing the interests of the community against those of individuals and holding the scales between individuals, to the local planning authority. There is a right to object to any proposed grant, provision for appeals and inquiries, and ultimately the minister decides.[64]

Most planning decisions, however, are not subject to the protections outlined by Buckley J—public inquiries are not the norm, and there is no

---

60 Discussed in *Khatun and 180 others v United Kingdom* (1998) 26 EHRR CD 212.

61 *Gillingham v Medway Docks* [1993] QB 343 (QB).

62 The docks had been granted planning permission at a time of high local unemployment but, in changing circumstances, effects on quality of life became more important. Quite openly, 361, rather than revoke the planning permission and pay compensation, the local authority sought an injunction in nuisance; the defendants claimed the planning permission as a defence.

63 Whether the sharp distinction drawn in the modern cases between statutory authority and regulation is appropriate is something that would merit further examination, given the role of statute in the nineteenth century in areas that would now be subject to regulation; see chapter 1 above.

64 [1993] QB 343, 359.

right of appeal (only judicial review) against the grant of planning permission. This far-reaching role for planning permission is matched in the very same paragraph by a more circumspect suggestion:

> It has been said, no doubt correctly, that planning permission is not a licence to commit nuisance and that a planning authority has no jurisdiction to authorise nuisance. However, a planning authority can, through its development plans and decisions, alter the character of a neighbourhood. That may have the effect of rendering innocent activities which prior to the change would have been an actionable nuisance.[65]

The Court of Appeal in *Wheeler v JJ Saunders Ltd*[66] endorsed this narrower approach. The plaintiff in *Wheeler* was a vet who claimed that the foul smells from the pig farm next door amounted to a private nuisance. The odours had become a problem following intensification of pig farming, which had been granted planning permission notwithstanding objections from the Wheelers. The defendants accepted that, apart from the planning permission, there was a nuisance by smell, but they argued that, because they had obtained planning permission for the pig sheds,[67] any smell from the pigs living in them could not amount to a nuisance. The Court of Appeal held that planning permission does not amount to a simple defence to private nuisance: 'the Court should be slow to acquiesce in the extinction of private rights without compensation as a result of administrative decisions which cannot be appealed and are difficult to challenge'.[68] But nor is planning permission necessarily wholly irrelevant. Staughton LJ concentrated on the change to the character of the neighbourhood, and thought it clear that the permission in this case did not make such a change: 'it is not a strategic planning decision affected by considerations of public interest'.[69] Peter Gibson LJ acknowledged that 'a major development altering the character of a neighbourhood with wide consequential effects such as required a balancing of competing public and private interests before permission was granted' may indicate that the 'public interest must be allowed to prevail'.[70] So it seems that some planning permissions may be significant in a private nuisance case, through their strategic nature and careful balancing of interests, bringing about a change in the nature of the locality.

[65] Ibid. This is familiar from the Court of Appeal decision in *Allen v Gulf Oil Refinery Limited* [1980] QB 156 (CA) 174 (Cumming-Bruce LJ); [1981] AC 1001 (HL).

[66] *Wheeler v JJ Saunders Ltd* [1996] Ch 19 (CA). The parties had previously been business partners.

[67] Trowbridge houses, which are apparently a more noxious system of keeping pigs than on straw bedding in Nissen huts, which had been used before.

[68] [1996] Ch 19 (CA) 35 (Peter Gibson LJ).

[69] Ibid, 30 (Staughton LJ).

[70] Ibid, 35. Peter Gibson LJ found that the extent of the nuisance was not the inevitable result of implementing the planning permission.

In 2009 the Court of Appeal revisited the question of planning permission and private nuisance. In *Watson v Croft Promo-Sport*,[71] the claimants alleged that the use of land as a motor circuit caused a nuisance by noise, whereas the defendants claimed that planning permission rendered their activity reasonable within the terms of private nuisance. The Court of Appeal reiterated the proposition that 'planning permission as such does not affect the private law rights of third parties', but that the implementation of planning permission may 'so alter the nature and character of the locality as to shift the standard of reasonable user which governs the question of nuisance or not'.[72] In its focus on the implementation of planning permission, rather than the fact of planning permission itself, the Court of Appeal rather played down the question of 'strategic' versus non-strategic planning permission and the questions of process (compensation, appeals, balancing of interests) raised in *Wheeler*. The Court of Appeal's decision adds little to the existing case law because, in accordance with the judge's conclusion that the nature and character of the locality is a matter of fact and degree, the Court of Appeal concluded that the judge's decision could only be overturned if 'plainly wrong or perverse'.[73] That was not the case, and so the decision that the planning permissions had not altered the nature of the locality, which 'remained essentially rural', stands.[74]

Turning now to *Hunter*, the Court of Appeal found that the very general nature of the powers granted to the LDDC by statute meant that the case could not be dealt with as one resting simply on statutory authority.[75] The defendants also argued that the permission granted for the building of the tower precluded the existence of a nuisance. The Court of Appeal rejected the idea that planning permission might be a defence, since that 'would transform what had previously been a matter of legal right into one of administrative decision making'.[76] The narrower proposition that the character of the neighbourhood may be judged by reference to the neighbourhood with the development is, however, followed, although not examined.[77] Whilst not every implementation of planning permission changes the nature of the locality, the Court of Appeal did not address which ones would. If the Canary Wharf Tower did not change the nature

71 *Derek Watson, Julia Watson, Jill Wilson v Croft Promo-Sport Ltd* [2009] EWCA Civ 15, [2009] 3 All ER 249.
72 [32] (Chancellor of the High Court).
73 [36] (Chancellor of the High Court).
74 [19] (Chancellor of the High Court).
75 [1997] AC 655, 668 (Pill LJ). The defendants had pleaded that if a nuisance was the direct consequence of the statutory scheme(s) or the Enterprise Zone consent, the defence of statutory authority would arise. Alternatively, they argued that the grant of planning permission would give rise to the defence of statutory authority.
76 Ibid, 668, citing C Crawford, 'Public Law Rules over Private Law as a Standard for Nuisance: OK?' (1992) 4 *Journal of Environmental Law* 262.
77 Ibid, 669.

of a locality, it is difficult to imagine what might, and indeed Lord Cooke (in his House of Lords dissent) puts the Canary Wharf development within the *Wheeler* 'strategic planning decision affected by considerations of public interest' category, changing the character of the area.[78]

In the House of Lords, only Lord Hoffmann discussed the planning process in any detail. In his discussion of the television case (by analogy with the absence of a right to prospect), Lord Hoffmann turned to the 'ordinary' planning system. He apparently saw the normal requirement that planning permission be granted for the erection of a building as a justification for not using the law of private nuisance to control the presence of buildings. He characterised the planning system as:

> a far more appropriate form of control, from the point of view of both the developer and the public, than enlarging the right to bring actions for nuisance at common law. It enables the issues to be debated before an expert forum at a planning inquiry and gives the developer the advantage of certainty as to what he is entitled to build.[79]

Lord Hoffmann also explicitly said that the appropriateness of planning as the form of control for these types of problems does not imply that planning permission should be a defence to nuisance: 'It would, I think, be wrong to allow the private rights of third parties to be taken away by a permission granted by the planning authority to the developer.'[80] Planning permission is decisive in the case of the presence of a building because, apparently, the plaintiffs are claiming a 'new right of action'.[81] Planning permission is decisive for new claims, but not in respect of what is an actionable nuisance under existing law. This raises the normal problems associated with different rules for 'new' common law developments, in particular the aspect of historical coincidence as to what has been before the courts at the appropriate moment. Also, given that the analogy with 'no right to prospect' is not perfect, the novelty of the claim (in the sense of seeking to overturn established law) does not entirely speak for itself.[82]

In any event, normal planning rules did not apply in this case.[83] The House of Lords makes much of the 'expert forum' of the planning inquiry, even though there was none in respect of Canary Wharf Tower, and of the opportunity to make complaints at the application stage, even though that was limited in this case, and the loss of television reception was anyway

[78] Ibid, 722.
[79] Ibid, 710.
[80] Ibid.
[81] Ibid.
[82] The appellants before the House of Lords argued that the loss of prospect cases were an exception based on policy. Here the television signal is not unique to a single plaintiff, but enjoyed by the entire public, and can be remedied by means other than the pulling down of a building. Ibid, 681.
[83] Thornley, above n 19, ch 8, characterises urban development corporations as a way to 'bypass the planning system', 165.

never likely to have been anticipated by householders.[84] Lord Hoffmann acknowledged the absence of normal planning rules, and observed that 'The plaintiffs may well feel that their personal convenience was temporarily sacrificed to the national interest. But this is not a good enough reason for changing the principles of the law of nuisance which apply throughout the country.'[85] For all its brevity, this captures the heart of the problem. However, Lord Hoffmann did not pursue this insight into a more detailed exploration of the relationship between private law and the actual application of regulation in this case. Because it had already been decided that the law of private nuisance does not in principle interfere with the right to build upon land, the regulatory scheme and absence of normal planning procedures was of little importance in *Hunter*. The argument that planning law is a better process looks in fact like a red herring.

It is clear, however, that, in principle, the courts are willing to defer to some more competent body in the assessment of the public interest in some cases, either because the claim in private law is a new one or on the basis of locality (depending in turn, it would seem, on the nature of the planning permission). A preference by the private law courts for collective views of the public interest seems, for those of us with environmental concerns, to be basically a positive development, especially when the competing interests are individual property or economic interests. From a regulatory perspective, it is at first sight absurd that an individual private property claim can disrupt a careful regulatory scheme. At its best, regulation can make a more considered allocation of public and private costs and benefits than individual litigation can. But the story is a little more complicated than it might seem. Most obviously, we do not live in a world of perfect regulation; deference to regulators places a great deal of faith in the ability of regulators to get things right first time, and of course also in the regulatory process itself. Tort litigation is a way of reopening and reassessing existing regulatory judgments[86]—in *this* case, the nuclear power station (for example) was not safe, or the impact of the planning decision on neighbours was not reasonable. Moreover, the competition in *Hunter* is less between public and private interests than it is between

[84] As pointed out by Lord Goff. The technical possibilities for remedying the problem of poor television reception are also raised several times (the BBC installed a new transmitter, but cable or satellite television are also options), although these remedies neatly avoid considering the responsibility of the defendants: 666 (Pill LJ), 687 (Lord Goff), 711 (Lord Hoffmann).

[85] Ibid, 710. Lord Goff similarly prefers planning permission as a way of raising objections to development early, but acknowledges that no such opportunities arose in the particular case.

[86] See J Steele, 'Assessing the Past: Tort Law and Environmental Risk' in T Jewell and J Steele (eds), *Law in Environmental Decision Making* (Oxford, Oxford University Press, 1998). On the role of tort as an 'unofficial' way of approaching environmental disputes see D McGillivray and J Wightman, 'Private Rights, Public Interests and the Environment' in T Hayward and J O'Neill (eds), *Justice, Property and the Environment* (Aldershot, Ashgate, 1997); K Stanton and C Wilmore, 'Tort and Environmental Pluralism' in J Lowry and R Edmunds (eds), *Environmental Protection and the Common Law* (Oxford, Hart Publishing, 2000).

competing views of public interests—or, indeed, between competing conceptualisations of the 'public'. Thus, one question is how well those competing views were addressed within the regulatory process.

Unfortunately, there is no detailed consideration of the significance of the regulatory process as it actually occurred, rather than its ideal form, in *Hunter*. Whilst not explicit in the decisions, we might cautiously say that *Wheeler* looks like a flawed grant of planning permission,[87] based on inadequate information, and *Watson* looks like a dated permission.[88] These are good reasons for declining to defer to regulation—regulators may have missed relevant factors, and the idea that a regulatory settlement can be static is out of favour. We might also, again cautiously, characterise the distribution of the costs of Canary Wharf as regulatory failure.[89] None of these issues is discussed in the cases. Moreover, even in the absence of anything we might wish to categorise as 'regulatory failure', if we have an excellent assessment of the public interest by regulators, there will be winners and losers, some of whom bear disproportionate costs. Redistributing those costs is only occasionally a function of planning law, so if tort law bows out entirely, they will simply lie where they fall. Nor does the idea of locality provide a straightforward compromise between public and private law norm-generation. Most obviously, the nature of the locality is not always relevant, particularly in respect of a case about physical property damage. Nor is it obvious how a change to the nature of the locality would affect rights to television reception: as Pill LJ puts it, 'the evidence does not suggest other than the neighbourhood will continue to have a substantial television-watching residential component'.[90] It is also hard to see how this compromise will operate for other sorts of regulatory permission, pollution control or waste management licences for example. Much better would be a clear examination of the ways in which regulators have considered and accommodated competing interests.

The opposite question from the one asked by the House of Lords in *Hunter* is whether the contrived absence of planning rules, coupled with a decision-making process that more or less excludes local interests and the individuals and communities most likely to be adversely affected, should *increase* the scrutiny provided by private nuisance in respect of burdens borne in the public interest. This requires a far closer examination of the process by which decisions have been reached. Lord Cooke suggested that a failure to comply with planning law could convert the reasonable into the unreasonable for the purposes of private nuisance.[91] In *Hunter*, the

---

[87] In process and substance see S Ball, 'Nuisance and Planning Permission' (1995) 7 *Journal of Environmental Law* 290.

[88] Planning permission was granted in 1963 and revisited in 1998.

[89] The distributional impact was of course in many respects no accident.

[90] [1997] AC 655, 669.

[91] Ibid, 772.

defendant did not fail to comply, but protections were nevertheless removed.

Private nuisance as conceptualised in *Hunter* is not ideally suited to assessing the public interests at stake. Property interests do not capture the extent of losses in anything like an adequate fashion, constituting only a very small part of disruption suffered by some communities in the interests of different or broader communities. The focus on property in private nuisance arguably even exacerbates the disproportionality of any burden—not only are poor people less likely to have a good claim in property, but their property is (almost by definition) less valuable. Moreover, property rights provide fragile justifications for overturning collective, if contested, determinations of the public interest.[92]

To conclude this part, the relationship between planning law and private law is, quite appropriately, not straightforwardly hierarchical. There seems to be no single site for the generation of the norms that control development, although the two areas of law are allowed to influence each other.[93] Examination of the process of regulatory decision making would, however, allow a more considered approach to this relationship. Such an examination is not too far removed from what the courts are doing already—it is simply a case of making effective their abstract discussions of the regulatory framework.

D. THE ROLE OF LAW IN COMMUNITY CONFLICT

The facts of *Hunter* raise concerns about the absence of local engagement in decisions that profoundly affect local lives and homes, and perhaps also about the uneven distribution of costs and benefits. Private nuisance showed itself in *Hunter* to be inadequate—not because the plaintiffs lost, but because they failed to find any forum in which even a small part of their losses could be considered. To say that this is not tort law's job, throwing our hands up and moving on, would be acceptable if we could find alternative mechanisms—or, of course, if we are prepared to accept law's impotence in the face of brute economic and political power. Clearly politics provided no voice for the residents of Docklands; nor could public law have provided a forum through the 1980s.

The land use planning of the 1980s was characterised in part by conflict between central and local government, especially in Labour-dominated inner cities, and so especially with urban regeneration projects like

---

92 See, eg J Steele, 'Private Law and the Environment: Nuisance in Context' (1995) 15 *Legal Studies* 236.

93 For a discussion of the ability of private law to influence planning law see Crawford, above n 76.

Docklands.[94] Part of that struggle was ideological, about the efforts of central government to create more market-led (rather than community- or public authority-led) land use regulation. This was not limited to special deviations from normal planning in the 1980 Act. From 1980, planning authorities generally were exhorted to 'play a helpful part in rebuilding the economy' and to 'avoid placing unjustified obstacles in the way of any development', in fact 'always to grant planning permission, having regard to all material considerations, unless there are sound and clear cut reasons for refusal'.[95] By 1988, there was an even clearer policy presumption in favour of development: 'There is always a presumption in favour of allowing applications for development, having regard to all material considerations, unless that development would cause demonstrable harm to interests of acknowledged importance.'[96] This deregulatory policy was only ever partially implemented,[97] although Canary Wharf is a striking example of success in its own terms.

The legal framework and expectations of both planning and regeneration have changed since the 1980s, with considerable consensus around the need for public participation in decision making.[98] There is also a revitalisation of city-wide democracy and governance in London at least,[99] although potential disagreement between the Greater London Authority (including the Mayor) and local boroughs means that this can complicate as much as resolve local democracy. In regeneration policy, the rhetoric (at least) is all of participation, engagement and collaboration, moving beyond partnership with just the private sector to looking at the third sector and local communities,[100] although not necessarily local government.[101] The meaning of 'regeneration' has also developed, increasingly moving beyond economic and infrastructure development to include sustainable development objectives, that is, social and environmental as well as economic development.[102] 'Legacy' for a deprived and culturally diverse area of

---

[94] See Thornley, above n 19, 180–82.

[95] Department of the Environment Circular 22/80, 'Development Control: Policy and Practice' (HMSO, 1980).

[96] Department of the Environment, Planning Policy Guidance Note 1, 'General Policy and Principles' (HMSO, 1988), para 15

[97] Nor was it always single minded. On 'dramatic swings in government attitudes' see P Healey and T Shaw, 'Changing Meanings of "Environment" in the British Planning System' (1994) 19 *Transactions of the Institute of British Geographers* 425, 431.

[98] On the development of public participation see J Holder and M Lee, *Environmental Protection, Law and Policy: Text and Materials* (Cambridge, Cambridge University Press, 2007) pt V and ch 3.

[99] See the discussion in M Tewdwr-Jones, 'Governing London: The Evolving Institutional and Planning Landscape' in Imrie et al (eds), above n 40, 58. The lack of democratic control of Regional Development Agencies outside of London is another matter.

[100] For a discussion of the always crucial theme of public engagement see Raco, above n 50.

[101] For a discussion of the role of the state and others see, eg J Davies, 'The Governance of Urban Regeneration: A Critique of the "Governing without Government" Thesis' (2002) 80 *Public Administration* 301.

[102] Davies, ibid; Imrie et al, above n 40.

London was a significant element of the success of London's bid for the 2012 Olympic and Paralympic Games, and long-term regeneration benefits have a high profile in efforts to justify the huge cost of hosting the games. The complex governance structures for delivering the games are very different from the Docklands approach (including central government, local boroughs, London-wide government and the private sector), and there is far more awareness and discussion of the need to engage with local communities. Nevertheless, the pressure to complete inevitably emphasises national interests and produces more in the way of simple consultation than it does bottom-up regeneration.[103] Whilst there is clear progress from the 1980s, actual delivery in terms of local peoples' needs and hopes for regeneration will no doubt be debated for many years.

Beyond these general political changes, EC and, to a lesser extent, international law provide hard legal mechanisms for bringing local views into the decision-making process, even if the role of these views remains in the hands of decision makers. Environmental assessment (including both environmental impact assessment (EIA) of projects 'likely to have significant effects on the environment by virtue, inter alia, of their nature, size or location'[104] and strategic environmental assessment of plans and programmes 'likely to have significant environmental effects'[105]) demands public participation.[106] This is bolstered by the Aarhus Convention, an agreement of the UN Economic Committee for Europe,[107] which promises public participation in environmental decision making. These legal moves have led to greater willingness on the part of the English courts to demand participation. Famously, the House of Lords in *Berkeley* said of the EIA Directive:

> The directly enforceable right of the citizen which is accorded by the Directive is not merely a right to a fully informed decision on the substantive issue. It must have been adopted on an appropriate basis and that requires the inclusive and democratic procedure prescribed by the Directive in which the public, however misguided or wrongheaded its views may be, is given an opportunity to express its opinion on the environmental issues.[108]

103 See the discussion in Gavin Poynter, 'The 2012 Olympics and the Reshaping of East London' in Imrie et al, above n 40, 132.

104 Directive 85/337/EEC on the assessment of the effects of certain public and private projects on the environment [1985] OJ L175/40 as amended by Directive 97/11/EC [1997] OJ L73/5 and Directive 2003/35/EC on participation [2003] OJ L156/17, Art 2. Under Art 1(5), the Directive does not apply to projects adopted by national legislation.

105 Directive 2001/42/EC on the assessment of the effects of certain plans and programmes on the environment [2001] OJ L197/30, Art 3.

106 Although the contribution of environmental assessment to local democracy is far from straightforward. For a discussion see Holder and Lee, above n 98, ch 14.

107 Convention on Access to Information, Public Participation in Decision-making and Access to Justice in Environmental Matters (Aarhus, 25 June 1998) available at http://www.unece.org/env/pp/documents/cep43e.pdf. For a discussion see M Lee and C Abbot, 'The Usual Suspects? Public Participation Under the Aarhus Convention' (2003) 66 *MLR* 80.

108 *Berkeley v Secretary of State for the Environment and another* [2001] 2 AC 603 (HL) 615.

Of government policy making on nuclear energy, Sullivan J has said (somewhat contentiously and obiter) that

> Given the importance of the decision under challenge . . . it is difficult to see how a promise of anything less than 'the fullest public consultation' would have been consistent with the Government's obligations under the Aarhus Convention.[109]

By contrast, nearly 30 years after the constitution of the LDDC, the Planning Act 2008 provides another deliberate effort to sidestep local pressures in the interests of the wider public. Again, there seems to be a 'perception that strategically important development projects in London have been thwarted by local community-based opposition and an overly bureaucratic, old-fashioned and slow planning system'.[110] Decisions on major infrastructure developments, such as electricity generation, transport or waste facilities, will be taken by a new Infrastructure Planning Commission rather than, as in the past, by the Secretary of State following a public inquiry. This Commission must decide in accordance with the relevant National Policy Statement, drawn up by the Secretary of State subject to parliamentary scrutiny,[111] unless to do so would lead to a breach of legal obligations (contained in EC or international law, for example), or the Commission 'is satisfied that the adverse impact of the proposed development would outweigh its benefits'[112] (although it is anticipated that the costs and benefits will usually have been considered in the National Policy Statement). Quite how this will work out is not yet clear, but the hope of the government is to deal with all of the 'general' questions about infrastructure development in a single high-level debate, calling on the national interest as a trump card when it comes to the local siting of projects.

The centralisation of planning, now and in the 1980s, is not simply cynical; it is seen as a way to enable nationally or globally important developments that are locally unpopular. Also, there are far more protections built into the Planning Act 2008 than there were in the Local Government, Planning and Land Act 1980: powers are more constrained, some consultation is still required. Most importantly for current purposes, statutory environmental assessments mean that local consultation cannot

---

[109] *R (on the application of Greenpeace) v Secretary of State for Trade and Industry* [2007] EWHC 311 (Admin), [2007] Env LR 29 [51]. The decision was ultimately overturned on the narrower grounds of legitimate expectations, given that government had promised consultation; K Morrow, 'On Winning the Battle but Losing the War . . .' (2008) 10 *Environmental Law Review* 65.

[110] Imrie et al, above n 40, 16, citing London First and Department for Communities and Local Government.

[111] A National Policy Statement is subject to scrutiny by Parliamentary Select Committee, and can be referred to the floor of the House.

[112] Planning Act 2008, s 104. The National Policy Statement will also flag particular things that will require local consideration.

be avoided. It is not yet entirely clear how environmental assessments will feed into major infrastructure planning, but they will have to do so.[113]

Legal obligations of public consultation of course provide no easy solutions to the assessment of competing public interests, let alone the relationship between private law and administrative law. Aside from anything else, consultation can be pro forma, it can be manipulated by the powerful and it can be ignored in fact if not in law. But the politics of these decisions are clearly on the agenda, and the status of EC law means that they cannot be as easily overridden as local democracy was in the 1980s. Arguably, improved process makes greater deference to administrative decisions in private law adjudication less problematic, but a proper examination of process, and a direct discussion of how that affects the relationship between tort and administration, is vital.[114] As well as opportunities for participation in decision making, this might include an examination of the ways in which interests were weighed, whether the decision was subject to challenge in any forum other than the private law courts[115] and whether compensation of any sort (not necessarily financial; for example, public space might be provided) is available within the regulatory process.[116]

---

113 Environmental Impact Assessment will be the responsibility of the developer at the time of application for permission for a project. Given that the National Policy Statement sets the framework for the decision, and there are no substantive obligations in the EIA process (ie no minimum environmental standards), presumably unless general environmental issues are flagged in the National Policy Statement as a possible reason for turning down an application, the EIA can only feed into conditions for planning permission, or perhaps the 'adverse impact outweighs benefits' criterion. Any pre-judgment is, however, of questionable legality, and certainly not within the spirit of the Directive. The National Policy Statement should be subject to Strategic Environmental Assessment under the Directive as well as sustainability appraisal under the Planning Act.

114 The human rights context provides a modest starting point for bringing process into private adjudication. *Marcic v Thames Water Utilities* [2004] 2 AC 42 (HL) is a good example. But in *Hunter* itself, the plaintiffs took their dust case to the European Commission on Human Rights, claiming breach of their rights to respect for their homes and private lives under Art 8 of the ECHR, *Khatun*, above n 60. Whilst Art 8 applies, it is not an absolute right, and interference can be justified if it is 'necessary in a democratic society' and 'in accordance with the law'. The Commission notes the 'legitimate aims of the economic well being of the country' in the Docklands development scheme. Given the scale of the public interest and the limited suffering by the applicant, the Commission 'cannot find that a fair balance has not been achieved'. The applicants also claimed that the conceptualisation of remedies in terms of market value of property amounted to discrimination on the grounds of poverty under Art 14. The Commission found this to be manifestly inadmissible, on the basis that 'there are no other persons in "relevantly" similar situations to the applicants. There is no evidence that there are persons in the same category as the applicants who have been treated more favourably.'

115 And there is still no appeal against the grant of a planning permission. For a discussion see the Royal Commission on Environmental Pollution's 23rd Report, 'Environmental Planning', Cm 5459 (HMSO, 2002).

116 Financial compensation is unusual in planning law, the conditions for compulsory purchase being narrow. The requirement in a planning permission that infrastructure be provided is more widely available, subject to conditions. It has always been controversial due to concerns that planning permissions might be 'bought' from hard-pushed local authorities, and

If deference to regulation does seem appropriate, that does not necessarily imply a straightforward hierarchy. The degree of interference with
private interests will still be significant, and there is no reason to expect
the prioritisation of physical damage (for practical as much as conceptual
reasons[117]) to disappear. In addition, deference might take the form of an
award of damages rather than an injunction. The dominance in principle
of injunctive relief in private nuisance sharpens the conflict between
planning permission and private law, since the grant of an injunction
against a permitted development would in effect overturn that
permission.[118] However, there are hints in cases from *Wheeler* onwards
that an award of damages in lieu may be an appropriate compromise in a
case with significant public interest dimensions. The Court of Appeal in
Marcic and the High Court in *Dennis* both pursue this possibility,[119]
although *Watson* seems to reassert the more traditional approach.[120]

I am not suggesting that this is straightforward or uncontroversial. It
sounds perhaps disturbingly public law-like, as well as worryingly similar
to the mess of public authority liability in negligence over the past decade
or so. It also arguably converts private nuisance into a more fault-based
tort, as the question becomes whether the regulatory permission has been
carefully implemented. However, the space for legal debate would continue
to be provided by the private interests of claimants, with a more realistic
appreciation of the public context for those private interests. The real, if
modest, benefits of private law (protection of individuals, obviously, but
also the provision of an 'unofficial' forum, the ability to revisit and contest
decisions from a particular individual rights perspective) in a heavily
regulated world would survive in that world.

E. CONCLUSIONS

Hunter v Canary Wharf raises serious questions about competing public
interests and the role of different areas of law in generating the norms that
apply to neighbourhood disputes. A perfectly reasonable response to this
paper would be to say that is not, never has been and never should be the
job of private nuisance to address disagreement over competing public
interests. I see two difficulties with that response. The first is that private

---

due to the likelihood that investment in infrastructure during the implementation of planning
permission is more attractive when property prices are already high.

117 M Lee, 'What is Nuisance?' (2003) *LQR* 298.
118 See, eg S Tromans, 'Nuisance—Prevention or Payment?' [1982] *CLJ* 93. Note McLaren's
discussion of the move to balancing interests in the award of an injunction, above n 58.
119 *Marcic v Thames Water Utilities* [2002] QB 929 (CA); *Dennis*, above n 7.
120 The Court of Appeal overturned the first instance decision not to grant an injunction,
which seemed to have been based largely on public interest arguments, and granted an
injunction restricting the days and type of use of the motor racing circuit.

law (and the protections it provides) will find itself increasingly circum-
scribed in a world dominated by collective determinations of the public
interest unless it engages in a realistic analysis of those determinations.
Private law debate tends to underestimate the prevalence of regulatory
decisions; few private nuisance cases are likely to be unaffected by
regulation. The second difficulty is inherent in any effort to keep different
areas of law in neat separate compartments. An examination of *Hunter v
Canary Wharf* demonstrates that no more appropriate forum was
available, in law or politics. This is not just about who won and who lost
(and, whatever my sympathies for the local, although not static, population
of Docklands, the rights and wrongs of the Docklands development are
actually far from clear[121]), but about the absence of a forum for proper
consideration of disagreement.

In the ongoing working through of the relationship between private
nuisance and planning, we can at least see that the resolution will not be a
simple hierarchy applying across the board. The common law continues to
create its own standards, even whilst it simultaneously defers to certain
norms generated elsewhere. A closer examination of the process of
decision making, whilst not comfortable in private litigation, is a crucial
element of any further steps towards a more subtle relationship between
private nuisance and planning. Even the special statutory arrangements for
the regeneration of Docklands, which had more or less entirely excluded
local people and their representatives from decision making, seem to have
had little impact in the private law courts; the House of Lords in particular
preferred to discuss 'ordinary' planning law. The quality of the administrative decision could usefully have had a clearer role in private nuisance.

---

[121] Foster, above n 2.

13

Fairchild v Glenhaven Funeral Services Ltd (2002)

KEN OLIPHANT*

A. EUROPEAN TORT LAW IN THE ENGLISH COURTS

The House of Lords' decision in *Fairchild v Glenhaven Funeral Services Ltd*[1] is undoubtedly a major recent landmark in the law of causation, providing for the imposition of tortious liability on the basis of a defendant's wrongful contribution to the risk of injury even where it cannot be proven that there was a causal contribution to the injury itself. This chapter, however, is not interested so much in the causation aspects of the case but in its use of comparative tort law material from a range of European civil law systems. It is such material that I have in mind when I speak here of 'European tort law'. This chapter considers the tort law of national systems, not the tort law of the European Union or the tort law inherent in the legal order established by the European Convention of Human Rights (ECHR), and focuses in particular on the tort law of civilian legal systems in Europe. *Fairchild* here provides the springboard for a wide-ranging inquiry into the use of such material in the English courts. Ultimately, I hope to demonstrate that *Fairchild* is a landmark case, not just for the law of causation, but also for the use of comparative European tort law material in the English courts.

B. *FAIRCHILD V GLENHAVEN FUNERAL SERVICES LTD* (2002)[2]

In three separate claims, heard together in the Court of Appeal and House

---

* I am exceedingly grateful to Colm McGrath for his research assistance and, in particular, for his help in formulating and developing the ideas in this paper.

1 [2002] UKHL 22, [2003] 1 AC 32.

2 This section draws upon my previous analysis of the case: K Oliphant, 'England and Wales' in H Koziol and B Steininger (eds), *European Tort Law 2002* (Vienna, Springer, 2003) 142, 144–50.

of Lords, three men were unlawfully exposed to asbestos dust in the course of separate periods of employment with different employers and subsequently developed mesothelioma, an invariably fatal cancer. They or their widows claimed damages from various parties responsible for the exposure (past employers, and in one case the occupier of premises in which the victim worked). The main obstacle in the way of the claimants was causation. The accepted medical evidence was that mesothelioma can be caused only by asbestos but that there was scientific uncertainty as to whether it results from a single exposure to a single absestos fibre or a number of fibres, or from cumulative exposure. When this evidence was considered in the light of the victims' work histories, it became apparent (as was found at first instance[3] and by the Court of Appeal[4]) that none of the claimants could prove on the balance of probabilities that any particular defendant was responsible for the mesothelioma in their case.

The House of Lords unanimously allowed the claimants' appeals, choosing by a majority of four to one[5] to set aside the orthodox approach to proof of causation on the facts at hand in order to avoid an outcome that would be 'deeply offensive to instinctive notions of what justice requires and fairness demands.'[6] Two considerations were paramount. First, the balance of justice and injustice favoured the tortiously injured claimant over the tortiously acting defendant. Each defendant was admittedly in breach of duty, and the injustice of imposing liability where there was no proof of causation according to the traditional approach was 'heavily outweighed' by the injustice of denying redress to the victim.[7] Secondly, insistence on the traditional rules would 'empty the [defendant's] duty of content'[8] and leave employers free to expose their workforces to asbestos with near-impunity (except, of course, in single employer cases). The decision built upon the authority of the earlier House of Lords decision in *McGhee v National Coal Board*[9] but, given the previous uncertainty as to *McGhee*'s proper interpretation, and in particular whether it represented a departure from causal orthodoxy at all, which was denied by the House of Lords in *Wilsher v Essex Area Health Authority*,[10] it is *Fairchild* that must be considered the decisive ruling.

---

[3] *Fairchild v Glenhaven Funeral Services Ltd (t/a GH Dovener & Son)* [2001] All ER (D) 12 (Feb).

[4] *Fairchild v Glenhaven Funeral Services Ltd* [2001] EWCA Civ 1881, [2002] 1 WLR 1052.

[5] Lord Hutton would also have found for the claimants but only on the basis that the facts provided sufficient evidence of an orthodox causal connection.

[6] [2003] 1 AC 32 [36] (Lord Nicholls).

[7] Ibid, [33] (Lord Bingham). See also [39] (Lord Nicholls), and [155] (Lord Rodger).

[8] Ibid, [62] (Lord Hoffmann). See also [155] (Lord Rodger).

[9] [1973] 1 WLR 1 (HL).

[10] [1988] AC 1074 (HL).

At the end of the first day of argument before the Lords, there occurred an exchange which provides the inspiration for this paper.[11] Having endured an extremely detailed analysis of the English case-law, with passing references to Australian, Canadian and American cases, and Roman law too, the senior Law Lord (Lord Bingham) intimated that their Lordships would be interested in modern European jurisprudence on the subject, and the claimants' legal team put itself to the task of tracking down relevant comparative material overnight. I am reliably informed that their efforts extended to an after-hours telephone call to the offices of the European Centre of Tort and Insurance Law (ECTIL)[12] in Vienna, answered by then ECTIL staff member, Bernhard A Koch,[13] who obliged by arranging for relevant material to be couriered to the UK. By this and other means, counsel were eventually able to refer the House of Lords to such works as Professor van Gerven's *Casebook on Tort*[14] in the Ius Commune casebook series, the European Group on Tort Law's collection, *Unification of Tort Law: Causation*[15] and Sir Basil Markesinis's *The German Law of Torts*.[16] Professor von Bar's *The Common European Law of Torts*[17] was not cited by counsel, but Lord Bingham (I am reliably informed) owned his own copy, from which he quoted in his speech.

C. EUROPEAN TORT LAW IN *FAIRCHILD*

The role played by comparative research into European tort law in the House of Lords' decision to depart from causal orthodoxy is hard to assess. Only two of the four majority Law Lords—Lord Bingham and Lord Rodger—expressly advert to the position elsewhere in Europe.

---

11 House of Lords, daily transcript, 7 May 2002, 137. The exchange is not recorded in the summary of argument that appears in the Law Reports, which (erroneously) makes it appear as if counsel introduced European legal materials of their own initiative. *Cf* Lord Rodger's observation, at [165], that it was at their Lordships' suggestion that the Commonwealth cases were supplemented by European legal material.

12 ECTIL is now the closely allied 'twin' of the Institute for European Tort Law, which was founded on 1 July 2002 as a research unit of the Austrian Academy of Sciences. It was upgraded to an Institute of the Academy on 1 July 2008.

13 Now Professor of Law at the University of Innsbruck.

14 W van Gerven, J Lever and P Larouche, *Cases, Materials and Text on National, Supranational and International Tort Law* (Oxford, Hart Publishing, 2000).

15 J Spier (ed), *Unification of Tort Law: Causation* (The Hague, Kluwer Academic, 2000).

16 Lord Bingham refers in his speech to B Markesinis and H Unberath, *The German Law of Torts: A Comparative Treatise*, 4th edn (Oxford, Hart Publishing, 2002), which appears to have been published between argument in the case (7, 8 and 9 May) and judgment (20 June). (The Hart website (www.hartpub.co.uk) gives the publication date as June 2002.) In argument, counsel referred to the third edition dating from 1994: *A Comparative Introduction to the German Law of Torts*, 3rd edn (Oxford, Oxford University Press, 1994).

17 C von Bar, *The Common European Law of Torts*, vol 2 (Oxford, Oxford University Press, 2000).

1. Lord Bingham

Lord Bingham begins his opinion by stating the issue arising on appeal and summarising the facts of the three claims before the House. Then, in a section headed 'Principle', he considers the well-known 'but for' test and various dicta which deprecated its mechanical application in situations where it led to injustice. It seemed to his Lordship to be 'contrary to principle to insist on application of a rule which appeared . . . to yield unfair results'.[18] There follows a review of the English cases under the heading 'Authority', leading to an extended analysis of 'the wider jurisprudence', the key part of his opinion for our purposes. Lord Bingham notes that the problem of attributing responsibility between several duty-breaking defendants when none of the possible candidates can be shown to have actually caused the harm is universal and has vexed jurists in many parts of the world for years. At this juncture, he cross refers to Lord Rodger's analysis of classical Roman law, before quoting from a number of texts (von Bar's *The Common European Law of Torts*, van Gerven's tort law casebook in the Ius Commune series, and Markesinis and Unberath's *The German Law of Torts*) which stress the unfairness of denying the victim redress and the preparedness of various legal systems to adopt special rules to prevent this. He then considers a number of Code provisions in translation—§ 830(1) BGB (supporting his analysis here with reference to the well-known *Palandt* commentary[19]), Article 926 of the Greek Civil Code, § 1302 Austrian Civil Code and Article 6.99 BW (Netherlands Civil Code)—finding that these too appeared to support the imposition of liability in the circumstances in question.[20]

His focus then narrows to a number of specific types of case. The first is the hunters' scenario, which has attracted specific attention in several countries. Lord Bingham refers to a French case[21] and a Spanish statute[22] before turning to the common law, in respect of which he cites the

---

[18] [2003] 1 AC 32 [13].

[19] *Palandt, Bürgerliches Gesetzbuch*, 61st edn (Munich, Beck, 2002).

[20] He notes that the applicability of the Greek provision is disputed in Spier, above n 15, 77. As the relevant chapter was written by a distinguished Greek tort scholar, K Kerameus, it seems rather bold to commit even tentatively to the opposite view based on the translation of a single Code provision. We may also note that the applicability of § 830(1) BGB on such facts is disputed by some German scholars, because it must be shown that each of the several contributions to the risk would have been sufficient to cause the harm. See G Wagner, 'Aggregation and Divisibility of Damage in German Law'in K Oliphant (ed), *Aggregation and Divisibility of Damage in Tort Law and Insurance* (forthcoming) para 68. § 830(1) BGB is in any case inapplicable where one of the potential causes lies within the victim's sphere, as, for example, in both *McGhee*, above n 9, and *Barker v Corus UK plc* [2006] UKHL 20, [2006] 2 AC 572.

[21] *Litzinger v Kintzler*, Cass civ 2e, 5 June 1957, D 1957 Jur 493.

[22] Hunting Act 1970.

well-known decisions in *Summers v Tice*[23] and *Cook v Lewis*,[24] and the Restatement (Second) of Torts. Secondly, with reference to Norwegian[25] and English[26] authority, he considers the position of the road traffic accident victim who cannot prove whether it was impact with the ground or with another vehicle that caused the relevant injury. Thirdly, he considers the market-share scenario with reference to the celebrated Californian case of *Sindell v Abbott Laboratories*[27] and a decision of the Dutch Supreme Court (Hoge Raad) that was inspired by it.[28] Lastly, following a short review of some rather inconsequential dicta from courts in Australia and Canada, Lord Bingham considers mesothelioma cases in Australia, apparently maintaining the traditional causal requirement, and California, where the Supreme Court in *Rutherford v Owens-Illinois Inc*[29] expressly adopted a principle of liability for contribution to risk.

Lord Bingham's analysis to this point is notable for its seamless interweaving of civil and common law authorities.

His conclusion to this section of his opinion warrants quoting at length. He deals first with the specific issue of causation:[30]

> This survey shows, as would be expected, that though the problem underlying cases such as the present is universal the response to it is not. Hence the plethora of decisions given in different factual contexts. Hence also the intensity of academic discussion . . . In some jurisdictions, it appears, the plaintiff would fail altogether on causation grounds[31] . . . But it appears that in most of the jurisdictions considered the problem of attribution would not, on facts such as those of the present cases, be a fatal objection to a plaintiff's claim. Whether by treating an increase in risk as equivalent to a material contribution, or by putting a burden on the defendant, or by enlarging the ordinary approach to acting in concert, or on more general grounds influenced by policy considerations, most jurisdictions would, it seems, afford a remedy to the plaintiff.

He then ends his review of the wider jurisprudence with what may well be styled a manifesto for the intelligent use of comparative legal materials in the English courts:[32]

> Development of the law in this country cannot of course depend on a head-count of decisions and codes adopted in other countries around the world,

23 (1948) 199 P 2d 1.
24 [1951] SCR 830.
25 RG 1969, 285 (apparently cited in N Nygaard, *Skade og ansvar* [Injury/Damage and Responsibility], 5th edn (Bergen, Universitetsforlaget, 2000), 342, a Norwegian work which does not seem to have been published in English translation).
26 *Fitzgerald v Lane* [1987] QB 781.
27 (1980) 26 Cal 3d 588.
28 *B v Bayer Nederland BV*, Hoge Raad, 9 October 1992, NJ 1994, 535.
29 (1997) 67 Cal Rptr 2d 16
30 [2003] 1 AC 32 [32].
31 Lord Bingham specifically mentioned Italy, South Africa and Switzerland, referring to Spier, above n 15.
32 [2003] 1 AC 32 [32].

often against a background of different rules and traditions. The law must be developed coherently, in accordance with principle, so as to serve, even-handedly, the ends of justice. If, however, a decision is given in this country which offends one's basic sense of justice, and if consideration of international sources suggests that a different and more acceptable decision would be given in most other jurisdictions, whatever their legal tradition, this must prompt anxious review of the decision in question. In a shrinking world (in which the employees of asbestos companies may work for those companies in any one or more of several countries) there must be some virtue in uniformity of outcome whatever the diversity of approach in reaching that outcome.

In the next section of his opinion, Lord Bingham briefly considers 'Policy', referring to only common law sources, before reaching his 'Conclusion': the claims should be allowed on the facts. This outcome, he considered, was fortified by the wider jurisprudence reviewed in his opinion, as well as by the policy considerations.[33]

2. Lord Rodger

Lord Rodger's treatment of modern civilian sources is rather briefer. After a lengthy analysis of British and other common law materials, he gives his approval to the development of the law relating to causation to be found in the earlier case of *McGhee*, clearly enunciating the two main policy arguments—the potential injustice to claimants and the 'empty duty' argument—in favour of liability on the facts.[34] He then states that he derives support for that conclusion 'from what has been done in other legal systems', and continues:[35]

Broadly speaking, they appear to me to demonstrate two things: first, that other systems have identified the need to adopt special rules or principles to cope with situations where the claimant cannot establish which of a number of wrongdoers actually caused his injury; secondly, that there are considerable divergences of view and indeed uncertainty as to the proper area within which any such special rules or principles should apply.

He then considers the approach to comparable causation problems in Roman law, before turning to *Rutherford* and other common law authorities, and finally the position in European legal systems. In his view, that material provides 'a check, from outside the common law world, that the problem identified in these appeals is genuine and is one that requires to be remedied'.[36] He refers in particular to the position in France, citing the hunters' case, and Germany, quoting § 830(1) BGB in German and in

33 Ibid, [34].
34 Ibid, [155].
35 Ibid, [156].
36 Ibid, [165].

translation, referring to the preparatory works preceding the Code[37] and citing a case before the BGH.[38] The German experience, in particular, he considers to support his analysis.[39] With what may well have been intentional understatement, Lord Rodger concludes his comparative analysis thus:[40]

> At the very least, the cross-check with these systems suggests that it is not necessarily the hallmark of a civilised and sophisticated legal system that it treats cases where strict proof of causation is impossible in exactly the same way as cases where such proof is possible.

3. The Other Law Lords

As previously mentioned, none of the other Law Lords (Lord Nicholls, Lord Hoffmann and, dissenting on the question of principle, Lord Hutton) made any mention of modern European legal material, though each referred to at least one other common law jurisdiction.

4. Postscript: *Barker v Corus (UK) plc* (2006)

Four years after *Fairchild*, the Law Lords were called upon to resolve two issues not decided in the earlier decision: first, whether the *Fairchild* exception applies where the victim was himself responsible for one of the relevant periods of exposure (answer: yes), and secondly, whether, where the exception does apply, each defendant is jointly and severally liable for the full loss, or for only a proportionate share reflecting his contribution to the total risk (answer: the latter).[41] This time there was no reference to European tort law materials, though they were cited by counsel.[42] The decision suggests that recourse to civilian legal sources remains exceptional and somewhat inconsistent, even where important and novel questions of principle come to the House of Lords.

---

37 *Motive zu dem Entwurfe eines Bürgerlichen Gesetzbuches für das Deutsche Reich* (1888).
38 *BGHZ* 25, 1 October 1957, 271. Lord Rodger cites van Gerven, above n 14, as a source for both the French and the German case.
39 [2003] 1 AC 32 [167] and [169].
40 Ibid, [168].
41 *Barker*, above n 20.
42 This is not mentioned in the summary of counsel's arguments in the Law Reports, but it is affirmed by J Stapleton, 'Benefits of Comparative Tort Reasoning: Lost in Translation' (2007) 1(3) *Journal of Tort Law* Art 6, 37.

D. EUROPEAN TORT LAW IN THE ENGLISH COURTS GENERALLY

1. Research Aims and Methods

Fairchild prompts further reflection on the extent and nature of the use of European tort law materials in other cases before the English courts. To assess the extent of such use, a set of structured searches of the Westlaw electronic legal database was employed, seeking in the first place to identify English decisions which make use of European tort law as defined above. Several combinations of free-text and keyword searches were used, employing six main search categories: (i) country name (France/French, German, etc); (ii) national supreme court name (BGH, Cassation, Hoge Raad, etc); (iii) leading authors (Bussani, Koziol, Kötz, Markesinis, Spier, van Gerven, von Bar, Zimmermann, Zweigert, etc); (iv) primary sources of national law, including civil codes (code civil/code Napoleon, BGB, etc), the numbers of fundamental code provisions (823, 1382), and collections of reported cases (Dalloz, NJW); (v) sources of transnational or comparative tort law literature (Principles of European Tort Law/PETL, Trento, etc); and (vi) particular legal categories (Negligence, Nuisance, Defamation, etc). Cases using European tort law in the context of private international law (eg as the foreign law applicable to a particular dispute) were excluded, as were a variety of other red herrings (eg decisions by French J or about German spies). The cut-off date for the searches was 1 March 2009. For reasons of time, the searches have not yet been extended to the English Reports, even though occasional cases prior to 1866 do make use of European tort law.[43]

2. Basic data

Twenty-four cases were identified in which European tort law material has been cited since official law reporting began in 1866 (see Appendix for a complete list). With one exception,[44] all decisions date from 1987 or later. *Smith v Littlewoods*[45] in that year was the first decision in which European

---

[43] Eg *Card v Case* (1848) 5 CB 622, 136 ER 1022 (liability for injury to sheep done by ferocious dog), where counsel (at 626–68) refers to Art 1385 of the French Civil Code in the course of a lengthy comparative discursus also embracing Mosaic, Athenian and Roman law. No other English tort case was thrown up by a search of 'civil code' in the English Reports. *Becquet v MacCarthy* (1831) 2 B & Ad 951, 109 ER 1396 (citing Art 1384 CC) concerned the enforcement of foreign judgments. However, a search of 'code civil' produced too many hits to review in the time available.

[44] *Manton v Brocklebank* [1923] 2 KB 212 (CA).

[45] [1987] AC 241 (HL).

tort law was used in the House of Lords. Eleven decisions were decisions of the House of Lords, nine of the Court of Appeal and four of courts of first instance. In some cases, European tort law was used by courts at different levels, but only in *White v Jones*[46] was such material used both in the Court of Appeal and the House of Lords. In the other ten House of Lords decisions citing European tort law, no such material was cited in the Court of Appeal. Only in *Campbell v MGN*[47] and *Douglas v Hello!*[48] was there reference to European tort law in a lower court (the Court of Appeal), but none on appeal.

One identified case, *A v National Blood Authority*,[49] refers extensively to other European systems, mentioning nine other EU states. However, the question there was the correct interpretation of the EC Product Liability Directive,[50] so the decision did not raise the issue of the comparative use of material from elsewhere in Europe and is excluded from further analysis below.

The majority of cases related to the tort of negligence (13, including *Fairchild*). The only other substantial category of cases (five) was that dealing with breach of confidence/informational privacy.

Excluding collegiate decisions, the judges who have had most frequent recourse to European tort law have been Lord Bingham, in four opinions in the House of Lords (*Fairchild*,[51] *East Berkshire*,[52] *Transco*[53] and *Rees*[54]) and one judgment in the Court of Appeal (*Kaye*[55]); Lord Goff, four times in the Lords (*Smith*,[56] *Henderson v Merrett*,[57] *White v Jones*[58] and *Hunter*[59]); and Lord Steyn, three times in the Lords (*Arthur Hall*,[60] *Rees*[61] and *McFarlane*[62]) and once in the Court of Appeal (*White*[63]). No other judge has referred to European tort law on more than an occasional basis.

---

46 [1995] 2 AC 207 (CA and HL).

47 [2002] EWCA Civ 1373, [2003] QB 633.

48 [2005] EWCA Civ 595, [2006] QB 125, rev'd sub nom *OBG Ltd v Allan* [2007] UKHL 21, [2008] 1 AC 1.

49 [2001] 3 All ER 289 (QB).

50 Council Directive (EEC) 85/374 of 25 July 1985 on the approximation of the laws, regulations and administrative provisions of the Member States concerning liability for defective products [1985] OJ L 210/29.

51 *Fairchild v Glenhaven Funeral Services Ltd* [2002] UKHL 22, [2003] 1 AC 32.

52 *D v East Berkshire Community Health NHS Trust* [2005] UKHL 23, [2005] 2 AC 373.

53 *Transco Plc v Stockport MBC* [2003] UKHL 61, [2004] 2 AC 1.

54 *Rees v Darlington Memorial Hospital NHS Trust* [2003] UKHL 52, [2004] 1 AC 309.

55 *Kaye v Robertson* [1991] FSR 62 (CA).

56 *Smith v Littlewoods Organisation Ltd* [1987] AC 241 (HL).

57 *Henderson v Merrett Syndicates Ltd (No 1)* [1995] 2 AC 145 (HL).

58 *White v Jones* [1995] 2 AC 207 (HL).

59 *Hunter v Canary Wharf Ltd* [1997] AC 655 (HL).

60 *Arthur JS Hall & Co v Simons* [2002] 1 AC 615 (HL).

61 *Rees v Darlington Memorial Hospital NHS Trust* [2003] UKHL 52, [2004] 1 AC 309.

62 *McFarlane v Tayside Health Board* [2000] 2 AC 59 (HL).

63 *White*, above n 58.

Excluding *Fairchild*, where nine different European legal systems were cited by Lord Bingham, the only national systems specifically cited are Germany (17 cases, including *Fairchild*), France (13 cases) and the Netherlands (two cases). In three cases, there was reference simply to unspecified civilian or continental systems.[64]

Courts were more inclined to refer to academic writings (nine cases) than they were to refer to specific cases (seven cases) or specific national codes (three cases). In six cases, there was simply a general reference to the law of a particular country without indication of any specific source. Courts relied extensively on translated extracts or summaries of European material, but there is evidence to suggest a direct sourcing of such material, from untranslated primary or secondary sources, in four cases: *Fairchild*,[65] *Hunter*,[66] *Yearworth*[67] and *Campbell*.[68]

Looking specifically at the secondary literature, the most-cited author was Markesinis, with three books cited and several articles,[69] and the most-cited book was his *The German Law of Torts*[70] (nine cases). Van Gerven's Ius Commune casebook on tort[71] was the second most-cited book (four cases).

E. USES FOR EUROPEAN TORT LAW

The use of European tort law was classified according to six different categories:[72]

1. Outcomes: the court attaches weight to the outcome that would be reached on particular facts in another system (eg whether the claimant would or would not recover damages).

2. Arguments: the court attaches weight to the underlying arguments of legal principle or policy which point towards or away from a particular outcome.

---

[64] *Kent v Griffiths (No 2)* [1999] PIQR P192 (CA); *Carty v Croydon LBC* [2005] EWCA Civ 19, [2005] 1 WLR 2312; *Arthur JS Hall*, above n 60.

[65] *Fairchild*, above n 1.

[66] *Hunter*, above n 59.

[67] *Yearworth v North Bristol NHS Trust* [2009] EWCA Civ 37, [2009] 3 WLR 118.

[68] *Campbell v MGN Ltd* [2002] EWCA Civ 1373, [2003] QB 633.

[69] H Lawson and B Markesinis, *Tortious Liability for Unintentional Harm in the Common Law and the Civil Law* (Cambridge, Cambridge University Press, 1982); B Markesinis J-B Auby, C Waltjen and S Deakin, *Tortious Liability of Statutory Bodies: A Comparative Look at Five Cases* (Oxford, Hart Publishing, 1999); Markesinis and Unberath, above n 16, and previous editions of the same. S Deakin, A Johnston and B Markesinis, *Markesinis and Deakin's Tort Law*, 6th edn (Oxford, Oxford University Press, 2008) and earlier editions, was not included because its focus is on English rather than European tort law.

[70] Markesinis, above n 16.

[71] Van Gerven, above n 14.

[72] Taken from J Stapleton, above n 42, with the addition of two further categories: Inconsequential Reference and Rejection.

3. Principles: the court attaches weight to the legal basis on which the outcome is reached (eg whether the claimant wins on the basis of loss of chance or material contribution to risk).
4. Conceptual arrangement: the court attaches weight to the categorisation of the principle applied according to its relationship to other legal categories (eg whether it is a principle of contract law or tort law).
5. Inconsequential reference: the reference does not fall into any of the above categories because it is too vague or only a passing reference.
6. Rejection: the court expressly declines to attach weight to the European legal material.

How each English court reference to European tort law should be classified was inevitably a matter of impression, at least to some degree, and the results certainly do not lend themselves to quantitative statistical analysis. The survey below is purely qualitative, not quantitative. It seeks to identify the different possible uses for European tort law in the English courts, giving illustrations of each use, with the addition of some fairly limited critical comments.

1. Outcomes

The simplest and apparently most common use of European legal materials was simply as a means of counting outcomes, whether to identify a single dominant view or merely to stress the range of possible approaches to difficult legal problems. A truism of comparative law scholarship is that the actual patterns of decision in different systems very often conform, even if different legal analyses are employed to reach such decision. Lord Goff, for example, in a resonant dictum, has stated:[73]

> [S]ince we all live in the same social and economic environment, and since the judicial function can, I believe, be epitomised as an educated reflex to facts, we find that, in civil law countries as in common law countries, not only are we beset by the same practical problems, but broadly speaking we reach the same practical solutions. Our legal concepts may be different, and may cause us sometimes to diverge; but we have much to learn from each other in our common efforts to achieve practical justice founded upon legal principles.

Though more than one judge has warned that a simple 'head-count'[74] or 'poll'[75] of other national systems cannot determine the development of the law in England, analysis of outcomes may yet serve a number of purposes. First, it may indicate the genuineness of the problem with which the English

---

[73] *Smith v Littlewoods Organisation Ltd* [1987] AC 241 (HL) 280–81.
[74] *Fairchild*, above n 1, [32] (Lord Bingham).
[75] *McFarlane*, above n 62, 81 (Lord Steyn).

court is faced, which was the starting point of Lord Rodger's comparative analysis in *Fairchild*.[76] Secondly, it may point to potentially better solutions available elsewhere, in a fashion somewhat reminiscent of the way in which modern management techniques highlight examples of 'best practice' with a view to encouraging emulation. Such examples may be seen as 'cross-checks'[77] on the results reached by English law. As Lord Bingham observed in *Fairchild*, an English court should engage in 'anxious review' of any decision resulting from the orthodox application of established principles that offends basic justice if a different and more acceptable decision would be reached elsewhere.[78] In his view, European legal material 'fortified'[79] the English court in departing from an established approach, insofar as is allowed by the rules of precedent. Where English law lags behind the law of another system, for example, in its (erstwhile) failure to protect the interest in personal privacy, and the rules of precedent leave the judge powerless to respond, the foreign example may also be cited to strengthen the call for legislative intervention.[80]

Thirdly, foreign outcomes may be cited for reasons of 'moral support', for example, with a view to seeking safety in numbers, or, a related aim, to show that English law is not out of line with other systems. Thus, an English court may stress the diversity of legitimate responses to difficult issues that transcend national boundaries. In *Hunter v Canary Wharf Ltd*,[81] Lord Goff said that it was 'of some interest' that the same conclusion—interference with television reception giving rise to no cause of action—had been reached in German law, thus demonstrating 'that English law is not alone in reaching this conclusion'. And, in *Douglas v Hello! (No. 1)*, in the claimants' initial proceedings for an injunction, Sedley LJ found it 'relevant', in considering the proposed development of a horizontal right of privacy in English law, to note the application of laws for the protection of privacy in France and Germany in cases of non-state invasion.[82]

The diversity of opinions that may legitimately be held about a difficult question of principle, morality or policy was emphasised by the House of Lords in its consideration of wrongful conception in the cases of *McFarlane v Tayside Health Board*[83] and *Rees v Darlington Memorial Hospital NHS Trust*.[84] In the former case, Lord Slynn observed in relation

[76] See above, text accompanying n 35.
[77] *Fairchild*, above n 1, [168] (Lord Rodger).
[78] Ibid, [32].
[79] Ibid, [34].
[80] *Kaye v Robertson* [1991] FSR 62 (CA) 70 (Bingham LJ).
[81] [1997] AC 655 (HL) 686.
[82] [2001] QB 967 (CA) [127].
[83] *McFarlane*, above n 62.
[84] *Rees*, above n 54.

to judicial practice in France, Germany and the Netherlands that 'different courts have taken different views on the difficult legal and ethical issues which arose', supporting the proposition 'that the law is still developing and that there is no universal and clear approach'.[85] In the same case, Lord Steyn's 'tour d'horizon of comparative jurisprudence'[86] also took in European tort law alongside the law of other common law jurisdictions and emphasised the variety of solutions adopted. His conclusion, repeated in *Rees*,[87] was that the majority of countries probably would not allow a claim for maintenance costs in a wrongful conception case, but this survey was heavily weighted in favour of common law jurisdictions: the only two European systems cited were Germany (in favour of recovery) and France (said to be against).[88] Lord Bingham, by contrast, noted that an orthodox application of familiar and conventional principles of tort law, in both common law and civilian systems (he expressly referred to Germany and the Netherlands), would have produced a contrary result.[89] For policy reasons, however, he considered that a parent who conceives after a negligent sterilisation should not be able to recover the child's maintenance costs, even to the extent to which these were increased in consequence of the parent's disability. This is therefore an example of an explicit English judicial departure from the majority approach of European systems.

Lastly, consideration of outcomes may be a step in a process of ongoing harmonisation of European tort law. In *Fairchild*, Lord Bingham stressed the virtues of 'uniformity of outcome whatever the diversity of approach in reaching that outcome'.[90] He had in mind, in particular, the undesirable inconsistencies that would result if employees of a single multinational company, working for it in different countries, were subject to a multiplicity of employers' liability rules.[91] Harmony of outcome is also a theme of at least one other Bingham judgment. In *Transco*,[92] he gave as one of four reasons for declining to assimilate liability under *Rylands v Fletcher* with negligence the increased disparity that would result from such a decision between English law, on the one hand, and the laws of France and Germany, on the other, all three systems currently affording a form of strict liability protection in disputes between neighbouring landowners.[93]

85 *McFarlane*, above n 62, 73.
86 Ibid, 80.
87 *Rees*, above n 54, [33].
88 *McFarlane*, above n 62, 80.
89 *Rees*, above n 54, [314].
90 *Fairchild*, above n 1, [32].
91 Ibid.
92 *Transco*, above n 53.
93 Ibid, [6].

2. Arguments

The view that comparative legal material is primarily of use for the arguments employed is neatly encapsulated in a dictum of Lord Steyn:[94] '[t]he discipline of comparative law does not aim at a poll of the solutions adopted in different countries. It has the different and inestimable value of sharpening our focus on the weight of competing considerations.'

In principle, European tort law can play a number of different roles in the development of arguments in English courts. First, a European decision may be the source of an argument applied by an English judge. At first instance, Cazelet J's judgment in *Greatorex v Greatorex*[95] provides a good illustration. Considering whether there is a duty of care not to injure oneself so as to avoid secondary psychiatric harm to a near relative, Cazalet J quoted from a decision of the BGH[96] of which a translated extract, from Markesinis *The German Law of Torts*, was produced to the court by counsel. The BGH found that 'to impose such a legal duty, except in very peculiar cases . . . would be to restrict a person's self-determination in a manner inconsistent with our legal system'. Cazelet J acknowledged the force of the argument, which he included amongst a set of policy considerations that together outweighed the considerations pointing to recognition of a duty of care.[97]

Secondly, European tort law may be used to lend added validity to an argument already accepted in the common law (*cf* moral support, above). For example, Lord Goff observed in *Smith v Littlewoods Organisation Ltd* that it is not only in common law countries but also in civil law countries such as Germany that the force of the floodgates argument is accepted.[98] This seems to indicate a concern to highlight commonalities between the common law and civil law, without going so far as asserting acceptance of the common position (if indeed there is one) in a majority of systems. The same analysis may also be applied to *Hunter v Canary Wharf Ltd*,[99] where Lord Goff, considering liability for interference with television reception in England and Germany, claimed that 'the underlying policy considerations appear to be similar',[100] though he did not explore this in any detail. He perhaps had in mind his previous observation, in relation to German law, that '[w]ithin the boundaries of his land the owner may in principle deal with his property as he wishes'.[101]

---

[94] *McFarlane*, above n 62, 81.
[95] [2000] 1 WLR 1970 (QB).
[96] *BGHZ* 11 May 1971.
[97] [2000] 1 WLR 1970 (QB) 1987.
[98] [1987] AC 241 (HL) 280.
[99] *Hunter*, above n 59.
[100] Ibid, 686.
[101] Ibid.

A final use of comparative European materials is to negate an argument relied on by one of the parties to the English case, for example, to demonstrate that allowing a claim of a particular sort does not result in an opening of the floodgates of liability or other practical difficulties. So Lord Bingham, dissenting in *D v East Berkshire Community Health NHS Trust*, noted that French and German law accepted in principle that a parent whose child was taken into protective care on mistaken grounds might have a claim against the care professionals, and observed that 'in neither of those countries have the courts been flooded with claims'.[102] Similarly, Lord Steyn in *Arthur JS Hall & Co v Simons* (abolishing the so-called barrister's immunity) attached 'some significance' to the fact that the absence of an immunity in other EU countries has apparently caused no practical difficulties.[103]

3. Principles

There was no case that could be said to have expressly 'transplanted' a European law principle into English law, notwithstanding the influential theory according to which this is the typical way in which legal change occurs.[104] In *Fairchild*, Lord Bingham considered a number of the principles adopted in other European jurisdictions which allowed the imposition of liability in cases of causal indeterminacy—reversal of the burden of proof, loss of chance, alternative liability, market-share liability—but the principle eventually adopted by the House of Lords—material contribution to risk—more closely resembles that applied in the Californian *Rutherford* decision,[105] if indeed it is correctly called a principle at all, so significantly hedged in it is with factual preconditions. Nevertheless, *Fairchild* identifies the role played by functionally equivalent principles in different systems, an approach that is also evident in Lord Goff's opinion in *Smith v Littlewoods Organisation Ltd*.[106] He noted there that liability for harm caused to neighbours by trespassers on the defendant's land (eg by starting a fire) was limited even in those countries recognising a general duty of affirmative action by a variety of principles, eg in France by the requirement that the danger to the claimant must be *grave, imminent, constant . . . nécessitant une intervention immediate* and that intervention must not involve *risque pour le prévenu ou pour un tiers*.[107] These requirements, he thought, were 'consistent' with the limits

---

102 *East Berkshire*, above n 52, [49].
103 *Hall*, above n 60, 680–81, citing Markesinis *Tortious Liability*, above n 69.
104 Cf A Watson, *Legal Transplants: An Approach to Comparative Law* (Edinburgh, Scottish Academic Press, 1974).
105 *Rutherford*, above n 29.
106 *Smith*, above n 56.
107 Ibid, 271, citing Lawson and Markesinis, above n 69, vol 1, 74–75.

recognised by English law on the steps required of a person under an affirmative duty to prevent harm being caused by a source of danger which has arisen without his fault.[108]

Sometimes an argument that English law should attach weight to a principle recognised elsewhere may be rebutted by pointing to a counter-example. In *Henderson v Merrett Syndicates Ltd*, for example, considering whether English law allows concurrent liability in contract and tort in relation to pure economic loss, Lord Goff briefly adverted to the French doctrine of *non cumul* (non-accumulation) but stressed that this was not indicative of the civilian approach to the problem as a whole, as concurrence was allowed (for example) in Germany.[109]

An alternative comparative analysis of principles may point to the lack of any functional equivalent to a common law principle in civilian systems, with a view to excising or limiting the role played by the principle in English law. The utility of referring to civilian as opposed to common law materials in such a case is easily grasped. The classic example is *D v East Berkshire Community Health NHS Trust*,[110] where Lord Bingham (dissenting) and Lord Nicholls both highlighted the absence from other systems of any principle equivalent to the duty of care in the common law, in response to counsel's argument that there should be a shift away from the duty concept in English law in favour of a 'modulated'[111] (per Lord Nicholls) approach to breach of duty. Lord Bingham was in favour of such a move, but Lord Nicholls and the House of Lords majority were opposed. Though Lord Nicholls was attracted by the flexibility offered by such an approach, this was insufficient to outweigh the disadvantages resulting from the subsequent uncertainty in English law.[112]

4. Conceptual Arrangement

In several cases, the English courts have contrasted the conceptual arrangement and categorisation of particular principles of English law with those of another jurisdiction. In *White v Jones*, in the Court of Appeal,[113] Steyn LJ noted that other systems—specifically those of Germany and the US—adopt a contractual solution in the case of the intended beneficiary under a will who does not inherit because of negligence on the part of the testator's solicitor, and expressed his preference for a contractual as opposed to tortious approach, while accepting that as a matter of precedent

---

108 Ibid, citing *Goldman v Hargrave* [1967] 1 AC 645 (PC).
109 *Henderson*, above n 57, 184.
110 *East Berkshire*, above n 52.
111 Ibid, [92].
112 Ibid, [94].
113 [1995] 2 AC 207 (CA).

the contractual solution was impossible.[114] The contrast in the legal categories implicated in England and Germany was also noted in the House of Lords (before which Prof Markesinis appeared as counsel for the claimants), where Lord Goff admitted that—whatever the attractions of the German approach—the common law contractual requirement of consideration was fatal to the adoption of the same solution in English law.[115] Though the German contractual concept of transferred loss, *Drittschadens-liquidation*, underlined the need in justice for a remedy on the facts, the situation before the Lords was not strictly analogous to those in which the concept was applied.[116] For the Law Lords too, then, it was necessary to push at the more readily opened door of tort liability, rather than the securely locked door of liability in contract.

The different conceptual context may also point the way towards a simple or more natural solution in English law than that adopted in another European system. In *Yearworth v North Bristol NHS Trust*,[117] concerning the availability of damages for non-pecuniary damage following the defendant's negligent loss of the claimant's sperm samples, there was very extensive citation of German materials both at first instance and in the Court of Appeal, but the Court of Appeal declined to attach any significant weight to the BGH's decision[118] that the destruction of his sperm constituted a personal injury to a hospital patient because of the special features (relative to English law) of the German law of non-pecuniary loss. At the relevant time, the governing Code provision (ex-§ 847 BGB, now replaced by § 253 BGB) allowed the award of damages for non-pecuniary loss only where there was personal injury and in other strictly limited circumstances.[119] English law's approach to non-pecuniary loss is not so limited, and damages for purely mental injury are (arguably) available even in a property case by way of an action in bailment.

Lastly, the reference to conceptual categories may be intended to support the denial in English law of a remedy on facts that would lead to liability elsewhere. In *Chagos Islanders v AG*,[120] Sedley LJ dismissing an appeal against the striking out of a claim against Her Majesty's Government for forced removal of the islanders from their homeland, refers in passing to the likely success of such a claim before the French courts,[121] but he quickly emphasises the different legal contexts in France

---

114 Ibid, 236–37.
115 [1995] 2 AC 207 (HL) 266.
116 Ibid, 264.
117 [2009] EWCA Civ 37, [2009] 3 WLR 118.
118 9 November 1993 (Sixth Civil Senate) *BGHZ* 124.
119 [2009] EWCA Civ 37 [22]. See also *Yearworth v North Bristol NHS Trust* Exeter County Court, 12 March 2008 [135] (Judge Griggs).
120 [2004] EWCA Civ 997, *The Times*, 21 September 2004.
121 [2004] EWCA Civ 997 [20].

and England. In France the claim would be against the state, an institution that is not known in English law, which recognises the Crown as the repository of prerogative and statutory powers: 'the State [sic] has no tortious liability at common law for wrongs done by its servants, from ministers down'.[122]

5. Inconsequential Reference

Comparative European material was cited but given no substantial weight in several cases identified in this survey. Citation of comparative material before the Court of Appeal appears to be especially likely to lack discernible influence, no doubt because that Court is more constrained in its ability to occupy new ground than the House of Lords. In the oldest case emerging from this survey, *Manton v Brocklebank*, Lord Sterndale MR noted that the French Civil Code, and the Biblical, Athenian and Roman systems of jurisprudence, were 'relevant only so far as they throw light on our law',[123] but did not proceed to consider expressly whether any such illumination could be derived for the purposes of the decision at hand (presumably not). More recently, Court of Appeal judges have frequently limited their comparative analysis to somewhat bland generalisations,[124] imprecise analogies,[125] polite acknowledgement of material cited by counsel,[126] an expression of interest in finding out how other systems would deal with a particular type of case[127] or simply a passing reference to the approach elsewhere without any indication of the weight to be attached to such evidence.[128]

Of course, similarly inconsequential references to European tort law materials are also to be found in the House of Lords. For example, in

---

122 Ibid. The reasoning is not easy to follow, as Sedley LJ purportedly denies that English law has any concept of 'state' at all.

123 [1923] 2 KB 212 (CA) 218.

124 Eg *Kent v Griffiths (No 2)* [1999] PIQR P192 (CA) P202 (Schiemann LJ), discussing whether the ambulance service owes a duty of care to persons whom it is called to attend ('Although the policy issues are largely common to all jurisdictions, approaches vary throughout the Commonwealth and in civil law countries'; no details given).

125 *Douglas v Hello! Ltd (No. 6)* [2005] EWCA Civ 595, [2006] QB 125 [113] (recognition of a celebrity's right commercially to exploit private information about himself, including photographs taken of him on a private occasion, has 'echoes' of the *droit à l'image* in France and the 'tort of publicity' in Germany).

126 *Carty v Croydon LBC* [2005] EWCA Civ 19, [2005] 1 WLR 2312 [83] (Mummery LJ) ('some interesting papers on relevant topics' in D Fairgrieve, M Andenas and J Bell (eds), *Tort Liability of Public Authorities in Comparative Perspective* (London, BIICL, 2002)).

127 'It would be interesting to know what answers French and German law would give in the present situation': *A v B plc* [2001] 1 WLR 2341 (QB) [39] (Jack J).

128 *Campbell v MGN Ltd* [2002] EWCA Civ 1373, [2003] QB 633 [34] ('[i]n some jurisdictions [sc. France and Germany] it is an actionable wrong to publish a photograph of a person taken without consent').

Hunter v Canary Wharf Ltd,[129] Lord Cooke agreed that a German decision cited by Lord Goff was 'of interest as a matter of comparative law and some help',[130] but did not specify what sort of assistance it in fact provided.

A final form of inconsequential reference to European materials is where they are cited in a passage from an earlier case that is quoted in a subsequent judgment without specific comment on the comparative material.[131]

6. Rejection

It is perhaps surprising that a consistent rejection of the utility of European tort law materials in the English courts—as opposed to the rejection of a particular analogy on the facts for specific reasons—seems to have been made explicit by only one judge, Lord Hoffmann. Others may share his scepticism, but have not made it express. In *Wainwright v Home Office*,[132] counsel referred to the protection of privacy interests in German law, but Lord Hoffmann, delivering the only speech in the Lords, made no reference to other national systems in Europe, while indicating his concern that recognition of a new remedy might 'distort' the common law.[133] In *Arthur JS Hall & Co v Simons*,[134] he cuttingly observed that '[l]egal cultures differ', and declined to attach significance to 'overseas experience' (not just in the civilian world), at least on the facts of that case.[135] This scepticism also appears in Lord Hoffmann's extra-judicial writings, as in the following curt rejection of the utility of comparative investigation into the tort laws of civilian systems:[136] 'Comparative law does not help. Continental lawyers have the same problems but their answers are hidden by obscurity or absence of reasoning.'

It is important to note that Lord Hoffmann's extreme scepticism is distinct from the measured acceptance that uniformity of outcome or approach is not always desirable, given relevant differences between jurisdictions. Lord Steyn, for example, has observed that 'the discipline of comparative law . . . reminds us that the law is part of the world of

---

129 *Hunter*, above n 59.
130 Ibid, 720.
131 Eg *Carr-Glynn v Frearsons* [1997] PNLR 343 (Ch) 356, where Lloyd J quotes Lord Goff in *White v Jones*.
132 *Wainwright v Home Office* [2003] UKHL 53, [2004] 2 AC 406.
133 Ibid, [52].
134 [2002] 1 AC 615.
135 Ibid, 695.
136 Foreword to R Stevens, *Torts and Rights* (Oxford, Oxford University Press, 2007) vi.

competing ideas markedly influenced by cultural differences'.[137] On this view, comparative law serves as an aid to identifying when harmonisation should be pursued, and when national differences are desirable.

F. CONCLUSIONS

It is possible to draw a number of conclusions from the above survey relating to the frequency of citation of European tort law material, the types of cases in which it is cited, the judges by whom it is cited, the types of material that is cited and the uses to which it is put.

First, as regards frequency of citation, it is important to emphasise that bare figures—24 cases since official law reporting began—do not tell the full story. In 11 of those cases, the comparative material was cited by the House of Lords, the first such citation dating from only 1987 (*Smith v Littlewoods Organisation Ltd*). Subsequently, there have been (on my count) 119 tort law decisions in the Lords.[138] So European tort law has been cited in approximately one in ten House of Lords tort cases since 1987—a small but not insignificant proportion. Of course, citation of comparative common law (especially Commonwealth) materials is much, much more frequent.

Secondly, as regards the types of cases in which European tort law is cited, it should come as no surprise that a majority of cases identified in the survey concern the tort of negligence and breach of confidence/informational privacy, as these are perhaps the areas where the law has been most volatile in the period in question. My impression—difficult to substantiate statistically given the limited hard data—is that European tort law is introduced most often when the court is facing difficult and novel questions of law, morality or policy, for example, when it is asked to break new ground by departing from well-established and fundamental principles (*Fairchild, East Berkshire*), to adopt a solution that is doctrinally problematic (*White v Jones*), to recognise new protected interests (the privacy cases) or to address issues regarded as problematic across jurisdictions (*Fairchild* again, and *McFarlane/Rees*); or, alternatively, when the House of Lords is asked to review its own approach under the 1966 Practice Direction in light of the perception that it is out-of-line internationally (*Arthur Hall v Simons*). In short, such material is particularly relevant in 'landmark' cases. Needless to say, there are probably countless cases that fit in these categories where no European tort law material was cited.

---

137 *McFarlane*, above n 62, 81. See further C van Dam, 'Who is Afraid of Diversity? Cultural Diversity, European Co-operation, and European Tort Law' (2009) 20 *King's Law Journal* 281.
138 Westlaw keyword search.

Thirdly, as regards the judges by whom such material is cited, it must be noted—again, as no surprise—that it is mostly members of the House of Lords. This is largely explained by the nature of the cases where comparative analysis is most frequently engaged in—landmark cases dealing with novel and difficult issues. However, it must be noted that only a small minority of judges, even in the House of Lords, makes frequent use of such material—in fact, only three: Lord Goff, Lord Steyn and Lord Bingham. All three have written extra-judicially about the virtues of comparative law.[139] Goff and Bingham have both been President of the British Institute for International and Comparative Law, a position which Bingham continues to fill. Goff, who evidently had a deep knowledge of German law in particular, was previously an academic, which may have made him more open-minded towards non-traditional sources. Steyn trained in a mixed system (South Africa), so was predisposed by his training to accept the influence of civilian legal theory. All three have now retired from the bench, leaving a worrying gap because there is no obvious front-runner to become the leading judicial comparativist of the next generation. Lord Rodger, a distinguished Roman lawyer, would be well suited to assume this mantle, but may not have the inclination.

Fourthly, as regards the types of material that is cited, we have noted the strong bias in favour of France and Germany—also to be expected, as those countries are generally regarded as the leading representatives of the Romanic and Germanic legal families. The more likely facility in the French and German languages as opposed to (say) Italian or Swedish may also be a factor, but perhaps a stronger influence is the range of comparative material that is available in English translation or summary. Academic writings were cited more often than Code provisions or cases, and it seems that the majority of references to the latter were by way of translated extracts. Markesinis's *The German Law of Torts*, with translated extracts from the BGB, cases and other sources, has been cited significantly more frequently than other works. It was first published in 1990. The more recently available comparative tort law casebook by van Gerven is structured round a comparison of three systems—England, France and Germany—though it does contain some material from elsewhere. Translated materials from a wide range of countries is to be found in Lawson and Markesinis's *Tortious Liability for Unintentional Harm in the Common Law and the Civil Law* (1982), but that is now somewhat dated. A wider range of national systems is covered in several

---

139 See, eg Lord Goff, 'The Search for Principle' (1983) 69 *Proceedings of the British Academy* 169 and 'Judge, Jurist and Legislature' 1987 *Denning Law Journal* 79; Lord Bingham, 'A New Common Law for Europe' and Lord Steyn, 'Interpretation: Legal Texts and their Landscape', both in B Markesinis (ed), *The Clifford Chance Millennium Lectures: The Coming Together of the Common Law and the Civil Law* (Oxford, Hart Publishing, 2000) 27 and 79, respectively.

more recent works,[140] but without anything more than occasional translation of primary legal sources. Only rarely is there reference to original
language materials.[141]

Lastly, as regards the uses to which European tort law is put, the
previous section showed that it is employed in a wide variety of ways, with
the emphasis sometimes on outcomes, sometimes on arguments, sometimes
on principles and sometimes on conceptual arrangements. It sometimes
supports an extension of liability in tort (*Fairchild, Arthur Hall*),
sometimes a restriction of liability (eg *McFarlane/Rees*). Reference to
civilian legal material may be useful if the intention is to challenge a
general principle of the common law which has no precise equivalent in
the civil law (as in *East Berkshire*), or simply to expand the range of
arguments and possible outcomes that can be taken into account.

It would be hard to argue that any particular decision would have been
resolved differently had there been no recourse to comparative material,
not least because so few judges explicitly attach weight to it, but I believe
that European tort law has been at least a contributory factor in several
recent advances or changes of direction in the English law of tort.

G. AND FINALLY: *FAIRCHILD* AS COMPARATIVE LAW LANDMARK

On the basis of the foregoing analysis, I would suggest that *Fairchild* is a
landmark case in promoting the reflective use of comparative European
tort law materials in the English courtroom for the following reasons:

1. It appears to be the first case in which counsel were expressly requested by
   the House of Lords to introduce such materials.
2. The breadth and depth of the comparative analysis, especially on the part
   of Lord Bingham, and the way he seamlessly interweaves common law
   and civil law sources, go beyond any other English judicial analysis of
   European tort law before or since. The number of civilian systems cited
   (nine) comfortably exceeds that in any other case.[142] The decision reflects
   the new era of European tort law scholarship which has moved beyond

---

[140] Eg von Bar, above n 17; the series *Unification of Tort Law* by the European Group on Tort
Law (including Spier, above n 15); and numerous publications by the Trento Common Core
project, the European Centre of Tort and Insurance Law and the Institute for European Tort
Law.

[141] But see, eg *Fairchild*, above n 1, [158]–[159], [167] (Lord Rodger).

[142] Excepting *A v National Blood Authority* [2001] 3 All ER 289, on the EC Product
Liability Directive, which, for reasons given above, text accompanying n 49, cannot be regarded
as a fair comparator.

two- or three-way comparisons of different systems, and looks as far as possible at Europe as a whole.[143]

3. This comparative analysis played a significant role in encouraging a radical departure from established fundamental principles. In other cases, by contrast, the comparative material supported the maintenance of the status quo (*Transco*), a policy-motivated restriction on the application of ordinary principles (*McFarlane/Rees*), or the removal of a policy-motivated restriction on the application of ordinary principles (*Arthur Hall*), if it was relied on at all. Perhaps the nearest rival to *Fairchild* in this context was *White v Jones*, but *White* ultimately followed the established approach of the courts below,[144] whereas *Fairchild* went directly against what was (following *Wilsher*) the prevailing tide.

4. Lastly, *Fairchild* is a landmark case because it is the first occasion (so far as I know) on which an English judge, acting in a judicial capacity, has expressed an enthusiasm for the harmonisation of the tort law of different national systems: 'In a shrinking world . . . there must be some virtue in uniformity of outcome whatever the diversity of approach in reaching that outcome.'[145] Who now will take up Lord Bingham's clarion call?

APPENDIX: CASES CITING EUROPEAN TORT LAW (BY COURT AND YEAR)

In the House of Lords

D v East Berkshire Community Health NHS Trust [2005] UKHL 23, [2005] 2 AC 373.

Transco Plc v Stockport MBC [2003] UKHL 61, [2004] 2 AC 1.

Wainwright v Home Office [2003] UKHL 53, [2004] 2 AC 406.

Rees v Darlington Memorial Hospital NHS Trust [2003] UKHL 52, [2004] 1 AC 309.

Fairchild v Glenhaven Funeral Services Ltd and Others [2002] UKHL 22, [2003] 1 AC 32.

Arthur JS Hall &Co v Simons [2002] 1 AC 615.

McFarlane v Tayside Health Board [2000] 2 AC 59.

Hunter v Canary Wharf Ltd [1997] AC 655.

White v Jones [1995] 2 AC 207.

Henderson v Merrett Syndicates Ltd (No 1) [1995] 2 AC 145.

Smith v Littlewoods Organisation Ltd [1987] AC 241.

---

143 See especially the works cited in nn 14 and 17 and, for a broad overview of European tort law scholarship, the *King's Law Journal* special issue, 'European Tort Law', ed K Oliphant (2009) 20(2) *King's Law Journal* 189.

144 See especially *Ross v Caunters* [1980] Ch 297.

145 *Fairchild*, above n 1, [32].

In the Court of Appeal

Yearworth v North Bristol NHS Trust [2009] EWCA Civ 37, [2009] 3 WLR 118.
Carty v Croydon LBC [2005] EWCA Civ 19, [2005] 1 WLR 2312.
Douglas v Hello! Ltd (No 6) [2005] EWCA Civ 595, [2006] QB 125.
Chagos Islanders v AG [2004] EWCA Civ 997, *The Times*, 21 September 2004
Campbell v MGN Ltd [2002] EWCA Civ 1373, [2003] QB 633.
Douglas v Hello! Ltd (No 1) [2001] QB 967.
Kent v Griffiths (No 2) [1999] PIQR P192.
White v Jones [1995] 2 AC 207.
Kaye v Robertson [1991] FSR 62.
Manton v Brocklebank [1923] 2 KB 212.

At First Instance

A v B Plc [2002] EWCA Civ 337, [2003] QB 195.
A v National Blood Authority [2001] 3 All ER 289.
Greatorex v Greatorex [2000] 1 WLR 1970.
Carr-Glynn v Frearsons [1997] PNLR 343.

Index